THE BASIC EXPERIENCE AND THE DEVELOPMENT OF THE SELF

LUCIANO RISPOLI

THE BASIC EXPERIENCE AND THE DEVELOPMENT OF THE SELF

DEVELOPMENT FROM THE POINT OF VIEW OF FUNCTIONAL PSYCHOTHERAPY

PETER LANG
Bern · Berlin · Bruxelles · Frankfurt am Main · New York · Oxford · Wien

Bibliographic information published by Die Deutsche Bibliothek
Die Deutsche Bibliothek lists this publication in the Deutsche Nationalbibliografie; detailed bibliographic data is available on the Internet at ‹http://dnb.ddb.de›.

British Library Cataloguing-in-Publication Data:
A catalogue record for this book is available from The British Library, Great Britain

Library of Congress Cataloging-in-Publication Data

Rispoli, L. (Luciano)
[Esperienze di base e sviluppo del sé. English]
The basic experience and the development of the self : development from the point of view of functional psychotherapy / Luciano Rispoli ; [translation by Jessica Ibbotson].
p. ; cm.
Translation of: Esperienze di base e sviluppo del sé. Milano : FrancoAngeli, 2004.
Includes bibliographical references.
ISBN 978-3-03911-750-5 (alk. paper)
1. Self psychology. 2. Child development. 3. Child psychotherapy. 4. Adolescent psychotherapy. 5. Functionalism (Psychology) I. Title.
[DNLM: 1. Self Psychology. 2. Adolescent. 3. Child Development. 4. Child. 5. Mental Disorders--therapy. 6. Psychotherapy--methods. 7. Self Concept. WM 460.5.E3 R595e 2008]
RC489.S43R5713 2008
155.2--dc22

2008041444

Original Title: Esperienze di Base e Sviluppo del Sé.
L'Evolutiva nella Psicoterapia Funzionale, FrancoAngeli, Milano, 2004

Translation by Jessica Ibbotson

Cover design: Eva Rolli, Peter Lang AG, Bern

ISBN 978-3-03911-750-5

Hochfeldstrasse 32, Postfach 746, CH-3000 Bern 9, Switzerland
info@peterlang.com, www.peterlang.com, www.peterlang.net

Printed in Germany

*This book is dedicated to all those who have managed to discover real love,
and who have, with patience and courage, learnt to feed it,
discovering the joy of giving love and the wisdom of giving themselves.*

Contents

Foreword

Studies in flow and process have taken on an increasingly important role in clinical therapy and psychotherapy in recent years. There is a growing need to respond to criticism about the scientific accuracy of clinical psychotherapy, the many doubts raised by ever more demanding patients, as well as attacks launched by scientists in other fields, such as the neurosciences. All this forces us to seek a greater understanding of the deeper mechanisms that underlie and govern the therapeutic relationship and the process of change.

This isn't simply about evaluating the *results* of therapy, as we previously tried to do, (i.e. trying to assess whether therapy resolves the symptoms or not, instead of trying to shed new light on what is actually happening while therapy is underway, what the therapist's actions and presence really set off in the patient, and what Rispoli calls the *modalities of therapy*). If we know the elements that go to make up the *plot* of a course of psychotherapy, then we can improve our tools so that they produce exactly the desired elements and obtain results that are more effective.

This book provides us with a new point of view, a new contribution in this direction, concerning both therapy and technique. Based on his long experience as a psychotherapist, and on years of research, Rispoli explores the events that constitute the nucleus of the therapeutic process, its very bones, i.e. what the therapist really brings about during therapy. Rispoli pitches his study at a level set halfway between the two levels more commonly dealt with: the overall, general aims of therapy (which would be too vague and generic) and the specific techniques applied (the operative tools used step by step).

This is, in a certain sense, a return to investigations made on the question of *factors of change*, the importance of which is enormous when applied to the above. This investigation must lead to a coherent and fertile debate between the various different currents and models of psychotherapy.

Rispoli's argument is rooted in that particular area concerned with understanding the interwoven relationship between *psychic processes* and *physical processes*. He does this first by tracing the most recent scientific developments, as well as the long and rich road of contributions made by the specific field of body psychology until he reaches Functional Psychology, in which field he has specialised for a number of years.

What really happens then during therapy? The phenomena described by Rispoli are as numerous as they are evocative They regard the human organism's deepest psycho-biological mechanisms (or Functional Processes, as they are referred to here): body memory, peripheral memory, and old traces that can be found on several planes of the Self and on the different Functional levels which, together, constitute the Self in its totality. These mechanisms refer to movements, postures, muscle tension, breathing, the autonomic nervous system (responsible for the 'fight or flight', and 'rest and digest' responses, the emotions, memories, fantasies, the symbolic world and so on. Functional Psychology looks at all of these levels simultaneously, considers the Functional processes underlying them, searches for the nuclei that lie at the base of our behaviour, attitudes and the different ways in which we relate to others: i.e. the psycho-physical Functions of the Self.

Where does the study of the complex phenomenology of the individual as a whole lead? It leads to the identification of several Functional processes which, according to Rispoli, are the foundations of life itself, and which represent what lies *at the root* of whichever form of behaviour we adopt in any given circumstance or context.

The Basic Experiences of the Self are a specific group of experiences that are of critical importance during child development. These experiences, if allowed to unfold fully and positively many times, with the help of the child's parents and surroundings, become genuine, stable capacities in the life of every individual.

For Rispoli, therefore, psychotherapy and child development are linked in that the central part of every course of Functional psychotherapy is based on the *reconstruction* of any Basic Experiences that have been found to be deficient, incomplete, suffocated or tainted by emotions and experiences belonging to completely different situations. The capacities linked to each Basic Experience are not, in effect, only necessary during development, but they are also at the root of the mechanisms governing life itself, and are therefore indispensable at any age.

At this point, the book talks, in great detail and with precision, about the methods that allow us to reconstruct the Basic Experiences more effectively, the methods that allow us to really *change* the old traces of the patient's past, the old tracks that their behaviour and the way they relate to others run along, automatically and subconsciously.

The author's idea is that a clearer understanding of what effectively happens during therapy (probably every course of therapy, regardless of the clinical model adopted by the individual therapist) will allow us to refine techniques and render the therapeutic process itself scientifically more successful, as well as more stable and profound. In the light of studies conducted from a multidimensional point of view, the therapeutic process has been revealed as being divided into typical, or *developmental* phases, in which elements such as the patient-therapist relationship, transference, and perception are continually modified, from the beginning of therapy right to its final outcome.

In this analysis, Rispoli demonstrates an ability to go beyond the clinical model he originally started with, in order to create a general discussion on our current thinking. This meta-theoretical point of view overcomes limits and breaks down barriers, providing a meaningful and significant contribution to the attempt at understanding the care relationship, regardless of the context or the techniques used. The aim is to build bridges between the various clinical models, to merge the study of psychology and studies in factors of change into a single theory, and to proceed towards the *integration* of the various clinical approaches.

Basically, what Rispoli is trying to do is to forge a deep link between theories of the cognitive type (which tend to look mainly at modalities of functioning, feedback circuits and the actuation of behaviour patterns) and theories based on dynamic psychology (which look at the way the inner world is structured, the tissue of present and past emotions, and levels of unawareness, depth and the subconscious).

By looking at the *Functions* (as Functional psychology does) rather than at *parts* of a system, we can contemplate the system as a whole, without fragmenting or dividing it, whilst at the same time examining its mechanisms in detail, giving concrete and copious indications on how to proceed at the practical, operative level.

A large part of the book is then dedicated to the description of all the various Basic Experiences. This description is ample, but it is also simple in its essential lines, and this simplicity reflects the simplicity of the concept of the Basic Experiences itself (whilst at the same time remaining complex and multidimensional). The reader will hear about Experiences that we are all familiar with, but which take on a new meaning, both in reference to everyday life and in terms of the way therapy proceeds. *Being Held* and *contained*, being able to *Let Go*, the capacity to *Just Be*, to *Abandon Ourselves to Others*, *Contact*, *Being Seen*, *Being Noticed*, *Tenderness* etc. are all crucial conditions for a child's life, as has been amply covered in literature on the subject. Rispoli attempts to examine these Experiences in all their psychophysical aspects and in all their components, in order to place them within the context of a comprehensive overview, in which each one assumes the same importance as all the others, none of which must be neglected. Nor should their presence be neglected within our society, in a world that risks losing the very components that are indispensable if we wish to live even faintly full or satisfying lives.

However, this book also deals with the Basic Experiences that regard our *activation*. It examines their full and positive functioning, just as it does any possible alterations that can occur. *Opening ourselves*, *Taking*, *Giving*, *Assertiveness, Making Choices*, and many others, become reference points in child development, but also in our lives as adults, in order to be able to live life with the fullness to which we should all be able to aspire.

Other Experiences laid out in this volume present more unexpected or interesting aspects. *Calm Strength*, *Relaxed Attention*, and *Affectionate Aggressiveness* all refer to capacities that are all too often misconstrued, ignored, or given insufficient value. These should, on the contrary, be given the same (if not greater) importance than hard strength or forms of expression that are more violent. *Anger* and *Hate* are without doubt also Basic Experiences, but if they end up prevalently substituting softer or calmer strength, if they cancel out tenderness and trust, then they limit our life potential and lead to a condition of permanent stress which certainly cannot be considered to be completely healthy.

The parallelism that the author proposes between life and therapy continues through the more detailed sections dedicated to each Basic Experience. For each one, the author includes a therapeutic technique (either in group work or in individual therapy) designed especially for the reconstruction and recovery of that particular Experience. In this way, Rispoli's book is full of elements of interest to the professional, as well as the less specialised, reader, including clinical aspects which are necessary, if we are to provide fuel for a debate on the new frontiers of psychotherapy.

Alongside each technique, the book includes the feelings and reactions of patients and participants at workshops, therapy groups and in training programs taking place in various countries in Europe and the Americas.

These descriptions increase the human-interest factor and allow us to look right into these methods of intervention, which overcome the traditional confines between clinical models, putting us into direct contact with patients' stories and the transformations that these techniques bring about during the recovery of the Basic Experiences of the Self.

This book is coloured with a universe of voices, comments and reactions, which are of extreme interest to those dipping into the world of psychotherapy for the first time. To us therapists, these descriptions are already familiar, yet they have an advantage, in that they demonstrate the *way* in which change comes about with absolute clarity. They show the stage each patient has reached in his or her recovery of the Basic Experiences, and better illuminate the road that each patient really takes (no matter what clinical approach he may have chosen) towards healing and wellbeing.

Marcello Cesa-Bianchi

Introduction

Development in Functional Psychology

One of the first goals I set myself when I sat down to write this book was that of bringing together all the recent findings about childhood to form a comprehensive overview child development. I wanted this overview to go beyond children's mere scholastic, neurological, psychomotor, or emotional capacities, and examine their *basic functions* (i.e. the functions at the very root of their behaviour, expressions and sensations) from *all points of view*, not just from a cognitive, symbolical, or emotional viewpoint. The school of thought which best allowed me to address all the above criteria was the school of Functional Psychology, together with data and experience gathered from the application of the Functional perspective during clinical and pedagogical activity, training and research.

For many years now, our teams have focussed their attention on childhood and adolescence, through direct involvement in the school environment, training projects for teachers and childcare workers, multidimensional methods of assessment aimed at evaluating children's real conditions, as well as preventative intervention for children, parents and teachers, and specific workshops aimed at "rebalancing" the personality and the Self.

All of the above activities successfully used the tools and methods of Functional Psychology, such as observation protocols, specific methods for the analysis of results, workshop techniques for children and training programmes.

Functional Psychology therefore represents one of the possible hypotheses upon which we could base a new *integrated method* of looking at the individual, studying him as a whole, on all his many levels and planes of functioning. Moreover, it represents a possible response to the challenge of complex thought, and the ever more pressing need to unite the various personality theories (which have concentrated, by degrees, on different aspects of human functioning and which now demonstrate the need for a concerted effort towards synthesis on a larger scale) into an *integrated* whole.

It was therefore necessary to reorganise the data obtained from our extensive direct experience, and the tools and the methodologies adopted, to make them useful and communicable on a wider scale. More urgent still, however, was the necessity of reformulating current knowledge on children's functioning during the various phases of their development in the light of an *integrated theory*.

In this way, I have attempted to outline a model, taking the complexity of the human organism into consideration, which could act as a *framework* to the development process. I wanted to shed light on the way in which a living being's *deepest functional processes* (the *Functions* of the Self) take shape, one at a time, during the numerous *formative situations* during his growth and life. On the other hand, it was necessary to clarify exactly what those *formative situations* were and how they develop. Functional Psychology has defined these significant moments as the *Basic Experiences*. It was crucial, too, to understand what *alterations* can interfere with these Basic Experiences if they are not given sufficient attention and facilitated within the child's environment, and what the *consequences* of these alterations are, whether in the short term, over the long term or later on in adult life.

This offered the possibility of writing not only a scientific text, but also a *textbook of pedagogy*, as well as a *guidebook* for parents, for teachers and for childcare workers, combining an overall view with a more thorough vision of children's functioning at many levels.

It is no longer enough just to refer to *emotional intelligence*, even though this concept represented a not indifferent leap forward in our approach to the way children function. Today we need to think about *integrated intelligence*: a Functional intelligence that extends to all levels of functioning of the Self.

However, if we wish to talk about child complexity in a concrete, rather than a vague, way, then we must examine the phenomena at an operative level. To this aim Functional Psychology, as we shall see, has isolated both the *Functions of the Self* and the *Basic Experiences* (each of which is comprised of a specific configuration of Functions).

This method of dealing with complex thought provides us with an approach that is both global and at the same time operatively detailed. By actually looking at the various Basic Experiences and the various Functions, we can understand human beings' basic functioning, (the processes at the root of their multiform and complex behaviour), without getting lost in endless sidetracks and details, constantly keeping in mind the unity of the individual.

Moreover, the concept of *Polarity* that I have developed (whereby the movement of each Function or Basic Experience is seen in terms of a range between two extremes, two polarities) can make it much simpler to interpret people's overall functioning.

The history of each individual's personal development can be interpreted innovatively, therefore, as their *Functional Development*:

- by shedding light on the way the Functions organize themselves and become more complex during growth (emotions, posture, movements, language, breathing, imagination, symbolism);
- by analysing how the *Basic Experiences* unfold in relation to the surroundings;
- by tracing the developmental history of the various parts of the body (divided into Districts) with the aim of clarifying how the child moves and expresses himself, and what innermost sensations and feelings were transmitted to him during growth by that part of the body.

From all of this, we can identify clear and precise *guidelines* that can concretely help parents, teachers, and childcare workers to understand what it is that *really happens* during childhood, and the deeper *consequences* of adult behaviour towards children.

This book is not, therefore, a "difficult" text, reserved just for specialists. It is a text that is open to everyone, a *story* about our children's activities and about what we were like when we were little. It is a story that leads us by the hand, calmly and gently, in that it talks about our own daily experiences and essentially about the way we experience life. Much common knowledge about the world of childhood has been shown to be mistaken. Much of it is also confusing, and often contradictory. Today, however, science can provide us with very precise data, which can help us to proceed in the direction of well-being and deep-rooted harmony for our children.

By gradually looking at each single Basic Experience, we can see clearly and concretely how important it is that every single one of them unfolds in the right direction. We can also see what we as adults can do to ensure that these experiences unfold in precisely that direction. Sometimes just a small effort on our part can bring about surprising results that could easily prevent subsequent distortions, or pain and suffering that is impossible to quantify.

We must bear in mind that the more conspicuous dramas of prostitution, paedophilia, child labour, and physical mistreatment are not the only problems for children (all over the world). There is also, above all, a much more diffuse condition that is still present today: a condition where children's basic needs are *not taken into consideration*, of insufficient *protection* during the delicate period of development, a passage through the Basic Experiences that fails to be *full* or *positive*.

This has more serious consequences than might commonly be thought, because it undermines an individual's very life skills, the elements which allow them to lead a full and satisfying existence. And even if they are not obvious straightaway, these negative consequences are subsequently very visible indeed in the alterations and pathologies that patients report during therapy: not so much in the more classic symptoms as in the many minor dysfunctions, which taken together represent an authentic *mutilation* of an individual's vital capacities.

For this reason, this book aims to integrate aspects of a *developmental* nature with more strictly *therapeutic* aspects, enriched with practical examples taken from experiences of Functional psychotherapy with both individuals and groups. Today, in fact, studies in psychotherapy and child development should no longer be kept separate, but instead woven together within the context of a global and integrated theory, which no longer divides aspects of growth and vital functioning from those of prevention.

Functional Development in Psychotherapy

An outline of development is not just useful for following child growth but it is also useful within processes of change in psychotherapy.

The link between the two aspects is particularly close and significant precisely because the core of the therapeutic process is intimately linked to the history of the individual's personal development; indeed it consists above all in gathering up and reconstructing the patient's previously interrupted lines of development.

This is even more clear if one considers development not as a succession of stages leading from a state of partiality to a state of maturity (in the subject's drives and relationships) but rather as a *process in which the Functions gradually become more complex* within an organism that is *already* whole and integrated. In other words, we should consider development as *a passage through the various Basic Experiences* where we consolidate capacities that are already an innate possession of the organism, and adapt them to different contexts and circumstances.

In Functional therapy, therefore, "regression" does not mean returning to pathological events in the patient's life, before an adult "genital" phase; rather it means getting back to moments and functional processes when the individual's integrity and completeness were still present, before environmental factors started undermining the Basic Experiences.

A non-full or non-positive passage through the Basic Experiences prevents the consolidation of an individual's life skills, and manifests itself in alterations in one or more functions, on one or more planes of the Self.

In a course therapy which takes into consideration not just thoughts and emotions but also sensations and inner functional processes, it is much more likely that very strong feelings and memories resurface from adolescence, from childhood, or even from the perinatal period which had hitherto been hidden deep down. We can define these as "regression" phenomena in the sense of a voyage into archaic functional processes (rather than into the past, per se), in order to discover and remove buried traces, the outcomes of the problems experienced as children. These traces consist of infantile movements and facial expressions, tears and smiles which need no longer be held back, physical sensations from when we were little, weak voices and self consolatory gestures.

All of this brings us back to patients' developmental history, and to a period in which this development suffered blows, interruptions, or alterations.

It is quite rare that we are able to track down a single traumatic event in patients' lives. Much more often it happens that a whole series of negative conditions, frustrations and displeasures emerge, caused by the surrounding environment, which have ended up accumulating to form strata in one particular direction. These negative conditions, when repeated, lead to the restriction of one or more functional processes linked to the particular Basic Experience which haven't been allowed to unfold in a full and positive way.

If a little girl is continually stopped in her vital Bursts of Energy[1], and in her natural desire to express herself with her full voice, over the years (and

1 Capital letters are used when the precise denominations given to the Basic Experiences are quoted.

not in response to a single reprimand, or a single punishment, no matter how severe it is) she will end up having a feeble voice, or one that is too high, without the full and joyous vigour that every voice should be able to express. This behaviour is neither conscious, nor can it be controlled voluntarily, because if she were asked to open out and increase the volume of her own voice she would be completely incapable of doing so even if she wanted to. She would not be able to express Bursts of Energy and vitality using the appropriate voice.

The same Function, "voice", can, however, suffer other alterations, linked to different forms of negative conditioning, which ends up limiting or impeding other important capacities in a person's life such as managing to Confront Others, saying "No" firmly, expressing a different opinion, openly showing Anger or disappointment, using a Full and Calm Strength or supporting their own convictions.

In the first example, the little girl has been hindered in a very specific Basic Experience, that of Joy and Vitality. In the examples that follow, in contrast, different Basic Experiences have been involved and damaged: Opposing Others, Anger, Calm Strength, and Assertiveness.

The link between development and psychotherapy is evident, therefore, in the patients' histories themselves.

Development in the context of a course of psychotherapy

The link that we are talking about can be demonstrated practically with a few short patient histories.

Lina

As a child, Lina's face had already taken on an increasingly *sad* expression; a constant, fixed sadness, which was present regardless of what was going on around her, whether it be a moment of joy or sadness. All too soon Lina had had to take on tasks of great responsibility in the family: look after her sick mother and her younger sister, look after the household, run the apartments that the family owned, and even take charge of her father's floriculture business. Lina's smile disappeared little by little from her face, to be substituted by a constant mask of profound sadness, which the patient still carried with her as an adult.

The therapeutic process could not, therefore, overlook the necessity of re-mobilizing her *facial expressions*, practically and repeatedly, not just to make Lina conscious of her bitter and sad bent, but above all to rediscover a new smile and recuperate (through therapy touching on the various planes of movement, voice, emotions and value system) the *Experience* of *Joy* that Lina had lost since she was a little girl.

Antonella

As a child, Antonella had had to learn to keep "composed" She was careful not to make inconvenient, exaggerated, tomboy, or mischievous movements. She could not run freely or chase her playmates. She could not throw herself on the ground for fear of dirtying her clothes; she could not play without control and without rules. She had to maintain a careful and measured comportment at all times.

When Antonella arrived in therapy, she was awkward and rigid in her movements. She was afraid to take on any activity which required freedom of movement: at the seaside she never dived into the water, she didn't swim unless there was something to hold on to nearby, she didn't practise sport and she didn't like dance, with its complicated moves to be memorised and carried out with effortlessness and agility.

Movement, then, had to form a central part of her course of therapy. If Antonella wanted to recuperate the vitality that had been suffocated and extinguished, then she had to re-experience the movements that had been lost. She had to rediscover, one by one, the vital movements that she too had possessed (in an era prior to the alterations), as well as fill them out with new nuances; picking up the *process of development* that had been interrupted at that moment.

Functional psychology (as we will see in more detail later on in the book) takes all levels of an individual's functioning into consideration (grouping them into four main areas: cognitive-symbolic, emotive, postural-motor and physiological), and it acts on the complexity of phenomena and of human functioning. Consequently, Antonella's therapy could not just be limited to the level of *movement*. That is to say, the course of therapy had to centre on recuperating the *Experiences* of *Bursts of Energy* and *Vitality*, recovering the movements intimately connected to all those Functions that had been damaged or altered by the difficult situations that had blocked Antonella in her childhood.

It follows, then, that the therapy also had to intervene in the way that the patient *saw* herself, as a "person who is incapable of measuring up to situations where ability plays an important role." The therapy had to intervene on Antonella's *symbolic* plane, i.e. on the fact that she attributed negative values to displaying herself, to anyone who willingly puts them self to the test, to throwing oneself with ease into new activities for which one is not sufficiently prepared. Antonella's *memories* of moments when she had managed to have more effortless and joyous movements (although few) had to be valorised as much as possible, and we had to attempt to reopen lost and suffocated memories of when there were still bursts of energy, and darting, happy and uninhibited movements.

With the Function of *making plans*, Antonella had to be helped to build concrete opportunities into her own life which would provide her with bursts of energy and

> movement: enrol in a dance school, go on trips, try a riskier sport and throw herself into relationships with light-heartedness.
>
> In an *integrated* course of therapy, however, even *muscle tone* had to play an important role. Antonella had to recover the elasticity and springiness necessary to allow her to pass from immobility to movement, and to fast movement in particular. Her *breathing* had to return to a slightly state of sympathetic arousal to give her just the right dose of excitement without breaking out into anxiety. The positive *emotions* of joy and enthusiasm had to be associated with fast and darting movements, whilst her negative *fantasies* of being ridiculous, inadequate, or of risking danger by throwing herself into things had to be toned down, helped by a revival of profound *sensations* of pleasure and a new way of savouring the sensations offered by vitality.

All of this represents, essentially, an authentic *return* to the moment when the *path of her development* was interrupted (or at least hindered) and demonstrates once again the profound link between child development and psychotherapy.

Functional Psychotherapy: an "integrated" therapy

Another objective of mine in writing this book was to take the results of years of work and research dedicated to the functional processes at the very root of the *therapeutic process* and make them useable. The aim of this was to genuinely improve the efficacy of treatments on a practical level, to make the results more stable and the probability of a therapeutic success more certain. What I am talking about are the functional processes that, regardless of the theories and methodology adopted by the individual therapist, in a certain sense constitute the *common foundations of every course of psychotherapy* and of every good psychotherapist. The common intention and interest of all psychotherapists is that of studying human organisms' deepest functional processes ever more completely, seeking the unity between body and mind that has for too long been fragmented into opposing parts, compressed into partial aspects or seen from limited angles.

The way of the future is undeniably a *multidimensional* vision, able to unite *all* the aspects that contribute to health and well-being, excluding nothing. It has become increasingly necessary to create an *integrated theory*, which links up all the different findings and theories that have appeared in close succession on the psychotherapy scene.

There is no doubt that it is the whole organism that gets ill and not just a few of its parts, a few of its structures, or a few psychological instances or constructs, whether they be biological or psychological. The self-same psycho-soma dichotomy has been completely overcome and is inadequate to describe how a living organism works.

However, to be able to proceed fruitfully along this path, we need to first carry out a complete reform in our way of thinking. An *integrated* theory cannot lie in the sum of the various existing theories. An *integrated* theory cannot consist in a mix made up of a few psychoanalytic techniques, a few cognitive methods, a bit of body work, and so on.

An integrated theory requires that several of the basic assumptions behind the pre-existing theories, those no longer supported by contemporary scientific knowledge, be abandoned once and for all. It also requires that we reach a different, "higher" level of theory and method construction. All of this is already underway, and Functional Psychology is a clear example.

The *Theory of the Functions* represents a significant epistemic and methodological leap forward, because it leaves the concept of "static structure" behind. It goes beyond the concept of a "system divided into parts", and embraces the wholeness of the individual (of the living organism), which it sees in terms of the *organisation* of the body. *This organisation regulates a series of processes* on all possible planes and levels. The body's internal organisation can be clearly detected and can be operated on in a clear, deliberate, and effective way.

Living beings are *whole* and *integrated*. The Functions express *wholeness* and they are profoundly *integrated* among themselves. *Every single Function* is an expression of the whole person; and each Function can be studied in its particular and detailed course. The Functions are neither abstract nor unlimited in number. They are working concepts which can be accurately listed because they refer to an individual's *basic functioning*; functional processes that then govern the individual's various behaviour patterns in life's different situations, and which are already well documented.

The *Functions* and the *Basic Experiences*, then, are multidimensional elements that relate to the individual as a whole and to his basic functioning, and as such they can be considered as *important and sophisticated foundations for an integrated theory and methodology*. With the Functions and the Basic Experiences, it is also possible to form an exact *diagnosis* for that person, draw up a concrete and detailed *program of therapy*, with a specific direction in mind, and carry out and *intervene, multidimensionally,* as appropriately and as effectively as possible.

In seeking a deeper comprehension of what happens in therapy, in trying to understand what it is that the therapist really puts into action, or what determines change, we must not abandon the theory at a general level, nor must we neglect the actual procedures, techniques and tools present at a practical level. This book therefore includes clinical cases, descriptions of the techniques adopted, the analysis of the effects of therapy and patients' experiences. However, what happens in practise must always be conceived within the context of a general theory, i.e. it has to be governed by a *theory of technique.*

The aim is to delineate a *theory of technique* that is also innovative, and which attempts to take the potential efficiency of care (and prevention, too) beyond existing levels.

In my opinion the discussion of a *theory of technique* is still relevant, in that nowadays we are all too often faced with a flood of new techniques that fail to examine their real effects, their effectiveness, their coherence or their compatibility with other techniques. All too often, there is a tendency to *collect* techniques, sometimes of the most far-flung and disparate nature imaginable, without a theory of reference that could allow them to be used correctly and productively.

This phenomenon is yet more evident when it comes to using the body in psychotherapy. Lately, it would seem that there is a veritable race towards everything that is *physical*, probably because the returns offered by body therapy with respect to the intensity of the effects, impact and results with patients of body therapy has by now become widely known. However, what happens all too often, unfortunately, is that techniques are adopted without taking into consideration the significant research that has already existed in this field for many years and the progress that has already been made. Sometimes it seems that new elements are discovered where the self same elements have were already being studied years ago.

Moreover, a basic misunderstanding still weighs against body mediation therapies. One cannot just move the body and use what emerges within the framework of pre-existing clinical theories. An *integrated* psychotherapy cannot just be any theory, which *also* uses the body. Besides, the body is always present whether we acknowledge it or not, regardless of the type of therapy: even if it is only lying on a couch. The body is always interacting, whether you look at it or not, whether you touch it or not, whether it is moving on the couch or around the room.

Integrated psychotherapy, on the other hand, must be characterised by a *specific theory on the mind-body relationship*; and this becomes even more evident when we start delineating it precisely with the help of Functional thought.

It is not about deciding whether to intervene on the *soma* or the *psyche*, but about discerning *how to intervene* on the body and the psyche, and *to what aim*.

To give an example, a patient in therapy could be made to explore the world of movements and then examine the feelings that emerge. But if his movements are altered (e.g. always rigid, or small and limited, or agitated, or without strength) he will only know how to carry them out in his habitual, altered manner: his feelings and reactions won't be that dissimilar from feelings and reactions that he normally has in the course of his everyday life. At most, he will gain a greater awareness; but it is very unlikely that awareness on its own can manage to alter his "rigidity", or his "holding back", or his "agitation", or his "weakness", as well as all those problems connected to the above alterations in movement.

In another example, this very patient could be asked to participate in a group sequence on Tenderness, a game about Tenderness, requiring (among other things) a well-determined type of movement, soft and tender, which he is unable to carry out in a full or substantial way. He may enjoy himself in this group game, but his deep functioning will not be altered; on the contrary, he will probably reinforce the stereotype that he currently has of himself.

Parallel examples could be made for the imagination, the voice, for life strategies, for value systems or for memories.

An integrated psychotherapy works in neither one way nor the other, but instead it *directly modifies the way a patient moves*, re-mobilising the "Movement Function" in its entirety, deep down within the individual. It also, at the same time, modifies everything that the alteration of this Function implies in terms of emotions, feelings, memories, potentiality, and symbolisations. An integrated therapy acts on the entire altered functional process (which arises from the altered movement), restoring, one by one, Tenderness, the capacity to Let Go, Calm, and Strength to the subject.

A program of therapy should above all consist in *rebalancing* the whole Functional organisation of the Self. Emotions that are too conspicuous have to be put back into perspective, the imagination and forward planning that are deficient must be allowed more space, limited postures and sensations that are too isolated from a patient's awareness must be integrated with the other Functions of the Self.

Functional processes that have been closed, stereotyped, limited or cut off need to be reopened. At the same time, the Basic Experiences must be recuperated: they must be gone through, rebuilt and recuperated so that they once again take part of the individual's permanent baggage of abilities.

Integrated Psychotherapy implies, therefore, a methodology which includes a theory of development, an etiopathogenic theory, a theory of treatment, a theory of the therapeutic process, and a theory of technique: remaining constantly within an overall vision that incorporates the various psychotherapy models at a higher and more wide-ranging level.

All too often, somatic or expressive activities are offered without a specific aim in mind, with no basic theory to back them up, let alone a theory of technique. At best, they are only borne out by the therapist's personal experience, or simply by the tradition of passing on certain techniques. In this way, offering expressive or body mediation techniques still means offering experiences without an overall therapeutic project.

Another scenario is that expressive or body mediation techniques get carried out as an add-on to other clinical models, or they remain separate experiences, divided from the "main" therapeutic setting, which is the only one considered to be "genuinely valid and scientifically founded".

It also happens that single psychophysical techniques are considered erroneously as a therapy in their own right. They get elevated to the status of a complete therapeutic system, even though they possess no general theory on human functioning, no theory of development, no etiopathogenic theory, no theory of technique.

In reality, body movement (to continue from the previous examples), whether you use it for dance, painting, or for any other type of expression, is always tied to overall *mind-body* functioning. What really interests us, therefore, is a mind-body theory, a theory of the organism's overall functioning, because it is this that allows us to *understand* the meaning of a given person's movements, and which allows us to *modify* that person profoundly and concretely on the plane of movement itself.

The answer lies in being able to frame, within a complex and complete system, the reasons *why* we make patients perform a given movement in therapy, *when*, *in what way*, and *what change we wish to bring about in the patient.* It must not, on the contrary, just be a case of generic experimentation, or of seeking lost spontaneity. Years of practice and research tell us extremely clearly that profound and stable changes very rarely come about (and only then in certain specific conditions of the functioning of the Self) by merely reliving experiences, or by merely experiencing and seeking lost spontaneity. Change comes about because of a complex and precise journey that touches many levels of an individual's functioning and which proceeds along a precisely-determined course.

The above misunderstandings do nothing to further current knowledge or increase treatment potential. They do nothing to ease the eternal debate about the effectiveness of psychotherapy as opposed to the exclusive use of pharmaceuticals. They in no way help the advancement of our knowledge about the mechanisms that cause illness or those which contribute to health.

These misunderstandings prevent us from fully exploiting the vast and innovative contribution that an all-encompassing mind-body theory could bring to the clinical world. They prevent us from integrating the various contributions produced over the years by different psychotherapeutic models productively and innovatively. And it is precisely this *integration* that could take us closer to a more complete understanding of human functioning, opening up the barriers between Psychology, Medicine, Biology and Physiology in order to finally aim towards a full, successful and integrated management of individual and social health and well-being.

To finish, I would like to express my thanks to Teresa Sorrentino for her affectionate collaboration throughout the whole book in general. I would also like to thank her in particular for her direct collaboration in the realisation of chapter 4 on Needs, Functions, and Basic Experiences of the Self, on the crucial and complex chapter 5 on the Basic Experiences during development, and on chapter 12 on child and adolescent therapy.

I would also like to thank my wife Paola Bovo for her constant loving support as well as her painstaking help revising this book.

My thanks also go to all those who believed in the book and who waited for it with unswerving faith, strongly encouraging me to make it a reality.

Chapter 1

The Development of Knowledge

Transformations in scientific thought

Over the last century, we have seen profound and significant transformations within the scientific world. We have been witness to changes both in the way we deal with problems and in the different methodologies that have been progressively adopted in the study of complex systems.

The situation in the field of the human sciences is even more delicate. We are still a long way off from a definitive and cohesive understanding of the laws that govern man's psychological and physical functioning. What we have at present is a series of different models, a series of approaches that allow us to consider human experience from different perspectives, e.g. medicine, psychology, the neurosciences. What is more, each of these branches is itself divided into different models and interpretations.

However, if we look closely at the history of clinical psychology and psychotherapy, a conspicuous trend emerges. The various clinical approaches can actually be seen as different angles from which one can study the individual and his psychological and relational functioning. As time has gone on, each model has shed light on different phenomena, on specific parts of this complex universe, focussing techniques on just those aspects. For this reason we can affirm that the psychological systems existing today are not in fact contradictory alternatives but rather *complementary* (at least for the most part).

Today, however, we are facing a new phase in the history of the human sciences, a phase characterised by an emphasis on caring for the individual *as a whole*, responding to the challenge of the *complexity* of this field of research whilst bearing in mind that it is a *unified whole*.

We are now able to interpret an individual's functional processes, the way he lives, thinks, relates to himself and to others, as well as his mind-body relationship, no longer based on partial or limited elements (cognitive processes, neurobiological structures, behaviour, self-image, emotions, or bodily processes) but in a new way which deals with all the phenomena that determine life and its relational processes. The time has come to be able to look at the individual in an *integrated* way, combining all the knowledge accumulated by the different models and techniques; connecting and integrating all the different approaches and experiences with the legacy of data collected, especially recently.

Subjectivism vs. objectivism

One of the causes of such violent and, at the same time, pointless, clashes between the different scientific approaches can be attributed to the dichotomy between *subjectivism* and *objectivism.* Several currents in the scientific world, and in the world of psychology in particular, have been careful to keep their distances from the "medical/organic" model, focussing almost exclusively on individual sensations, on feelings, on subjectivism. Several branches of the neurosciences and psychiatry have, on the other hand, continued to sustain a marked objectivism.

At a conference on the advantages of combining psychotherapy and pharmaceuticals in treatment, there were, among others present, a Neuroscientist and a Psychoanalyst. The first maintained "without a shadow of doubt" that psychotherapy could provide the patient with "support", but that in reality it was pharmaceuticals alone that were the healing agents. The Psychoanalyst, who was also apparently in favour of associating the two methods, let it be known that pills are only useful because when the patient takes them he is introjecting the "good breast", and therefore he can do just as well without them, or take a placebo in their place.

Rose, an American neuroscientist with a more open frame of mind, argues, on the other hand, the necessity of research integrating the two viewpoints. Siegel (1999) retains that a convergence between the various areas of research is fundamental, given recent findings indicating that interpersonal relationships influence the development and functioning of neurobiological structures themselves.

More and more scholars are becoming aware of the necessity of an all-encompassing vision that integrates both subjective and objective levels.

They believe that this can be achieved through research projects that consider the uniqueness of each single subject's feelings and emotions, but which also take into account elements that exist objectively.

Chronically hunched posture, constant shallow breathing, or cold, sweaty hands are some simple examples of elements that are in part subjective (being linked to different emotional reactions from person to person). However, are also clearly objective, in that they are elements that can be easily noted by any observer of an individual's psycho-physical functioning (as long as they are competent).

This concept could fuel much future research. For example: we could study the effects of a determined course of psychotherapy on the quantity of seratonin (the drug used for depression) produced by the organism itself. Readings could be taken before and after treatment and before and after a single sitting, in order to analyse to what extent the changes produced can be found at the different levels of functioning, right up to the neurophysiological level. Moreover, we could compare different types of psychotherapy in order to verify which of them has the biggest effect on these levels, and, consequently, which of them brings about the most deep-rooted change in the individual as a whole.

Hydraulic, homeostatic and stimulus-response models

As Science has evolved, new perspectives have gradually replaced old ones, and new ways of thinking have replaced earlier ones.

The mechanistic forms of logic that characterised science at the beginning of the last century, based on linear causality, have been abandoned. Similarly, concepts attributing the triggering of behaviour to *hydraulic models* of build-up and release have also been surpassed. Tension does not always *build up* to the point where it triggers a reaction, and it is not always the case that a reaction finishes when "what was bottled up" has been "released".

Today we know that there are functional processes that are set off independently of real situations, favourable environment, or pressure from inner needs. For example, explosions of rage in choleric individuals are set off at the slightest chance and seem to become increasingly uncontrollable. Sexual desire is more intense when sexual activity is present than following a period of abstinence. Obsessive behaviour becomes more repetitive if it is left uncontrolled. Eating, sleeping, and smoking all seem to have functional processes that intensify more with fulfilment rather than with abstinence.

Even the principle of homeostasis is no longer considered valid for every system. Today, for example, we know that there are *non conservative* systems whose energy levels can increase or decrease. Living beings do not react like feedback circuits designed to maintain a *status quo*: life is in fact variable, or wave-like. Feedback processes are complex because they do not merely modify the causes of the process, but also the effects and intermediate stages of that self same process.

Even within *Stimulus-Response* (S-R) or *Stimulus-Organism-Response* (S-O-R) models, emphasis is shifting towards *what* happens within the organism and *how* it comes about. The organism is no longer seen as something that is different for every individual, remaining, however, invariable over time. The organism itself is a delicate and complex variable, which is continually subject to the influence of both the Stimulus and the Response. The most recent models therefore, are typically of a *Stimulus-Organism-Organisation-Response* (S-O-O-R) type, where *the organism continually organises and modifies its own internal organisation*, responding to both the external environment and also to its very own actions and interactions.

The concept of *organisation*, therefore, takes into account the existence of complex feedback cycles that have an effect on the organism (and therefore on the way it which it relates with its surroundings), constantly transforming it. It also explains the profound influence that the organism and its transformations have, in turn, on the feedback systems themselves, and on the modality and functioning of such retroactions.

Systems

The most recent formulations take into account the fact that even the most apparently simple phenomena belong in reality to a *complex system.*

A structure, of whatever nature it may be, cannot be considered merely as the simple sum of its parts. Subdivision of a "spatial" nature, whereby the whole is divided into smaller parts or categories, does not permit us to fully understand the way the structure or the system itself actually *functions.*

The concept of parts has, undoubtedly, allowed us to analyse various "dynamics" between the parts themselves, understood as "forces" which push in different directions; but it is not able to fully explain how these parts *function* or how they contribute in their complex correlation to the life of the system as a whole.

If we do not take into account the fact that the entire system functions as a whole, we run the risk of losing a global understanding of its workings, and we therefore risk falling into the trap of excessive specialisation and compartmentalisation, which is undoubtedly one of the evils of certain currents in modern science.

A form of logic based on parts or categories rarely manages to encompass a vision of the system's *organisation*, and therefore the parts or categories end up being considered either as alternates to each other or in opposition to one another: in other words, in *conflict* with one another. If we treat a pain in the stomach, we don't look to see whether the eyes are tired, nor do we look at the emotions underlying the discomfort, nor do we check to see whether the breathing is fluid and open, because apparently the stomach has "nothing to do with" these other aspects. Even if we did not ignore other parts of the body or the person, we would end up setting them against each other and against the rest of the organism, which has been left out of the equation.

Thus, even the theory of systems has evolved. Scientific currents are abandoning the concept of "conflict between parts" and subdivision in categories, in order to approach that of *inner organisation,* and consequently that of *possible deficiencies or alterations within the body's organisation.*

We can join Morin in saying that the paradigm of complex thought helps us to envisage the "unity/multiplicity of every entity, instead of heterogenizing it into separate categories, or homogenizing it in an indistinct whole. It incites us to recognize the multidimensional character of every reality studied." (Morin, 1985, p. 202)

On the other hand, the problem cannot merely be resolved by thinking in terms of "structures" because the very idea entails thinking in terms of something that is difficult to modify. It also requires us to consider the elements in a structure as *real things*, when in fact they are not "things" at all.

> Structure is an atrophied concept, says Morin, which takes us back to an idea of order (rules of invariance) rather than that of organisation [...]. The "structuralist" vision [...] tends to reduce the phenomenological aspects of the structure to the structure that generates them (Morin, 1982, p. 136).

Organisation, on the contrary, is *active*: it implies the idea of the employment and dispersion of energy; it produces the "degradation of the system and of itself... and the regeneration of the system and of itself" (Morin, 1982, p. 137).

It is exactly for this reason that the field of clinical psychology has resisted considering the Self as something that goes beyond "mental images" and mere subjective experience. The fear was that we would have to resort to a model that ended up being too similar to a structure, to elements characterised by a "material" existence, and by an over-simplistic outlook.

The concept of complexity, however, has gradually helped us to rise above these fears, and to go beyond a purely experiential conception of the Self, which was unable to encompass the functioning of the whole organism and the interaction between the body and the mind, between emotions and psycho-physiological systems, between images and neuro-endocrine apparatus.

Holism

The concept of *holism* is based on the laudable aim of maintaining the overall unity of the subject, overcoming the fragmentation and specialisation that causes us to lose sight of the central elements of human functioning, life, health and well-being.

Prigogine has always maintained that modern science must be truly *holistic*. Modern science must not hide behind specialisations or fragment itself into separate details, attempting to reunite all the various different branches of knowledge into a coherent whole.

What Prigogine was referring to was the idea that science could form a bridge between *being* and *becoming* in the natural environment, and between the different aspects of nature in connection with us (in particular with respect to human beings and their relationships), as well as the different models we use to interpret their functioning.

Recent studies on the mind (Eccles, 1990; Ross, 1996) have demonstrated that the various parts of the brain and its neurons are less specialised than we previously thought, and that they are able to modify their tasks if necessary.

The brain itself therefore presents a basic unity, over and above the various Functions to which its different parts are allotted. This type of organisation demonstrates the validity of theories that take the concept of the whole into consideration, without which it is impossible to grasp the meaning of a living organism.

Pascal said that it was impossible to understand the parts without understanding the whole, just as it is impossible to understand the whole without an accurate knowledge of its parts.

Holism can, however, fall into the very trap of reductionism that it aims to oppose. This happens if the "whole" is seen as a broad totality, divorced from any detail; if it is understood as a simplification of reality; or if it is not seen as having the dynamism of *organisation*. Holism in that case remains vague and generic, and is unable to get to grips with the innermost details of life's smallest functional processes.

> The problems of the system cannot be reduced to a whole-parts relationship, and the holistic paradigm neglects two fundamental terms: interaction and organisation (Morin, 1982, p. 136).

Organisms

The concept of the *ecosystem* has further contributed towards a change in current thought. However, it has been applied primarily to the natural world. With the theory of *chains of interaction* and *life cycles* we can better understand the levels of interaction between the parts that constitute living, cyclic chains, and we are able to study where an ecosystem breaks down and why.

Further progress has been made in this direction, however, providing an understanding of how systems modify themselves *throughout their whole organisation*, what their *general* and at the same time *specific,* conditions are, and which living forces open up or block them.

The theory of systems, according to Morin, had only seemingly defined the problem. We can only reach a new principle of knowledge (cognition) if we perceive the system not just "as a general term but as a generic and generative term, in short, a paradigm" (Morin, 1982, p. 130).

> If the idea of the system remains "theoretical" it completely fails to touch the disjunction/simplification paradigm it sought to overtake by overturning reductive atomisation. On the contrary, its very "holism" becomes reductive because it reduces the system to a single idea: "the whole" (Morin, 1982, p. 144).

Conceptions that regard the *living organism* as a system, and which attempt to rise to the challenge of *complex thought*, are characterised by a few basic elements:

- They take into consideration the *organisation* of the system itself, its continuous levels of plastic modification, in response to both external and internal stimuli, operating change both externally and internally;
- They look at the organism as an ensemble of *complex feedback cycles* which interact with both the environment, the organisation and the actual feedback cycles themselves;
- They keep in mind the *wholeness* and *unity* of the system-organism, without falling into a vague and reductive idea of a "whole" which fails to take into account the system, with all its vital, specific and detailed phenomena;
- They are able to get right down even as far as the *very small and detailed elements* within an organism, in order to be able to study them and intervene at an operative level, without losing sight of the whole or resorting to the concept of "parts" or "categories";
- The are able to reach the depths of the system, to the *functional processes that are at the root* of its actions, of its "behaviour", of its interactions;
- They take into consideration all the levels of the system's functioning, all its planes and possible processes;
- They create a model integrating the various approaches, with differing points of view and with different scientific outlooks.

Steps towards a reform of thought

Scholars today are tending towards a truly modern science, which both Morin and Prigogene refer to in different ways. It is not a static or mechanistic science, nor is it a science that compartmentalises or divides. Nor is it, on the other hand, an indistinct, metaphysical, holistic conception.

On the contrary, it is the science of a universe in constant change, a science that accepts the idea of *complexity* without abandoning the task of understanding and explaining it. It is a science that attempts nonetheless to give a mathematical form to the *laws of chaos*.

The search is well underway for a new level that can overcome classic *determinism* on the one hand, with its excessive reductionism, its cause and effect linearity, its laws that are solely quantitative, its simplification and its disjunction, and a purely *chaotic* conception of reality on the other, seen as unrepeatable and impossible to study, comprehend or predict.

How can we keep in mind the nature of the whole without losing the study of its complexity? How can we overcome the dichotomy between subjectivism and objectivism? How can we go beyond neo-positivism without falling, on the other hand, into the pure irrationality, which states that nothing can be studied, understood, or reproduced? How can we overcome the notion of parts?

One possible answer to these questions is to take the system's *Functions* into consideration: i.e. their basic functioning on every possible plane: the psychological, motor, postural, psycho-physiological and neurobiological planes.

As we will see in more detail in the next chapter, *Functional thought* deals with the system-organism, with systems' processes of *organisation*, with the connection between subjectivism and objectivism, with the study of the "whole" without relinquishing the idea of getting down to specific detail at an operative level. For a long time now, the Functional school has been studying not only the mental and psychological planes of human functioning, but also its physical aspects: the complex mind-body interactions that characterise human life, in its complexity and entirety.

The concepts of the *Functions*, the *Functional processes,* and the *Basic Experiences of the Self* are an innovative response to modern science's call for a new epistemology.

Chapter 2

Functional Psychology

The first functionalist movement

The attempt to overcome mechanistic scientific notions in the search for new ways of looking at reality is certainly not a new one. One of the most interesting paths taken has been that of Functionalism, a current of thought that emerged in the United States in opposition to Wundt's *Structural Psychology*.

Functionalism was a school of study and thought that grew out of *evolutionism*, developed principally within the spheres of pedagogy and philosophy. It has remained, however, unexpressed as far as the field of clinical psychology is concerned: both perhaps due to the fact that the time was not yet right, and because the American school of thought (from which it originated) changed course immediately afterwards along the strictly pragmatist lines of *behaviourism*.

Normally, psychological functionalism is associated with the Chicago school (Dewey, 1896; Angell, 1907), but the important contributions of scholars such as James, Hall, and Cattel cannot be overlooked within its framework.

James sustained, even as early as 1890, the need for a method which was both phenomenological and genetic/functional, with a Darwinian outlook, although profoundly revised in its epistemological approach. For James, psychic reality is a stream of consciousness that must be represented in its immediacy (above and beyond any possible metaphysical, positivistic or idealistic structures) concretely tied to an *organism in interaction with the surrounding environment.* Man is seen as the product of action and emotion no less than that of thought and reason. Not even interior activity can be seen as separate from physiological factors or from necessities and needs.

The theory proposed by James-Lange (1892) considers *the physical elements of emotion as almost the primary font of human's ability to feel.* Here, a dualistic approach is starting to be replaced by a holistic one, whereby a patient's psychic life is seen as a global experience in continual transformation, as a process, as a current in motion.

Even more clearly, for Dewey (1896), the objective of psychology is to study the organism as a whole, in its functioning in relation to the environment. This relationship is not however considered in a Darwinian sense, i.e. as something endured by the individual through the species, but as the active adaptation of the organism to the environment and the active adaptation of the environment to the organism.

There is a *circular* causality uniting the phenomena. To give an example, a reflex arc is actually a circular concatenation of reflex arcs, impossible to break down into two just units, i.e. stimulus and response. In this approach, psychic phenomena such as the sensations, the emotions, perception, learning, and reasoning, although distinguishable for their particular characteristics, cannot be examined as *separate* elements but only as elements in reciprocal relation with each other, and in their interaction as a whole with the surroundings.

One of the essential texts of functionalism is Angell's manifesto, *The Province of Functional Psychology* (1907). In it, he makes clear that Functionalism aims to discover the modalities of man's functioning, not analyse mental content "in vitro", so as to avoid the risk of attributing (by defining them as structures) an absolute character to fluctuating or evanescent formations. Mental activity is part of a wider complex of biological forces, and contributes to the efficient running of all organic activities in which the Psychologist and the Biologist are strictly related.

Objections have arisen from some quarters that functionalism was nothing other than a sort of "psychophysiology". However this is, if anything, a quality rather than a defect, because it confirms that functionalism strove towards determining the reciprocal relations between physical and mental aspects within the human organism; and, what's more, in an era in which the necessity for a similar reform of thinking had not yet been clearly identified.

Woodworth (1918), in his dynamic psychology, insists on the physiological causes of behaviour. Between S (Stimulus) and R (Response), there is a living organism with its complexities and different levels of functioning.

With Carr (1925), the functionalist school reaches its greatest development, together with the idea that a more general and global theory is necessary. For Carr, in fact, many of the currents in the field of psychology had hitherto developed theories regarding only limited sectors of human functioning, differing as they went along according to the point of view taken.

Functionalism lost ground perhaps with the decline of the Chicago School. One of its most promising followers, Watson, took his distances in order to dedicate himself to the study of the most visible and concrete elements of human functioning: their *behaviour*. At the same moment, the entire American school underwent a sudden shift towards Pragmatism, in relation to the evident necessity for economic and social expansion of that period.

Nevertheless, the Chicago School's basic methodological imprint was not lost with the decline of the school itself. We can find it, elaborated in different ways, in numerous contemporary theories. Today, the matrix of functional thought still possesses the same nuclei and catalysts of extreme interest that it did at the beginning of the last century, for numerous sectors beyond the philosophical and pedagogical fields.

It is true that functionalism wasn't much interested, even in its period of maximum expansion, in other fields; but only because no-one at the time attempted the task in a truly convincing manner. On the other hand, we must not forget that, at that time, clinical psychology had long been occupied with, and dominated by, the conflict between the two great currents of thought, or opposing interpretative models of reality. The first was derived from the "idealist" school of thought (which was allowed to develop more in Europe and which was incarnated above all in Freudian psychoanalysis); and the second was derived from "pragmatism", (which gave birth to behaviourism and the systemic school of Palo Alto, and which was diffused principally in America).

Today, however, we can affirm in all certainty that functionalism (if freed from certain extremisms and simplifications resulting from its historic context), can be of surprisingly contemporary interest, and can be considerably developed with new epistemic, theoretical, and technical formulations.

The birth of modern functionalism

Modern functionalism is the result of a different process to that of the first functionalist movement, in that it is rooted above all in clinical practise, and research relating to the field of the complex relations between the body and the mind.

The field of Body, or Somatic Psychology was the first to deal with the mind-body relationship. This branch of Psychology was originally derived from the first formulations of Wilhelm Reich in the 1920's on the cardinal concept of the *functional identity* between the psyche and the soma. Since then, Body Psychology has developed numerous and varied movements in America and Europe. However, the various schools of Body Psychotherapy haven't always developed adequate reflections on what was happening in clinical practise and on the relevant phenomena that emerged during trials, because they were swept up by the desire to explore new paths in this increasingly fascinating field of study. More often than not, they gave precedence to the exploration of new techniques, starting with the use of the body with its many possibilities of expression.

Among those interested in a reform of the underlying theory was the Naples School, which had specifically dedicated itself to the construction of a more adequate theoretical framework since the beginning of the 1990's. Their aim was to construct a scientifically innovative theory able to put the complex field of the mind-body relationship in better focus.

Whilst the Naples school had its roots in Body Psychotherapy, it soon began to take up the threads of the first functionalist school, together with Reich's promising theories, and the developments that the latter had subsequently undergone over time. Thanks, also, to the results of studies carried out in those years on the processes involved in therapy on one hand, and on child development on the other, the Naples school began to form *modern functionalism.*

In so doing, the Naples School of Functional Psychotherapy was obliged (as we will see better later on) to go beyond the confines of body psychotherapy and its traditional theoretical principles, and venture out on a wider plane. It embraced the study of complexity and theoretical reform suggested by modern functionalism, together with the possibility of *integrating* the different points of view that the various clinical approaches had maintained up until that point.

Practise in Psychotherapy uniting body and mind brought about intense phenomena, such as the recovery of inner sensations connected to very early moments in the patients' lives, changes regarding not just cognitive and emotional, but also psycho-physiological and neurobiological levels, and the effects encountered on different levels of functioning. These have all helped to open up a new scientific course towards the challenge of complex thought. From this has arisen a new way of looking at living organisms: a perspective that is multidimensional, a way of thinking about reality, which allows us to contemplate both the global overview and the operative detail. This in turn has reinforced the conviction that the way systems are *organised* internally must be taken into consideration, together with their *functioning*. These elements, by their very nature, entail a different and truly modern vision of complex phenomena. This is the direction that modern functionalism has taken during the course of its development.

In this way, we have reached a new form of thinking. This new epistemology seeks to avoid as much as possible basing itself on the concepts of "structure" and of "parts". It avoids being reductive or deterministic, and it seeks to interpret not just individuals but also every "organism": families, groups, institutions, geographic areas, or cities, in a way that does justice to its innate complexity.

In fact, even when referring to the workings of a typically "structural" system such as a city, the concept of "parts" has been demonstrated to be inadequate. There is no point talking about living standards and well-being if the single zones of the city are seen as being in competition with one another. For example, restoring and pedestrianizing historic centres has led to the worsening of living standards in the surrounding areas. Town centres are improved (when indeed measures do actually lead to improvements) at the expense of the outskirts.

Even the subdivision of systems into "sectors" is no longer convincing: it is not true that the merchant sector has contrasting interests to those of civil servants or professionals, because an improvement in the *life* of the city brings advantages for everyone.

All too often, however, the idea of *contrast between parts* has prevailed (even in wider systems such as regions and states). The only possible activity, therefore, can be that of mediating between contrasting parts, instead of a *general improvement in living standards*, which concerns and affects everyone, across the board.

The *interdependence* between territories, if we see the Earth as a single *living organism*, is perhaps more evident than in the past, but it must always have existed. The proper working of nuclear reactors in Russia cannot but interest the other countries (as the Chernobyl disaster has shown); mad cow disease in England produced a widespread crisis throughout Europe; the impoverishment of the Amazonian rainforest puts the entire planet in danger.

Stress as an example of multidimensional interaction

Another area where the interaction between different levels of the individual, of the *human organism*, can be clearly seen is that of *stress*. At this point research has confirmed the profound ties that cause an organism under stress to become ill, to lose its capacity to conserve health and well-being. Today it is clear that stress is linked to many illnesses, in particular cancer, heart problems and diabetes, the weakening of the body's immune system in general, skin diseases and even a greater risk of drug addiction.

Until recently, however, the distinction was still unclear between short-term, or *positive* stress and permanent, or *chronic* stress, truly harmful for the organism. Nor were we aware of the mechanisms that led to chronic stress.

Research conducted in recent years on the argument (Rispoli, Di Nuovo, Genta, 2000) has gone right to the root of this subject. It gives us a complete picture of the phenomenon of stress, discovering all the links in the chain leading from "macro", (the external situation where the stressful stimulus transpires), to "micro", (biological or physiological levels where chronic stress becomes a pathological condition).

Today we know that stress even produces alterations at a neuronal level, leading to the degeneration of synapses, neurons, and relative connection patterns (Siegel, 1999). We know that difficulties and traumas suffered during childhood accentuate physiological reactivity and hormonal responses to external circumstances, and that this increased reactivity remains over time and characterises states of chronic stress (Perry, 1997). We have ascertained that stress also begins to anchor itself in the organism, and remain there, through alterations in breathing and basic muscle tone (Rispoli, 2000).

The "filter" with which a subject impacts and evaluates a stressful stimulus is not, therefore, purely cognitive. Rather, it is made up of a more or less altered state on a number of levels (emotional, muscular, symbolic, neuronal, vegetative). The first alterations develop, as we will see in the course of this book, as *traces* left by the relations between a child and its environment, and whether or not the latter was able to satisfy the child's fundamental needs, on *all the above levels.*

On the one hand, the interwoven nature of the relationship between mind and body, and between the various levels of the Self, has become increasingly evident. This interweaving has, on the other hand, shown itself to be increasingly complex, as it comprises the planes of the emotions, symbolism, imagination and fantasy, the planes of movement, posture, body language, muscle tone, and systems like breathing, inner perceptions and sensations, as well as the autonomic nervous system, heart and circulatory, neuronal and immune systems, right down to the exchange between neurotransmitters and osmotic and liquid exchange in the organism's tissues and between its very cells.

Overcoming the mind-body dichotomy

During the course of many years of practice in Psychotherapy, intervening on the body as well as the psyche, it had become clear that the concepts of "body" and "mind" continued to perpetuate a metaphysical and idealistic schism, born perhaps with Platonic thought, and propagated nonetheless by an Aristotelian culture, based on linear causality, within a deterministic and reductive scientific paradigm. The concepts of the body and the mind ended up representing (and what's more, in a way that was static) entirely abstract entities, with the defect of remaining too vague. When it comes to it, what do we mean by the words "body" or "mind"? Just about everything; and this renders them concepts of very little use both at a clinical, descriptive level and at the level of operative methodology.

Labelling a person's physical unease as "psychosomatic", didn't in fact explain what was happening within his organism. The phenomenon could not legitimately be explained by the simplistic assertion that the body had become ill as a result of conflict within the psyche, as if the body were just a blank canvas onto which we projected what happened in the world of the mind.

After more extensive observation, however, the psyche and the body did not appear to be separate entities at all. In reality, it has never been possible to find a single clinical case in which the ailment was exclusively physical or purely psychic.

As far as the notion of complex systems is concerned, similar observations have been made regarding the same dichotomy. Morin maintains that the concept of complex thought cannot remain limited by the contraposition between "physical" and "psychic".

Several researchers in body psychotherapy have gone as far as to talk about the "emotional" body, the "expressive" body and the "energetic" body, overflowing ultimately into ideas which are no longer linked either to the concept of the body or to the unity of body and mind. The body in this way becomes a totalising whole that does not allow us to examine the human being's real planes of functioning, or to gather the richness of their differences and specificity.

In order to overcome the mind-body dichotomy it was necessary to envisage human organisms' basic unity, without erroneously creating a reductive or mechanistic model, divided into "parts" separate from the whole, or creating excessively vague or abstract totalities.

The Functional concept of the Self

The standpoint of modern Functionalism emerged, as we have seen, from the necessity to go beyond the *impasse* of the mind-body dichotomy, and to satisfy the strongly perceived need for *multidimensionality*, bringing together the verbal and the nonverbal in psychotherapy.

Modern Functionalism also emerged from the need to trace a *new paradigm that could allow us to go beyond the partiality inherent in the various psychotherapeutic approaches* and their theoretical referents, in a comprehensive and general vision, without ignoring any of the aspects brought into focus by the different existing clinical theories.

Seeing the Self as just an assortment of *mental images* and subjective experience has proven itself unsatisfactory and limited. Was it possible to go beyond a merely "experiential" notion of the Self without falling into the trap of thinking in terms of a structure, a material "thing"?

The only way to do so consisted in an authentic conceptual and epistemological leap forward. This consisted in the formation of an approach that looked at the human organism not in terms of parts, nor of structures, and not even as mind-body categories, but as something that could represent at the same time the whole and its details, and which grasped the basic functioning at the root of human life.

This "something", this new element capable of bringing about a genuine reform of thinking, lay in the concept of the *Functions*, the *flow of the human organism's functioning on its various levels.*

The Self can therefore be seen as the *organisation of all the Functions of the human organism*, on all its possible planes and levels of functioning: memories, symbolism, fantasies, mental images, forward planning, time, rationality, as well as the emotions, too, and also movements, posture and body shape, sensations, muscular tension, the respiratory system; the neurological system, and the autonomic nervous and immune systems.

In this case, the concept of self image (taken into consideration on the basis of precedent experiential conceptions of the Self) is none other than a type of *Function*; one Function among many, and not the only or most important one. They are part, along with many others, of a larger and more complex system that is not limited to just that which is "mental".

On the other hand, the Functions are not parts or pieces of the organism. Evaluating the human organism according to its Functions avoids the risk of once again compartmentalising the unity of the individual, given that it is *the Self, in its unity and entirety, that presents and expresses itself every time in each and every one of its Functions.*

Chapter 3

The Development and Integration of the Self

The Functions

What are the human organism's Functions and how are they organised?

If we look at the various scientific disciplines that deal with man's functioning, we can easily make out the different Functions that these approaches and viewpoints have focussed on in their particular field of research and intervention. However, in order to identify them more precisely, it is important to remember that a Function, in order to be defined as such, must respond to several fundamental criteria:

– It must refer to a deep-rooted functioning of the individual, and not to the levels of action or behaviour;
– Its progress must be able to be studied over time;
– It must be connected to a "polarity";
– It must be able to clearly demonstrate possible alterations.

If we look at the various psycho-physical planes, and the various Functions that make them up, we can conceivably divide them up into four larger areas: the *emotive* plane, and *postural-muscular* plane, the *physiological* plane and the *cognitive-symbolic* plane.

The need to consider four larger groupings arises for two reasons. Firstly, it helps us to obtain clarity, if only from a graphic point of view. Secondly, it is because observation has shown that when divisions occur in the Functional processes (thereby losing, in the case of ailments and pathologies, their original integration), it is much more likely that they do so according to these four groupings. Each area of the Self can become wholly altered. Expressions like: "The subject has an atrophied emotive plane", "That person has an modified physiological level", "This is a hyper-cognitive individual" have each of them very specific meanings.

The first of these Functional areas of the human organism, the *Emotive* plane, represents the particular colouring with which the individual, right from the beginning of his life, perceives to the world around him; which therefore is neither neutral nor banally equivalent. Emotions cause us to make choices, they cause our preferences, and they make us draw closer to or take our distances from people or objects. Objects, events, and people are always associated with particular emotional states.

Within the sphere of the emotions, we can distinguish:

- *positive moods*, which draw us towards people or objects, which prompt us to form sentimental ties, which give us a consistent impulse to live: love, tenderness, joy, happiness, serenity, trust, hope, sense of humour, sociability and good manners towards others;
- *negative moods*, which allow us to put up opposition or to defend ourselves from attacks (anger, hate), to move away from what we don't like (oppression) or to escape from dangerous situations (fear);
- *feelings about ourselves*, which consent us to differentiate ourselves from others (autonomy), they allow us to elaborate, with tenderness towards ourselves, the loss of loved things or people (sadness); which contribute to our relationship with ourselves and the way in which we perceive ourselves (Self awareness, self-esteem, self-confidence, insecurity, bravado, discouragement);
- *basic mood*, the general atmosphere of each individual's affective world, the deep-down, most undifferentiated state of the emotions: well-being or unease, being in a good mood or a bad mood, tranquillity, agitation, positivity or negativity.

Emotions can be openly expressed, or they can remain suppressed and concealed. Sometimes they can take up so much space in a person's life that they become *pervasive.*

The *Physiological* plane covers numerous sub-planes because it comprises all the organism's internal systems and apparatus. These systems assure functioning at all levels:

- *the respiratory system*, which (together with the mobility of the diaphragm) represents one of the most important *regulators* of the organism as well as many other physiological subsystems;
- *the heart and circulatory system*;
- *the digestive system*, with its related dietary problems;
- *the central nervous system* and the various neurobiological structures and organisations that make it up;

- *the neuro-endocrine system*, with its chemical mediators and neurotransmitters, fundamental for transmitting information through the whole organism;
- *the autonomic nervous system*, which has the capacity *parasympathetic activation* (the system related to calm and well-being) or *sympathetic activation* (alarm systems, vigilance, immediate action);
- *the immune system*, which has been linked ever more clearly to affective relationships, states of stress and the emotions;
- *perceptions and sensations*, which represents the entire, vital scope of information which reaches us both from the outside and from the inside, including pain thresholds: a crucial alarm bell for the organism;
- *basic muscle tone*, with its states of hyper- and hypo-tension, which should normally be linked to the exertion to be sustained, independent of the degree and scope of the movement in question;
- *thermoregulation*, often completely incongruent in psychiatric patients of a certain severity;
- *arousal processes*, which contribute to our attention span, the capacity for movement and action, especially with regards to every type of pleasure;
- *inflammatory processes*, which can be either chronic or acute, and which comprise states of pain and soreness.

Today, research has proven that there is a marked interconnection between all of these systems, and with the world of external relationships. The latter is a two-way process, in that the individual is influenced by his surroundings, just as the surroundings are influenced by the individual through his own attitude and actions. Recent research has also shown the neuro-endocrine and neurobiological systems to be involved in this interconnection.

Deficiencies in the maternal relationship have significant effects on the neuro-endocrine system. This can appear over the long term, or even in adult life; for example, in the subject's capacity to cope with stressful situations (Weiss, 1997).

Cerebral circuits develop in relation to the degree to which they have been *activated*. Experiences can consolidate our existing neuronal connections, they can cause us to develop new synapses, or they can prevent the destruction or "pruning" of unused synapses and neurons. They can even have an effect on the sheaths that insulate the individual neurons, increasing the speed with which electrical signals can be sent (Siegel, 1999).

The *Postural-muscular* plane is an area more traditionally studied by Body mediation Psychotherapy, especially with regards to Non Verbal Communication: it is generally known as *body language*, and has various sub-planes:

- *posture*, which assumes a central role in communicating with ourselves and with others;
- *movements and gestures*, which can be conscious and aimed towards a specific purpose, or rather subconscious and uncontrolled; and which can, moreover, take on characteristic modalities for each individual: expansive or subtle, slow or fast, strong or weak, ample or limited, explosive or restrained;
- *strength*, seen in this context as being the individual's ability to intervene directly on his surroundings through muscular capacity. This can also be expressed or repressed, and includes the strength to move or to endure;
- *the structure and form* that the body has gradually assumed over time, which can be well-balanced or imbalanced between top and bottom, right and left, between fat and thin.

The *Cognitive-Symbolic* plane comprises a whole series of Functional processes more widely associated with the traditional theoretical models, in the areas of psychology, psychiatry, and neurobiology. These processes should not however be considered purely as "psychological" or "mental", but rather as processes that are always *psycho-physical*, seeing that they always involve the whole person, even at a physical level, and which must therefore be regarded in relation to their specific purpose, rather than whether or not they exist "materially". We distinguish:

- *memories*, which can regard the recent or distant past, with a prevalently positive or negative colouring;
- *consciousness*, the extent to which a person knows himself and his own functional processes;
- *rationality*, i.e. the ability to evaluate the elements of a problem or of reality logically, to weigh them up and compare them;
- *control*, which represents the capacity to keep up with what is happening in and around oneself;
- *fantasies*, i.e. thoughts which erupt into the consciousness without being voluntarily evoked by the subject, more often than not with negative or disturbing connotations;
- *imaginative processes*, which the individual can organise and concentrate towards a project (to predict the outcome of his actions or words, ad-

justing and modifying them until they find those most suited to the project in hand);
- *the structure of time*, which place past experiences or future goals closer or further away from us;
- *symbolism*, seen as the system of profound meanings and attributes that each one of us assigns to the more significant human and social events, such as birth, life, masculinity and femininity, childhood, maturity, old age, work, play, sexuality and so on. This value system is expressed not only through our dreams but also continuously, impregnating the way each of us feels about the world around us.

The complete picture of the Functions so far identified can be seen in fig. 1.

Fig. 1. *A general outline of the Functions*

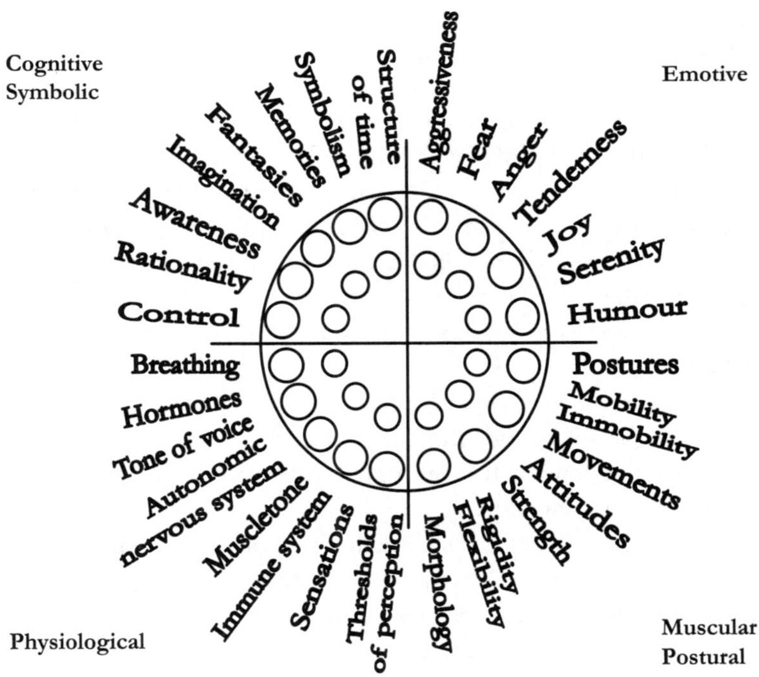

The Body and body memory

Taking a closer look at the history of psychotherapy in recent years, we can trace a history of the "body in psychotherapy".

It was in the twenties that Wilhelm Reich first hypothesised the existence of a link between the psyche and the soma so profound and complex that he considered it necessary, even indispensable, that psychotherapy must work on not just the mind, but also the body.

In actual fact, Freud's formulations had already started outlining the necessity of taking physical processes into account when studying psychological functional processes. In Freud, this aspect presented itself, in accordance with the science of the time, as "biologism" in his theory of the drives. After Freud, too, a good deal of attention has been given to aspects relating to the body, but often only concerning child development.

However, the body could not carry on being considered important only when it came to child development. It is undoubtedly present in the therapeutic relationship itself, in its processes of communication, even if the therapeutic model only provides for the gathering of verbal input, symbolism, the fantasies, or cognitive information. The body exists in silences, in the tone of voice, in the patient's movements, in the positions that the therapist assumes in relation to the patient within the setting. We talk and act with our bodies even if we do so implicitly or subconsciously. In addition, during therapy both the body of the patient and that of the therapist are 100% present.

That is why in the end, clinical psychotherapy has always recognised the importance of the body, though often implicitly. Interest in the body has always been active, and it has prompted numerous scholars to look out over this fascinating landscape.

As far as psychoanalysis is concerned, it is enough to bring to mind Ferenczi's active technique, Alexander's corrective emotional experience, Winnicott's psycho-soma and his *holding technique*, Balint's primary love concept, right up to Kohut and Stern's formulations on the Self, Sapir's somatic relaxation and This and Veldman's thesis on *haptonomy*.

Other clinical models present us with similarly significant examples: behaviourism, with its concepts of *modelling* and *flooding*, gestalt, with its interest in how the body represents itself, and how it represents itself to others, Schultz's studies and his somatic autogenous training techniques, cognitivism for its idea of feedback on a psycho-physiological level, and systemic therapy especially with regards to its techniques for family sculpting.

Reich, however, remains the one who formed the most direct, profound, and systematic approach to the body in psychotherapy. His concept of the *identity* between psyche and soma opens the way to the great discovery that our emotional history, as well as the history of the way our lives develop, is written in our bodies, as well as in our minds, right from the moment we are born.

However, the body has also been dealt with by the *encounter groups* that went on in the 1960's and 1970's in California, based on Schutz's ideas; by oriental physical disciplines; through dance, movement and "antigymnastics" experiences, used to "cure" patients. Psychometrics has played its part, too, as has the whole *body therapy* school of thought, with Baker, Raknes, Lowen, Sharaf, Boyesen, Pierrakos, Kurtz, Stattman, Boadella, Marcher, Painter, Estrada Villa, Levine, Pesso, Heller, Liss, not to mention the various schools and theories pertaining to " massage".

A lot of water has passed under the bridge since Wilhelm Reich expressed his ideas on the *identity* between body and mind in the twenties. Many concepts have widened, changed, or become more specific. This is also thanks to advances in our knowledge of the way small children function, and to progress in neuro-psychology and in psychophysiology.

To start with, scholars explored the way the psyche influences the body (that which is "psychosomatic"). Next, scholars explored the opposite phenomenon, (that which is "somatopsychic"). The influence exerted by the weather and its physical elements (barometric pressure, humidity and temperature) on people's moods had already been known for some time. Researchers then realised that assuming a certain posture induces the corresponding mood, even if such emotions were absent from the subject's actual lives. A sad face creates a state of sadness; drooping shoulders give a creeping feeling of discouragement. Very intense massages carried out by physiotherapists frequently bring out uncontrollable emotions in their patients, often to their great surprise (e.g. crying, sadness, joy).

Today, among the many contributions that the study of the body has made to psychotherapy, one of the most important has been the recent discovery of an actual *body memory*, or, rather, a complex and structured *peripheral memory*, which has its own existence, often quite independent of the central memory. The peripheral memory is made up of *traces* of past events, particularly during childhood, which have limited the full development of the Self, interfering with the satisfaction of the child's fundamental needs, and with the protection necessary in order to reach adulthood fully and harmoniously.

Functional Psychology[1] has organised and completed this discovery by studying both what the possible traces are and the modality with which these traces present themselves. The traces are essentially made up of *permanent alterations* in several of the subject's psycho-physical Functions, i.e. the values of these Functions are permanently oriented in the same direction, limited to the same *polarity*: a prevalently hyper- or hypotonic basic muscle tone, prevalently "closed" posture, breathing that is almost always shallow[2].

So far, we have identified the following Functions as part of the peripheral memory:

- basic muscle tone;
- thresholds of perception, such as pain and touch;
- posture;
- breathing;
- habitual movements;
- kinaesthetic perceptions and proprioceptions.

Basic muscle tone

The same movement can be carried out with different basic muscle tones, varying in proportion to the level of exertion required by a specific task. If I lift a plastic cup or a bag of books onto the windowsill, my muscles shorten by the same amount, but their basic tone is very different. This basic tone can lose its modularity in various areas of the body, it can lose its capacity to change according to the task in hand: it can remain chronically high or low; it can become unsuited to various situations. An altered basic tone produces unwitting moods and emotions: a sense of suffused anger due to tension in the arms, a sense of defeat from drooped shoulders, fear which spreads due to a hardened thorax. A tightened throat produces a plaintive and sad voice or a weak and fragile one.

1 See L. Rispoli (1993, 1998a, 1998b).

2 See section intitled "The Oscillation of the Functions", later on in this book.

Perception thresholds

There are people who have become hypersensitive to touch and who feel pain, at times unbearable, at the slightest touch, over most of the surface of their bodies. The sensation that derives from this state can only be one of fragility and vulnerability. On the contrary, other subjects have modified their pain thresholds, making them very high, becoming desensitized even to a strong pressure. This produces a sensation of being able to endure suffering, but at the same time it causes considerable difficulty in perceiving any kind of sensation on their skin, even pleasurable sensations or tender caresses.

Posture

Over time, postures can lose their original ductility and flexibility and become repetitive. The habit of adopting specific subconscious postures and falling back on the same body stances, has an intense effect on both third parties and the subject himself. For example, there are people who "bear the weight of the world on their shoulders", others who always keep their head down giving off an obvious signal of submissiveness, others who keep their arms too close to their bodies, sign of an evident inability to occupy the space around them.

Habitual postures represent a serious limitation to the flexibility of relationships and a subconscious source of malaise.

Habitual movements

Subconscious and uncontrolled movements constitute one of the most interesting chapters of body memory and the subtle influence that the traces of the past have even now over the present. Commonly, researchers have tended to study the more "deliberate" aspects of non verbal language, the ones that have a very precise symbolic and conventional meaning[3], but involuntary movements are much more important for revealing problems

3 See P. E. Ricci Bitti, S. Cortesi (1977), R. A. Hinde (1972), D. Morris (1977).

and mechanisms that have stuck over time, and which assume a significant importance in people's lives.

There are subjects who are unable to suppress tiny movements and jerks, because of a lurking anxiety, undermining their basic tranquillity and confidence. Other times we note that a subject's feet endlessly writhe and cross over each other, transmitting a sense of fragility and an obvious difficulty in drawing strength from the ground beneath them. There are people who frequently carry out movements that draw energy upwards: they often touch their face, their hair, and their eyes. They "take everything upwards", congesting the upper part of their bodies. They are often exceptionally cerebral and controlled individuals who suffer from headaches, throat inflammations, or conjunctivitis. Others move without stopping, continuously changing their position, as if they were never comfortable, never at their ease, as if they always had to adjust themselves.

Subconscious and habitual movements are a very rich source of information about people's real, underlying state.

Breathing

Breathing represents an important "general regulator" for the organism, because it acts directly upon system imbalances such as the autonomic nervous system, heartbeat, and the neuro-endocrine circuit linked to anxiety.

Permanent alterations therefore have a significant effect on well-being (or vice versa on discomfort) and on the emotions at a profound level. Halted breathing is a sure sign that fear is blocking the diaphragm; breathing that is always in the upper half of the thorax demonstrates a subconscious thrust to face the world head-on; uncoordinated breathing gives little certainty, breathlessness brings about a suffused sensation of anxiety; shallow, quiet breathing doesn't give the subject sufficient energy or vigour. Sometimes, we overdo it, breathing in too much air too quickly, "gulping" air, cutting off a large part of our capacity for movement towards the world, towards the outside: we feel choked and without energy. Other times, we exhale slowly, in an extremely controlled way, anaesthetising a large part of our sensations, diminishing our capacity for contact, and creating an excessive sense of detachment[4].

Kinaesthetic perceptions and proprioceptions

Even the perceptions that arrive from within our bodies can undergo more or less permanent alterations, transmitting a whole series of messages that no longer have anything to do with external stimuli. Some examples: the sensation of being off-balance whilst walking communicates a sensation of frailty and an inability to exercise control; excessive lightness stops us being able to feel the weight of our presence in the world, and, vice versa, the sensation of excessive weight makes us feel in difficulty when it comes to bursts of energy and vitality. If our insides move around too much, it gives us a sense of disgust for life; an empty sensation rushing downwards from the pelvis to the legs provokes fear and fragility; a closed throat makes it difficult for us to make our voice heard, tension in the legs can increase our feelings of anger and irritability.

Conclusion

The persistence of the above types of alteration over a long period constitutes a genuine *memory* of past events. It is not, however, a memory in the traditional sense, linked to precise scenes from the past, but rather a memory that continues to exert an influence over the present, conditioning a person's whole functioning, almost always completely subconsciously. Anger that has become fossilised within the muscle tone will give us a subtle and constant underlying sense of rancour; a sense of acute pain puts us in a continuous state of alarm; breathing too gently prevents us from having adequate sensations of vitality; hunched shoulders will give us a sense of sadness and solitude.

4 For a detailed analysis of breathing, and in particular on diaphragmatic breathing, see L. Rispoli (1993).

The original integration

The Functional conception of the Self consists of the combination of all the Functional planes and processes, together with the laws regulating their functional processes and interactions, even during the neonatal period. It therefore follows that, if the Self is formed in this way for its own survival, the various Functions of the Self cannot but be completely *integrated* right from the beginning.

In addition, within the context of scientific findings developed over recent years, the concept of an *Integrated Self* is gaining ground, compared to the idea of an ego made up of purely rational and symbolic Functions.

Studies on the capacities of newborn babies confirm this type of hypothesis. Meltzoff and Borton's experiment (1979), taken up by Stern (1985) because of its importance, confirms them all. Three-week-old babies were blindfolded and given either a smooth dummy (pacifier) to suck or one with protuberances. Afterwards, the blindfolds were removed and they were allowed to see both dummies. The babies, after briefly comparing the two visually, watched the ones that they had sucked for a longer time, and with greater emotivity. In this way, they demonstrated that they recognised them and that they were already able to directly associate the image with the tactile sensation, without passing first through the construction of a tactile schema, the construction of a visual schema, linking the two schema, and then arriving at a coordinated visual-tactile schema, as sustained by Piaget (1952).

A child already possesses, therefore, the capacity to "translate" a perception received on one plane of the Self (tactile) into another plane of the Self (visual), before he is a month old, even if he has not been stimulated towards learning. This is possible only if a close interrelation already exists between the planes.

A further proof of the Self's original state of integration is the fact that no newborn child has ever demonstrated incongruences or contradictions between different Functions (if they are generated, it only happens later on).

We can note, for instance, that when the newborn wishes to be breastfed, or angrily refuses something, or is in a state of pain or displeasure, there is an essential consistence between the way he cries, his movements, his facial expression, his physiological condition (from breathing to heartbeat), his emotions and also probably the mental images he sees. They express the same condition, both internally and externally.

If a "colourful rattle" intensely interests a newborn (let's say at six months of age), we observe that all the Functions of his organism "move" in the same direction, to express a coordinated and integrated whole. The child opens his eyes wide to be able to look closely at the rattle, he smiles, he expresses approval and joy with his face and by excitedly waving his little arms, jumping up and down on his high chair, reaching forward with his body and arms as if to grasp it. He accompanies this movement with expressive sounds, to show interest and to request the desired object, making little cries, and making repeated vowel sounds and smacking his lips. It is evident that he is experiencing intense desire and that he is also anticipating the arrival of the rattle with his imagination at the same time, "foretasting" the pleasure that he will have shaking the rattle, admiring its colours up close and perhaps feeling its smooth roundness with his mouth. At the same time, his physiological apparatus function in tune with his movements and emotions. His autonomic nervous system is in slight sympathetic arousal (slight in that it is only a pleasant and calm excitement, not anxiety). The heart beats a little faster because of the emotion, but in moderation. His breathing is slightly accelerated, but still low and diaphragmatic because he is not in a state of alarm (the confusion between *excitement* and *agitation*, frequent in adults, is not yet present). The child, moreover, is conscious that he likes the rattle and that he wants it, he clearly remembers that it has already entertained him (it is superfluous to say that he recognises it perfectly), he imagines that it will give him pleasure again when he has it in his hands (although he can't foresee *everything* that it will do). The *positive* value that he had attributed to it has been reinforced (and will be further reinforced if the game continues to afford him pleasant sensations and stimulate his curiosity) and the rattle will *represent* a symbol of playful fun more and more, because of its colours and the funny noise that intensifies every time his little hand shakes it.

In Functional terms, all of this is the clear sign of the congruence that exists between the various Functions of the Self: emotions, movements, facial expressions, physiological systems, memories, imagination and prefiguration, symbolism and conscious attention.

The baby organises his relationship with his surroundings using all the Functions of the Self. He builds a "model" of the world through which he can interact. He learns to recognise which elements remain constant, the ones that Stern (1985) defines as the first "envelopes of experience", which include being breastfed, the way his mother changes him or gives him a bath, the changes in attitude which prelude a change of mood or a temper tantrum. The newborn manages to recognise the parts of the experience that are invariable, even where the invariant is "change" (for example the way the muscle tension in the arms relaxes when the baby goes from a state of alarm to being "held" firmly and safely in the arms of an adult).

These first "concerts", uniting parts of various experiences into an amalgamated whole, later on become "narrative envelopes": i.e. events that take on a sense of development and continuity, where the child comes to perceive himself as the only unvarying element, as the protagonist that can communicate and narrate them. This phase corresponds with the birth of complete self-awareness and the full consciousness of continuity, where in the past only the organisation of the Self had this complete continuity.

What do these envelopes of experience contain, however? What do they consist in? *How* do we arrive at the learning of these unvarying elements and *how* do we construct them?

These questions bring us back to the theory of the Functions of the Self. Learning would be impossible if there was no initial integration between the different Functional levels, since it is the Functional levels that, interacting together, determine what the emotional-postural-physiological-creative constants of a given experience are. In other words, envelopes of experience are made up of none other than Functional processes, such as memories, mental images, perceptions, sensations, the movements of internal apparatus, intimately linked with a given association, and from the characteristics that the newborn has managed to "abstract" from the extremely variable events surrounding him.

The *molar* unit of functioning (i.e. the smallest and most basic unit) must then consist of a cross section of *all* the Functions (although they are still at a simple stage and have not yet become complex) that can be identified within the Self, gathered around a particular sequence of events, taking on a particular form.

These forms, the way in which the Functions are connected between themselves, are none other than a human being's first fundamental experiences in life, which I have termed the Basic Experiences because of their importance (please see chapter 4).

The child, in effect, consolidates these Basic Experiences more and more each time he goes through them in different contexts and situations.

He learns to interact better and better with his surroundings and manages to influence events in the desired direction, completing his development.

Here we can begin to glimpse the existence of *ranges of functioning*, i.e. the presence of many nuances spanning from one *polarity* to another: from hunger to satiety, from tenderness to hardness, from tension to relaxation, from fast movement to slow movement, from pleasure to pain, and so on. While there is a state of *mobility* and *integration*, the newborn is able to move freely (with his behaviour and responses) through all nuances of the various ranges, responding adequately to all situations.

The organisation of the Functions

All Functions are present from the beginning of life. Development does not consist in the addition of new Functions but rather in the fact that the Functions become continuously more *complex* and *hybrid*. The existing Functions gradually take on new nuances as the child interacts with different situations and encounters new experiences. "Hybrid", in this sense, refers then to the birth of new "nuances" as the child meets a primary emotion (or any other Function of the Self) in a new context. "Joy", for example, can become happiness, enthusiasm, contentment, and passion. The basic emotion "opposition" can become hate, isolation, intolerance, low esteem, hostility, or rancour.

However, although the Functions become more complex over the course of an existence, they can never operate independently of each other: it is only together that they represent a complete functioning of the organism.

A Functional conception of the Self of this nature allows us to embrace the subject's whole life sphere, taking into consideration both mental and physical Functions; or, rather, just *Functions* of the very same, indivisible psychophysical unity.

The Self, then, is a "sum of Functions"; *an organised and organic ensemble of Functions* which determine the identity and the complexity of the individual.

Seeing the Self as an ensemble of Functions allows us to understand more clearly how it is that we develop a sense of continuity over time. It is precisely their internal organisation that imparts a sense of continuity to the sea of experiences and to the varied nature of events. The internal organisation is itself *continuity*, continuity over time and continuity between the different planes of the Self (Rispoli, 1993, p. 17).

This internal organisation (complex and at the same time unitary) is not just a subjective sensation of the individual, because it is made up of visible and concrete Functional processes on various levels, far beyond any sort of self-image. It is therefore the organisation to provide continuity over time and continuity over different planes of the Self.

If it is true that the Self changes constantly over time, we can hypothesise that these changes do not come about through completely separate situations, but rather through *continuing modalities of change*. We can envisage configurations that evolve following rules inherent within the very organisation of the Self. We could therefore talk about *multiplicity* and *complexity* without contradicting the idea of *integration* and *unity*, without even having to resort to the notion of continuity as a subjective illusion. It is precisely this concept of internal organisation, the internal organisation of the Functions that allows us to get away from conception of the Self as merely experiential.

The integrated Self persists in everyone, it *is* everyone; quite aside from what *type* of Self is contained in the subject's consciousness. It is the presence of this internal organisation that allows us to live and interact, independently of the form and content contained within a few of its Functions, such as consciousness, subjective experience, and conscious and subconscious images.

The sum of *all* the organised and integrated Functions *together* determine the individual's experiences and life. On the contrary, the experiential Self merely constitutes the *contents* of a few specific Functions.

On the other hand, the "theory of complex thought" (which allows us to approach living systems) gives us further confirmation of this self-regulatory capacity both within systems as a whole and within their components. Processes of "self-regulation" are at the root of these systems: they are mechanisms that the system, in its complexity, uses in order to coordinate its activities (Siegel, 1999, p. 7).

Seeing the Self as an organisation of Functions can also help us understand more clearly what it means to have, or not to have, a consistent "sense of Self". We can also see the consequences of a fragile and eroded nucleus of the Self, or how a loss of this primary continuity can lead to a dispersal of identity or a series of negative self-images.

The Self, therefore, can be defined Functionally as the *organisation* that allows the organism to function on various planes; such as the ensemble of the psycho-physical planes themselves and the processes that characterise them.

A Functional viewpoint allows us to go beyond the simplistic categorisation of conscious-subconscious: in every Function, indeed, a given process of a given content can be fully present or more or less stifled ("repressed").

Complexity and practicability

Although Functional thought widens the field of investigation, the danger of becoming vague and generic is averted by the fact that it allows us to examine given Functional areas with great *precision*, right up to specific single Functions, such as respiration, movement and forward planning.

On the other hand, it also prevents the individual being compartmentalised because the *entire Self* expresses itself in every Function. For example, taking the *movement Function* into consideration, it is the whole person's *way of moving* that gets analysed, and not just the single movement of their foot or arm or head. Similarly, joy is not a "piece" of the Self, but the whole person that is participating in, living, and expressing joy *at that moment.* It is not just the lungs that breathe but also the whole body. It is the combination of all the fantasies, and of their manifestations, that constitute the *fantasy Function*, and which reveal the individual as a whole. Symbolism, i.e. the values present in the individual's inner world, is not a part of the individual that can be opposed to other parts, but rather it, too, refers to the characteristics of the individual and to the way the individual functions as a whole.

Another advantage of the Functional model is the possibility of descending from the most external and accessible planes bit by bit right down to the tiniest modalities of the "micro", without losing oneself in a thousand details, a thousand particulars. Widening the investigation to all planes of the Self, not just to those more commonly taken into consideration, we meet with the difficulty inherent in an excessive amount of data. If we want to concentrate just on *movement*, we find ourselves faced with thousands of tiny movements: there are an infinity of movements in the face alone, even in the modest amount of time limited to an observation session. It would be impossible to gather them all in the space of a therapeutic session. It is even less possible to take into consideration the movements of the whole body, let alone adding posture, muscle tension, sensations, fantasies, and memories. Yet, when we talk about the *movement Function*, we mean the way the whole person moves and not the thousands of movements that they make in a given space of time. We can see whether the movement is expansive and free, if there is strength or not, if it is rigid and nervous, if it is narrow and repressed, if it is gentle, if it is towards others or closed in on itself, if it is to take things or to push things away. We can gather, in short, what the totality of the individual's movements express, and how the *movement Function* is progressing at a general level. In the section on the oscillation of the Functions, we will see how each Function can be analysed in a precise and analytical way.

Investigation and research can be carried out within just the one plane. However we must reach it gradually, consciously and correctly, using the method best *suited* to that plane, and we must never lose sight of the simultaneous presence of both the overall picture and its specific details, both the singular elements and the overall view, with all the assonances and dissonances that this implies.

The Functional vision of the Self takes into consideration a functioning that is all-encompassing, within which all Functions have an equal contribution to make, they all have *exactly the same importance.* The Functional model puts to one side the pyramidal notion of the individual, where the mind controls all the rest, hierarchically. Instead, it offers a more *circular*, or, better still, a *spherical* notion. All Functional planes contribute *jointly* to the organisation of the Self.

To use the words of Morin, a "macro-concept" substitutes the idea of a single Functional plane at the summit of everything else "in which the interrelations between constitutive terms are circular" (Morin, 1982, p. 132).

We are currently following the example of the individual-organism, but the value and innovativeness of the Functional viewpoint lies in the possibility of applying it, with extremely interesting results, to other organisations: couples, families, groups, teams, institutions, companies, territories, districts and towns.

Alterations of the Self

By overcoming the imprecision and approximation associated with the older "typologies" (from those theories based on libidinous development to those linked to the structure of the personality), the Functional approach allows us to analyse the events which have intervened on all planes and sub-planes, and their reciprocal interactions, as a whole, for every single practical situation. In so doing, every single alteration of the Self can be analysed, without lapsing into vagueness or losing sight of an overall, or holistic, vision. This is only possible if we take into consideration all the modifications that can occur within each Functional process, each sub-plane, and each area. Above all, we must examine the modifications that can occur in the laws of functioning that govern and determine the interconnections between the above.

We can essentially identify three different types of alteration.

a) *Divisions.* These occur more frequently between the larger spheres, which have been subdivided in the way that they have been, precisely because there is a strong tendency for them to become separated from each other. However, divisions within the same sphere are also very common, as indeed they are within the very same sub-plane.

Because of these divisions, what happens on one plane no longer produces similar events on the other planes, i.e. events that proceed in the same direction. For example, we can have emotions that are not present at the rational and conscious levels, movements that express feelings that are different from what the person perceives, physiological states of fear without there being external stimuli, postures that contradict the tone of voice, tones of voice that contradict what the individual is saying, and so on. Some Functional processes become uncoupled from the rest of the Self, forming a sort of *short circuit.*

Naturally, no plane can become completely separated from the others, but in some cases, the only link that remains is very deep down, in the original nucleus of the Self, which has been suffocated by the stereotyped forms of the false Self. As a result, the Functions can pull in opposite directions at more superficial levels (get closer to others and at the same time push them away, value and deprecate at the same time).

The interactions between Functions can become indirect or contradictory.

b) *Hypertrophy or hypo-trophy.* A Function can develop in the same way as the others, in harmony within the overall working of the individual, or it can undergo alteration during its development: becoming hyper-trophic, exaggeratedly present and expanded, or, on the contrary, it can become hypo-trophic, underdeveloped or almost absent. Some obvious examples would be people with overdeveloped emotivity or with a hypertrophic rationality, people with very few memories, an absence of strong movements, or tender movements, or people who find it difficult to conceptualise or use their imagination.

These disharmonies translate themselves into a tendency in the individual to accentuate all those aspects linked to hyper-trophic Functions in their life and relationships. These aspects continue to be further stimulated in a spiralling crescendo. We can begin to see at this point how important it is not to proceed randomly in therapy, because the therapist could end up confirming aspects that are already too developed, accentuating disharmonies instead of leading towards re-establishing harmony.

Let us take the recent debate on the damage that children could suffer watching too much television as an example. A Functional type analysis allows us to understand, in a concrete and specific way, whish people are really at risk from too much television, i.e. children who have already developed their imagination, surreal and fantasy planes to the detriment of the capacity to act and "feel" in the first person.

c) *Scleroses.* Psycho-physical Functional processes can undergo alterations in their very functioning. When only a few movements become possible, an emotion "fixes" itself, an idea takes on a repetitive nature, even becoming obsessive, a posture becomes a prison; we can say that this Functional plane, or that area, has become rigid, or sclerotic. It has lost its fluidity and elasticity.

The "ranges" (that the organism has at its disposition) of responses, stratagems and capacities, become more or less limited in all areas of the Self: from conceptualisation, movement, perceptions, emotions, right down to the subtle mechanisms of the internal physiological apparatus, delicate microcellular, biochemical and bioelectric functional processes. It is not rare to find situations of limited mobility: fixed emotions or expressions, stereotyped movements, coactive fantasies, modified perception thresholds, altered muscle tone, a dearth of ideas and creativity. These stereotypes or limitations in the various ranges of possible responses to both external and internal events, are the cause of serious difficulties in life. They do not permit the individual to exploit a variety of modalities, allowing the subject to interact effectively with his surroundings, rather, they permit only repetitive and automatic modalities, which force the subject to commit the same old "mistakes", even if he is aware of them and tries consciously to avoid them.

The first alterations and disharmonies start to emerge within the equilibrium of the Self thanks to the impact of frustrating or adverse conditions within the individual's surroundings, as figure 2 demonstrates. The first rudiments of a sclerotic way of relating to the outside world also start to appear, i.e. the subject is no longer in profound contact with all the parts of the Self: the false Self has begun to form.

Divisions are represented graphically by a *separation* between the circles relative to the various areas (or Functional planes); *hypertrophy* and *hypo-trophy* are represented by the *size* of the circles. Functions that are *sclerotic* are shown as having *thicker* outlines.

This method of representation allows us to make very detailed diagrams on the patients' actual present conditions and on the interventions to be made during the course of therapy (allowing us to actually plan the course of therapy)[5].

The *Functional* approach has rearranged both old and recent knowledge, starting to construct a global, all-inclusive theory of the Self, taking into consideration how the Functions work as an ensemble. Functional theory allows us to understand how each Function is connected to the others: e.g., what the links are between movement and other Functions such as the emotions, the sensations, symbolism, and the imagination.

Functionalism provides us with a unitary and comprehensive framework regarding, contemporarily, all psycho-physical Functional processes. The therapeutic relationship itself is seen and studied on all planes upon which it intervenes, through all the modalities of communication put into action. These modalities correspond to various aspects of the Functional conception, relative not only to the patient's Self, but also that of the therapist.

5 The use of such diagrams in diagnosis and in planning a course of therapy is covered in chapter 10, through the study of an actual clinical case.

This vision completely overtakes abstract typologies, since it allows us to read the actual person in terms of his various components. In particular, it allows us to look at what has been modified during his past through the multiple *traces*, which remain clearly visible on many planes of the Self. In this way, we can examine past relationships beyond just the patient's memories and fantasies, and intervene as a result, directly and concretely, on the traces and consequences left by these relationships, and finally manage to modify them.

Fig. 2. *Functional diagram detailing an actual clinical case*

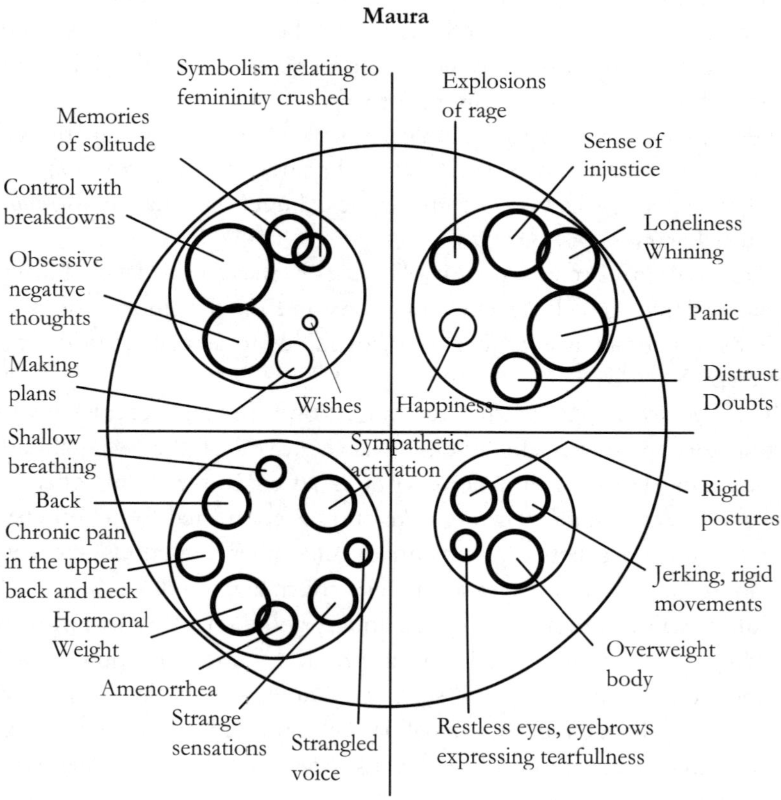

The negative *consequences* of unsatisfactory affective relationships during childhood can crystallize themselves within each one of the Functions of the Self, where they help to worsen the alterations within the whole equilibrium of the Self, continuously and often imperceptibly.

These *consequences* can also remain condensed, along with their load of emotions and sensations, within any one of the Districts of the body.

In both cases, the capacities that children should consolidate as they go through the Basic Experiences will result as being lacking, limited or altered.

We will be dealing with all of this in later chapters, outlining child development according the Functional vision.

Laws governing the Functions of the Self

At this point, it is possible to try to summarize modalities of functioning of the Self through several *laws* and their relative *corollaries*. It should be clear that these are not "laws" in the deterministic sense used by the so called exact sciences. They do, however, represent hypotheses or attempts to describe the *oscillation* of the phenomena interpreted by the general theoretical model of the Self, and as such, they allow us to make predictions on their functioning and to verify what actually happens. Every "law" is complemented by a *corollary*.

1) *All of the Functions are interconnected and integrated with each other, and they are present from the very beginning of an individual's life.*
– *No completely new Function forms over the course of the individual's life, but the pre-existing ones become more complex and specialised, enriching themselves with new nuances.*
2) *The Functional processes can suffer alterations, due to a negative impact with the surroundings. These alterations can be of the following types: a) separations and divisions, b) scleroses, rigidity and decreased mobility (size, modularity, mobility), c) over- or underdevelopment (hypo- or hypertrophies). All of this can be read from the exterior as the false Self.*
– *These alterations tend to cause the Functions to become separated, particularly into four main areas or groupings, and to start functioning independently from one another, in short circuit.*

3) *The disconnections are never total. The Functions stay connected, nevertheless, at deeper levels, through what can be termed the "original nucleus" or "integrated nucleus" of the Self.*

– *A course of therapy must therefore aim to regress the patients to the deep nuclei of the Self, when the Functions were still integrated. In order to get there the therapist must use and follow the Functions that have been least altered, and where the false Self is less embedded.*

4) *Changes on a single Functional plane can only produce corresponding relevant and stable changes on another Function of the Self if both planes have not been too altered. If not, the changes induced by reflection in the other Function will be minimal, unstable and distorted. Changes induced by reflection in the second Function can go in a different direction from changes brought about in the first Function, in accordance with the level of division or alteration present between the two (even going in a completely opposite direction to the changes obtained in the Function where we have directly intervened).*

– *It is crucial to act as far as possible on all Functions in therapy, re-mobilising them and recuperating their original integration, using specific therapeutic techniques which work on numerous Functional planes at the same time, and which produce changes in the exact same direction in all of them.*

An alteration never affects just one Function, but rather multiple Functional levels and planes of the Self, each one in a different way according to the different life experiences that the individual went through as a child. The traces of the past are the alterations of these Functions. It is only by looking at all the Functions as a whole that we are able to fully understand the patient's history.

It follows that it is very difficult to modify the whole person with all their planes of functioning by intervening on just one of them. If we induce a sense of calm, it does not necessarily mean that the patient's breathing becomes deep and calm; a tranquillizing massage can, contrary to the therapist's intentions, produce feelings of fear; talking about happy memories can provoke deep sadness. All of this depends on the insistence of the old traces, which come to the surface regardless of the actual real life situation. The Functions in this case have lost their original integration, becoming disconnected, more or less seriously, closing themselves in a short-circuit. In order to obtain a profound and stable change, it is almost always necessary to act on several planes of functioning, sometimes on all of the Functions. This action must be integrated at both a theoretical and a practical level.

Now, as we will later see in chapter 7, this can be done if we take the knowledge and experience of the different clinical approaches into consideration, not in an eclectic way, nor adding up different techniques, but constructing a theory that combines the scientifically valid aspects with a corresponding theory of technique.

Functional theory is revealing itself to be useful and effective in finding a way to unite the various clinical models, also because analysing all the Functional levels can show us, quite clearly, which Function each of the various models of psychotherapy acts on, and therefore how they can be joined together effectively.

The Oscillation of the Functions

The Functions alternate between two opposite polarities, with a movement that roughly traces a sine-curve; allowing the individual to have a complete range of all possible movements, emotions, strength, posture, physiological equilibrium and symbolic values at their disposition, e.g. *small movements-big movements; sadness-joy; tenderness-toughness; strength-fragility; parasympathetic response-sympathetic response; control-loss of control.* The more *complete* and *intact* the ranges at the individual's disposition, the greater his potentialities in life. A full life consists in being able to oscillate and range freely and fully between one pole and another as circumstances, needs, and desires require. The two poles are not opposites at all: rather, the complete fulfilment of one helps the individual to reach the complete fulfilment of the other. Life does not consist at all in finding the "middle road", but rather in the possibility of reaching intensity both in one position and the other, both poles. There is no good pole or bad pole. Both have a profound meaning in our existence.

In figure 3 we have represented the movement, over time, of a Function that has remained intact and complete.

Fig. 3. *A complete range*

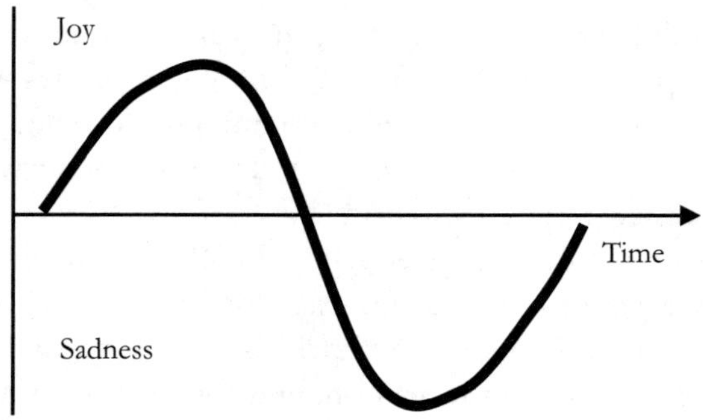

Amplitude

One of the first possible alterations in the oscillation of the Functions consists in the diminution of the amplitude of the range (figure 4).

Fig. 4. *Limited range*

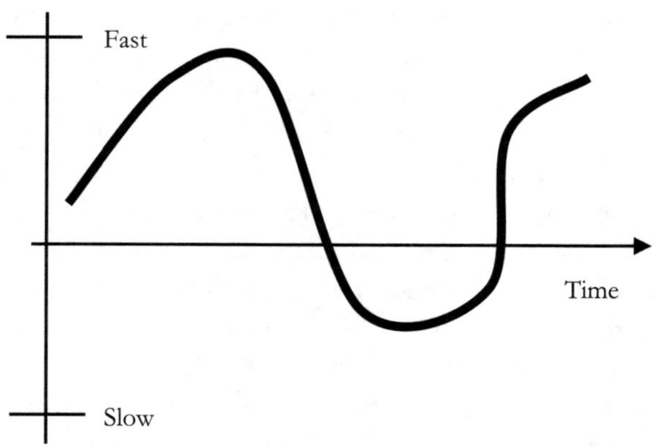

A child's movements, for the reasons explained repeatedly above, can all have become too slow, even when speed would be indispensable in order to seize an opportunity, to act rapidly or to transmit a spurt of energy and vitality. Chronically slow movements do not even, in actual fact, enjoy the full potentialities of that pole. Rather than being calm and tranquil, they are resigned, discouraged, and indecisive, whereas chronically fast movements are in reality agitated, frantic and imprecise.

Modularity

Modularity consists in the individual's capacity to pass from one pole to another within the same polarity, more than once, continuously, softly, and gently. The range could even be limited, but the individual still has the possibility to express, in equal measure, both strong movements (even if not totally strong) and weak ones. A lack of modularity, on the other hand, produces preponderance towards one pole rather than the other (as figure 5 clearly demonstrates). The person referred to in figure 5 not only has *little strength* in his movements, but he also seldom uses the little that he has.

Fig. 5. *Deficient modularity*

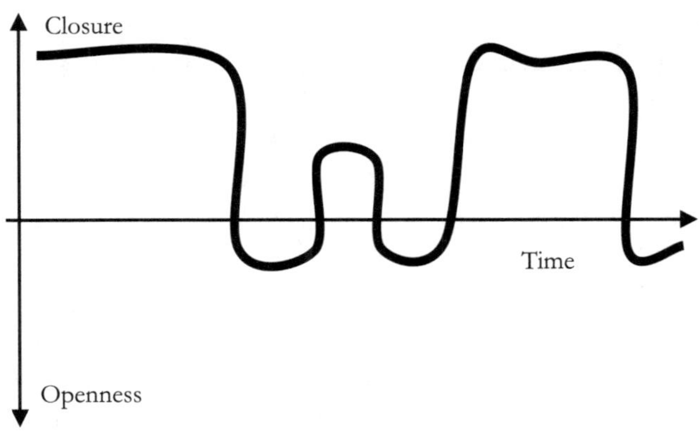

Mobility

Lastly, limited mobility prevents the subject from passing *rapidly* from one pole to another: there is a viscous inertia that keeps him on one of the two fronts for a long time, much longer than necessary. For example, someone who suffers an affront at a party could move to fast and happy movements after having been aloof and immobile for a short time; but, on the other hand, he could have great difficulty in changing the modality of his movements and unleashing himself in a joyous dance. It is not a case of incapacity, of being limited to that dimension, because that person is able to be quick and dance joyfully, as well as show spurts of movement: the problem is being able to rapidly abandon one modality for another, being able to change gear rather than remain mixed up with the previous condition.

Some other examples of mobility, indispensable for a rich and meaningful life, are: managing to open up again after the conditions requiring us to close in on ourselves have been removed, being able to "let go" when there is no longer any need to hold on, not staying angry too long.

Fig. 6. *Poor mobility*

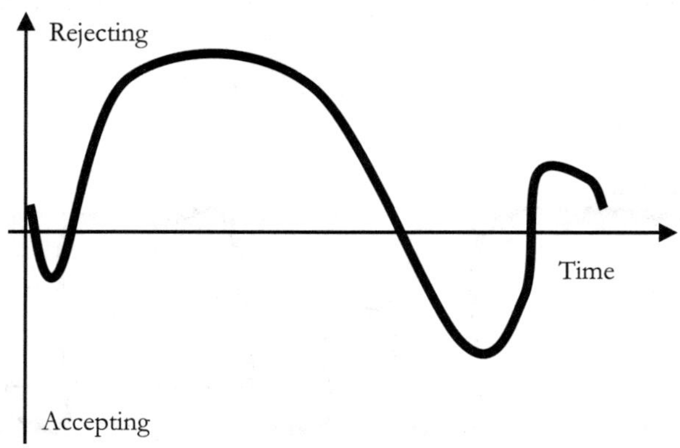

As we have been able to see from these few, simple examples, the theory of the Functions brings us a very deep and analytical breakdown of the functioning of the individual: the precise movement of his Functions, exactly how they are altered in every detail. Consequently, therefore, we can learn the patient's history and the episodes of his life that have lead to it all.

Chapter 4

Basic Needs and Experiences of the Self

Needs and the development of the Self

Recently, studies that demonstrate the multiplicity of our instincts and drives (or of manifestations that could be seen as such) beyond sexual and survival instincts have been gaining ever more ground, starting with Bowlby's attachment instinct (1969, 1973, 1980). Gradually, the spotlight has moved from visions of a biological nature towards theories regarding the child's relationship with his environment, motivational, relational, and interpersonal theories.

On the other hand there is no longer any sense in placing instinct and environment at odds with one another, given that scholars have been able to verify both the presence of genetic tendencies and the fact that these tendencies modify themselves gradually throughout the life of the individual. The most important capacity in Man's baggage undoubtedly remains that of being able to *learn* and to modify his own innate behaviour patterns.

Besides, the concept of the *drives of the Ego* has been shown for some time now to be rather limited, a limitation that has not been similarly encountered in actual observations of the world of children. Even the concept of the *drives of the Id*, in the sense of an uncontrollable and dangerous magma that pushes and creates profound anxieties in the newborn has been brought into question (Balint, 1965, 1968).

On the other hand, science is proceeding ever more in the direction of a concept of the Self as a system and as an organisation, towards an all-encompassing theory of the Self.

Light has been shed on various levels of mind-body processes by numerous scholars. Studies on newborns by Bower (1977), Eimas (1971), Eisenberg (1969), Haynes (1965), Hutt (1968), e more recently by Stern (1985); studies on non verbal behaviour by Ekman and Friesen (1968, 1969) and by Brannigan and Humphries (1972); Hall's research on spatial distribution (1966), and research on "ethological" and biological functioning by Hinde (1972, 1974), Lorenz (1949, 1966) and Timbergen (1983); Argyle's research into non verbal interaction (1975); psycho-physiological studies by Selye (1974, 1976) and Laborit (1973, 1974); Bernstein's discoveries on perception and motor control, Tuvey (to name but a few of the many studies that have been made in recent years) have therefore made a significant contribution to the formation of an overall framework of man's functioning, from an all-embracing, rather than a limited or compartmentalised point of view.

In this vision, therefore, the *quantitative* conception of impulses, the idea of a "hydraulic" mechanism of build-up and release, has been overcome. Instead, we can begin to think about impulses in a *qualitative* sense: i.e. we can conceive of the objects or goals of our impulses as *Directions* in which the child moves (and towards which the child will move his whole life), indispensable for his psychophysical well-being and for maintaining his health and equilibrium. Impulse objectives consist in all the fundamental needs of existence such as heat, nutriment, being held, moving, curiosity, and so on.

The latter could be represented, for example, as shown in the figure below.

Fig. 1. *The fundamental needs of the Self*

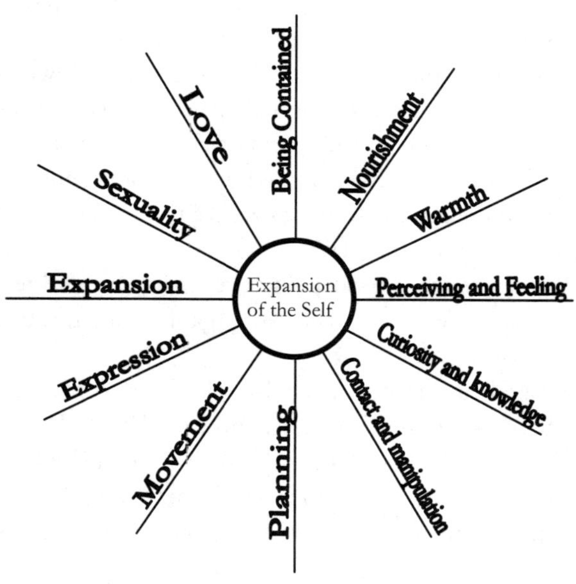

The individual is driven by these fundamental needs (all of which must be satisfied); not in the mechanistic sense of an energy that accumulates and then has to be *released*, but rather as the individual's need to find, throughout his life, experiences that proceed in these *Directions*, indispensable for his well-being.

A healthy child (just like a healthy adult) will always seek out such experiences; and his mobility and elasticity will allow him to satisfy the fundamental needs with varied and differing objects, because they are (at least to a certain extent) interchangeable. When a child no longer manages to accept different or varying objects in order to procure warmth, or nourishment, or joyousness, his mobility has already suffered a limitation, which has begun to impinge on a full and healthy development of the Self. In this way, we can observe babies crying desperately if they lose their dummy (or pacifier), incapable of using another; or babies that absolutely cannot manage to fall asleep if they don't have their own cushion, or if they are not in their own cot.

However, it can also happen that these Needs, not fully satisfied, end up becoming mixed up with one another. This is the case with people who resort to eating to make up for a lack of affection, or those who resort to sex because they crave contact, or those who seek power over others instead of the need to love. These drives never manage to find true satisfaction because they do not regard the real object of the individual's need, but rather a "contiguous" need which becomes more and more swelled and altered.

For this reason it is crucial that all the fundamental needs of the child are recovered in therapy, reconstructing a sense of satisfaction and fulfilment above all in those areas where there have been strong confusions or deficiencies.

The Basic Experiences of the Self

Proceeding along this path in clinical practise and research, I arrived at the need for more answers on the process of change in psychotherapy. What is it that really happens at the most fundamental levels of this process? What is it that the patient-therapist relationship really puts into action?

Using a multidimensional point of view, I realised that the altered Functions did effectively end up being modified; and a large part of the therapist's work was effectively aimed (consciously) at obtaining this result. As the number of sessions increased, concrete changes could be observed on various Functional levels: memories opened up, stereotyped postures were transformed, suppressed tenderness once more came to the surface, fragile movements gained strength, fantasies lost their load of negativity and terror.

However, there was something else that occurred during therapy, which could not be explained merely by the work carried out on the Functions. Yes, the work on the Functions was already much more articulated, complex and precise than techniques aimed years ago at "freeing" the body (or guided visualisations used to create new symbolic references, or interpretations on transference, or the modification of cognitive patterns). Yet, the mere fact that the intervention was more circumscribed and intentional was not enough to explain what was really happening during therapy. What was happening in all those moments when the relationship between the therapist and the patient took on an unusual quality, an uncommon intensity, a configuration that resembled something very close to what happens between a "good" parent on the one hand and a little boy or a little girl, tiny children, on the other?

What was the therapist putting into action during those moments? What was he "touching" to cause such extraordinary results?

The solution to these problems was both complex and simple at the same time. It could be hypothesised that the therapist was helping to recompose something that had become fractured, rarefied or altered in the patient; *something that, once recovered, allowed them to reoccupy lost spaces in their lives, ways of being that had long been buried, corners of emotions and sensations that had been hidden and trapped in the folds of disappointments, pain, desperation and inner emptiness.* The lowest common denominator, however, was, therefore, *fullness*; a fullness that had already existed in the patient's past. Moreover, recent scientific discoveries on infancy corroborated the hypothesis that right from the beginning the child feels their relationship with their parents totally, with the participation of all levels of his organism.

In order to proceed further in my research and answer these fundamental queries, I started to reread the notes of all the various cases treated in therapy closely. Through reflection on the techniques used during the sessions (techniques perfected through years of therapeutic practice) and on the effects produced in the patients in terms of the changes brought about, one basic idea took form more and more clearly. At the end, regardless of the techniques used, what was really happening within the therapeutic relationship was the recovery and reconstruction of particular *modalities of relating*. These modalities are *what characterise a positive parental relationship, or the life of children before negative impacts intervened to close channels, capacities, and movements.*

The vividness with which incredibly archaic sensations and experiences re-emerged in patients also helped me to understand the basic essence of the therapeutic process, that of recovering the lost vitality and mobility of archaic experiences that play a very important role for the child and its development.

These experiences, which I have termed the *Basic Experiences of the Self*, are the bricks with which we build our lives. If we pass through them many times with a positive outcome, they will go to create a reservoir that we can draw from as and when we need to: in order to be able to live a given situation to the full, in order to make what we desire come about, to interact effectively and successfully with others and with reality.

"Letting Go", for example, is a fundamental part of human existence. We could not live if we were not able to Let Go every so often, instead of remaining in a continual state of alert and concentration. "Letting Go" is an Experience that the child is already capable of living right from the beginning, and which he will go through over and over again in the initial phase of his existence (and in later phases, too). It is by continually passing through this Experience that the human being can become familiar with it in differing environmental conditions, through the different nuances that can characterise it, in differing contexts.

Little by little, the Basic Experience of the Self is consolidated, assuming different colouring. In this way, it becomes a permanent part of the individual's *stock of knowledge and capacities*. Subsequently, as the need (or possibility or desire) arises, the subject will be able to turn to these capacities. He will be able to "Let Go" to lessen the weight of a situation at work, he will be able to "Let Go" in order to step back a pace from a stressful period of concentration. He will be able to "Let Go" in order to decrease the tension of a relationship that is too difficult or excessively controlled.

On the other hand, for human beings to develop, improve and refine all the capacities necessary for independence, autonomy and social success, they really need time and they need to follow a specific path. Given that human life is far more complex than animal life, human capacities cannot be contained within their genetic inheritance, or at least only along general lines. Most of the adaptive functional processes are acquired and consolidated over the course of childhood and adolescent development. All this serves to build up a store of knowledge far more articulated than that of the animal world, to acquire more abilities, with more detail. Each of these capacities must be furnished with an elasticity and mobility suited to the most widely-differing situations, in order for the individual to be able to face and resolve the most disparate problems.

A list of these Fundamental Experiences can be seen in figure 2. Each one is important in order for us to be able to live well. Every single one of them, if reconstructed and relived positively, can contribute towards creating a store of possibilities and capacities that we can draw from as and when we need or wish to.

As I continued my research and studied the various clinical cases, analysing the common elements and phases in therapy[1], the list of the Basic Experiences gradually changed. The Experiences appear below subdivided into groups, the differences within which are, in effect, different nuances or colourings of the very same Basic Experience of the Self.

Creating a list of the Basic Experiences, i.e. boxing them into "categories" is rather stretching and simplifying the question, but on a practical level, this subdivision has proved itself very useful.

The Basic Needs and Experiences

We now know that for children to grow and maintain their state of well-being, health and harmony, there are some specific conditions that must be fulfilled. Life can exist only within precise and fairly limited parameters; and not just from the purely physical or chemical point of view (such as temperature, humidity and radiations), but also from the emotional, sentimental, and relational perspective.

1 See L. Rispoli (1998a) and chapter 9 of this book.

Fig. 2. *The Basic Experiences of the Self*

Being Held
Being Held, Being Contained (Being Stopped)
Protection

Being Taken Up
Being Taken Up
Being Carried

Letting Go
Letting Go (Daydreaming)
Just Being
Abandoning ourselves to

Contact
Contact (Fusion)
Being Nourished (Absorbing)

Active Contact
Taking (Asking, Seducing, Drawing others to us)
Giving (Hugging)
Giving to Ourselves (Consoling Ourselves, Finding Balance)

Love
Being Loved (Belonging, Being Carried inside by the other person)
Loving (Carrying the other person inside us)
Positive Continuity (Memories)

Sharing
Opening Up (Sharing)
Pleasure in Others
Pleasing Others (Showing Ourselves)

Tenderness
Needing Others
Tenderness
Fragility (Softness)

Receiving Attention
Being Seen
Being Listened to
Being Understood
Being Helped
Being Encouraged

Vitality
Joy (Excitement, Bursts of Energy)
Vitality (Energy, Impetus)
Playing (Running, Throwing Ourselves into)

Well-Being
Well-Being (Harmony, Wholeness)
Pleasure (Vagotonia, Mobilising towards the lower body)

Sensations
Perceiving
Sensing (Sensations)
Amazement

Control
Losing Control (Explosions)
Loosening Control (Head Bent, Collapses)
Soft Attention

Strength
Original Strength (Detachment, Space)
Soft Strength
Calm Strength
Open Strength (Letting Out)
Changing Others (Moving)

Aggressiveness
Affectionate Aggressiveness
Aggression

Authority
Presence (Determination)
Authority (Standing, Confidence, Knowing Our Own Value)

Assertiveness
Assertiveness
Making Choices
Making Plans

Negativity
Anger
Hatred

Autonomy
Opposition
Separation

All human beings therefore have *fundamental needs*, which must be respected and satisfied throughout their whole lives (all the more so during childhood).

As we have already seen, these Needs are, in a certain sense, the Directions in which the Self expands, in which the individual develops as a complete organism. What, however, is the relationship between these Needs and the Basic Experiences?

The Basic Experiences are simply the way in which these Needs are *put into practise* (which are none other, as the reader will remember, than the general lines along which human life must develop). The Basic Experiences are concrete life and relational experiences where the individual proceeds in the direction of the fulfilment of these Needs. The Needs, then, are *incarnated* in the Basic Experiences, in the opportunities that the latter actually represent, in all their specificity and detail. They fit into specific contexts, compared to the paths of development seen from a more general point of view.

Concrete intervention must centre on the Basic Experiences, at diagnostic, therapeutic and preventative levels. It is the Basic Experiences that furnish us with practical indications on what to go and evaluate in children at a given scholastic level, what we can find in the problems related to drug addiction, what to go and alter to rebalance the organisation of the Self during childhood and adolescence from a preventative point of view.

The study of the Fundamental Needs remains, however, a very useful tool for identifying the *limits* within which the healthy development of human beings is really possible. In addition, therefore, it helps us to evaluate to what extent the trends existing during a certain era remain within these limits, or whether indeed they risk overstepping them, demonstrating at the same time in what way and what dangers they might have for the human race's integrity and harmony.

The Functions and the Basic Experiences

Earlier, we talked about the "Functions" in infant development, and now we are affirming that this process has more to do with much more complex and articulated systems. What, then, is the relationship between the Functions and the Basic Experiences of the Self?

Stern, dealing with the question of life's first experiences, revealed that the child learns to "read" the elements that are common to these experiences and link them very closely. The child, therefore, characterises the given event in a systematic way: hunger and breast feeding, the return of his mother, being held, and so on[2]. As we have already seen, Stern retains that these elements get contained in unitary systems, in so-called *envelopes of experience.*

In other writings, as well as in chapter 2, I had added to Stern's reflections the idea that these groups of elements connected to a given experience are fundamentally none other than the various Functions of the Self gathered around an event that follows a more or less constant pattern. This idea subsequently developed further. Today, the hypothesis is that all the Functional planes of the individual, profoundly interconnected and congruent with each other, go to form not only a simple "envelope of experience", but also something much more significant and important: that is to say a Basic Experience of the Self, which, if consolidated and reinforced repeatedly with a positive outcome, will become capacities, or in other words, the wealth of the individual.

For example, in the Basic Experience of "Just Being", of staying calmly in one place without anything else to do, the child experiences the possibility of loosening his level of activation and alertness. Lying in his cot, pleasantly lazing, his movements become calm, relaxed and without any precise sense; his eyes wander in the distance, his breathing becomes calm and diaphragmatic, his voice reduces itself to soft murmurings. His thoughts, too, are calm and slow, as are his perceptions. A parasympathetic state (or the "rest and digest" response) takes the upper hand; his desires loosen as if they were a liquid, with no precise form.

We can note that during this experience (just as with the other Basic Experiences of the Self), all the Functional planes (such as thought, posture, voice, emotions, desires, etc.) are (at least at first) *in harmony* with each other, making the experience full and complete. As long as repeated negative impacts from the child's surroundings have not disturbed the Experience of "Just Being", as long as "Just Being" has not been made difficult by excessive stimulation, fears, or anxiety on the part of the parents, then the

2 D. Stern (1985).

child will feel an intense feeling of well-being and pleasure in "Just Being", a pause between one period of activity and another. If this Experience is gone through positively over and over again, it will consolidate itself, and the child will conserve this capacity to stop and stay calm in his own company, without having to do anything other than be with himself, even as an adult.

Every Basic Experience is an ensemble of functions, each of which takes up a particular position within its own range (between one polarity and the other). Passing from one Basic Experience to another means, when it comes down to it, having the capacity to change the Functions in their various ranges, suiting the individual's way of being to different contexts.

A Basic Experience is determined by a particular constellation of nuances, of polarities. Unlike Just Being, Vitality and Exuberance are characterised by accelerated movement, deeper breathing, a vigorous muscular tone, an intense level of physiological activation, vivid images, and joyous emotions.

In any case, the *Basic Experiences* must have a repeatedly positive outcome to ensure the child continuity in the existence of the Self (without precocious, brusque interruptions), the conservation of their original integration, an harmonious and full development of all the psycho-physical Functions and the acquisition of as rich a baggage of capacities as possible.

Last of all, it must be pointed out that when we refer to the "emotions" as *Functions*, we are referring to the individual's subjective experience, i.e. what that person feels in a given situation; whilst the *Basic Experiences* that carry the same name (Joy, Tenderness or Anger) are not the same thing, in that these Basic Experiences are made up of all the Functions on all the various planes of the Self, as well as the corresponding Function "emotions".

Chapter 5

Basic Experiences in Functional Development

Introduction

In this chapter, we will be examining each Basic Experience of the Self, its specific meaning, and its influence on our lives and on human development right from childhood. As we examine each of these Basic Experiences, we will be highlighting each of the most specific and characteristic Functions that they bring into play.

I have tried to adhere to the "story" of these Basic Experiences in the life of the child, how it is that they evolve positively and the alterations that they can undergo: how, why, and their consequences in adult life.

What can emerge is a very useful and practical guide for parents (and also teachers and childcare workers) who wish to accompany their children's development actively, and who wish to work towards ensuring that all their children's life capacities form fully and harmoniously.

Moreover, an example has been provided of Functional therapeutic techniques for each of the Basic Experiences, each of which is specifically aimed at reconstructing that particular Experience. Each technique is followed by a description of its effects on the patients who have undergone it, as well as the patients' personal experiences and reactions to it (particularly in therapy and training groups). The aim of these descriptions is to demonstrate practically, and with greater clarity, the course of the therapeutic process and the profound meaning behind the reconstruction of the Basic Experiences of the Self. It must be specified, however, that seeing as it is very difficult to calibrate the techniques to recover just one Experience in a totally unambiguous and circumscribed way, many of the techniques actually touch on at least a couple of Basic Experiences.

The choice of the techniques has been made, in part, based on their significance, but also essentially on the availability of accounts relating to the personal experiences and reactions of the patients. There are, as we have already said, numerous other techniques. The collection of techniques that I have so far developed covers the entire list of the Basic Experiences of the Self – there are, in fact, copious techniques at the therapist's disposal for each single Experience.

In this chapter we will also see how the various Functions converge, in their specific configurations, to form each Basic Experience: what the *symbolic* content will be, what the prevalent *images* are, what type of *control* is necessary, what the most suitable *muscle tone* is, what the most appropriate *breathing*, *posture*, *voice*, and *emotions* are.

It will also be interesting to follow the progress of the Basic Experiences over time, i.e. what characterises the different Experiences during life's various stages. In fact, if (as we have already said) the baby goes through the various Experiences repeatedly with a positive outcome, these will gradually take on a stable connotation and become a genuine *capacity* at the individual's disposal. If, on the other hand, external circumstances obstruct this passage or make it difficult, the Experiences will not be full or complete, and they will therefore exhibit altered characteristics, because the Basic Need at their root has not been fully satisfied. We will see how this can happen: how, in these cases, the Basic Experiences become "polluted" by elements belonging to other Basic Experiences or to other personal experiences and emotive contents that are not in harmony with the Experience in question, thereby strongly limiting its potential.

Being Held

Being Contained

The Experiences relative to Containment (in both the strictest and the loosest sense of the word) are among the most archaic Basic Experiences of the Self. We already live in the condition of *Being Contained* fully and at length in our mother's womb: a condition that generates a very near complete sense of tranquillity and security. All little ones, however, even after birth, have innumerable opportunities to feel "inside", i.e. inside something soft and warm. It is enough just to think of how tiny a newborn is and how totally cocooned he must feel when he is held in an adult's arms in contact with their body.

Even afterwards, children continue to seek out the sensation of Being Contained. They curl up next to their mother's body, almost underneath her; they love hiding under the cushions, in a protected corner, or covered by something that contains, envelops, and reconstructs that old sense of tranquillity. Very often, when we were very little, we sought refuge under the covers, even hiding our head beneath the blankets, when we were scared at night. There are people who only manage to sleep if they are covered by a sheet or a blanket, or only if they are tucked in tightly.

Being Contained is not unpleasant, as some people sustain. Neither, however, is it an unattainable, "lost condition" that we aim for our whole lives. It is just one of the Experiences that are fundamental for the development of a human being and which, like the others, is never fully abandoned during our existence. People will continue to seek occasions when they will be able to feel (at least partially) Contained.

For example, it is pleasant to snuggle up close to our partner every so often, or among the cushions on the bed or the sofa. It is healthy to allow ourselves to be "little", every so often, a baby in the presence of someone or something bigger than us that encircles us and annuls almost all thought.

Being Held (Being Stopped)

Being Held is another nuance of this primary Experience, and this time the parent has an active role. The child feels that he is being looked after, he feels attentive, firm hands Holding him: as a result, he calms down and can allow himself to *Let Go* completely. Being Held in the arms is an important experience, which is repeated countless times during infancy. Every time, this experience confirms the child's vital sensation that he does not have to look after himself (at least in this first period of his life), and that he can savour life and the world around him without responsibility or care.

Even as adults, however, we should always seek moments in which we don't have to hold ourselves up completely on our own, in which we leave our cares and responsibilities to someone else, or at least share them. It is enough just to let a friend help us carry out a task, or to ask someone to accompany us to a delicate appointment, to feel Held and "supported", even though in this case we are Held only partially, with different nuances.

This Experience leaves a clear mark on our musculature, fixing it in our body memory. It is for precisely this reason that when we hold someone firmly in our arms they can finally let go.

Ersilia, a patient undergoing group therapy, after having taken part in the experience of "running away and being caught", said that she wanted to run even further away, so that she could feel even more *stopped*! Being caught and Held had in fact given her a very intense feeling; and together with that feeling, she had profound sensations of warmth, strength, and well being. In actual fact, once the body is Held firmly, then it really can *let go*. One is almost forced to let go, and we can experience the pleasure of not having to keep going, of not having to strive any more.

The *Holding* technique (used in some forms of body psychotherapy and in therapy for autistic children) is based on exactly that, on the body memory of having been Held when we were little. After an initial phase of irritation and oppression, sometimes followed by a violent attempt to free himself, the patient is overcome by a new, profound, and healing tranquillity.

Many animal species conserve this archaic memory even as adults. If you hold a little bird in your hands, it tends to fight to free itself, but if the hold is firm (and gentle) and prevents almost all movement in the little animal, it stops stirring and straining to escape, and finally rests calmly in the hands of the person who is Holding him. Mammals, being nearer to us in the chain of evolution, present behaviour of this type even more.

Functions

What is going on within the body memory? What happens to our musculature while we are Held firmly, intensely and gently? What does *letting go* mean? It is the Function *muscle tone* that "lets go", assuming a relaxed, hypotonic state, typical of when we don't need to be active, abandoning ourselves as if we had nothing to do. Yet, although the latter is among the most important Functions in this Basic Experience, other configurations must correspond to the same Experience, belonging to all the other Functions. All lead back to the typical relaxation associated with Being Held: the *mood* is of serene tranquillity and feeling softly cocooned, *movements* are almost completely absent, *thoughts* fluctuate without focussing on anything in particular, *breathing* is deep and diaphragmatic and produces an intense state of *vagotonia*. There is no state of alarm, there is no danger, there is no need to maintain a state of *attention*, and there are no unexpected or disturbing *fantasies* of danger. In the *symbolic* Function, "Being Held" is experienced as a precious gift and not as a situation of weakness, danger, or dependence; it has, in short, no negative connotation.

Stopping children when they really need to be stopped, when their excitement has become over the top and risks overflowing as if it would never stop, is in fact very good for them. Those interminable, over-intense tantrums, those surges of anger that go on long beyond even the little one's own endurance, excitement for a game pushing them to go way beyond tiredness: these are all situations in which children demonstrate a profound need to Be Stopped because they are not capable of getting out of the short circuit of activation on their own.

If we really do care about the child, if we are meeting their profound needs rather than "ordering them about", then Stopping them is not harmful. On the contrary, they find it necessary and pleasant: the children are very glad to "give in". What's more, we all go through moments when Being Stopped is a necessity and a pleasure that we desire deep down, but that we are not always capable of recognising at a conscious level, and it is a need that we should not underestimate.

Newborn babies are intensely aware of how they are being Held by an adult. They are content to be in the arms of someone with a calm, secure grasp and once there they are tranquil, even if the person is a stranger that they have never met. On the other hand, they grow gloomy, cry, and want to go back to their mother if the grasp is unpleasant, nervous, detached, or hostile.

Alterations

As we were just saying, the Experience of Being Held and Contained can suffer harmful interference if a baby is not Held with a calm, secure and decisive grasp; but it can also occur when the child is not Held often enough.

Many parents still believe that it is right to leave the newborn to cry for a long time to get them accustomed to crying less, so as not to "spoil" them, and they end up (though unknowingly) neglecting the fundamental need for Containment.

The Experience of Being Held and Contained will therefore be neither full nor complete, and this capacity will not be present and developed within the individual's personal baggage of functioning as an adult. He will therefore find it difficult to allow himself pleasant moments curled up on the sofa, among his bed cushions or in the arms of his partner. He will lose the regenerative resource of being able to become small for a while and playfully allow himself to be helped or cuddled. Rather, he will perceive being small and needy as unbearable weakness. Often, an authentic trace will remain in the child's body memory of when the hands Holding him were not secure and reassuring, and as adults, they find themselves with an unexplainable "fear of falling".

If, however, the subject has not developed at least a little *Control* and *Strength* as an alternative to Being Held, it can happen on the contrary that they continue to seek support disproportionately as adults. On the surface, it seems that these people manage to ask for help, and that they are prepared to accept help when it arrives, but in reality they just go round in circles, asking for help from everyone, everywhere, without adequately evaluating where it is that help can actually be obtained, without managing to tap that deep, unfulfilled need. In so doing, they continue to be afraid of not finding help, or they remain with the desolate certitude that help will never arrive.

There is another important consequence linked to not having been Held and Contained well: the child's incapacity to pause every so often, and just be, without having to do anything in particular, without running after impossible dreams ad infinitum, victim of a continual background level of excitement. This type of alteration is becoming very diffuse in recent generations: children are left to their own devices too often, alone with the television and computer games, filling up their time with unrelenting excitement and stimulation. They no longer have a moment's peace, pleasant repose, or stasis. Children today are losing the pleasant sense of "Being Stopped", and they are becoming increasingly restless, volatile: they never stop moving; they are becoming children who have spilled "over the top".

Holding and Containing means setting precise and clear limits. Limits are never a tragedy for children, if they have a clear and comprehensible meaning, and if they are set with genuineness, firmness, and authority. On the contrary: the child accepts clear limits with relief and pleasure. This helps him to Stop himself when necessary, without going beyond his own stamina and capacities, without giving in to the constant excitement of novelty or the stimuli of today's society, which is continually pushing us to go further, to the detriment of our inner equilibrium, health and profound well-being.

On the contrary, another alteration can affect the Experience of Being Held and Contained, i.e. when it has been excessive and the subject associates the Experience with imposition, or violence, whether it is physical or psychological. Being Stopped has become, in this instance, a genuine case of "being trapped", suffocating the child's vitality, impeding his movement rather than letting him feel the pleasure of a soft and tender acceptance. Anger ends up becoming a part of this particular Basic Experience, completely denaturing its profound essence. Once the individual reaches adulthood, he will find even the slightest physical contact aimed at Holding him unbearable, he will perceive it as oppressive and violent, even when the other person has clearly shown tenderness. Anger, suppressed inside and continually fed, even if unconsciously, will tend to come out in explosions of resistance and intolerance precisely when there is the prospect of letting go or of accepting help or support.

All of this clearly demonstrates the central role that reconstructing the Basic Experience of Being Held and Contained plays in any course of therapy, a role of extreme delicacy and vital importance.

Holding

In pairs. Person *A* lies on their side. Person *B* lies down behind their back and, with a gentle touch, encourages *A* to breathe deeply and to let go a little. Person *A* is then locked in an affectionate embrace. They can struggle, they can scream; pleasantly losing control until they stop, calm and tranquil, held by the warmth of *B* behind them.

As soon as Irina felt restrained, she let out a shout. The person holding her was frightened and to be honest he let go of her. It was a huge disappointment for Irina, because she did not feel at all held but rather alone for the umpteenth time, the useless winner (of a fight that wasn't a fight at all). When she was little, she had become used to continually fighting against her mother, often shouting in her effort to win the argument. The same thing had happened in this experience: fighting, winning, without being able to finally taste the new sensation of finally being caught and held.

Emily, on the contrary, was seized with anxiety when she realised she was locked in her partner's grip. She started moving, as she had never moved before, struggling and screaming out of control. She gradually became calm when she felt that she was held firmly but also very affectionately. She might perhaps have been able to give one last violent shove and free herself, but in the end she realised she really didn't want to at all! Towards the end, she felt that the arms holding her were completely fused together and she felt a hugely pleasant sensation of calm. Emily had had a very difficult experience of being blocked as a child: she had been immobilised and frightened at any sign of rebellion or strength towards her own family. Now her anxiety had finally melted away and she could remain in the arms of another person, a tiny little girl again, held with warmth and protection.

Marina, who had had similar experiences, managed to finally scream and struggle without restraint too: but instead of her initial fear, a sudden, unimaginable sense of calm descended on her. She felt completely stunned, and her usual worries and nagging thoughts were completely absent.

Marisa was completely surprised to find that she could finally manage to stay wrapped in the arms of another person, happy and serene. Before her therapy, she had found even the mere idea of being "inside" suffocating and cramped.

Protection

Protection is a natural corollary of Containment. The only difference is that Protection is slightly more intentional. Protecting is an act that is aimed at distancing the child from danger. It aims to make the child's life easier, and to reassure him of the fundamental role that his parents play for him.

Alterations

When this Experience has not been undergone fully and correctly during childhood, the individual will obsessively seek Protection throughout his life without stopping to ask himself who it is that really can offer it to him, and who it is, on the contrary, that he should absolutely avoid because they are untrustworthy and incapable to satisfying this unfulfilled need.

Difficulties with various types of *positive authority* (evident sources of Protection) are often a result of deficiencies and alterations in this very need for Protection, sometimes acknowledged by the subject, and sometimes denied and completely subconscious.

Cradled from behind our shoulders

Lying down on their sides, the therapist holds the patient from behind his back, first using just his hands, and then in a whole body hug, giving protection and making the patient feel tiny, held and contained. The two should feel as comfortable as possible.

Sergio relives early events in his life vividly and dramatically. His mother had been about to die, and as a little boy, he had felt completely defenceless, overshadowed by the threat of death. The fear that had been unleashed at that time returns now with this experience. But, little by little, his partner's gentle but sure hold of his back loosens the grip of anxiety, and starts dissolving the old traces caused by the lack of protection, instilling in him an unfamiliar sense of serenity: "It's good to open up", Sergio later remarks.

Anna feels her load of tasks and duties (which had recently been weighing her down) suddenly melt away. Finally feeling protected, she weeps, quietly and softly, and she finds it difficult when the contact behind her back has to end.

Atena becomes intensely aware of an old need for protection and when she abandons her back to the other person, her thoughts draw to a complete standstill.

Caterina felt like a tiny little girl, and she really liked it, but when she went as far as imagining herself in her mother's tummy, she became terrified and burst into floods of tears. The supportive and comforting hug behind her brought her back to her present sensations and allowed her fear to dissolve and she began to feel well, protected and reassured once again.

For Malina, the cuddle was intense and lovely. The sensation that she was being contained without her having to run away (as she normally did in life) gave her a previously unimaginable sense of calm, and the sensation of being fed like a tiny baby. A deep pain dissolved and was gradually absorbed completely.

In this type of technique, it is very important and reassuring being able to "Give", without worrying too much about how the other person is receiving. In order to be able to experience the conditions of both Giving and Receiving fully, the two concepts must be completely separated, without the paralysing load of responsibility, worry, and duty.

Being Taken Up

Being Taken Up

Newborns have a large *motility*, but they do not yet possess *mobility* in space. To move from one place to another, they must be Taken there by a parent. Naturally, this Experience doesn't just represent a mechanical means for the child of getting from one place to another, rather it is directly related to the joy of seeing the person he loves come closer, seeing the smiling face bending over him, feeling lifted up easily by a force draws him in close, towards his father, his mother, his big sister. The whole experience of being brought nearer is exciting: feeling light, flying high, seeing the face of the loved one come closer and being able to touch it with his little hands, being able to feel cuddled and kissed, his face touching the other person's.

It's no coincidence that all children love being thrown in the air: they can once again feel the sensation of lightness and "flying" that they felt every time someone lifted them from their crib, from their pram or from their bed and lifted them upwards towards them.

Being Taken Up is something else as well: it is the fulfilment of an expectation. It is the passage from one state to another, from *being on our own to being with a parent*, or rediscovering a loved one after a pause for sleep, for siesta, or for relaxation. A movement contains a "burst of joy", the beauty and excitement of an impulse. It is a movement with enormous vitality.

Functions

The full expression of this Experience involves the *emotion* of joy, but also the child's complete trust that the adult will definitely Take him up and bring him in close. On the other hand, an intense *excitement* is present, anticipating the moment when he will be Taken up, permitting the child to foretaste it with his *imagination*. The excitement slightly activates the *sympathetic nervous system* although he is far from being anxious; his *breathing* is just slightly more intense and more accelerated than normal. *Muscle tone* is activated, ready to aid the movement and joyously grasp the adult. His *gaze* is intense and fixed on the object. His *voice* expresses excitement, and there is no *fantasised* fear of falling.

Alterations

Even though being completely "Taken Up" proves more difficult as an adult than it did when we were children, we are continually Taken Up, grasped. This happens physically when we are Taken by the arm, when someone puts their arm around our shoulder, when a friend Takes hold of us by the shoulders, when we are Taken, sexually. It happens metaphorically when we are helped or our case is Taken in hand by a lawyer, a doctor or a psychotherapist.

It is easy to imagine what the consequences could be if someone is not Taken Up well as a child: he will never let himself be grasped and he will not be able to bear any contact whereby he feels Taken.

Sea Anemones

This is an experience for groups of 6–8 people. Kneeling, the group forms a tight circle on the carpet. It is a sea anemone. The participants' arms are the anemone's tentacles and filaments waving in the sea. In turns, each person stands on his feet outside the circle. The anemone's tentacles touch him, lift him up and they make him slide head first into the centre of the anemone. The anemone closes, and the person inside is moved, rocked, his position is changed, he is softly "chewed up", and the anemone absorbs him. At the end, the anemone softly deposits him on the outside of the circle. The anemone is once again alone, the participants are in close contact, waving: almost as if it were the dance of an anemone in the sea. When the last participant has been "digested" and deposited outside, the anemone rises up and continues to move, waving. Then he stops. All the tentacles and filaments weave in and out of one another for a last contact, and then they separate for the last time.

It is the first time that Amalia has felt such a strange, and at the same time, tranquil pleasure. She completely let herself go and she found it fantastic. She could have carried on for hours.

Françoise feels intense sensations of well-being. She feels as if she were immersed in an ocean: everything and nothing at the same time.

Francesca finds diving head first into the centre of the anemone impressive, as if she were falling into a deep space. Once she is inside, she savours the movements that the anemone imposes on her: sometimes fast and sometimes slow.

Mary feels lightness and well-being: she felt completely held and cradled.

Being Carried

Being Carried does not just apply to being moved from one place to another. The newborn lives a very intense and multifaceted experience just *being* in the arms of a parent. From up there he can see what is going on around him much better: it's a perfect vantage point, also because it moves exactly as the adult moves, and so he therefore finds himself at the centre of the action, in the world that interests him.

Let us examine the practice, so widespread in ancient civilisations (and which still exists today), whereby children are Carried tied behind a parent's back or slung diagonally from the shoulders. The baby follows everything that his mother does, staying in close contact with her (in some cases, the contact is skin to skin). The child can follow what gives him the most pleasure, observing the world without having to worry about where he is going, without having to care for himself or his situation: it doesn't matter where because he's always in contact with his mother.

Moreover, this contact is intense, and full of different elements, all of which are very significant in a baby's life: his mother's intense smell, her voice, her taste (if his mother's skin is within reach of his mouth), and above all, her "movement". The child perfectly recognises his mother's gait and abandons himself to it. The vibrations that are transmitted to him, both from his mother's larger movements and the little bumps that arrive directly from the jolts of walking, are very pleasant for him and he feels as if he were being constantly rocked.

Sometimes, during therapy, when patients re-experience precisely such vibrations and little bumps, very old sensations of being Carried are suddenly reopened, bringing back intense emotions that had been buried and forgotten over time.

Milly was asked to lie down on the couch and relax her head in the therapist's hands. He moved her head gently from side to side. This experience is profoundly regressive, and Milly rediscovered very early feelings and sensations. The movement of her head brought back a strange feeling of nausea that she had not felt for a long time. Then she became literally rigid when she was moved with those little tiny movements, which were transmitted to her like vibrations. A storm of emotions welled up inside her when she heard the words "let go" and an old and silent weeping flowed over her.

I asked her if she knew what had happened to her between the ages of one and two years old. Milly responded that she saw the image of herself at the age of one and a half, running but there was no-one to lift her up into their arms at the end.

Didn't she have any memories of being held in her parent's arms?

No, she did not have a single one. On the contrary: it seemed impossible that this had ever happened!

In reality, these minuscule movements are exactly what the baby feels when he is in his mother's arms while she is on her feet, going about her everyday tasks. They are little swaying movements, little jolts, a slight rocking. Milly became rigid with emotion when she felt these little head movements that reproduced the same sensations as that remote period: the sensations of Being Carried. Milly must therefore have gone through this

Experience, so important in the life of a child; it is just that the Experience had not been full or satisfying. Alternately, it might simply be that the Experience had been positive enough, but that it had finished too quickly and its traces had been suffocated by subsequent feelings: not being Carried any more, the pain and displeasure of not being able to have the thing she had desired so much.

This can help us to understand that the traces of particular positive Experiences are sometimes not absent, but rather buried very deep down. This example also shows us how important it is to recover them in therapy, bringing them to the surface, so that they can form a positive, present and working support in the patient's life.

Another nuance of this Experience is being Pushed in the Pram, and it is just as important in the child's life. Even though there is no physical contact, the sensation of being able to travel about protected and secure, able to enjoy the world around them, is equally enjoyable and significant. The same vibrations and sensations are present as when the child is being Carried.

Later, when the child is older, he will still be able to have the opportunity of going through the Experience of Being Carried even though he is walking on his own legs. Besides the occasions when he can still be held in his parents' arms, the adults also Lead him by the hand. The reason why many children love being pulled is not, in most cases, that they don't want to walk, but rather that they want to be Led, just as when they were little. As children, we can "hang" on our parent's arm and leave ourselves to be Led without having to worry about where we are going, about what route to take, just like when were are Carried in our parent's arms. We let ourselves be pulled along, and in the meantime our eyes can settle on a shop window, on the dog at the corner of the street, on the girl walking next to us, on the colours of the street poster. We can enjoy the world a little longer without too many responsibilities, and let our thoughts wander to what fascinates us without running any danger.

When we grow up, there are still lots of opportunities for Being Led. We are Led when someone in our group of friends decides on the programme for the evening, or what film to watch, or when we leave our partner to organise a holiday, deciding where and when. Even being involved in a project for work takes up this Basic Experience, just like when we put our faith in a trusted architect for the work on our house.

Functions

The Functions that most characterise Being Carried/Led are at the *symbolic* level, because of the positive significance that the person attributes to letting go every so often and letting someone else take on the responsibility of choosing and leading. The person's *feelings* are of trust and calm, indispensable if he really is to place his trust in another person and have faith that the decisions that they will make will be good for him as well.

One of the techniques developed in Functional Therapy in recent years reconstructs exactly this experience of being Led by the hand, as if the patient were a little child.

Alterations

Naturally, Carrying or Leading, like all the aspects of the relationship with the child, needs to maintain a fundamental respect, which must never be lacking. Otherwise, Drawing others towards us risks becoming aggressive, and will take on the useless connotation of "dragging" instead.

Chiara is slowly losing all the exasperated control that characterised her life and symptoms. Her partner, however, is not content with the huge progress she has already made and tries to push her harder, to make her go further than her progress in therapy will allow. At this point, taken beyond her own capabilities, Chiara *counter-reacts* ending up restraining herself, stopping herself, falling back on her old perfectionism and her old uneasiness, her reliance on men, her difficulties in dealing with her colleagues. It is the same with children: if a child is pulled along beyond his own ability, he always ends up falling over and hurting himself; if he is allowed, on the contrary, to calmly experiment within his own limits, he will manage to run fast and well.

Being excessively urged on in this Experience can provoke a reaction of rejection, extreme negativity, and feeling paralysed. If a little boy is pushed too hard in his schoolwork, pushed beyond his capabilities, or dragged ahead, rushing the stages of his education that would ordinarily have allowed him to reach the same objectives with a timing and a modality more in keeping with his personal development, his enjoyment of schoolwork will decrease. It will weigh him down or become a source of anxiety, until it becomes a real obstacle. The same thing could happen to those children who are hauled from one after school activity to another without time to breathe (swimming, catechism, music lessons, gymnastics).

All too often, parents "drag" their children insensitively in the direction of their own preferences rather than leaving space for the children's desires to arise and develop naturally, without really being aware of their real limitations. All of this makes the real Experience of Being Led impossible, and the whole business simply ends with the negative or pathological consequence that the children convince themselves that they are incapable, that they have disappointed their parents, that they are unable to cope with important situations, or that they are unable to bear comparison with others or measure up to their judgement.

If, on the contrary, we are never Carried or Led, or accompanied step by step in life's important situations and helped to understand what path we should take or what phases we should go through to get to a particular goal, or ability, or dream, the consequences will be an extreme difficulty in gradual learning processes. These children will find the first stages of learning new things very difficult: either they are already very good at something and they already know how to do it at a high level, or they tend to give up completely.

Cradling the patient's legs

While the patient is lying on his back, hold his legs in your arms, gently cradling them as if he were a little tiny baby.

During this experience Alessandro feels, with a great sense of relief, that he can perhaps start to trust others, for the first time in his life.

Jolanda feels her body to be tiny and fragile like that of a little baby, and at the same time, she feels gratified by the experience of being held and carried.

Anna really perceives herself to be a newborn baby, completely abandoning herself to the adult.

Marco bursts into heartfelt tears when he feels "carried". He recalls happy memories from his past that had been buried and forgotten for too long: for example when he used to help his mum, or when he received flattering compliments for his results at school.

Luigi feels permeated by a huge sense of peace because another person is looking after him and holding him without having to do anything to be accepted.

Letting Go

Letting Go (Daydreaming)

Children are well aware how healthy it is to be able to Let Go every so often during their intense day's activity. We are not talking about lazy children, who find it difficult to socialise and make contact and who often sit silent and sad in a corner. We are talking instead about healthy, vivacious children who have lots of energy and who are continuously active. These children have moments when they pause to "Let Go". They interrupt their activity, allowing themselves a rest that is different from sleep.

Sleep "shuts out" active life in some way. It forms an unconscious parenthesis. These breaks, on the other hand, are conscious moments inserted into active life, moments when we can savour the old pleasure of not having to do anything, suspending our activity and vigilance, also, above all, at the muscular level. Breaks during which we let go are fundamental in order for us to preserve our health and well-being, so as not to accumulate excessive excitement, anxiety, or stress. In a book I wrote some time ago (Rispoli, 1995) about the prevention of stress in the workplace, I had already suggested the practise of taking "micro breaks". What they consisted of were brief moments, fitted into the day outside and during working hours, when we "Let Go" for a few moments: with a deep sigh, moving away from the place of work, relaxing our muscles and posture, emptying the mind of thoughts, thinking of something pleasant, completely different from the work we are doing.

Functions

One of the ways that children manage to Let Go is to Daydream: their eyes get lost in the distance, their body *movements* stop, *muscle tone* relaxes, their *thoughts* become vague, almost liquid. Children can start Daydreaming while they eat, after having played a particularly intense game, while they are drawing, or whilst watching another child. They often Daydream, as they did when they were younger, lying on their bed watching the ceiling and getting lost among the imperceptible geometric forms drawn by shadows, reflections, pictures, the design of the wallpaper and stains on the walls.

Daydreaming has none of the negative values that parents almost always attribute to it, in the fear that their children will lose intelligence and become stupid. On the contrary, Daydreaming is a breath of fresh air and a boost for the whole organism, and therefore, for the intellect.

This is because all the Functions normally involved in activation and concentration modify themselves in the direction of relaxation and a break, letting the individual and his psychological, biological and physiological levels to recuperate energy. During Letting Go, it is principally the individual's *muscles* that rest. The body rests its whole weight and it is completely relaxed. *Movement* is strongly restricted and slow or they are movements aimed at stretching to relax tension. The eyes are softened without concentrating on any one object. The *breathing* is calm and slow, setting off yawns of relaxation. The individual is profoundly in contact with their own *sensations* whilst their thoughts wander without any fixed objective. All of this happens is a *mood* of tranquillity and well-being.

Alterations

It can occur, however, that a child is stimulated by adults too much or too often, or that he has not been able to live through the Basic Experience of Letting Go because other connected Basic Experiences have been damaged that were necessary for it to be able to be realised satisfactorily. In fact, if a deep fear has crystallised within the child, if he has not be Protected sufficiently, if he has not felt sufficiently reassured, held and sustained, then the necessary conditions will be lacking for him to be able to go through the Experience of Letting Go.

If this is the case, the child will be lacking an indispensable resource for finding energy and vitality when he grows up. This is the case for adults who are hyperactive, dedicating every second of their lives to some activity, even when it is not indispensable, even when they have to invent one. These adults are incapable of enjoying sweet idleness, *lazing around.* They are incapable of sitting down to enjoy a good book, a beautiful view, or the sun on the beach.

Touching pain

Massage in pairs. In turns, each partner massages the source of pain, making the pain more concrete and delineated and less cosmic, less all-encompassing.

Francesca has a sensation of pain and irritation diffused through her whole body, but with the slow massage, she realises that the painful sensation that she feels originates in her chest. This makes the pain itself less intense and unbearable.

Gaia realises that the massage has finally dissolved the terrible pain that she felt in her legs, until it completely disappears.

As soon as she feels her partner massaging her back, Claudine feels a pain like a violent blow, but she also feels at the same time that the hands of her partner limit the area and the intensity of the pain more and more.

Tino clearly feels the need for strong pressure and heat on his aching shoulder blades.

At the beginning, Mariano just felt an indistinct state of anxious suffering in his stomach, his belly, and his back. In reality, it is his abdomen that is rigid and tense, causing all the discomfort. As the massage progresses he manages to perceive the pain as being increasingly localised in a precise point of his intestines. At this point, he is also able to distinguish other vital sensations, of which he was normally unaware, in even more detail: a pulsating pain in one part of his body, the sensation of having a "knot" in his belly, and cold shivers running down his legs while the pain is dissolved and calmed, finally arriving at a quiet and restful sense of well-being.

Just Being

Being able to Just Be is a natural consequence of being able to Let Go: we can say that it is the most general aspect of it. Letting Go means "deactivating" vigilance, action and control systems. More specifically, Letting Go implies, above all, the relaxation of muscles, breathing, movements, and thoughts. The case of Just Being is a little different in that not everything is deactivated. When a baby "Just Is" in his cot, without doing anything in particular, he moves his legs randomly, moving his hands around, touching parts of his own body. Letting Go can be brief or for a few instants, whilst Just Being is a deeper condition that requires a comfortable position and a good ability for getting in contact with ourselves.

Neck and Shoulder Massage

Massage deeply at the point where the neck joins the shoulders, with movements that go from the centre outwards. Hold the shoulders in your hands so that the patient can let them go and so they no longer have to support them. The massage descends from the shoulders a little way along the arms. A long massage of the neck, moving upwards towards the base of the skull, then place your palm on the nape of the neck and move the head from one side to the other. Massage the nape of the neck where it joins the skull. Massage in circles from the nape of the neck towards the head, as if you wanted to make the head fall backwards. Hold the back of the head with your hand and pull it upwards a little, lifting it slightly as if to reopen the flow of something that runs downwards from the head, through the neck and into the back. With one hand on the neck and the other on the crown of the head, rotate the head gently in several directions, with gentle movements, until it abandons itself to the hands of the therapist. With one hand, massage downwards towards the back (whilst the other hand is on the neck) between the shoulder blades, slightly lifting the patient's back: the head can hang backwards even better, relaxed. "Cup" your hands under the patient's head and then calmly leave it for a while, calm and protected.

Long, intense shivers run through Alida's body, mobilising her organism's deeper physiological Functions and leaving her in the end with a sensation of peace and calm.

Mariella finds the massage wonderful, and at the end she feels that her internal perceptions have been strongly modified: her hands feel enormously heavy, and her body feels light and waving like a thin piece of paper.

Serenella, once the initial fear caused by the currents of energy running along her arms and legs has passed, experiences intense well-being. Bice feels that her head is light as a feather and the rest of her body is very heavy. Rosamaria feels her mind empty itself, together with a sensation of lightness because she has lost all sense of responsibility. When Amanda starts to feel the possibility of abandoning herself to the pleasant sensations caused by the massage, an intense alarm signal is set off within her. She remembers several episodes in her past when she has suffered, but with a sensation of compassion and tenderness towards herself.

Initially, Lorella feels a strong sense of pressure on her forehead, which disappears after the massage, leaving instead an intense tingling sensation, together with the impression of flying.

Contrary to the shivers in her body, the warmth of the massage helps Emanuela to let herself go.

Vigilance prevents Marilena from completely abandoning herself to the hands of the other person. On the contrary, her attention obsessively returns to her head and hands, and to the countless thoughts that never give her a moment's peace and which converge on her old fear of being "abandoned". Marilena's facial expression and behaviour remind the therapist so vividly of a very small child, that he asks her what happened to her in her first two years of life. In this way, he makes the discovery that when Marilena was exactly one year old her baby sister was born, but she died soon afterwards!

Abandoning ourselves to

The third aspect of this group also has Functional characteristics that are very similar to the first two. As with the other groups of Basic Experiences, it is basically a different nuance of the self same Fundamental Experience. In this version, Letting Go and Just Being are themselves made possible by the presence of another person. The child abandons himself, letting go yes, but in the hands of an adult: someone who inspires trust, someone who cares for him and looks after him.

Alterations

Whether the child has gone through this Basic Experience fully and well or not has hugely relevant consequences in his life as an adult.

There are people who do not even know what it means to Trust themselves to another person, who have to do everything on their own, relying only on their own resources.

There are people who never Abandon themselves, not even in love. On the contrary, they run away when they glimpse the possibility of a more intense relationship that could involve them more deeply. They always have reserves about their partner because they cannot accept the idea of completely opening up and placing themselves in the other's hands.

There are others who, on the contrary (although only apparently on the contrary), spend their whole lives searching for figures that they can Trust themselves to, upon whom they can lean part of their weight by whom they can let themselves be Led. They desire this with all their hearts, but they almost always end up being disillusioned, their hopes unfulfilled, and expectations disappointed. Actually, precisely because the Experience of completely Abandoning themselves to an adult has been partial or dissatisfactory, both those who don't trust themselves and those who obsessively and continually seek figures to rely on have considerable difficulty in distinguishing, separating and discerning who it really is possible to Abandon themselves to. They do not realise what the other people they are in contact with are really like, deep down. They cannot "sense" whether these people are trustworthy or not, or whether they are seriously interested in looking after them and taking on their problems. It occurs, therefore, that both of these types of people have experiences that "turn out badly", often suffering great pain and distress, because they Abandon themselves to the wrong people.

> *Leaning ourselves and being lifted*
>
> One person is on their feet in the middle of the group. The others are standing around them. With enormous delicacy, the members of the group start to take a little of his weight upon themselves, until they completely lift him up and cradle him gently in their arms. In the end, the person is delicately placed on the mat. A moment of contact and then they detach themselves.
>
> Elisa cries with huge sobs while she is in the centre of the group, while she is taken up, supported, and cradled. Her worries about putting other people to trouble, which prevented her from fully trusting others at the beginning of her course of therapy, have significantly decreased, giving her the possibility of experiencing abandoning herself in someone's arms like a baby in a completely new and unreserved way. She never thought she would have been able to be lifted up by others and really be able to afford to do so.

Contact

Contact (Fusion)

A little child demonstrates the desire to be held in his mother's arms (or those of his father, his aunt or his babysitter, for that matter) without doing anything else. He does not need to eat, nor does he seek any particular cuddling or tenderness. He does not even want to play. He simply desires to be in Contact with his mother. He leans his face on her shoulder, skin to skin, and stays like that for a while, without doing anything else, other than feeling the Contact.

Another little girl, a little older, holds her best friend's hand while they are out for a walk in the park. She does not wish to pull her along, nor does she wish to be pulled. She has no desire to convince her of anything, nor does she wish to demonstrate gratitude or comfort her with her affection. She just wants to feel Contact and enjoy it calmly.

A dog curls up next to his mistress. He does not want to be stroked; he is not trying to demonstrate that he is loyal and tied to her forever. He is not trying to show her that he is at her orders at her feet. He is taking some Contact, absorbing it with all of himself.

To understand more about this simple, and at the same time complex, Basic Experience, we take the *amoeba* as an example. The amoeba is quite a simple protoplasmic animal in the scale of evolution. It has very linear behaviour but is already able to react entirely with the surrounding environment. When the amoeba perceives a pleasant Contact it stops, expands, and absorbs anything positive that the surrounding environment can offer it. When it senses something unpleasant, the amoeba contracts itself, retreats, moves further away.

The amoeba does not have particular aims or hidden agenda, nor does it reason in a refined way. On the contrary: it does not reason at all. The amoeba simply "feels" the exterior of the other living being that it has entered into Contact with.

The whole living world "feels" beyond reasoning or trying to understand things through the filters of rationality. This feeling comes about through Contact; this contact comes above all through the skin, but also through *looks*, *sounds*, *smells*, the *imagination*, and the *emotions*. It is less a case of perceptions (the interpretation and sorting of external signals) and rather one of *sensations* that arrive as little filtered as possible, i.e. *seeing* rather than looking at anything in particular; *hearing* rather than listening to the contents of a conversation, *sensing* rather than smelling specific perfumes.

We often talk about Contact, but we often do not know what it actually is. In actual fact, it is very hard to describe it in words in a clear and exhaustive way. Of course, Contact passes through several sensorial organs, among which, as we have said, touch is very important. Contact, however, is not merely to do with touch. Contact is a flow of sensations passing from one person to the other, which the organism absorbs openly and fully.

There is no giving and taking in Contact. It is simply an exchange. Contact has no aim other than Contact. It is an experience of very deep nearness to the other person, almost a fusion; without, however, the aim of demonstrating anything, trying to make the other person like us, ingratiating them, or showing them gratitude.

Contact also contains an element of being inside the other person, feeling how they are, perceiving reality as if we were in their stead. This happens almost automatically, as soon as the channels are opened. There is no forcing or dishonesty. Neither is it an unequal relationship where one person is little and dependent and the other a magnanimous adult bestowing a little of their love. Contact implies a melting of the boundaries between the two, and the flow of sensations leads to a deep comprehension. Empathy is nothing other than Contact: a Contact that allows us to take the other person's feelings and emotions within ourselves.

Contact does not necessitate that we be "worried" about the other person. It simply means "exchanging" the flow of sensations.

Why is it that Contact often works better with a dog or a cat than with a fellow adult? It is because the dog is not *worried* about his master, and he therefore procures evident pleasure from caresses and Contact. Likewise, the master isn't much *concerned* what it is that he's giving his dog, how he's giving it, whether the dog is accepting it or refusing it, whether the dog loves him too or instead couldn't care less, if he will be grateful or if he would love another master in the same way. Nobody torments themselves so much for a dog, as often happens with another human being (especially if they are of the opposite sex); and therefore Contact with a dog is often a full and effective form of Contact.

Functions

The other Functions, apart from the *sensations* (undoubtedly the most important) that apply to the Experience of Contact are above all *thoughts*, *emotions,* and *symbolism*. The *rationality* must not interfere with excessive forms of judgement caused by the fact that the subject has been educated to control himself and social conditioning. The *thoughts* must be free from preconceived ideas. The value that the person attributes to Contact on the *symbolic* plane must be positive, too. Contact must not, moreover, be distorted by inopportune sexual overtones, caused by the physical proximity, nor by the fear that other people are always dangerous enemies, nor should it be deprecated as if the other person were moved solely by self interest or the wish to obtain something. Lastly, the *emotions* are of pleasure for its own sake, calm and intense: the pleasure we felt when we were little and leaned ourselves against our mother's body, without doing anything other than melt ourselves into the Contact.

In this Experience (just as in all the Experiences that we are talking about, for that matter), the word "Contact" doesn't just refer to skin-to-skin Contact, rather it refers to the Experience of Contact in its widest sense: a global and general modality, lived and felt by the whole person, with all the levels and planes of the Self. In order to reproduce this Experience exactly, *all* of the Functions must assume the same direction; they must *all* concur in the right way in order to create the Experience of Contact's specific modality of functioning. There cannot be true Contact if the visual Contact is missing, if there is no Contact with the other person's emotions, if we do not feel the other person, or if we do not perceive what the other person perceives.

When the Experience of Contact is firmly rooted in all its aspects, then it is possible to recover it when we need to, even in situations in which the other person is not physically present and near. In this case, all the Functions will likewise be activated by the memory itself, just as if the person were right there.

Alterations

Why do we lose our Contact?

When a child does not receive enough nutriment, interest, attention, or affection, then he has to start trying to obtain all these things on his own. However, he is too young in the course of his development to worry about these things, when he should still be tranquilly immersed in the adults' care. Instead, he is forced to increase his self control and triple his efforts to obtain what is crucial for his existence and which ought to come naturally from the love surrounding him.

All of this isolates him from Contact with other people and from the calm and pleasant sensations that can arrive from the outside. Contact becomes limited to a form of Contact based on the urgent need to survive, on a need that is always struggling to be satisfied. It is no wonder then that the Contact becomes anxious and worried. Contact with another person becomes too finalised: it is more like desperate clinging, during which, instead of feeling the other person, we just feel our own dramatic state of need.

During our frenetic and stressful lives, we constantly risk losing our capacity for Contact. Yet we must understand that if we and future generations continue in this direction, we will lose a functional process that is truly at the base of life that no technological innovation, no matter how sophisticated, can ever substitute.

In reality, it is precisely Contact (despite the fact that this is not its primary motivation) that allows us to understand who the other person really is, to feel what they are like beneath the facade, beyond the parts that the other person consciously and voluntarily chooses to display on the exterior.

This capacity is clearly present in the animal kingdom. A dog *senses* if the man in front of him (or another dog) is an enemy, if they are afraid, if they are about to attack, or if they are really a friend. Dogs choose the person they feel to be most favourably disposed towards them to be their master or mistress. My little dog was a sort of "weathervane" regarding the patients who came to my clinic: the more closed, absorbed in themselves, angry or afraid of her they were, the more she barked at them (and not because she didn't know them). Her behaviour towards these people gradually changed as the therapy went on and they became more open, they softened and became sweeter and better disposed, in short, as they recovered their capacity for real Contact.

When a man or a woman comes to me to tell me how tragic their choice of a partner was, when they tell me what a despicable and negative person their partner is, I can be sure there is a significant incapacity for Contact. How can it otherwise be possible that they could have lived for so long alongside another person without realising what that person was like deep-down? Nor can we consider (apart from in very particular cases) the hypothesis that their partner has radically changed in a short space of time: nuances can change, but the basic tonality of the person cannot.

It is clear that when they are first in love, people tend to show the best part of themselves and to hide the negative part. However, if we have the capacity of deep Contact, the capacity to sense and feel what the other person really is, we cannot fail to notice that person's innermost and hidden aspects. We cannot fail, in short, to perceive what the other person is really like. Being able to discern what other people are really like allows us to be able to discern when it is that we can really open up, when we can abandon ourselves, and whether we can really trust someone or not.

Contact as the basis of various forms of relationship

Contact has no aim other than Contact, but it is, at the same time, a primary Basic Experience, which numerous other forms of relationship can be based on. Profound Contact can help us to understand the real nature of the person standing before us; it can be the foundations on which we build profound affection or love. It can be the glue that binds the most sincere and long-lasting friendships and should be the backbone of the relationship between parents and children.

Contact can also be the loadstone that brings about and helps to maintain sexual excitement and eroticism. Many forms of difficulty in sexual arousal, particularly in men, are due to a deficiency in their capacity for Contact. They therefore try to make up for this deficiency by becoming sexually more active. They try to "do" many things during intercourse and put their fantasies and imaginings into action, increasingly frantically, as if all this could really serve as a remedy to the situation. But the more they try, the less they manage to "feel" the woman they are with and sense the Contact and the pleasure of the sensations that could reach them. The less they feel, the easier it is for them to lose their arousal, in an evident downward spiral. For this reason it is important not only to be able to perceive Contact, but also to know how to conserve it, feed it, and how to avoid suddenly losing it.

Contact needs gentle and calm adjustments if it is to be maintained. It needs little movements. Prolonged immobility reduces it (causing further worries), as do activity and frenetic movements.

The capacity for Contact, or being able to feel others, is therefore far more important that we can possibly imagine. For this reason, we should try to create and spread the ability to recognise this fundamental value in life at a cultural level, and try to re-establish it fully in this high-tech and high-speed society.

Amoebas

In groups. Each person lies on their back on the floor. They start to make little movements as they breathe. Their breathing is pulsating inside them and they expand with every breath. Then, continuing these movements, they start to move about, sliding their backs along the floor head first. The Therapist says, "Let's move around without thinking, without knowing where we are going or why. We are amoebas who move around, pulsating. Pulsating and breathing. Amoebas don't have an aim, they don't move in any particular direction. They just move along the floor, pulsating. Amoebas don't think, they just move and feel, nothing else. One amoeba can meet another amoeba, but it feels only the contact. It doesn't have to do anything for the other amoeba. It doesn't have to repay what it receives. Amoebas don't worry about other people. Amoebas don't have a head or feet or hands, but just one big, smooth outer surface that can enter into contact with other surfaces, with other amoebas. If the contact is pleasant, the amoeba stops and absorbs the pleasant contact through its membrane. If the contact is unpleasant, the amoeba simply retreats, in the search of more positive sensations. The amoeba feels the other contacts and stops when the contact is good, absorbing it, feeling the contact with no aim other than simple and pure contact. Then, after one last encounter the amoeba gently detaches itself from the others and, pulsating as it breathes, remains alone with the sensations that it has absorbed".

Anna found it very difficult to let go of her thoughts and her state of vigilance. Alicia, on the contrary, didn't find it at all difficult imagining she was an "amoeba". She was scared at the beginning that she would feel too fragile in contact with the other bodies, but when she tried it, she realised that her fear was unfounded and she felt relaxed and on a par with the others.

Monica felt very good. She felt protected. She felt that the need she had for unseen contact had been fulfilled.

Ilaria feels the same wonderful sensation that she felt a while ago, at the beginning of her course of therapy, but now she felt better able to enter into contact with the others, and she felt her movements to be less finalised and less conditioned by thoughts. She clearly realises how important it is to be able to abandon oneself to contact for contact's sake: a completely primordial feeling, pleasant in itself, with no other aim than simply being in contact. Her experiences of contact before had been too finalised by excessive, and sometimes "invented" concerns, influenced by deep-seated fears.

A contact like this would have been impossible for Graziella a while ago, whereas now, with the group, this difficulty melts away (at least partially), in part due to the movements that she finally manages to carry out, each of which had been suggested by the therapist. Graziella manages to slither along the floor head first. These movements allow her to diminish her level of control and tension.

Feeling contact through the spine

In pairs. One person lies face down, turned a little to one side, with their back towards the other person. Their partner sits behind them without touching them. The therapist asks, "What do our backs feel? Is the presence behind us reassuring? Is it someone who is close to us and who is looking at us with affection? Or is the other person distant from us, lost in their own thoughts looking at something else? Try to feel beyond what you know rationally. What can your back tell us? What sensations is it transmitting? Is it tranquil, serene, or is it restless? Does it feel warm or cold? Is the presence behind us someone who wants to take care of us? Or is it a dangerous or hostile presence? Is it someone who could hit us, or hurt us?

Now the person sitting behind places a hand on our back. Then they start a slow, gentle massage. What are the sensations in our back now? How do we feel about this contact? The hand moves faster and more lightly. It almost never stops. The partner places their hand at random on different parts of the back. The hand is lifted up and placed down, ever so lightly. What does our back feel? Is it tranquil and calm? Worried? Now the hand moves even faster. It is agitated. Frenetic.

Suddenly it stops. The hand becomes heavy. It starts a back massage, taking the muscles it its open palm, and loosening them, moving them. The massage is calm. It comprises the whole back. What does our back feel now? Is it pleasant or unpleasant? What do we feel about the presence behind us? We are in our sensations and not in our rationality. We stay in our sensations a little bit longer. Then the hand readies itself to leave the contact. One more moment, almost like saying goodbye, and then it detaches itself.

Marcella feels a sense of danger behind her when there is no contact; Ippolita feels that the presence behind her is familiar. Marinella experiences a strong shiver down her spine not knowing what is behind her – her feeling of expectation is part excitement, part fear. Mercedes feels that the presence behind her is known to her, but that the other person is far away, detached. Adele experiences fear and anxiety, even. For Juana, the sensation is one of distrust, and Elisabetta felt a male presence giving her warmth and protection. Geraldina senses her partner's presence and their curiosity. Laura feels pleasure and warmth at the centre of her back.

Almost everyone finds the last phase of the exercise, that of the massage, reassuring and pleasant. Just as newborn babies feel the strength of the hands around their little bodies, no matter how delicately the parent is holding them, so the group feels the strength of the hands massaging them. Some of the group require a longer massage in order to recover the benefits of such intense contact, others are able to enjoy the positive effects of the experience straight away.

Lighter contact is experienced as positive only when the entire spectrum of sensations in the back has been fully opened and is perceived by the individual, otherwise the connotations arising from this contact can result as been very uncomfortable (for Ippolita), anxious (for Geraldina), ambiguous (for Luisiano) or frightening (for Adele); whereas the experience for Laura is that it is playful and Laura finds it gentle and sweet.

Being Nourished (Absorbing)

All of these primary Experiences are basically Experiences of "nourishment": in the sense that something warm and loving passes from the adult to the child, just like mother's milk. Breastfeeding is the strictest example of nourishment. However, during breastfeeding there is an intense and important play of affective relation. Love, understanding, tenderness, and protection pass from the mother to the baby in the same way as the mother's milk.

It is for this reason that we have termed all the Experiences of contact that include Absorbing "Being Nourished". It is for this same reason that we use this term to define the objectives of a series of specific therapeutic techniques. In the Experience of Being Nourished, the accent is placed on Absorbing, and on the person who is doing the Absorbing.

Naturally, in therapy this does not include nourishing patients in the sense of giving them food (although we can do something similar by giving a sweet, a biscuit or a little chocolate every so often during a session). Nourishing during therapy takes the form, as we were saying before, of letting positivity, attention, interest, and affection flow towards the patient.

Alterations

There is so much that could be, and indeed has been, written about this Basic Experience. Here, we can only add one further contribution to the subject, by underlining (perhaps a little more clearly) the link between deficiencies in this Basic Experience and the fact that many people, deep down, are greedy for food, continuously searching for the emotional nourishment that was completely insufficient during their childhood. People try to "fill themselves up", but they are never full because it is not food that they really need. What's more, people find it hard to feel full if their childhood and adolescent development took place in an unfavourable environment, leading to the closure or stifling of their internal sensations.

Lastly, we must highlight the fact that the phase of Nourishment during therapy is, and will always remain, one of the most important phases in the process. We often make the mistake of passing on to successive, more "adult" phases too quickly. Sometimes we can unconsciously push the patient towards independence from therapy and the resolution of their current problems without having dedicated enough time to good "Nourishment". In so doing, we risk interrupting precisely the process whereby the patients deepest needs and deficiencies are reconstructed, which the patient is more unlikely to be able to continue during their adult life.

Passing along the mat

The group lines up along the two opposite sides of the mat (along the long sides). One person lies down at one end; face downwards, just outside the mat, breathes deeply, and then starts to enter within the space of the mat, first with his hands, then with his head. The hands of all the members of the group caress the person entering within the area of the mat (from the exact point where the mat starts and not before) calmly and gently, sometimes remaining still to allow contact. The person slowly advances, soaking up the warmth, the caresses and the contact from this tunnel of hands and then passes out of the space of the mat at the other end. The contact as the person leaves goes right up to the point where the mat finishes and not beyond. The person completely leaves the mat, withdrawing even their feet (this is the last contact before leaving); and then they sit on the floor for a little while, listening to their sensations. In the mean time, another person starts the passage.

Although it seems to allude to a new "birth", this technique is linked at a more general level with a return to the state of being little and being nourished, with being able to stock up on warmth and contact and then leave, to face the world with renewed energy. The difference between this technique and others based on receiving lies in the "active" movement of the patient through the mat, their freedom to choose body positions and the timing of their movements and stay.

For this Experience, too, the ability to live it to the full is linked to the modality in which the other Basic Experiences related to it have been experienced in the person's life.

This experience provokes a strange mixture of happiness and sadness in Rita. Lia finds the experience extremely disturbing at the beginning, but then she manages to calm down only when she recognises whose hands are caressing her. Nora has an old sense of oppression clearly linked to her past; then, little by little she manages to make such good use of the experience's healing qualities that she doesn't want to leave.

Active Contact

Taking (Asking, Seducing, Drawing Others to Us)

There is no doubt that, in the light of present knowledge, a newborn baby already has an enormous capacity to influence his surroundings with strength and determination. Whilst it is true that he experiences many moments of pleasant passivity during which he absorbs, receives, allows himself to be moved about and abandons himself, this does not mean that he doesn't have other moments when he becomes very active, full of initiative, leading the adults instead of just being led.

A baby has varying degrees of activity, and Active Contact is one of the oldest and most important. Children do not just wait for Contact to arrive as a concession from the adult, rather they learn very quickly to take it for themselves. They can do so with a tender smile, by waving their little arms towards their mother so that they can be picked up, or by asking with their voice in a way that is completely unequivocal.

The newborn baby already possesses this capacity for Active Contact when he is born; it is enough to think of how he touches his mother's breast while he is being breastfed in order to feel more pleasure, in order to sense her more intensely, to adjust himself and her breast better. Anyone who has spent time with babies can certainly bring to mind how frequently they make a tender and joyous gesture of Active Contact when they are being held, taking their parent's face in their hands and drawing it to their own, smiling, one forehead against the other.

In the animal kingdom, it is common to see a cat rubbing itself up against his owner's legs or hands (with his side and his back) until he manages to steal a caress or a stroke (often even when his owner doesn't really want to). My Dalmatian used to ask me even more directly by tugging at my hand with his paw.

Functions

Among the many Functions involved in Active Contact, the need for a relaxed, visible, and direct *movement* towards the desired object or person emerges immediately. In babies, it is the arms and hands that first play an important role in Drawing the other person to them, but as they grow, being able to move using their legs will go towards "completing" this movement.

For this to happen, however, there must be a strong inner drive to move with determination, and for there to be this inner desire, the child must be able to *imagine* every little step of his own movement, progressively bringing him nearer to the realisation of his desire. The imagination, then, serves as a genuine means that will, by allowing the child to prefigure the joy of the final result in all its vividness, push the child and motivate him towards Active Contact.

Naturally, the *voice* also fully participates in the overall expression of this "movement". The voice, with its tones, its nuances and its sonority evidently affects the people surrounding the child, transmitting both his joyous and appealing desire and his calm trust that it will be fulfilled.

Within the picture of the child's immediate request, the verbal content of the request is just as important: how precise the words that he uses are, the clarity and non-ambiguity of the question, the ability to express *concepts* (an expression of the rational Function) in a direct way.

Alterations

All too often, with man cubs, the natural capacity to Ask is suffocated and repressed.

Christine related, at the end of the therapeutic experience termed as "Amoebas" with a group, that she had felt an enormous sadness. It had been wonderful glimpsing the possibility of Contact with the other "amoebas" (the other members of the group), but she hadn't stopped close to them very long because she was afraid she would disturb them with her presence, so she hadn't made any Active movements to take a pleasant and healing Contact for herself, too.

Christine was considered by the group to be the "spiteful" one. She had been like that as a child, too. How was it possible that a "spiteful child" was unable to go and take something good for herself, that she was even paralysed by the fear of disturbing the others?

When we become "spiteful" (like Christine as a child), in reality it is not because we are insensitive, and could not care less, at all. On the contrary, spiteful children are very aware of the adult and they know how to read his slightest reactions. No spiteful child wants to provoke the other person too much and make them explode in anger and then suffer their violent reaction. Spiteful people long, deep down, to attract the other person's attention and make them listen, in order to obtain the fulfilment of their wishes and needs, but they have unlearned how to ask for these things directly.

Asking is therefore fundamental in obtaining what we want. Little children have no doubt at all whether to Ask or not: it is totally natural for them to do so. Only later, when their capacities have been suffocated by an unwelcoming environment, does difficulty arise in Asking, for fear of refusals, shyness, and inhibition in movement.

One patient used to fall from her bed at night when she was a little girl. She used to lie on the floor until the next morning because it was impossible for her to call her parents to ask for help. She used to remain, terrified, on the floor!

It is precisely when we do not Ask that our expectations can become exaggerated and our disappointments even more bitter. We too often take for granted that the other person should be able to understand exactly what it is that we want, and we put ourselves in the position of passively waiting. However, in reality, it is very rare that two people manage to be in complete harmony all of the time. More often, the other person has no idea what it is that we expect from them or how much value we attribute to a specific action on their part. That which we do not ask for openly is unlikely to arrive, or be given to us.

Unfortunately, many people end up thinking that if a particular gesture or such-and-such an attention doesn't arrive *spontaneously* from other people, they completely lose their affective value: and so what's the point of Asking?

Children, however, show no difficulty in Asking: they do so with vigour and determination. A mother's embrace is not devalued a bit by the fact that it was given on request. Quite the opposite! The child's sensation is of a pleasant little triumph because he has managed to obtain what he wanted. You can read it in his face, in that sweet smile of great satisfaction.

It is not Asking that isn't right, it's begging! All too often, to avoid Asking for what we want in a clear and direct way, we end up adopting a constantly *complaining* demeanour, as if life had nothing good to offer us and we are forced to beg for even an affectionate glance.

The request is expressed in a plaintive tone because complaint expresses the anticipation of disappointment. Beyond what might really happen, the child is sure (due to his negative fantasies and his previous frustrating experiences) that his request will be met with an inevitable refusal.

What has happened to the child to so compromise his capacity to Ask? Where do his negative fantasies come from? In order for the child to continue to have a healthy impulse towards action, the child must have obtained the real fulfilment of his desires; he must, of necessity, have obtained the adult's attention and affection many times. Conversely, if the adult is too rigid, not letting himself be influenced by the little one's soft and persuasive movement, then the child's positive imagination (the motor behind his movement) will be transformed into thoughts with negative connotations, or fantasies in which there is no success, or in which the other person fails to understand his request, in which the other person is indifferent, or even in which the other person angrily turns against him.

When we beg, we undervalue ourselves: we feel unable to obtain what we want and we content ourselves (always in a passive capacity) that someone has been moved by pity to give us a few crumbs. However, if it's up to the other person to give us something, they will always give us what they want to, and not necessarily what it was that we were expecting.

As in all "polarities", a healthy functioning of the gamma *asking ↔ expecting* lies not in one or another of the two poles, but rather in being able to use both as the occasion demands. If we Ask all the time, constantly, we lose the joy and the pleasure caused when other people foresee and satisfy our desires. Vice versa, constantly expecting others to guess what we want ends up making us lose the possibility of obtaining what we wished for, inevitably leading to bitter disappointments.

The healthy functioning of this polarity doesn't even lie in a useless and negative "happy medium": veiled requests, giving things to be understood but only up to a certain point or seeming to say what we want without actually saying it are all stereotypes. This is another dysfunction of *asking ↔ expecting* and it leads neither to the full joys of Asking, nor the profound satisfaction of being understood. A healthy functioning lies in the ability to pass easily from one pole to another. It lies in being able to pass easily from one extreme to the other: Asking clearly and explicitly when the occasion demands it, and trustfully waiting when it is possible and pleasant to trust ourselves to the attentions and intuition of the other person.

Taking something for ourselves

Taking something for ourselves that we know will do us good is extremely important for life itself. It is a nuance that is even more active than just Asking. We can Draw other people to and Take them to our side; we can obtain their affections, we can trigger interest and love. "Seducing", in its literal sense, has no negative connotation. It does not mean deceiving, deluding, or making someone believe something that is not true. Neither does it mean enchanting someone using our mere outward appearance. The verb "to seduce" comes from the Latin *se-ducere*, where *se* refers to self and *ducere* means to lead, thus the verb means *leading to oneself.*

If we retain our capacity to ask for things joyously, leading the other person to us, moving them, arousing (like cats do) the desire to give us a stroke or a cuddle, we will have no problems in Seducing others, in the most positive sense of the term.

Many patients are amazed when, as their course of therapy progresses, they meet with more success with the opposite sex than ever before. This is none other than the consequence of having recovered the Basic Experience of Active Contact, Leading the other person to us.

Drawing someone distrustful towards us

In pairs. One person pretends to be the one who is distrustful of the relationship between the two. They think that the only solution is to separate. They no longer believe in the relationship. They are disappointed that their love is no longer returned. The other person wins back their trust little by little, with the right words and gentle contact.

When Veronica gets into the part of being in the condition of mistrust and disappointment, she can feel that the other person has felt difficult moments just like her. Often, the fear of losing the one we love can make us forget the fact that they have they same fears about us. Many people share similar experiences and backgrounds and this constitutes a sort of common background which draws us closer and unites us. Discovering that our partner has the same fears that we do can, in some way, prevent our sense of loss from becoming the false certainty that we have already irredeemably lost the other person.

When Gianluigi plays the role of the pained and disheartened person, he feels exploding within him the old, violent pain from when he and his wife divorced, and he was forced to separate himself from his ten-year-old son. He, too, had suffered a painful separation at the same age when he had been taken away from his family in Africa and taken to his grandmother's house to study and he did not see them again for a long, long time.

His experiences as a boy have become mixed up with his relationship with his son, and Gianluigi feels the same old sensation of sadness and loss when he thinks about the fact that he will be able to spend much less time with son after the divorce.

Now, however, in his experience in the pair, Gianluigi manages to finally place the weight of his pain in his partner's arms. He manages to let himself be held, crying softly, and yet with a new sense of serenity. This act of letting go will be a small but important step for Gianluigi in dissolving that knot of old sensations that were binding his recent experience as a father to his old experiences as a boy himself, without hope of extricating himself.

Alone, searching for others

One person is on their own in the centre of a circle with his eyes closed, playing with the hands of the others. The others move away. The person in the middle stretches his hands out to find the others but he cannot find them. He feels alone. Instead of staying trapped in one place, he moves around and goes looking for them, advancing towards them. He finds them and gathers them all in, one by one, squeezing them to him. At this point, the other members of the group give him gentle and affectionate contact.

With her eyes closed, Martha plays calmly with the hands of the other members of the group surrounding her. Then the others move away and her hands can't find anyone, despite the fact that they keep searching. She doesn't like finding herself on her own, but she doesn't fall into dejection or fear, as she would have done at the beginning of her therapy. Helped by the therapist's encouragement, by that warm and familiar voice that reaches her as if it came from within her very self, she continues to search, reaching out her arms because by now she has a certain amount of trust in the fact that sooner or later she will find someone.

Thus, when she feels the contact of the other hands again, a beautiful sensation of joy erupts within her. Martha takes the others, and then she lets herself be taken up by them and have her whole body massaged.

Graziella, on the other hand, is not at the same point in her therapeutic journey. She does not manage to take the hands surrounding her very well, much less play with them. When the group's hands move away from her leaving her on her own, she does not go looking for them. She does not move. She will later say that this was because it seemed to her that she didn't mind being on her own. However, after a few minutes a strange anxiety petrifies her. She finds it hard to understand what is happening.

It is only when the hands of the group make her feel that she is no longer alone with their contact, that that indecipherable and intense sensation turns into a thought that can explain what she has been feeling: the fear that no-one would come looking for her, the fear that she had no choice about remaining alone.

Graziella's fear is very common. It is a fear that arises from not having passed through the Basic Experiences linked to really passing time with someone, with the continuity of relationships, fully and positively. All too often, those who consciously or unconsciously choose solitude do so not because they have really decided to, but rather in an attempt almost to pre-empt what they most fear, in order to avoid feeling possible separation or abandonment too keenly once they have become too tied to people in their lives.

Giving (Hugging)

The capacity for being active does not just lie in being able to go and get what we want. Children feel genuine pleasure when they are able to Give to others, when they Hug and caress others or when they show affection or love. A child does not so much ask whether mummy or daddy love them, more often they just vigorously declare, "I really love you!" My daughters used to welcome me on my return from a business trip running towards me on the stairs to Hug me, in a spontaneous gesture which not only gave a lot of pleasure to me, but also to them.

Alterations

Giving is a huge pleasure, which is completely ruined when it is aimed at getting something in return. The pleasure of Giving can have nothing to do with a bargain. Bargaining affection means robbing it of all value.

If the child gives something to the adult (a picture, a piece of school-work, a little letter) and the parent critically "evaluates" how good it is, rather than just appreciating it for what it is, the child will confuse Giving with Being Judged, and the child ends up losing the will to Give, or he ends up thinking of it as something to be exchanged, as a means to obtaining things (presents, affection, forgiveness, calming the adult's anger).

One of the difficulties in Giving serenely lies often in the anger that has been shut off and accumulated over time. It is impossible to be able to Give without expecting anything in return when rancour is eroding the nucleus of the person's innermost feelings.

On the other hand, it is extremely common for parents to accompany the act of Giving with "conditions", i.e. with precise requests that the child must fulfil or have fulfilled (you can't have the new gameboy game if you don't do your homework).

Furthermore, parents are often prompted to Give (beyond the child's real needs) to calm their *own* anxieties: that the child eats enough, that they grow well, that they don't get ill, that they keep loving the parent in question.

In this circumstance, the pleasure of Giving freely is undermined even more, setting off a mechanism of *do ut des*, or Giving in order to accumulate "brownie points" in our favour. This happens when we are adults, too.

During moments of confrontation or disappointment, we end up throwing everything we have Given in the other person's face, often listing the efforts and energy we have spent in detail, heaping it all up on the "scales".

Undoubtedly, Giving also includes some receiving: Giving and receiving are interwoven. The child Gives without thinking, but he also receives without thinking. Parents also Give to their young one without expecting a return, and without expecting to be thanked (or at least they ought to). However, it as also true that in so doing they too receive, and a lot at that.

Even though Giving and receiving are interwoven, that does not mean that they should be *confused.* They can become confused over the course of an existence if the relative Basic Experiences have not been passed through fully and positively. We can Give with the obsessive expectation of receiving, and we can receive with the constant worry that we have to give something in return.

It is therefore necessary that during therapy these two elements be separated once more. It is important that the patient manages to receive without worrying about having to Give something in return (at least once in their existence), just like a little child in the arms of a good parent. Therefore, during group work in pairs, it is vital that the other person playing the role of the good parent manages to Give without expecting "repayment", and that he, too, manages to recover in therapy the pure pleasure of Giving.

Only afterwards, in real life, can we then rejoin the experiences of Giving and receiving in a healthy way. "Giving well" means receiving as well; "receiving well" also undoubtedly means giving the other person the profound satisfaction of having done something good for us.

During an experience of back massage in pairs at a group therapy session, Maria feels agitated. She feels like she is making an exaggerated effort to massage the other person and that she is shaking because of the effort.

When Maria was little and she used to try to give her mother a kiss, her mother used to retreat. Maria was left, impotent, completely paralysed by a mixture of rage and sadness.

She really does want to touch other people, but she only does so fleetingly and with great effort, because she feels that other people can be irritated by it (just like her mother when she was little). Massaging disturbed her because it became mixed up with her sense of compressed rage, the fear of irritating the other person and her sense of impotence. She felt she might "hurt" the other person.

In an experience especially designed for her by the therapist, Maria is on her feet in the middle of a circle. The others touch her with a light pressure until she can clearly feel the boundaries of her own body. She is then helped to free herself from her old rage by making her give in to the sweetness of being cared for by the group. She is cradled gently and touched softly and affectionately.

It is only after this phase that we can pass on to the next stage, i.e. that of transforming the results of her old experience in touching and hugging. For this reason, the therapist asks her to lift her arms upwards and a little forwards to feel them immobile and impotent one last time, just like she felt when she was little, but this time with intense emotion. And then, however, she is finally helped to rediscover the pleasure of being able to cuddle the people around her, very aware of the contrast between her old sense of impotence and this new experience, feeling the concrete strength of the embrace and being able to modulate this into a tender hug. Tenderness, warm embraces, and calm strength are all expressions far removed from the full aggressiveness of anger.

Little children touch other children's bodies or adult's bodies without thinking about whether what they are doing is right. If, on the contrary, they receive little or bad physical contact, they will start to worry about what a touch should be and they will attach a negative connotation to their capacity to Give. This worry becomes magnified, what's more, by the fact that they cannot manage to "see" the results of their touching (as with many people, when they are adults, when they have lost contact with their sensations). They no longer feel their own sensations and therefore they are unable to feel the other person, in a sort of genuine "blindness".

Therefore, to recover the pleasure of Giving, they must also, (first and foremost) recover the real, practical sensations that touching another person makes us feel, digging below the surface of the old bad impressions that make us worried and afraid of every gesture, no matter how small and delicate, towards another person.

Hugging

One person is on their feet in the middle of the circle, held by the hands of the other members of the group who keep their hands placed on him so that he can feel the limits of his own body. The person is rocked slightly, to soften any possible old sensations of being "crushed" and to make them feel instead softness and affection. The person in the centre puts their hands above their head (without touching anyone else) feeling the old sensation of immobility and impotence. Then, instead, he hugs the people around him, feeling how different this new experience is, and feeling the concrete strength of the embrace and the possibility of modulating this strength, feeling tenderness and, at the same time, a warm embrace, both of which are very different from the much-feared aggression of his old fantasies.

A strong trembling takes hold of Elena's body when she is in the centre of the group. A sensation of fear opens up within her. She feels that the others are far

> away, too far away for her to be able to reach them with her hands, whilst at the same time she feels a consuming need to feel them near, and to be able to touch them and feel herself embraced in return. In the meantime, she remembers that when she was little, every time she tried to hug her mother, the latter always ended up keeping her at a distance with one excuse or another. She clearly remembers her arms vainly reaching upwards to ask for her mother to pick her up.
>
> It is exactly this sensation that Elena feels while she is in the centre of the group with her arms in the air. Tears start gushing, ever more convulsively, which in their turn melt away when, on the contrary to what happened to her as a child, Elena feels that the others come closer, hug her, and allow her to squeeze and hug them.

Giving to Ourselves (Consoling ourselves, Finding Balance)

Within the area of Active Contact, we must not neglect an element of vital importance in life: the capacity to Give something positive to ourselves as well.

Coming out of a bad mood, or out of periods of depression and closure, overcoming difficulties easily: all these depend largely on the individual's Self-consolatory capacity. Children know how to Give themselves pleasure right from the beginning, in the mother's womb. The image of the foetus sucking its thumb is well known by now (demonstrating that this gesture is linked to pleasure and not to breast-feeding as was commonly thought, preceding it). Images that are less well known are those where the embryo takes its head tenderly in its hands, or hugs itself, or even when it enjoys itself rocking and sliding backwards and forwards in the uterus.

Alterations

If, however the sensations of well-being and pleasure have been suffocated by anxiety and growing worries during development, by ever more pervasive and relentless negative fantasies, Giving to oneself loses meaning and effectiveness. The child tries to reach the calm and self-consoling pleasure that he once had, but, not obtaining the same effect, he will continue with insistence, even to the point of exasperation, until these actions form authentic "tics", unconscious gestures or obsessive behaviour patterns[1] and compulsions.

> Ennio, following a group workshop where the participants were asked to hug themselves and give themselves tenderness, said that he felt that cuddling himself had done him a lot of good: just as if it had been someone else cuddling him.
>
> As a child, he had been painfully lonely. He had conveyed this finally by describing one episode that summed it all up. Once, when he was five or six years old, he had felt very ill while he was in bed in his room, alone. His parents were in the house next door, which backed on to his room. Ennio started to scream, beating his fists on the wall to call them, all to no avail! His physical discomfort kept increasing and he ended up vomiting, still on his own. He felt completely abandoned!
>
> The self-consolatory experience recovered during therapy brought back old memories and sensations for Cinzia, too. When she was six or seven, she absolutely did not want to go to school. Every morning she felt sick, her stomach hurt and she found it difficult to breathe. She was always terrified of being left, of being abandoned, whether it was at school, at a party or in a big department store, but she never managed to talk about it openly. While she rocked herself, she felt an intense sadness and she cried. It seemed to her that once she had broken through her closure and her tough outer shell, she would never be able to stop crying. However, together with her sadness she felt, for the first time in her life, a profound tenderness! She had given tenderness to herself and she had felt it from the others!

Love

Being Loved (Belonging, Being Carried inside someone)
Loving (Carrying someone inside of us)

The chapter on Love is about a very large area of the Self, which touches many other Basic Experiences of the Self at a deep level, or which at least makes them possible. If the child is really Loved, then they will also be held, nourished, protected, seen, and understood. Yet, this is not always the case. Many parents Love their children, even with an intense and visceral

1 A classic example is that of trichotillomania, or the tearing of hair, a gesture which is very similar to the childhood habit of repeatedly curling a lock of hair in their fingers, helping them calm down or sleep. This gesture, however, is much more intense and violent, searching for a soothing effect that is no longer there.

Love; but all too often, they lose the capacity to really feel what is genuinely positive or negative for their offspring. This happens for two reasons.

The first reason is that the parents have also suffered deficiencies in their own Basic Experiences (during childhood and adolescence), leaving areas of confusion, dysfunctions, difficulty in establishing contact with themselves and others. These negative effects are passed on to their children, from their children to their grandchildren and so on and so forth, like an endless chain. These generational chains must therefore be interrupted, intervening with both "curative" and above all "preventative" methods.

The second reason is that this state of confusion is increased by the contradictory messages and disvalues sent out by today's society, culturally conditioning the "job" of being a parent (acting directly on the children through the channels of communication that are omnipresent in their lives, such as television, videogames and the internet). All too often, parents are diverted away from their children's real needs: everyone claims to be an expert and everyone expresses their opinions publicly as if they were pure truth. There is no space left for the scientific rigour that could be of such great value in this field.

Functions

Loving, then, involves, more than ever, the *entire* scope of the Functions of the Self: the *emotions*, first of all, but also the *rationality* (despite the fact that popular wisdom continues to insist on placing the heart and the head at odds with one another), *memories*, the *imagination* (helping us to express our feelings in ever newer ways). Moreover, Love should be given a powerfully positive *symbolic* value, so much so that we are continually prompted to search for new Experiences of Love. We Love with all our *senses*, with our *breathing*, embracing, caressing and drawing near to the loved one with our *movements* and a full and vibrant *muscle tone*. Love implies a slight, pleasant activation of the sympathetic nervous system, and a pleasant and joyous exuberance. Love brings about *sensations* of profound pleasure and well-being.

Alterations

However, it can occur that adults do not know how to receive the child's Love with the same intensity and spontaneity. How many parents, tormented by their own problems in life and work, are unable to enjoy the Love of their little ones if not during moments when they have a moment's peace and are more inclined to open up. Love that is not "welcomed" produces frustration and pain in the child. His ability to Love is compromised, becoming mixed with anger and bitterness. The child starts to use Love as something that is no longer natural, but as something that is artificially constructed and forced, as an opportunity to "blackmail" others in order to get what he wants: "Then I won't love you anymore!" "I only love you if...".

Being Loved is an experience that comes into the natural flow of things. Normally, a child doesn't worry if they are Loved or not: they know they are! But if Love fails to arrive punctually from their parents, if they don't encounter *loving* comprehension, tenderness, warmth and attention towards their basic needs, children will begin to doubt whether they really Are Loved or not. What should have been natural and taken for granted becomes a source of "worry": something that is missing, for which we feel an acute need and which we have to "procure" in some way.

Countless fears, countless doubts, countless reasons for doubting that they Are not Loved crowd the negative *fantasies* populating the child's imagination. These come out again in the subject's adult life: sometimes a loved one's reassurances are not enough – there are always countless clues that "demonstrate" that the loved one doesn't really Love us or that they don't Love us anymore.

On the other hands, the obsessive search for Love can lead to confusing Love with food, or with power over other people, or with possessiveness and jealousy. Other times it can lead to seeking Love in exchange for our own submission, loss of independence or excessive compliance; or rather, on the contrary, it can prompt us to seek Love with force and violence.

Therapy

Being Loved and Loving are experiences of a *global* nature that must be reconstructed throughout the entire course of therapy rather than through specific phases or methods. We cannot think that we are really helping our patients, modifying them deep down, touching extremely old and painful experiences, if we do not truly Love them. A psychotherapist cannot fake on this point. The patient's capacities for contact and feeling the other person, once recovered, would allow them to realise it straight away and the process would come to an inexorable halt.

On the other hand, Loving patients cannot be an obligation or a sacrifice. It cannot be forced. If we manage to go beyond our more superficial sensations, reactions resulting from counter-transference, beyond patients' hardened and altered ways; we always discover their fragility, their neediness, and the tenderness within those who come to ask for our help. We can really manage to see the patient as a *little child*: frightened, needy, and completely abandoned to our care. We really become a *new parent* for them. At that point, our Love is neither difficult nor forced and it allows us to accompany this "little one" by the hand in a new path towards growth.

Loving has an aspect of continuity, which is less relevant in the other experiences. Loving means *carrying someone inside of us*, even if they are not present, or we have not seen them for a long period of time. Being Loved, on the other hand, brings with it the certainty that *the other person is carrying us within them*. It is a continuity of feeling that is not limited to the other person's mere physical presence at a given moment.

In "Love in the time of Cholera", Marquez describes this trait of Love masterfully, which the leading characters carry within them, despite long and varied vicissitudes, their whole lives. This Love, which has kept burning their whole lives, can only be consummated in the autumn of their lives, but this doesn't make it any less sweet or intense than in their youth.

It is easier to reconstruct the Basic Experience of Loving than it is to reconstruct that of Being Loved, even though the latter is basically what the therapy aims to recuperate throughout its whole course. As soon as the negative implications of transference have been overcome (and today this process is concluded in a much shorter period), the patient can reclaim the positive sensation of caring about someone like the therapist, so important for his existence, and carry this affection beyond the time limits of the session, carrying the therapist with him during his everyday life and feeling the therapist "at his side" in every moment.

It is much more difficult, then again, for the patient to reach the certainty that the therapist cares about him and that he can think about the patient as a loved one. The greater the patient's distrust and disbelief that this can really happen, the harder the process of recovering the Basic Experience of Being Loved becomes. When, however, this certainty manages to fully re-emerge, we can talk about a therapeutic success and we can say that the course of therapy is drawing to a close.

Belonging

When the Experience of Being Loved is profound and strongly felt, it brings about another extremely important consequence: a sense of Belonging. When we Love another person, to a certain extent the other person Belongs to us and we to them: not in the sense of obsessive and exclusive possession, but rather a sweet and pleasant reciprocal sense of Belonging to one another.

A sense of Belonging is the fundamental basis that allows the child to move around, come out of his protective shell, and explore the world. In order for the child to be able to adventure "outside", he must first have been well "inside": first, he must have fully felt Belonging. The strength and the fullness of our roots allows us to face the world with tranquillity in a vital oscillation between the protection of our own homes and going outside, whereby we will always manage to find new things that make us feel we Belong or rediscover old states of Belonging. People who break away from their roots or who stay forever in their protective shells almost certainly have significant problems with their sense of Belonging.

Being in contact with one's roots ↔ going out into the world is a polarity that is very close to that of the *known ↔ unknown*. A child constantly needs to find that which is "familiar". It is an extremely well-known fact that children love rereading the same story, drinking their milk from the same glass, using the same cushion and cuddling the same stuffed animal. Children adore coming back to things that they know or that are familiar, recognising them and feeling and hearing them again each time. However, they also love venturing out in that which is new, all that is unknown fascinates them and attracts their curiosity. Furthermore, it is precisely this continual return to that which is known that allows them to go out and discover all that is unknown with great serenity.

The therapeutic relationship and group work produce a considerable sense of Belonging, and they must be used with this aim. Recovering a sense of Belonging allows patients to start out once more on the path of discovering new things, and it allows them to rediscover the capacity to manage their communication and relationships with other people.

Ties

The group divides itself in pairs; each person chooses to work with the person they feel closest to. Each person holds one end of a rope that is two metres long. The couple starts out right up close to one another. Each person explores the presence of the other, the sensation of safety that comes of hugging and being hugged by the other person and the tranquillity of a relationship that is familiar. Then the couple explores all the movements that it can make whilst still keeping hold of the rope: every possible movement. "Let's feel what it's like to be able to move around in space with our bond, feeling that our companion is at the other end. Our movements can become wider and wider and we can set out to explore the world, still with our tie. We discover that it is possible to meet other people. Slowly and softly, we can enter into contact with other ties that fill up the space around us. The space is a whole series of ties that move gently. We can even interweave ourselves with other ties without losing the first one. We can untangle ourselves just as gently from other ties, without tearing any bond, without brusquely breaking anything. We can interweave ourselves in with still more ties, we can move other ties, we can meet other people and put ourselves in contact. Now the ties intertwine even more densely and we can discover the pleasure of contact with the person who happens to be near us in this tangle of ties. The ties weave together and tighten, at random, just like they do in real life. And we remain with whoever we find next to us in that moment, without looking for anyone in particular. We savour the pleasure of being with whoever is next to us at the time, without worrying about anything. We stay still for a while, calmly in contact with this person. Then, little by little, the ties start to untangle themselves once again. Softly, the ties unravel and we find ourselves once more with our tie, our companion, and we hug them with renewed joy. Only afterwards, slowly, can we then detach ourselves, we can detach ourselves from the whole group, and feel that we can carry this bond through our whole lives, inside of us."

Martina sees the history of her relationships in this experience and she relives her present difficulty in bonding completely with her most recent partner, but the experience comforts and encourages her, and she resolves to try again with a perhaps completely new sense of calm and confidence.

Marta is once again assailed by her old fear that ties with people she really cares about can melt away. Her fear gradually gives way to the profound desire (that she had always somewhat denied) for intense and lasting ties, even if only with friends; but she also feels the lack of a child painfully.

Françoise, at a very advanced stage in her course of therapy, found the whole experience very beautiful, being able to move away from her own tie without being afraid of losing it, with the awareness that she could take it up again without problems whenever she wanted.

It is important to keep the concepts of *being near* and *moving away* well separated, and consider them both as necessary and positive conditions. That is to say, we must not confuse the strong bond that links us to our partner with an impossibility of moving autonomously. In reality, these two poles are only apparently opposites, because the more intense and serene the relationship, the easier it is for both partners to live serenely and joyously even when apart, or when, in various moments, they are moving in different directions or motivated by differing interests. In a relationship where there is real, deep-down contact, there is no danger that "moving away" can destroy it.

Positive Continuity (full and open Memories)

For a small child, there is absolutely no doubt that a positive experience will always return following a period when it has been absent. If a newborn baby has been breastfed and is full, if he has been held in his mother's arms with love, if he has been understood and cuddled, then he will have no difficulty in letting go of her and being left alone for a while in his cot. He suffers no fear of abandonment; he has absolutely no fear that the warmth, affection, and nourishment have disappeared. For the newborn baby it is just a break, following which all of these good things will undoubtedly return.

The fabric of the Continuity of the Self has not yet been torn: if a normal positive experience ends, the child simply waits for another positive experience to arrive.

Functions

It is above all our *memories* that keep our past positive experience constantly alive and present; and not just visual memories or memories of words, but also the memory of tactile and kinaesthetic sensations, smells and flavours, the memory of emotions and experiences. The capacity of the *imagination* serves as "cement" where memories are incomplete or lacking: the memory is maintained full and whole through details that the imagination creates where necessary.

Logically, for the memories to be kept alive rather than cold and detached images, other Functions must be fully active and mobile. There can be no tactile memory if the capacity for physical contact is not fully open.

Alterations

If the fulfilment of the child's needs is late in arriving over and over again or if a child is not understood and surrounded by an adequate circle of affectionate care, then this Continuity will start to be undermined and the child will start to suffer from the fear of loss: every time a positive experience ends it could be forever.

If this is the case, it occurs that, as adults, we often start a new love affair with the fear of being left; we go on holiday feeling sad and tense because we are already scared that we won't be able to enjoy it to the full because it will be too short; we are unable to think that if a love has ended another, better one might come along; we don't throw ourselves into new relationships because sooner or later they are bound to end.

A friend's son was already sad in the first few days of an exciting and promising holiday by the seaside in Greece. When they asked him what was wrong, he replied that he was sad because the holiday would end soon! But it hadn't even started yet!

The Continuity of Positive Experiences, on the contrary, allows us to create a thread uniting one positive experience to another, from our past, present and future. It acts on our current sensations, but also on the memories of pleasant sensations that we have felt, as well as foreseeing those to come. Memories make it possible to imagine, with a certain intensity of detail, that everything that has shown itself to be pleasant is still close at hand, and it will happen again in the same way (or at least a similar one) on another occasion. Thanks to Positive Continuity, there is no reason to believe that things could be different.

Therapy

When a patient goes through a period of sharp improvement, and then (as is bound to happen until the changes made have become stable) they worsen again, it is their recovered sense of Positive Continuity that helps them not to despair. They can be sure that, if they felt good for a while, then their organism is capable of attaining that form of positive functioning, and that they will attain it again soon, and more permanently. If, however, their sense of Positive Continuity has not been completely reconstructed, then the person becomes discouraged, despite the huge steps they have made, because they feel that all the good things are over, that they have disappeared, and that they find themselves at square one again.

Patients' ability to transfer the positive effects of therapy out of the session and into their ordinary lives is tied to the recovery of Positive Continuity. In all the initial phases of therapy, benefits only last for the length of the therapy session, or just a few days afterwards. Little by little, however, as the Continuity of Positive experiences is rebuilt, changes tend to become stable and lasting.

For this reason it is vital that techniques and interventions be developed, aimed specifically at consolidating the Positive Continuity of the Self. All too often, when the patient reaches an important turning point, therapists passively allow the course of therapy to finish, despite the fact that the improvements have only occurred within the therapeutic space, rather than being long-lasting over time.

Something good in the past

The participants in this experience are all lying down, each on their own mat, with their eyes closed. The therapist proposes travelling backwards in time to find something good that happened to them in the past, or some very important thing that we have had in our lives, something that warmed us, that has made us happy, that made us feel satisfied; something that still gives us an intense emotion today, at the mere thought of it. Try to live all the sensations rather than just images.

After having completely sunk into her mat with deep, diaphragmatic breathing, Lia remembers that when she was a small girl she used to spend a little time in bed with her daddy before bedtime. The exclusive and tender relationship that she had with her father is something she has recovered in therapy and is now something that she manages to relive with her daughters.

Magda has also recovered a fine capacity to reclaim good experiences from her past. A clear memory emerges, among the other images, of a sunny day spent with her parents. There are not just images. Magda relives all the sensations and emotions linked to this memory.

When Silvana remembers people in her life who have passed away, she remembers their smell, too. She relives the smell of potatoes with sauce that her grandmother used to prepare for her, and the smell of the cork that her grandfather used as a building material for the nativity scene at home at Christmas.

However, it is not as easy for everyone, as it would seem, recovering a lovely memory. This is the case in fact for Angelo. He is at the beginning of his course of therapy, and no image, no memory comes to him. He finds it hard to let himself go. His breathing remains shallow and a little laboured. He is unable to find a comfortable position on the mat.

A memory, a very old need

Everyone is lying down. Go backwards in time to one of the oldest memories you have, a need from when you were little. Patiently reconstruct it, what you felt, the sounds, the images, and the smells.

At times it is incredible to see what fragments of memories and sensations resurface during these sessions: images from when the patient was in his cot as a newborn baby, the smell of mother's milk, faces coming towards our own when our parents curved down to pick us up, first meals, the bottle, the movements of our own little legs lying on our backs on the bed.

Memories this old don't always come to the surface, but when it happens, it is always because other functions have been opened up: the patient's deep body sensations, movements, perceptions of physical contact, etc. have been remobilised. Old memories are not therefore indispensable for the successful outcome of therapy, but they are an extra element that helps to make the recovery of the Basic Experiences of the Self that bit fuller.

Sharing

Opening Up (Sharing)

A child's "social" life starts before he even comes into the world. From the mother's womb, he can already perceive the existence of several people to whom he is linked, closely and intensely. He hears and recognises his mother's voice, but he can also recognise the voices of the people who live with her. In an interesting experiment, it has been demonstrated that a foetus who was used to hearing his father's voice talking to him through his mother's stomach every evening awaited this appointment with excitement each time the hour drew near.

The human being is, therefore, a "pack" animal, who lives right from the beginning in a network of relationships that are absolutely vital for him, and he needs to Share his experiences, emotions, ideas and plans with the others. Sharing is made possible thanks to his ability to Open Up to other people: Opening Up should be considered as a normal part of our lives and not an unusual or atypical element.

Alterations

The ability to Open Up can be compromised however, if the child has been conditioned to have an excessive sense of distrust towards strangers, a sense of danger outside the family, or fear of the unknown. In this way, the child will lose the benefits of an extended social group and a wide support network.

Then again, the child's sense of trust can be undermined from within the family too: if the child feels that he is not fully "accepted" in all his various expressions, if he feels that he has not been understood then he will start to close in on himself, becoming isolated. He will no longer wish to talk about himself. As a result of this process, as an adult he will convince himself that it is pointless to share his experiences, ideas, or plans.

Whilst the concept that Man is essentially irredeemably alone, and that loneliness is deeply rooted in his very existence, has been defended for many years, today we should, rather, think of life as being essentially made up of relationships and company. Human beings always perceive themselves *with* other people, even when they are alone, through memories, sensations, and images that accompany them. Being alone is pleasant every so often, when it does not mean, "being isolated". It is when we feel isolated that the painful feeling of loneliness arises, and not when we are alone from time to time.

Opening Up in three places

Workshop in pairs. The therapist sits down on the floor leaning against the wall. He settles the other person lying face up over his legs. The patient's back should be arched backwards over the therapist's legs. First of all, the area of the pelvis is relaxed (the pelvis should be positioned over the therapist's legs, opening up the posture, muscles and sensations); then the diaphragm is treated in the same way, the patient moving so that his diaphragm is resting over the therapist's legs, and lastly the shoulders (the shoulders should be resting on the legs of the therapist and the patient's head should hang backwards a little). While the person is lying down, the therapist helps them to open up with the touch of his hands, massaging them, relaxing their breathing, loosening their muscles.

The opening of the pelvis, diaphragm, and throat should always be accompanied with pleasant sensations, unless there are tensions encapsulated in these three fundamental parts of the body. Although this experience is mainly corporeal, it re-evokes intense and precise emotions, directly linked to the significance of the closure or opening of these parts of the body.

Brigitte doesn't have pleasant sensations as her pelvis is relaxed. Rather she feels a sense of panic when she feels the upper half of her body falling backwards, while the support of her neck is much more pleasant because it makes her feel taken up and carried by firm and secure hands.

Cristel, with the therapist's help, manages to live the experience with happiness and open trust, whereas only a short time before she had only been able to sleep if she was lying face down.

Jeanine finds the position of the pelvis painful, which she recognises as being an old reaction of withdrawal when her mother lost her patience and threatened, firmly, to hit her.

Petra felt such an intense feeling of pleasure and relaxation that she completely let go of her vigilance, arriving at the suspension of her consciousness, although she was far from sliding into sleep.

Pleasure in Others

In the Experience of Sharing, or being with other people, there is a genuine Pleasure, which is often not due to any cause in particular, other than simply that of "being with" another person. There is Pleasure in the presence of the other person. The child thoroughly takes delight in this presence, he delights when his mother is there with him, even if she is not interacting directly with him.

When we are together, the presence in itself of the other person produces Pleasure, without having to "do" anything or "expect" anything. Rather, in this sense, the profound and pleasant nature of this experience is given by the total absence of any task or duty. There is nothing that has to be done if not simply being together, in the same place, each feeling the presence of the other.

An excellent piece of advice to give to parents is simply to be with their children, letting them feel their presence, without necessarily doing anything together. There is no need to play with them all the time, or tell them a story, or necessarily talk about something or help them to do their homework. Often it is enough just to be near them, even if each one is occupied with their own activities. Active help is particularly counterproductive when it comes to homework, because it prevents children from managing on their own, getting themselves organised and managing their relationship with their teachers. The simple presence of a parent, on the other hand, helps them to calmly do their homework, using their own skills.

Parents, encouraged by teachers, are too ready and too quick to send their children to private tutoring. In theory, these lessons should help them to obtain good results in their studies, but they end up causing greater damage over time than the initial problems. At the end of the day, the child is never given the opportunity of discovering the best way for him to learn and organise himself. We need to learn to understand when direct help with schoolwork is necessary and, on the contrary, when it is in fact useless or even damaging.

It is much more useful to if we encourage children by staying with them while they study, with an attitude of affectionate nearness. Every so often, there can be a pleasant exchange of words, feeling each other's presence. And then, however, each throws himself back into his own work: the children feel supported by their parent's warm presence, and not only that, but the parents feel sustained by the pleasant presence of their children, too.

Pleasing Others (Showing ourselves)

Being together is a mutual pleasure. For this reason, it is extremely natural for the child to Please the other person. There is no false modesty and no narcissistic exaggeration in seeking our parents' approbation about our bodies and what we are able to do. Seeking to Please our loved ones is the very basis of "seduction", in the most positive sense of the word, just as we have analysed in the last section.

Children Show themselves off with pleasure and expect signs of approval. They Show their drawings, the sentences they have written, the music that they have learnt to play and the dance steps they have learnt. However, they also Show themselves and their bodies just as naturally. The child is happy when he is made aware of his own image, when his mother praises him, when she compliments him on his body and plays with it affectionately and without reserve.

Functions

Showing Ourselves also implies the expression of our personality and creativity. The *imagination* and *creative fantasies* therefore play an important role in this Experience. The world of the child's inner *sensations* is also intensely stimulated when Showing himself, in the sense that when we Show ourselves, we are made ever more aware of how our bodies work, how to express what feel what we feel inside to the outside world and what our bodies are like. Our *value* system is called into play as our self-worth is reinforced positively. We learn to appreciate ourselves and consider ourselves as able and pleasant, aesthetically, too.

It is for this reason, therefore, that this Experience takes on an ever greater importance in the child's later life, during his growth right up until adulthood. Knowing that we can Please others (although obviously not everyone, and not indiscriminately) is the basis for social success, positive relationships and being able to present ourselves for what we are and what we know how to do. On the contrary, if this basis has not been consolidated while we were young, we find it very difficult "offering" ourselves to others, in work as in friendship and love.

Embarrassment

If the child feels that he Pleases the other person, he will Show himself with pleasure. A physiological level of modesty, of embarrassment, is natural: but we feel it only in situations when we are not sure whether or not we will Please. With a stranger, for example, it is normal for a child to feel a little embarrassment. However, an excessive amount of embarrassment or an excessive need to show off indicates an alteration in this very old Basic Experience of the Self and the polarity corresponding to *embarrassment* ↔ *showing oneself with pleasure.* If the child has frequently felt that he doesn't Please his parents, or if he has been observed too often without admiration, with a continual sense of criticism, then he will end up believing he will "never please anyone", and he will be pushed towards a stereotyped functioning of continual and excessive embarrassment and shame. Instead of sweeping from one pole to another, he finds himself flattened at one extremity of the scale. He will never manage to Show himself with pleasure. Showing himself will always cause him suffering.

Exhibitionism also originates in an alteration of the same dynamic. For the child, "Showing himself" loses its connotation of a natural and calm Pleasure. The only difference is that the child discovers that shamelessly showing himself off creates a strange state of unease in the people around him and that by showing off he manages to put himself at the centre of everyone's attention, attracting the looks of all the adults. Exaggeratedly showing himself off will become a painful prison for him, but at the same time, it will be the only way that he knows to make himself seen and heard.

Exaggeratedly showing off has nothing to do with the calm pleasure of Showing oneself. Certainly, all children the clown a little, slightly exaggerating, when adults are watching them; but they feel no need to force this aspect (as the only way of making themselves seen). They lose neither his natural modesty nor the calm pleasure of Showing themselves. If they go over the top, then something is already altering.

This is the key for interpreting all the "excessive" fashions of today: clothing, make-up, piercing. Whilst wanting to be part of the "group", some young people do everything they can to "stand out from the crowd", to get themselves noticed more and more, Showing themselves excessively, in an attempt to compensate for the old feeling of not being seen enough, of never managing to Please. We are forced to Show ourselves as much as possible, we try to get ourselves seen in every possible way: appearing on the television in any modality, even the most shameless, even without any dignity whatsoever, becomes the most desirable object.

Tenderness

Fragility (Softness)

Adults in today's competitive society force themselves to be tough, strong, to resist, and not to allow themselves Soft feelings, all too often and for too long. We have to carry on, gritting our teeth, passing over others' suffering, without being able to ask anybody for help.

However, Tenderness is fundamental for the equilibrium of our existence. If there is no Tenderness, then there can only be toughness that ends up becoming unhealthy, sooner or later.

Functions

Tenderness is not, however, merely a question of *feelings* or an expression of our *reason*. People do not become tender or strong just by deciding to be so: other important Functions come into play, without which Tenderness cannot be authentic. *Movements* must be able to have the characteristic of softness: brusque and hard movements do not communicate Tenderness to ourselves nor to others. The *muscle tone* must also therefore be soft (softly elastic, though, and not lifeless). On the other hand we perceive Tenderness in another person thanks also to their *posture*, the way move their face and body, and from somewhat graceful, rather than stiff, positions.

One aspect of Tenderness, made up of slightly different nuances, is Fragility.

Many patients allow themselves Fragility only when their course of therapy is well underway, and they discover that feeling Fragile every so often is not a tragedy but rather a remarkably pleasant feeling of relaxation. Children do not feel their Fragility to be negative, nor do they despair about it. On the other hand, they never feel merely Fragile, but also pleasantly strong. Once again, the answer lies in alternating between the polarities: in this case *Strength* and *Fragility*. Unease arises when there is a sclerosis at one or the other end of the scale. Being Fragile all the time is certainly painful and intolerable, just as it is being strong all the time.

Whilst it is true that Tenderness in the young also has the aim of attracting the attention of the adult, obtaining care and help. It is not true that this is necessary only when we are young. Tender feelings are what we use to construct the central nuclei of positive relationships. Toughness indeed must only be used for real defensive needs, There cannot be satisfying positive relationships if hardness ends up prevailing. It is Tenderness that is at the basis of life's real values, and which creates harmony, serenity, and union.

Unfortunately, however, what is spreading is a culture of violent strength and of overpowering, or rather of pervasive and subtle aggressiveness. Hard feelings are stimulated more and more by the necessity to suffocate growing fears and anxieties, by the uprooting of sentiments, by the presence of technology that produces an excessive acceleration of our daily rhythms, and by a world which only offers us the opportunity to get rich and prevail over other people at any price, whilst values and utopias of equality and solidarity collapse, leaving a hole that is hard to fill. What's more, the scientific knowledge that could allow us to understand what human cubs really need to grow up healthy, harmonious, serene and with all their vital potential is not being spread in a linear and clear way.

It is for precisely this reason that we must work intensely and diffusely today with the aim of creating a decisive change of direction, and a full renewal of the "culture of life" and of Tenderness.

Little body on big body

Everyone lies down comfortably on the mats, relaxed, with their eyes closed. "Let's breathe. At every breath, our body gets a little bit smaller. We keep shrinking, smaller and smaller, more and more, until we are just large enough to fit into the palm of one hand. Let's imagine our little tiny body near our own body, lying down, really big. We are so small we can climb up onto the big body, and we settle on the belly. We cuddle up on the belly, feeling the breathing that is making us rise and fall slowly. How do we feel on the belly of the great big body? What emotions reach us? Let's stay for a while on this soft belly, without having to do anything but just be, listening to our sensations. Then, with our little tiny bodies we go away from the belly. We move and we settle on the chest of the great, big body. We settle there too, near the heart, we lie down and feel the contact, the beating of the heart, the life in this big, big body. What is it like being there? How is it different from being on the belly? We are in contact with our sensations. Also with our sensations of being a little tiny body on a great big body. We breathe deeply so as not to cut off the sensations and we remain in contact a little while longer. Then, slowly, calmly, we detach ourselves again and we move even further up until we settle on the neck, on the throat. We curl up, tiny, tiny, on the big, big throat, where we can feel the air passing with each breath. We curl up on the throat. We feel what it's like to be there, in this place, and how it's different from the other two. How do we feel, tiny, tiny on the throat of this big, big body? What sensations do we have? What emotions? We remain in contact a little longer before leaving the big body for the last time. A little longer. Then, gently, we move and we prepare ourselves to leave the big body. We let ourselves slide down the neck and throat until we arrive on the ground, and once on the floor, we lie down next to the big body, side by side. Us, tiny, tiny, shoulder to shoulder with the big, big body. Then, a really deep sigh, and we become big again."

The experience of being able to feel small can be experienced to the full if the contact with our parents' big body has been positive and reassuring, and if we have felt thoroughly held and welcomed. Laura, indeed, has experienced all the stages of the experience as pleasant: on the belly, on the chest and on the throat (which represent the successive phases in the child's growth). She was a cuddly toy made of soft wool on the stomach, and so she felt tender and gathered when she was there, and she felt really small, then she rode the heart, smiling, playing with warmth and calm, more like an older child, and on the throat she felt a breath of warm air and the warmth of the sun, and this gave her a sense of joy and serenity.

During the return to the phases of childhood in this regressive fantasy, it is not always the case that all three moments are experienced with the same level of pleasure: the level of pleasure depends on whether we have enjoyed full contact in the corresponding phases of our lives.

Martino savours a calm sense of rocking when he is on the belly; on the heart he still manages to feel ok in his own company, but on the throat, he feels alone.

Lola already feels lonely and sad when she gets to the heart, and when she sees herself on the throat, she feels a strong sense of suffering, which she expresses with a cry. Whilst she was able to abandon herself to the affectionate arms of her parents in the first phases of her life, in the subsequent phases of activation towards others (the heart) and the more adult expansion of verbal communication (the throat), Lola experienced serious difficulty, which is amply shown by the type of images that come up during this therapeutic workshop.

Marzia on the other hand just can't manage to imagine herself small: the only image that appears to her is that of a paper doll, inert on her belly.

Natascia is also scared of becoming small. Her whole body becomes extremely tense because she can see herself in the womb, cold and dark, with the sensation that her mother won't accept her because she wanted a boy instead. The impact of this huge rejection is transformed into a dramatic and painful phrase, which finally forms within her: "Why did you give birth to me!" During her life, Natascia had always tried to beat her fear *forcing herself* to love herself, without ever really completely managing it. That old pain erupts now in all its unaltered intensity.

At this point in the therapy, the therapist draws close to her, enters in contact with this pain, gently takes her in his arms and lets her feel little, reconnecting with the very old positive nucleus (after her birth) when Natascia had perceived a welcoming and loving mother. The therapy must now part from this deeper nucleus; to reconstruct fully the ability to "be held" in subsequent phases in her life too.

Sequence on Tenderness

Participants are asked to walk around, entering into contact with their sensations. "Little by little, we slow down and we stop. Let's listen to ourselves. Let's be with ourselves for a little while. (A soft music starts.) Gradually, a little gentle movement starts within us. At the beginning, this movement is shy and uncertain but then it takes form and space as a gentle and tender movement, a soft, soft rocking. We let it arrive; we let it come out into the open. A little, repetitive, rhythmic movement. A swaying that rocks us, which gives us tenderness. The swaying takes hold of us and continues, unchanging, gently moving us. A little tender movement, rocking us softly, softly. We abandon ourselves to the tenderness. The movement takes us and we move slowly around the room. The soft swaying rocks us. Now the tender movement takes our whole bodies. A tender movement, never forcing, that comes naturally and which finally gives us a little tenderness. Our hands touch our bodies giving us tenderness. We really need tenderness. Our hands give us tenderness; they touch us and hug us tenderly. We too have the right to a little tenderness: all the tenderness that we wanted in life but didn't get. We give in to the tenderness, without being afraid. We let our hands fall to our sides. We let go of everything and we let our tender movements carry us. An old, old tenderness. A tenderness that expands towards the outside bit by bit; like a field expanding from us towards the others. Our hands, our arms can brush the hands and arms of other people and the tenderness can flow like a river from one to another. We don't need to do anything in particular for the others. All we have to do is let the tenderness spread and expand. Little soft touches with our hands. Little tender touches. Then, gradually, we slow down and we let ourselves gently slide to the floor".

A memory of tenderness

Once on the ground, think of a moment in the past when you gave or received tenderness. Reconstruct the tender memory in all of its details (expressions, surroundings, voices, sensations, smells).

Pamela can only allow herself a little tenderness; a lot of tenderness irritates her, and expressing it openly on the outside is more than irritating, it's completely impossible! She is unable to find any moments of tenderness, going backwards in her memories: she can only find one in the recent past when her daughter was ill and she felt infinite tenderness for her. Besides, in her life, she explains, ever since her father (who she was very close to) died when she was 17, she completely stopped seeking tenderness or cuddles.

In reality, what she suffers from is a deep fear, born of a very old confusion between *expressing tenderness* towards other people and *needing* other people. Pamela doesn't want to find herself in the position of having to ask anyone for anything, believing that she will never again find the help and support that her father gave her (at least apparently). Yet, tenderness is not asking for something, it is not weakness or dependence.

Pamela's course of therapy cannot be limited simply to recovering memories (merely visual), but it must necessarily reach a full recovery of the Basic Experience of "tenderness", with sensations, movements, posture, sounds, breathing, and images of tenderness.

With Maura, on the other hand, the workshop on tenderness worked well and brought significant results. The expression of this sentiment, during the soft rocking motion with music, managed to open her up by degrees in a full and satisfying way.

The memory that she brought up also produced a small but decisive change. The image was from when she was about 5 or 6 and she was busy in the kitchen with her mother, chatting with intimacy and complicity. In the scene, her mother is beautiful, whereas until now Maura had only remembered her imperfections. Maura's mother had also been tender to her, although up till now she had never been able to recall a single moment of tenderness.

Elsa realised that tenderness towards herself is all too rare in her life: when she concedes herself something "good" she always ends up doing it too rapidly, too briefly, "on the hoof".

It was the music that allowed Enrica to rock herself with extremely pleasant infantile emotions, and she had an image of her body and the ground moulding themselves around each other.

Apparently, unimportant daily or habitual gestures and movements can also open up unsuspected sources of tender emotions in patients. Indeed Alba's memory is of her father's smile and warmth while she bit him playfully (one of the few moments of contact between them); Gianna's memory is her mother's goodnight kiss; Silvia's memory is of the affectionate nickname her father used to call her: "piccinuzza", or "little thing".

Needing others

Alongside Tenderness, another of life's great lessons is understanding that we all need other people. Young children know this well, and they are not weighed down by this condition, rather, they enjoy the benefits to the full, full of joy and happiness when their parents help them to change, bathe them, feed them or put them to bed.

Yet for adults, too, other people's help is en essential prerequisite for survival. Trying to take on every load, having to do everything on our own, never being able to ask for help, not only creates hostility in those around us, but it also creates unacceptable levels of stress, which lead, sooner or later, to violent breakdowns that are dangerous for our psychological and physical well-being.

Functions

The child clearly *remembers* how pleasant help is, and he looks for it again each time he needs it with great desire. He expresses this request for help, this Need for others with his whole self (*movements*, *voice*, *breathing*, *the autonomic nervous system*, words with a clear and direct *content*).

Alterations

Obviously, if help is always linked to disagreements, criticism, anger, irritation, rigidity, if it is slow to come or if it is very different to what we were expecting, if undesired and oppressive help arrives when there is no need for it, then the child will end us detesting it, he will deny that he needs it, and he will end up completely avoiding asking for help.

Marisa remembers every time that she used to wake up in the night when she was small, full of fear, breathless; she used to stay in this state of anxiety for a long time because she couldn't admit she needed her parents' help.

Most patients who turn to psychotherapy have a past with similar characteristics: having had to be strong too early, having to manage on their own, not being able to ask for help, not being able to allow themselves weakness or Fragility.

If an attitude of excessive strength and self-reliance intervenes too early in the life of a young human it leads inexorably to a dangerous alteration in the organism's overall equilibrium. We end up paying for it if positive changes do occur. A precocious self-reliance tears the very fabric of human existence, painfully interrupting what has been termed earlier in this book as the Continuity of Positive Experiences: i.e. the child's inner certainty that the pleasant and gratifying things that he has received are not lost simply because they have been interrupted. A baby has no doubt that the warm tasty milk will return when he is hungry again, and that he will be able to return to his mother's welcoming arms, that he will be able to play with the water and his favourite rubber duck again, that he will be taken out again out in the outside world, sitting nice and comfortably in his pushchair.

Leaning on others

The members of the group walk around the room. "We are walking around the room, abandoning ourselves to the movement. We let our legs carry us without thinking. We don't want to meet the others. Just touching them is enough to irritate us. We avoid them, quickly changing direction. We feel this sense of irritation, everyone irritates us. We don't want anything to do with the others. On the contrary, now we actually want to push them away. We touch the hands and the arms of another person and we push them, we drive them away. We can even push them away quite forcefully. We don't want to deviate our route any more and we make way among the others. We stop and we push the other person away. We do it quite forcefully and then we continue on our way. We carry on walking, fast now, going in different directions, without worrying about anything any more. We start to feel tired. The tiredness of our whole lives. We slow down. We really want to lean on something. We feel the weight. Walking, we brush our shoulder against another shoulder. We stop and we lean slightly, ever so slightly. Then we carry on walking, breathing deeply, with a light sound. We find another shoulder and we stop a bit longer. We leave a little of our weight, at least a little. We lean gently. Then we detach ourselves, we walk on, and we find another shoulder to lean on. We experiment with other ways of leaning. Still gently. We have a right to lean a little on other people in our lives: we hold ourselves up all the time! We try so hard! We always have a thousand things to look after! Just once in a while we lean on another person. We lean our heads as well. Softly. We leave a little of our weight: there's no problem. We can lean on each other in twos or in little groups. We shift our position to get comfortable. Our movements are gentle and slow. We lean even more. Bit by bit we move towards the centre of the room: there are more opportunities for leaning. We lean on the others, without worrying any more. Gentle movements. We get even more comfortable. We leave our weight and our thoughts. Then we let ourselves slowly, gently slide to the floor".

Angela doesn't want the others to come near and lean on her. She feels an intense wave of anxiety and suffocation at the thought. In reality, her duties have always been too present in her life, so much so that now her organism (independently of her will) refuses the obligation to help the others, escaping from support. Her course of therapy should allow her gradually to let go of her duties and manage to follow what she really desires.

Annamaria completely enjoyed the whole experience, on the other hand. At one point, she felt completely "immersed" in something dreamy, almost weightless, and fluctuating, with her thoughts becoming ever hazier and more relaxed. It was an exceptionally pleasant sensation that she hadn't felt for a long, long time.

Receiving Attention

Being Noticed – Being Listened to – Being Understood – Being Helped – Being Encouraged

The possibility of a child to have a happy and full development depends for the most part on this group of Basic Experiences: these Experiences are directly linked both to Showing Ourselves and to the ability to calmly recognise that we need other people in order to receive help.

The child needs to perceive himself as he is, he needs to see how he appears to the outside world, not just how he feels on the inside. He can do so only when the adults around him Look at him and Listen to him. The profound importance of these Experiences lies in the need to develop and share a positive sense of himself. A child moves through life learning the adult world's difficult and complex system of *values* and *meanings*. He must learn the *rules* and *laws* that govern relationships; he gradually becomes able to *perceive* his own and others' feelings. He must hone his own capacity for communication (made up of *words* and *reasoning*, *tone of voice*, *gestures* and *movements*, facial *expressions*, *posture* and *attitudes*).

It will take years before he is able to carry out such a difficult task, during which time he needs protection, first and foremost, but also encouragement and approval. All of this can be seen perfectly clearly in the mammal world. Elephants take two whole years to acquire the knowledge and capacities that will be indispensable during their adult lives; and during these years, they are helped and encouraged unreservedly. If a mother is busy at a certain moment and she has to move away from the herd, the others look after the little ones, so that support is never lacking. Just imagine how much support and encouragement is necessary for human beings' much more complex lives.

Each of the Experiences in Receiving Attention is as important as the others. Not one of them is less important.

A child needs to Be Noticed because he needs to feel that an adult is affectionately monitoring his progress continually as he goes about discovering the world. He needs to know that the adult's loving gaze is following, giving him a sense of security and approval. An parent's gaze is "nourishing" and reassuring for the child, but it must be free of anxiety, imposition, or excessive criticism.

However, the child also needs to Be Listened to in everything he says; the way he reasons and sees things needs to Be Understood; he needs to Be Encouraged for his progress and for the skills that he demonstrates.

It is attention in general, in all of its aspects, that is important for the child: Attention in listening seriously to what the child has to say; Attention in fully Understanding his feelings and experiences, in Helping him in his efforts and in Encouraging his successes. We can never give *too* much Attention to children, because it gives them strength, encouragement and confidence. Only once they have a "full tank" can they calmly set out to conquer the world.

It is only in this environment that a child will accept guidance with pleasure, and listen to advice and suggestions willingly. A child needs to learn functional processes and capacities step by step, because learning is gradual by its very nature.

Alterations

If the Basic Experience of Receiving Attention has not been undergone in a positive way, the child will not feel reinforced in his efforts to learn and acquire capacities. On the contrary, he will feel misunderstood, unjustly criticised, diminished, and discouraged. In these conditions, it is unlikely that he will continue to grow and learn in a serene way, just as it is unlikely that he will consolidate a positive self-image. He will tend to feel incapable of dealing with the difficulties he faces, or rather, on the contrary, he will delude himself that he is able to know and do things that are beyond his reach, and he will fall into subsequent disappointments, which will worsen his sense of discouragement. In other words, he will become depressed thinking that he is much worse than he actually is, or he will think that others are unable to see his worth (as is actually the case with his parents) and he will end up making rash moves that will work against him.

Above all, he will end up losing the ability to *learn gradually*, to learn in gradual phases and steps, putting the advice of those with knowledge and wisdom to good use, and welcoming suggestions and help along the road. He will either feel that he is able to do something straight away or he will give it up completely.

What we are constructing here is a vital capacity that we will need to use our whole lives, and not just during childhood. We need to learn, grow, improve our capacities, and acquire new ones throughout life. Those who have gone through the Experience of Receiving Attention non-positively will encounter serious difficulty in travelling this road. These are the people who for one reason or another refuse to have a Mentor in their lives, or who deny it even when they meet one, or who end up rebelling even if they have accepted and applied their teachings, denying having received anything important or useful from them.

Predicting the other person's needs

The group divides into pairs: one person plays the part of the "therapist/parent" and the other person is the patient. The patient lies down on the mat and the "therapist" starts to enter into contact with him, trying to see how small and fragile he is despite appearances, how tender and needy he is, deep down. He tries to perceive the needs of the other person, to see him, to understand him, to give a positive "therapeutic" response to these needs (a contact, a massage, listening...), taking him in as if he really were a little one needing to be looked after. It is pleasant trying to predict the other person's needs.

It is no coincidence that Carla finds playing the role of the parent familiar, but that she feels a huge sense of suffering when she is the little girl needing to be held and nourished. The lack of a good experience in this sense in her infancy appears even more clearly when an age old crying wells up inside her, and extremely intense sensations of suffering accompany the distressing thought that if she doesn't support herself no one will.

In the case of Lavinia, both experiences make her sad. As a child, she found no gratification or reassurance, but rather oppression, alarm and sense of being continually shifted about due to the awkwardness of the parent (or of some other adult that looked after her). As the mother, she is unable to understand what the other person needs: all that she manages to do is cry with him, drying his tears, but she still feels small and unsupported, in this role as well as the last.

It is clear that Lavinia is unable to live the pleasant potential of being a "mother" with serenity yet: she still really needs to recover the Basic Experience of being held well, with attention, love and the full understanding of her needs.

Alessandra felt very encouraged. It was marvellous having a parent who listened to her and understood her deep down. The massage that she received was exactly what she needed.

Vitality

Joy (Excitement, Bursts of Joy/Exuberance)

How many people end up leading opaque, grey lives, with no impetus or enthusiasm? If we look at young children, we soon realise what we are missing. Children have a marvellous capacity to break up monotony and dreariness; lighting up, becoming enthusiastic and getting passionately involved in every moment of their lives.

Joy should be the essential pivot that our existences revolve around. Contrary to the many debates and nit-picking on whether or not Man can be *happy* on this Earth, Joy is a concrete possibility that we can all conserve, even as adults, and which does not just belong to the "naive" world of childhood.

Functions

Joy is not just an *emotive* state; it is also essentially a *movement.* It is a sudden, fast movement, both in the psychological and the physical sense. It implies exuberance without constrictions, sometimes ample and intense, and sometimes it is just a tiny little tremble: but it is always a "movement". Yet, Joy is also a strong inner *sensation*, a shiver that runs all along our bodies, opening us up to happiness. Children know exactly what it means to throw themselves into a run, or to pirouette, or to leap, or to make a sudden dive. Adults who are able to relive this Joyous impulse in uncontrolled movement, in a crazy dance, when running along the beach, or by making wild passionate love know what it means too.

Just like other aspects of our lives, sex can fall into the habit of controlled, uneventful and boring movements, or rather it can remain a Joyous Exuberance, a movement of pure happiness, which overcomes us and others.

In our past as children, there are sure to have been satisfying experiences of Joy, just as in our adult lives. *Remembering* these moments, keeping them alive within us and reliving them in all their taste and flavour, helps the Experience of Joy even further.

If a child receives the new bicycle he dreamt of, every time the thought comes back to him he will shiver with joy. A new love can warm us through with uncontrollable joy each time we think of it.

Joy is also an expectation. It is being able to anticipate the good moments ahead of us with our *imagination*: a holiday, a pleasant meeting, the much-awaited return of a son or a daughter, a book, a delicious dinner, a daytrip, a desired goal at work, a break for a moment of peace or relaxation.

The movement of *joy* comes about largely due to what we *have*, what we get from others and from life. *Happiness* has more to do with being satisfied with ourselves and what we *are*.

Alterations

All too often, the Experience of Joy is altered when we are children: "don't run too fast", "don't be so silly, you look like an idiot", "compose yourself", "control yourself". Other times, the joyous moment is suffocated by the worrying of a parent, by their fears, by their sadness, which are transmitted to the child, becoming mixed in with the joy until it becomes almost unrecognisable. These alterations persist over time and are carried into the life of the adult, subsequently worsening: "grown ups have to be serious, life is not about having fun", and sources of worry are certainly not lacking.

Many people try to keep up an appearance of Joy by constructing a forced cheerfulness which, not being based in a real profound Joy, is seen by others as false and stereotyped. This type of forced jollity is very easy to spot, not least, because its effects on the person are very different from those related to real Joy.

It is well worth the effort, therefore, of recovering the moments in our lives in which we have experienced Joy or when there has been a movement of Joy, trying to give value to the Joy that there is in our lives at the moment, without having continually to return in our thoughts to causes of worry, sadness and pain. This does not mean "not thinking about things", quite the reverse! It means recovering the profound essence of the Basic Experience of Joy, whose thoughts of joy are an anything but negligible factor.

This means recovering, in a full and integrated way, a capacity that is indispensable if we wish to avoid living a life that is grey and tough, or characterised by sadness and suffering. For this reason it is decidedly preferable that we recover these moments of Joy in our past, experiences of Joy, Joyous exuberance, rather than forcedly constructing a jollity that, not being based on anything real, ends up being false and stereotyped, far more damaging than it is useful.

Exuberance, acceleration, flying

Everyone in the group is on their feet. The suggestion is made that they move around the room, calmly and serenely. Then, suddenly, a burst of joy, a joyous fluttering. Calm again, and then a run, short but fast, a sudden acceleration. A change of direction. A dive to one side. A jump of joy. An about-turn. A joyous quiver. A few jumps backwards, too. Move around lightly, softly: flying with their arms above or below those of the others.

Monica's fast and exuberant movements with her whole body communicate easily with the outside world. Only her voice appears to be inhibited. Slowly, however, with a joyous movement, she discovers (not by chance) at the end of the sequence that she feels like singing.

Lavinia has quite the opposite experience. Her first emotion is to feel ridiculous. She is awkward in her movements, so much so that her head starts spinning, her hands are paralysed and her feet are frozen. During her childhood, rapid or sudden movements had always been considered by her parents as signs of "idiocy": The true quality of a good girl was calm composure.

All too often, fast and "impetuous" movements in young girls are stifled; both when they are young and when they are a little older. All too often women lack joyous exuberance, leaving space for immobility and depression.

Remembering a burst of joy

Each person is lying down on a comfortable mat, resting well on their backs. "We can imagine that our mats are sloping backwards a little, and we slide ever so slightly in the direction of our heads. We can imagine that we are gently sliding backwards in time. To the left and right we can see images from our lives flowing by, frames and quick flashes. We go even further back, in the past. Images flash by. We stop at a moment in our past when there was a profound burst of joy. Perhaps the image isn't clear yet, but we stay with it. Bit by bit it comes into focus. Us, as tiny children, in a moment of joy, in a burst of joy during our past. We try to look at the scene more closely. We get right into it and we observe it in all its details: the facial expressions, the person, or people we were with, the movements we made. We try to notice our surroundings: if we were indoors, the details of the room we were in, or what the place was like if we were outdoors. Even if we can't remember all the details, we try to reconstruct them, in order to make the scene fuller and more complete, and at the same time more intense and more vivid. We don't need to be scared of repeating the scene before us many times. We stay within the scene a little longer. We try to notice the smells, sounds, voices and words too. We reconstruct the scene in all its detail, intensely and vividly. We stay in contact with the memory one last time before leaving it, before we leave that little boy or little girl in their moment of joy, in their burst of joy. Then, gradually, gently, we move away; we leave that scene, and we travel through time again, towards the present. Images flash by to the left and right, like the view from a train window. We are travelling fast towards the present. And we are here again".

The memory that Gabriella recovers goes back to 3–4 years of age, when she was on her parents' bed having a pillow fight with her older brothers. Gabriella, who was the youngest one, almost always ended up hurting herself and crying, with the sensation that the game was only fun for her brothers.

It is for this reason then that she has found it so difficult to play openly, to play with exuberance and joyous movements in her life, without this old fear rising up again, blocking off her vitality.

The scene that Fabrizia recovers is a moment of pure fun: in the kitchen with her brother wrapped up in colourful aprons, making biscuits in bizarre, funny shapes with their mother.

Mara, on the other hand, was unable to trace any joyous memory, and she found it strange because she had always imagined that she had had a lot of happy moments with her mother. While discussing her reaction during therapy, she realises, with remarkable fear, that this idyllic memory very probably bears little relation to the real situation and that actually, in her life, she had had many moments of suffering and loneliness buried under an apparent serenity. It was certainly no coincidence that Mara suffered from panic attacks.

When the therapist asked Mara what had happened to her at around 5–6 years of age, having linked Mara's facial expressions and posture (during the regression experience) to a precise moment in her childhood, Mara related that she went to a school run by very strict nuns, and that the severity and rigidity of that school had extinguished her joyousness.

Often the memories that come to light during these therapeutic experiences refer to a very precise moment and age in the patient's life. For example, Adele sees herself as an eight-year-old again at the swimming pool, diving from a thrilling height and swimming gracefully; or spinning dizzily on the swings after having twisted the ropes around themselves over and over. Mercedes had been given, at the age of five, her first little handbag. It was a delicious shade of water green and smelt intensely of painted leather. Rosa remembered sliding down a steep lawn on her behind with her dog in her arms.

The ticklish sensation that Elisabeth remembers is so vivid and present that it seems as if her parents are here with her now, gathering her up between them and tickling her, playfully.

When Angelo used to walk through the fields on his way to his rural school, he was content to pick a mango from a tree, or he used to feel happy when he rang the school "bell", which wasn't in fact a bell but rather a piece of metal tubing banged on a piece of railway sleeper.

Other memories go even further back, like that of Alma, who used to play on the slide with her sister while her father watched them tenderly and held her doll for her. When she relives this scene, she suddenly realises, for the first time, that her father really loved her.

Letizia remembered an episode that went as far back as when she was a year and a half old. She remembers her father picking her up from her pushchair, throwing her up into the air, and rocking her in his arms.

Vitality (Energy, Impetus)

Functions

A lot of time during therapy is dedicated to the reconstruction of this interior and exterior *movement*: a person's Vitality. In therapies that involve work on the body as well as the psyche, Energy is often mentioned. However, when we talk about Energy, I maintain that we must refer principally to a whole group of "movements" regarding not just musculature, but also the entire range of the organism's functional processes: its *fluids*, *heat* and *strength*. We are referring to the Vitality of the person on all levels of the Self, and not just on *emotional* plane. All the *physiological* apparatus that back up behaviour and emotive expression play a fundamental role in Vitality and Energy: blood *circulation*, tissue *oxygenation*, the *autonomic nervous system*, the biodynamic action of the *neurotransmitters*. All of this is Vitality and Energy.

No "happy pill" could ever replace a complex system of functional processes. Introducing some substance or other from the outside (lacking in the individual at that time), such as endorphins or dopamine, cannot suffice to make them reach a state of happiness. The elements (and not just neuro-chemicals) that contribute to such a state are so numerous that only the organism on its own is capable of producing all of the substances, internal regulations, and psychophysical conditions necessary for a state of Vitality and Joy.

If, indeed, we manage to remobilise the organism's central regulators during a Functional Psychotherapy session (open *diaphragmatic respiration*, rebalanced *muscle tone*...), then we can be certain that the level of endorphins and other neurotransmitters linked to well-being has significantly increased in the subject.

> *The body follows the arms*
>
> The whole group is standing in the room. The therapist suggests that they move their hands and arms. They are asked to swing their arms. The members of the group throw their arms in different directions. The arms drag the bodies behind them. They make the bodies turn, jump, and twist, leap). They fling themselves about with joy. Darting and leaping.
>
> The tingling that Giulio feels descending towards his toes dissolves the tension blocking his shoulders and arms, reopening and amplifying his sensations of pleasure.
>
> Mario is unable to recognise his own voice in this movement, and this makes it difficult for him to open himself up completely with his arms.
>
> Ludovico cannot throw his arms around, let alone let his voice out. He feels completely immobile and paralysed.

Playing (Running, Throwing ourselves into)

Everyone knows that Play represents an important form of experimentation for the young of any species, a way of preparing themselves for life, an essential activity that occupies the majority of their time. However, Play is not only a form of experimentation, it is also mobility, impetus, fun and joy.

It is a mistake to think that Play is only important during childhood and adolescence: Play is *indispensable* at any age. Play keeps us young; it helps us to reflect, to imagine, to predict events with precision, to respond rapidly to external changes, to make educated guesses and to refine our capacities for expression and exhibition.

Functions

Play helps us to establish contact with others, and not just "mental" contact. Play must by its very nature involve all of the areas of functioning of the Self: we must use our *imagination*, but at the same time there must be concrete *experimentation*; there must be *expression* and also *feeling*, there must be *movement* and also *reflection*, *intelligence* and at the same time loss of *control*.

If we stop Playing, we risk losing joy, mobility, and the ability to experiment, exuberance and the ability to continually find new enthusiasm.

Alterations

It may seem that this Basic Experience encounters no problems in the lives of children today, but this is simply not the case.

First of all, Play is too often associated with "toys" and it therefore risks losing the Functional characteristics that make it complete such as creativity, movement, and self expression on all levels. Then there is the fact that today we give our children lots of toys, too many toys, often as a substitute for affection or the time that parents are no longer able to give to their children.

Play can also assume even more limited characteristics, as is the case with computer games: the movements involved are always small and fast, repetitive and frenetic, presaging obsession, the input is almost exclusively visual, the goal to be reached (in the great majority of computer games) is violent: destroying enemies.

Then there is the fact that toys are almost all divided into toys for boys or girls, from a very early age. In this way, masculine and feminine stereotypes are already created and consolidated from birth. If you go to buy a toy for a child, even a very young one, any shopkeeper will ask you if they are a boy or a girl. Even today, boys are given war games, construction sets, alien monsters, balls, games involving movement; girls are given dolls, kitchen sets, baby carriages, games of patience. Boys are allowed Games involving strength, uncontrolled movement, shouting, and violence. Unseemly and vulgar Games and games involving fighting or strength are not considered to be "appropriate" for little girls.

Playing with such stereotyped roles certainly does not represent the complete fulfilment of this Basic Experience; it leads to substantial problems, whose consequences we inevitably find in adults. Men end up developing a strength that is completely lacking in tenderness or gentleness: a hard strength that turns into violence and which seriously wears the individual down over time. In women, tenderness without strength ends up becoming passivity, the inability to deal with problems head on, the inability to put themselves forward, complaining and self-pity.

Playing can also become altered in the sense that, for many children, it becomes an obsessive valve for letting off steam: they are unable to stop, or rather they pass compulsively from one game to another. It can become a way of creating a forced excitement, which would otherwise be missing from their lives. This is how the addiction to gambling starts: the need to constantly feed excitement because the subject is unable to perceive normal sensations, delicate or slight sensations of pleasure. Anxiety gets mixed with excitement: it is only in this way that these people are able to perceive something of their inner vitality. The problem is that when the game ends, they fall back into the same old absence of sensations, into greyness, and they return obsessively again to the search for violent excitement.

Therapy

Playing is a Basic Experience that must never be neglected during psychotherapy. Naturally, it would not be appropriate to reconstruct it right at the beginning of the course of therapy, but sooner or later the moment will come when the pleasure of Playing has to return, it needs to be helped and encouraged, starting from the therapy itself, whether it be individual or group therapy.

Crib, bed, legs

Everyone lies down on a mat. They bring their legs upwards and lean them against the wall. Memories and games with our legs and feet. Remembering an object that was in our bed when we were little. Movements of the legs in the air, moving around the room on our backs, reactivating old memories. Meeting the others and looking for contact with our backs.

During this experience, Carmina remembers the tableau of Mary and Jesus that was above her bed when she was small, and at the same time she feels, once more, the curiosity that used to prompt her to roll from one side to another in her crib. On the other hand, Monica sees the coloured carpet that used to be on the wall of her room and she feels pain in her legs that remind her of how her legs already felt uncomfortable when she was little. She currently suffers from rheumatism in her legs.

While Marina is playing with her legs, remembers the duck that used to hang over her bed and seemed to be watching her. Alma remembers her parents' big bed, and at the same time, the pain that she usually feels in her stomach and leg disappears as she breathes deeply.

Carmela manages to feel the sensation of entering into the other person's back with her own.

Well-being

Well-being (Harmony, Wholeness)

Much attention is given to the concept of Well-being nowadays. We seek it in an infinite number of ways, using an infinite number of techniques and surrogates, sometimes adopting empty and inanimate tools, or carrying out numerous strenuous and superficial activities. Well-being, however, can only come from our own deepest sensations. A child can reach a state of well-being only through satiety, contact and the fulfilment of his needs.

Functions

There can be no Well-being if the body in itself does not feel whole, if there is no sense of completeness, or if the Harmony and balance between the various Functions of the Self are not maintained. Well-being cannot exist solely in *thoughts*: on the contrary, our thoughts allow us to think any number of things, even as far as imagining the most negative eventualities, or the worst and most alarming possibilities. Only the full use of all of our psycho-physical *sensations* (nothing is ever purely physical or purely psychological) can constitute an adequate basis for Well-being and keep old and new distressing *fantasies* at bay. In a genuine and full state of Well-being our organism reaches a specific state of functioning, a hugely intense "state of grace", which has a significant effect on us, which all of our principal vital systems contribute to. Our *breathing* is calm and deep, spontaneously diaphragmatic[2]. The *autonomic nervous system* tends decidedly towards a para-

2 The subject's inhalation is slow. The diaphragm is not contracted and it expands downwards. The abdomen expands, therefore, not due to muscular movement, but purely that of the diaphragm. There is hardly any pause after the inhalation: exhalation takes place immediately, and is much faster that the inhalation, simply caused by the

sympathetic state (the system responsible for a state of calm and relaxation): the hands are dry, the skin has a lively colour, heartbeat is slow and calm, the eyes and mucous membranes are moist. *Muscle tone* is relaxed and soft, the person has completely abandoned; the eyelids are closed without effort and the mouth is a little open rather than tightly shut. The body has no need to make excessive *movements*, other than slow and calm ones when strictly necessary. Internal *sensations* are intense and extremely agreeable: heaviness, small sensations of energy flowing downwards, warmth in the central part of the body and coolness in the upper parts, swollen and full hands, the colours before our eyes are pale and soft. *Thoughts* are pleasant and fluctuating. There is a flow through the body of all the biochemical *neurotransmitters* and *neurohumors* that produce Well-being: endorphins, encephalin, P proteins, and the various components of the GABA circuit.

Well-being is not, therefore, the "absence" of physical sensations, quite the opposite! The body is present, and all its deepest and most profound functional processes must converge in order for the subject to be able to reach a state of Well-being. This is why we must act on the various Functional elements in concert if we are to reach this state or Basic Experience, in a genuine and concrete way.

We cannot, therefore, merely base the recovery of this Basic Experience on the ability to imagine (as is the case with classic techniques for Autogenic Training); nor merely on the bio-feedback mechanism; nor can intervention be founded on our personal willpower or cognitive strategies; nor can it be merely founded on slow movement (antigymnastics, the Feldenkrais technique), or on releasing energy (bioenergetics). We must also directly act on respiration, muscular tension, on the autonomic nervous system and so on. Intervention must furthermore lead in the right direction, so that we can arrive at exactly this precise, profound state: a state capable of completely regenerating our energies, recovering what it is that we have spent, and causing us to rediscover our vital equilibrium.

---

relaxation of all the muscles. The pause following exhalation (not too long) serves to intensify the parasympathetic effect, the effect of relaxation, produced by exhalation. Exhalation is neither withheld nor forced by muscular activity.

Alterations

If, however, all of these Functions have lost their mobility, if the child has been forced to remain in a constant state of tension, activity, or alarm, then he will no longer be able to reach a full state of Well-being. People clearly perceive that something is missing and they try to fill the in any way they can: with the obsessive search for sex, through gambling, smoking, becoming workaholics; or they try to loosen the grip of anxiety and search for the lost paradise of Well-being by drinking, or using soft or hard drugs.

Well-being is a necessary stage not only in therapy but above all in projects aiming to deal with the question of prevention profoundly and seriously.

Back Massage

Exerting a strong pressure with his whole hand, the therapist massages downwards from the neck towards the shoulders. He takes the muscles in his hands. Arriving at the shoulders, he holds the shoulders firmly in his hands, allowing the other person to let go completely. He massages each arm with his whole hand, squeezing it like a toothpaste tube, over and over again, squeezing right down to the tips of the fingers, as if trying to make something come out of the hands. Then the therapist massages the centre of the patient's back, from the neck towards the coccyx. The therapist massages with two fingers each side of the vertebrae, pushing and descending slowly downwards. He then massages, still descending downwards, the bunches of muscles that run along the sides of the spinal column (one immediately next to it, and one further out, almost on the flanks. The massage descends to the lower back, on the coccyx, down to the glutei. The therapist places his whole hand on the patient's back, leaning his whole weight on it, then places his other hand next to it, leaning his weight on the second hand as he lifts the first (as if the hands were "waddling duck's feet"). He proceeds in this way along the back over and over again. This is followed by a gentle massage and gentle cradling motion before ending. Or rather, the massage can proceed down the glutei and then squeeze along the legs, downwards, just like the arms. He then finishes by massaging the back with two hands rising along the centre and descending along the arms (to unify) not too slowly, and then passing the hands quickly (creating friction, shivers) from the head downwards as far as the arms and hands and downwards as far as the legs and feet; energetically and quickly.

Morena experiences pleasant feelings, as if something trapped in her back were bursting out. Shudders of happiness passed along her arms, and her hands were expanding and contracting as if they were made out of some spongy material. Nonetheless, when the massage reaches her buttocks and pelvis, a strong sense of anxiety is unleashed, together with the feelings of pleasure, linked to her feelings that she is losing her femininity with age. Morena is tired of paying excessive attention to her looks. This therapy could finally help her to attain a more serene relationship with her body, without having to compete with her physical beauty.

Despite the fact that back massage is profoundly linked to the old sensation of abandoning ourselves to others and of our parents holding our backs in their arms, Margherita did not feel herself to be taken up in the slightest, because her back continues to harbour many very strong traces of an old lack of support.

Arlette's back suppressed fear and unease, linked to the fact that she wore a plaster cast around her torso for many years, and therefore it also contains the anger that went with feeling herself to be undeservingly "imprisoned". Only a long, delicate and deep massage manages to unleash reactions that are initially painful (like little electric shocks), and dissolve the burden of those suppressed and suffocated emotions.

Pleasure (Parasympathetic state, Mobilising, Towards the lower body)

Many techniques and experiences used in Functional psychotherapy regard the possibility of rebalancing the organism, also from the point of view of alterations affecting the correct relationship between the upper and lower parts of our bodies. Many times, while measuring my youngest daughter's temperature, I have noticed that her forehead was burning but that her legs were cooler: the temperature varied from around 38°C in her mouth, to 37.5°C under her armpits, and even to a varying value below 37°C when her temperature was measured at the groin!

These temperature differences reveal imbalances in functioning at a more general level (in spite of all "symbolist" interpretations that equate the upper part of the body with noble thought and the lower part with instinct), and which reveal, in this instance, an "overloading" of the functions regarding the upper part of our organism.

A young man came into therapy because of a whole series of very evident and unnerving tics; he had had many tics, ever since he was a child, but all of them were in his face and in the movements of his head. He presented other differences between the upper and lower parts of his body as well: alterations in the tissues, the skin, and even muscular tension were only in the upper part of the body.

Today's society pushes children towards an excessive diminution of their Mobility very early on, particularly favouring verbal forms of expression over non verbal ones, cognitive aspects over motor aspects, the mind over the heart. This general tendency towards a division between the mind and the body and the idea of the supremacy of thought over sensation is the consequence of a civilisation based on a strong presence of "control", which is indispensable for imposing social order and rules that are not based on sharing, justice and equality.

From this state of affairs arises the constant need, during therapy, of taking patients' consciousness back down towards the lower half of the body, in order to rebalance, as far as possible, the general conditions of the Self and recover Well-being and sensations of Pleasure.

The recovery of Vagotonia, or the Parasympathetic state, also represents a constant aim of Functional therapy, given that it is the system upon which calm and relaxation are based, as opposed to a state of sympathetic activation which represents our alarm system, which allows us to concentrate, and which governs the fight or flight response.

Pleasure should not be considered as an atypical condition that can only be reached using special or artificial means. Rather it should be seen as a basic condition of human functioning, interrupted every so often by those external situations which require more concentrated or energetic action, or a suspension of sensations, but only temporarily.

Pleasure is not inconvenient, and nor should it be placed, moreover, in opposition with duty. People who have been overloaded with duties and tasks, and who do not alternate them sufficiently with moments of Pleasure, end up breaking down or becoming ill in one way or another.

Pleasure is a social Function. It is an important regulator in interpersonal relationships as well as in the basic health of adults and children.

Someone we like

Everyone is lying down with their eyes shut. "Imagine that you are with someone of the opposite sex that you like. We are in a pleasant and cool wood. We take in the colours, the sounds. There's a little stream. We walk hand in hand. Then we run in the fields until we let ourselves pleasantly fall to the ground. We look at the trees, birds, the stream. We touch the other person lightly, feeling the their arm, their face, their hair with our delicate touch. Then we imagine touching our face to theirs tenderly and gently. We cuddle this person, delicately at first, and then more and more strongly, absorbing all the sensations within us. Last of all, we remain lying down side by side, without thinking, a little lost".

Adriano found this therapeutic workshop very pleasant, and he made a new discovery. Indeed, despite not having chosen the girl that he continuously thinks about, but rather another girl that he had met in passing, he manages to find pleasant and even "familiar" sensations with her.

Ettore found this experience "beautiful" too. The nearness with the imagined person left him with a sensation of profound joy.

Emilio finds it very hard to choose one person among the many that he thinks about (as is often the case during his life), and he risks not being able to enjoy this imaginary experience at all. But then, perhaps for the first time in his life, he lets himself be guided by his more visceral sensations rather than his classic "rational" criticism, and manages to sink into a unexpected condition of tranquillity that brings back an image of the girl that first came into his mind, and he finally settled on her.

Sensations

Sensing (Sensations)

The Sensations are the principal means that human being have for orientating themselves in the world; like a dog's nose. The majority of our decisions should be based on our Sensations: on the capacity to Sense our own organism, Sensing how it reacts to different situations, what it is indicating us to do or choose.

Functions

An Amoeba opens itself up to a form contact if that contact is pleasant and gratifying. It does not base itself on suppositions, imaginings, or on the widest variety of thoughts imaginable. Vice versa, if the contact is unpleasant it closes up and moves away. Obviously, in order for us to manage to Sense ourselves we must first *conceptualise* what our inner sensors are telling us, locating it within the framework of our whole perception, and giving it a precisely determined *value*. To do so, the Sensations coming from our *muscles*, our *movements* and *posture* must be compared to the *memory* of other, more or less analogous, Sensations. Once again, the Basic Experience cannot be limited to just one or a few Functions, rather it embraces the human's entire functioning.

Alterations

In therapy, reactivating patients' capacity to perceive real and "current" Sensations is the most effective means of dissolving the pathological persistence of old feelings and traces of the past, along with all their negative effects. The Sensations need to be reopened when they are closed and altered within the context of the patients' lives.

Children are often forced to suppress what they really Sense when their parents do not believe them, or when the parents in turn have lost contact with their own Sensations. When a child says that he feels as if he were *floating*, that a *current is flowing inside* his legs, that his body is *expanding*, that he is *melting*, parents are not always able to understand. At any rate, it is improbable that a child will be encouraged to express his inner Sensations. Sensations can also be suffocated when parents insist that a child needs something when this is not actually the case, when we insist on interpreting what the child feels instead of letting him decide himself. Excessive agitation, alarm, and hyperactivity (around and within the child) can also prevent him from listening to himself with calm, concentration, and serenity.

The Sensations can also be blocked in other ways, for example in a child's attempt not to feel pain. However, along with pain, rage, or anxiety, the child risks blocking and burying his vital Sensations as well.

At this point, contact with ourselves has been interrupted. We do not Sense ourselves, we do not understand ourselves, and we are unable to look after ourselves effectively. We risk living a grey, flat existence, in a world without nuances of colour.

If, later, the Sensations begin to flow to the person's consciousness again because of a breech that has opened up in his control, the person will perceive them as strange, dangerous, or even alarming. This is the mechanism behind, for example, the combination of symptoms grouped under the term "panic attacks", i.e. Sensations that re-explode in an altered and virulent way after a period of almost total absence, like water bursting through a channel that has been blocked for a long time, whirling and gushing along, full of leaves, broken branches and mud, instead of flowing calmly.

Reopening the Sensations for what they really are, instead of being conditioned the traces left by negative experiences in the past, is a hugely important task that only a course of psychotherapy can carry out fully.

Massaging according to need

In pairs. The person who is massaging follows, for once, their own need to "manipulate" (an old need, already present in newborn babies). The person being massaged follows their own need to be helped, rather than the desire for one particular type of massage over another (the early need to be manipulated, a vital need).

Whilst Gaetano is being massaged, he meets with childhood images and early feelings of anger and hostility, which become even more intense when he starts to feel the other person manipulating his muscles. Only later, due to the precise, continuous and tranquillising suggestions given to the group by the therapist, does Gaetano manages to give in to the massage until the unpleasant sensations dissolve. Manipulating the other person, however, "kneading" them as if they were pizza dough, is immediately a joyous experience.

Ferdinando also enjoys playfully manipulating the other person's body, using his hands. He lets himself beledby his own desire to massage, completely abandoning himself to himself and his own perceptions: worrying thoughts disappear, leaving pleasant sensations in their stead, making his headache disappear. However, being manipulated by the other person turns out to be a terrible experience for him. Rushes of anger and pain succeed each other; evident traces of the negative connotation that touching must have gained during his childhood.

It is only through the pleasant sensations associated with touching other people's bodies that Ferdinando will gradually be able to overcome the distrust that has crystallised within his own body and recuperate the joy of letting himself go to another person's hands.

Perceiving

Amazement (Wonder)

As we have already seen, children love listening to the same story or looking at the same little book over and over again, or always drinking milk from the same beaker, always using the same cushion. Children adore rediscovering known or familiar objects, recognising them and feeling them again each time. However, they also love venturing out to explore new things.

These two ways of functioning are only seemingly opposites, and they constitute one of the most important bases for success in human life. This is due to man's huge capacity for adaptation.

Being able to classify what we Perceive, rapidly recognising it, without having to decipher all the details of our Perception each time, permits a fast and efficient comprehension of the surrounding world. Just one word, a sound, a part of a phrase is enough for us to be able to understand what the other person is talking about, or what song they are playing on the radio. It is sufficient to see just one detail of an object for us to be able to automatically read its complete form.

It would be disastrous if we had to analyse every single detail that we Perceive in order to be able to orientate ourselves in the world. "Known" elements provide us with shortcuts that are essential for life.

On the other hand, knowing how to see novelty even in what seems to be completely familiar and obvious is the basis of creativity; it is what has allowed human beings to be able to constantly find new ideas and new solutions.

In order for there to be progress and invention, at its root there must always be a basic ability to Be Amazed, the capacity to look at the world with naive eyes in order to discover new details, nuances and connections that habit normally prevents us from noticing.

This is what happens when, for example, we hear the sound of a word as if we were hearing it for the first time, disconnected from the automatic categorisation that we normally give it, so that in some way the word seems new to us. It is also what happens when a piece of music that we are listening to suddenly appears to us in all its fascinating novelty. This is what happens when someone we know suddenly Amazes us for some aspect of the way they go about things that we had never noticed. It is the same phenomenon that allows us to enjoy a view that we see every day as if it were for the first time.

All these are examples of a sudden departure from the stereotypes and rigidities of Perception. These rigidities arise because we automatically compartmentalise what we perceive as something already known to us, without having to really, thoroughly gather all its multiform elements, without having to read any more details, nuances or sensations. Wondering and Being Amazed at the world around us is not, therefore, an experience that is purely related to the realm of childhood, although it is more frequent and more intense during that phase in our lives. Our *senses* continuously transmit, even as adults, a multitude of fascinating, varied, and multiform signals to us. Knowing how to capture their richness and beauty is one of the secrets to a pleasant and full life.

Functions

Of course, if Perception is genuine, then it is also useful for there to be (almost automatic) *cognitive* filters that select signals and categorise them, because Perception is not just *feeling/sensing*, but also becoming aware of the sensory world. *Memories*, therefore, play a significant role in the compartmentalisation and recognition of the sensations that we receive. However, a certain dose of "subjectivity" is always present in the way in which each of us perceives the world around us. This subjectivity is in part due to the *emotional* colouring that human beings attribute to all objects, situations, and people within their perceptive environment. The world is never neutral; rather it carries intense affective values, right from a very young age.

However, in life, it is essential that we are able to perceive the people and situations that we are faced with sufficiently "correctly" and "objectively". Being able to perceive correctly allows us to make congruous evaluations and to act without making serious mistakes or incurring unexpected or bitter disappointments.

Alterations

If a child is not lovingly aided in his Perceptive discovery of the world, if his parents push him towards perceptions that he does not in fact have, if his parents confuse him by ambiguously masquerading reality, he will end up losing his capacity for open and full Perception.

This gives rise to two types of consequences.

In the first case, the child will be unable to Perceive his surroundings well: he will mix many of his Perceptions of reality with his *fantasies*. This will prevent him from realising the real nature of the situations and people that he is faced with beyond a superficial level made up of external images. When sensations and Perceptions have been altered and confused, they will, of necessity, be mixed with inner *fantasies*, which have a negative outcome for all those children who have not been able to experience the full satisfaction of their basic needs.

We carry all of these alterations into adult life. For example, many relationships end after an initial period precisely because we suddenly realise that our partner is in fact very different from what we initially perceived them to be. In actual fact, the other person cannot really have changed so radically in such a short space of time: rather, it was our own Perception to be unconnected with reality. Some other, very common, examples are the Perceptive misunderstandings that occur between people: "you said such-and-such – no, you haven't understood what I said – you shouldn't have done this to me, this of all things – but I haven't done anything, you've completely misunderstood." A small percentage of misunderstandings like this are a fairly natural part of human communication, but most misunderstandings like this are avoidable, because they are due to a deficiency in the Basic Experience of Perception.

The other possible consequence is that the child seriously undervalues the Perceptions that he receives; he does not trust them, closing them up little by little inside himself, feeling them less and less. In this way, essential threads that guide us in the world, the elements that our choices and actions are based on gradually *disappear*. The child becomes increasingly insecure and uncertain, less permeable to sensations, more closed in on himself. Positive and tender emotions end up losing their strength too, because they are not sufficiently supported by sensations that are more positive.

Therapy

A course of psychotherapy must therefore pay much attention to the recovery of Sensations and Perceptions. It must intervene, delicately and profoundly, to reopen them little by little, starting from the most simple and elementary ones, in order to restore the person with the basic tools that will allow them to orient themselves in life.

During a therapy group, Manolo becomes aware of an extremely simple and elementary fact such as that of "walking". For an instant he had abandoned the stereotype of walking automatically and was ecstatic to discover the movements he used to move around the room, all its relative, subtle Sensations: his feet as they touched the floor, his legs as they took his weight, the strength involved, and the sliding of one step after another. He felt almost as if he were a child learning to walk again; and, like a child, he managed to modify his habitual way of moving that had been too light, with his weight too much in front, so much so that it had prevented him from experiencing the joy of a greater stability and strength.

Compartmentalising our Perceptions allows us to recognise and act rapidly and effectively without losing ourselves in too many deviations. On the other hand, seeing things with new eyes allows us to renew interest in our daily lives, finding new attractions that we would otherwise lose, immerging ourselves fully in the beauty of our surroundings without getting bored. It allows us to renew our relationships and fall in love again: because nuances and sensations are an infinite world, which can never bore us.

Discovering the other person with our hands

Walking around the room with their eyes unfocussed, the group members are asked to feel their hands, to let their energy and sensations arrive as far as their hands. The hands are open to receive sensations from the outside. They explore the space around them with arms outstretched. "We enter into contact with the others, our eyes closed. We feel the others through the sensations in our hands, without thinking about anything else. We feel the sensations of smoothness, wrinkles, tissues, and skin. With our hands, we can feel the other person's muscles, their consistency. Feel the shoulders, back, arms, face. Little movements. Softly, softly. Feel what the other person is really like, beyond their appearances, beyond what we know about them. Maintain the contact. A calm, calm contact.

Mara lets her breathing become soft and deep, and when this happens, she perceives her hands like two great big receiving antennas that are exploring the world. The contact with the others is a new, wonderful dimension.

Rosa notices that, when every last thought has disappeared and her hands start exploring the space around her, strong vibrations start flowing down towards her hands from her shoulders, along her fingers, which become extraordinarily sensitive, almost as if there were no skin to attenuate the contact with the outside.

During the experience of exploring the world using just the perceptions of her hands, Francesca feels a huge need for contact, she feels the need to find the others and get close to them. But the sensation is a pleasant and calm one, not a breathless and spasmodic search for others: just the simple pleasure of feeling a good contact.

Control

Loosening Control/Relaxation (Head bent)

A significant percentage of today's most common psychological and physical problems are the result of an incorrect functioning of the Control ↔ Relaxation dynamic.

As we have already seen, life is characterised by a *sinusoidal* type movement, in waves, which alternately touches both extremes of the various "polarities" that characterise it. Each of these opposite poles has characteristics that are positive and fundamental for a full and harmonious existence. We must be able to reach each pole fully as life progresses along this wave-like course.

For the ancient pre-Columbian colonies, the Maya and the Aztecs, the divinity who created all the other gods was Quetzalcoatl, the serpent-god: an evident representation of life's sinuosity.

Control is also, therefore, a positive capacity because it allows us to choose, make decisions, to act with extreme precision (without missing anything that we should evaluate) in order to find the most effective and correct path. It is also true, however, that life cannot consist in just Control. Relaxation is just as indispensable, because it allows us to recharge our batteries, to recover a particular state, almost suspended and fluctuating, that we have experienced ever since we were young. If we allow ourselves to be transported by this state, we can enjoy the pleasant and restorative aspects of our surroundings even if they are not necessarily very important.

When the state of Control lasts too long, when it becomes prevalent without there being sufficient moments of relaxation, the organism cannot sustain the pace without a break and it finds alternative ways of diminishing this excessive tension. This is the origin of "holes" in our Control, i.e. bona fide collapses which can become dangerous because they erupt (with excessive intensity) in our lives; more often than not at the most unexpected and inopportune moments. If this happens when we are driving at over 60 mph, it is certainly a disaster. How many drivers, when involved in serious accidents, claim that they suddenly lost control of the vehicle!

Breakdowns and "explosions" from excessive control can occur in various ways. We may lose objects (being unable to remember where we put them), notes (even important ones). We may collapse into a sudden state of weariness, we can suddenly flare up in an unexpected fever with no evident physical cause, we can start to stumble all over the place as we walk and bump into things. We may hurt ourselves inexplicably, even if we are going about our daily routine at home.

All too often our society requires us to maintain levels of attention, concentration and Control that are untenable for the human organism, especially when we have lost, over time, the capacity to dissolve our tensions and let go of our Control from time to time, creating regenerative pauses. From very early on, especially at school, we are pushed towards an excessive Control, as if learning depended solely on attention and concentration, rather than a healthy and harmonious state in the whole human organism.

When we talk about Relaxation, however, it does not always mean, as some people believe, a "long, complete break", such as an entire night's sleep or a holiday in the farthest and most remote spot possible. Even sleep can lose its regenerative properties if we have become ill with chronic Control, and holidays are often a source of further stress, bad temper, and irritability. Practising sport and going to the gym do not necessarily create moments of genuine relaxation: they often end up fraying us even more because we become anxious about the results of our workout or because of the frenzied pace of the activities. Holidays, daytrips, sleep and sport are simply occasions that can aid Relaxation (but not always), however they are not the same thing as Relaxation itself.

We must be able to attain a state of Relaxation *during the course of our everyday lives*: reaching a series of breaks and pleasant moments naturally and gently as part of life's sinusoidal nature before these same waves take us back to new tensions and moments of vigilance. We have to be able to set aside time for even short breaks, as long as they are pleasantly regenerative, whenever we need or desire one.

When, for example during therapy, a state of Relaxation is reopened in people who suffer from chronic Control, they are not always able to recognise the feelings of well-being and pleasantness that it brings. On the contrary: Loosening Control can be frightening at first. Some people are so unused to Relaxation that they fight in order to avoid letting go: The situation is rather like a swimmer in the open sea who, letting himself be overcome by the fear of sinking and drowning, starts to become agitated, struggles to avoid sinking and to stay up. For precisely this reason, the swimmer will inexorably sink further and further down. In life, it is important that we learn how to "sink" every so often without wasting energy, letting ourselves softly go "under" (we can't drown), because we float naturally to the surface anyway, and we can rise to the surface again with renewed energy, we can breathe without danger and start swimming again at a good pace.

Functions

People who are unable to Loosen their Control are almost always unable to dive head first into the sea or do somersaults or twirls: Control is very much based on keeping the head rigid (muscular control) and well "centred on their shoulders", not losing it. Control is in the eyes, because it is with the eyes that the child, from a very early age, follows everything that happens around him with attention. It is above all the eyes that have to spasmodically increase their vigilance when things are not going well, as if the child hoped to fix things with them. Control means suppressing movements that are too fast, sudden, or exuberant. Control means maintaining an attentive, vigilant position, ready for action. However, it also means incessant *thought*, continually weighing up, and evaluating everything that happens.

There are *images* and *thoughts* in Relaxation, too, but they are much softer and more fluctuating, rather than being hard and concentrated.

Children are very familiar with the pleasant sensation of letting go of their vigilance with their eyes before they drift off to sleep. As the child gradually Relaxes in his bed at bedtime, the things and people around him appear to be a little smaller, more distant (perceptive distortion) and he can "drift away" and sink softly into sleep. Alternatively, the *images* of the storybook that the adult is reading him can dissolve his thoughts and favour their soft and gentle fluctuation. It is well known that when we are taken up with the thoughts and actions of a hard day at work we are unable to Relax even the little that is necessary for us to be able to fall asleep.

Alterations

What can have happened in the life of a child to make it so difficult for him to Relax? If his life is always full of causes for alarm, if his parents argue all the time, if his father or mother or sibling suddenly inundate him with storms of rage, if everything he does is criticised, then the child will be forced to increase his attention and vigilance. He will not be able to allow himself a moment's pause because Relaxing means he might be caught by surprise by something very dangerous. Little by little, over the years, this sensation that letting go means exposing himself to danger becomes crystallised within him, and it remains even when there is no longer any danger. The person will therefore end up being unable to tell whether or not the danger is real, only this indistinct and intense impression of fear of Loosening Control.

Even surrendering ourselves to sleep can become distressing when we have not been held sufficiently surely as children. If the child is not sure of returning to life, if on his waking he does not have the complete certainty of finding affection, warmth and help again, then he will not be able to drift off into unconsciousness with sufficient ease of mind, and he will fight sleep.

Many people have a fear of falling asleep. Sometimes they are afraid they might die and not wake up again. Many people lack the courage to go through with surgical operations because they are terrified of going under general anaesthetic. This fear must be resolved in therapy working specifically on the capacity of Loosening Control.

Therapy

During the therapeutic experience of "imagining we are sinking into the earth" as if it were a soft and protected nest where participants could "let go", Amalia had vivid, positive and pleasant images, which did not disturb her. However, she still felt that her eyes were tense and attentive. The eyes are often the last barrier to break down before patients give in completely.

Susy, a patient who was at an advanced stage in her course of therapy, saw, during the self-same experience of "sinking into the ground", the scene from far away, exactly as a child does when they are about to fall asleep. For the first time, unlike normal, she felt no fear.

Numerous techniques have been developed to help people loosen tension in their eyes, their head, letting go of their thoughts and hard concentration, and descending down into their bodies (almost as if we could emerge ourselves head first within our own bodies).

Sliding on and off the mats

Each participant lies on little mats on the floor of the group therapy room. They start rocking from side to side. The movement becomes more and more intense and it allows them to slide off the mat. Still sliding on their backs, they move along the floor head first, without looking where they are going, letting go of their heads and their thoughts until they slide on to another mat. They move around the room, sliding on and off the mats and meeting the other members of the group with a calm head-to-head contact.

Stefania feels a fluid with a huge energy, joy, and dynamism flowing through her whole body, together with an enormous desire to play.

Françoise feels an intense warmth reaching all the way down to her feet. The movement becomes less and less controlled and deliberate, more lithe and lighthearted.

Michelle almost manages to "lose her head" and she rediscovers the sensation of being little again, together with the joy and enthusiasm that are typical at that age.

Patients are not always able to make full use of the therapeutic experience proposed, above all when the experience is oriented towards the recovery of a Basic Experience that they lack. Indeed Colette, as well as not being able to let go and enjoy this free and uncontrolled movement, feels afraid of being crushed by the moving bodies.

Losing Control (Explosions, Collapses)

When life starts imposing an excess of Control then more decisive and intense movements are necessary to be able to pass to the pole of Relaxation/Loosening Control. Every so often, it is a good thing for us to be able to arrive at a complete Loss of Control, pleasantly exploding, going wild. These experiences produce not only joy but also a vital decrease in the level of tension and concentration. We need to be "crazy" every so often, deliberately "rebellious", uncoordinated, inconclusive, in order for us to be able tolerate an existence made up of wisdom, prudence and Control without damage.

Children know how to manage this well and they manage it without too many complications, for example, when they throw themselves to the floor, when they slide down the banisters or pirouette, dive or roll head-over-heels. But they also lose Control with pleasure when they shout at the top of their voices, or they have fun sticking their tongue out or pulling funny faces, or when they let themselves go in frenetic, silly or "subnormal" movements. The problem is that all too often irritated parents stop them telling them not to be so stupid!

This search for periodic moments where we can free ourselves of excessive rigidity and constrictions exists in many different cultures. This is precisely the Function of wild dances, or carnivals with costumes and rowdy pranks. This was precisely the Function of tribal rites involving dance, the Bacchanals, "vulgar" rites, the great religious meetings of the ancient Maya, the whirling dervishes, Voodoo, Macumba, and Condomblè rites.

An inability to Lose Control can become an even more acute problem if the society in which the subject lives does not offer opportunities of breaking with norms, routines, and stereotyped habits. If dances are made up of controlled and fashionable movements, if adult games lose their component of creativity, if parties are only private moments and rituals no longer "tribal", if sport has become simply obsessive and controlled training, if religious festivals force us to behave even more rigidly, then Losing Control gradually becomes inconvenient, unacceptable or simply very difficult. Moreover, things are getting worse since the invention of computers, computer games, internet, which require concentration, punctual attention, extreme vigilance, and small, controlled movements.

If Control becomes ever more obsessive and hard we will have more uncontrolled explosions, there will be an ever greater search for "stupefaction" through drugs, alcohol, irresponsible behaviour, crazy, death-defying acts, violence, killings and destruction (whether they be real or on the television), and rebellion against any semblance of law and order.

However not all of this, as we have already seen, can serve to restore a correct alternation between *Control* and *Relaxation* because it is merely the result of breaches in excessive Control, and represents a worrying pathology rather than a healthy expression of this polarity. Significant changes must therefore be sought through therapeutic intervention, or, better still, we must place our trust in preventative intervention to help new generations recover healthy and beneficial losses of Control.

We teach parents how healthy the little innocuous explosions of their children are, we teach them to help the process of Loss of Control rather than impeding it. On a social level, however, we also recover the pleasure of light-hearted community parties, costumes and pranks, wild and group dances, rituals that allow us to let go of our thoughts and worries, where we calmly lose our heads: without using external substances, without damaging ourselves, without becoming destructive. A truly effective way of preventing drug addiction lies also in the positive Experience of Losing Control (as well as recovering that of deep down Well-being) because people almost always use drugs as a way of escaping from the ferocious bite of Control and anxiety.

Losing Control, innocuously and pleasantly rebelling for ourselves and for others, has another important preventative effect, too. It prevents people from passively accepting the abuses of this unjust society; it liberates positive energy and the will to use their own strength to re-establish a fairer social functioning, closer to life's real essence.

Alterations

However, Losing Control must not be confused with the phenomena that are intensifying more and more today: the overflowing of violence, the fading of respect for others and for life itself, the continual transgression of community rules in the form of diffuse illegality. On the other hand, these are examples of cases in which the Basic Experience of Losing Control has not been experienced positively and it has not been acquired with its full potential of equilibrium and harmony. In these cases, we are talking, rather, of explosions of Control or serious dysfunctions in the *Relaxation ↔ Control* polarity. Control is unhealthy if it is not a real Control, if it has no limits, if it is not used to help us understand the world and act in harmony with it. When we are excessively limited to one of the two poles, not only does the other pole not work because it is almost absent, but the pole on which we are "Crystallised" also works badly. If we are excessively without Control this is absolutely not Relaxation: yes, the Control is almost absent, but the Relaxation is distorted and inappropriate.

The *Relaxation ↔ Control* dynamic therefore has extremely important consequences and significance for society. For this reason, then, a considerable part of Functional therapy, together with prevention schemes inspired by Functional Psychology, is dedicated to the Experience of Losing Control, to the recovery of desired, deliberate little explosions and breakdowns, freed from the grip of fear and anxiety, reconciled with their load of pleasure, richness of sensation, openness and vitality.

Freeing inhibited legs

The therapist traps the patient's legs with his arms, after having provokes them with a painful and irritating massage. The patient agitates his legs violently, without restricting/closing his voice or withdrawing his legs towards himself, until, with a last spurt, a last effort and a last shout he completely straightens his legs and pushes the therapist away. Or rather, the therapist provokes the irritation of the legs with a painful massage and then tires them out. The patient raises one knee at a time pushing against the therapist with effort and fatigue and then lets go. This is repeated many times. Afterwards, the massage no longer causes irritation and the legs are calmer.

Daniel, a man with a large build, a big, full chest and an imposing voice breaks into hidden and timid tears during the experience of freeing the legs. Since he was little he had had to develop his strength, not by choice but by necessity, because from the moment his father died all the weight of his family had fallen on his shoulders. Daniel had had to use more strength than he had wished or really needed to, so much so that during a fight with a classmate he had been terrified by the fear that he had actually killed him.

The therapist welcomes these tears, encouraging him to finally feel his weakness not as a defect but rather as a need, a need that he had never been able to grant himself until now. Daniel cries in the arms of the therapist, letting himself go almost as if he were a little child and he feels calm in this recovered sensation of fragility.

Clara bears the squeezing around her legs for a long time without feeling any sense of oppression or irritation. In this way, she realises, painfully, that she lives the exact same situation in her every day life; she tolerates and accepts bad treatment without rebelling, passively. Only when she has gone way beyond her limit does she finally free herself of what is oppressing her.

Relaxed Attention

Control that is excessively protracted is no longer effective control. Rather it becomes defective control. Similarly, living in a continual state of relaxation no longer constitutes a real recuperation of energy but rather a state of confusion, a lack of energy, and the inability to focus on precise objectives. Being limited to just one of the polarities means that not even that polarity can function correctly.

The two extremes are in fact only opposites in appearance. In reality, the more able we are to let go, the easier we find it to concentrate effectively. Vice versa, the more able a person is to control (real control) the easier they will find it to pass to a profound and healthy relaxation.

In other words, we can think in terms of a modality of attention that is not spasmodic, hard, or exasperated: what is known as *relaxed* Attention. We notice, for example, that when we drive a car with excessive vigilance, our hands squeeze the wheel too tightly, our muscles are tense, and our eyes are fixed straight ahead with great difficulty. In these conditions we tire rapidly, everything is done with excessive effort, in a hard way. If we take, on the other hand, the example of driving relaxed, listening to good music, enjoying a pleasant, flowing conversation: our *muscles* are not tense, the wheel slides gently through our hands, our *gaze* sweeps about in all directions. *Time* passes quickly and driving is not an effort: we are almost surprised to find we have travelled such a long way. Not only that, but an accident is also undoubtedly less probable when we use relaxed attention than when we use hard attention.

Relaxed Concentration is actually the way Concentration should be: it allows us to gather various aspects of the situation, we have a more overall vision, and above all it helps us to avoid stress.

Functions

Relaxed Attention does not act solely through our conscious *thoughts*. Rather it is our whole *organism* that puts it into action. It is a more global, *integrated* attention.

There is, therefore, a capacity for Relaxed attention that we can define "integrated", to distinguish it from the Relaxed attention based solely on rational and cognitive consciousness. Ironically, it is precisely the latter that ends up noticing less of what is going on. The sensations are, indeed, few, and the imagination ends up becoming excessively developed, substituting real perceptions. With *integrated attention*, on the contrary, there is no disassociation between the various levels of perception and attention: we can write and listen to good music at the same time, we can watch television and form ideas, we can make plans watching our child playing next to us. Children clearly show the existence of this capacity for simultaneous attention on several levels of the Self: as long as the attention is Relaxed rather than hard.

Strength

Original Strength (Making Space for Oneself, Taking one's Distances)

Strength starts very early on in human development. Newborn babies know how to channel their forces in the first experiences of Original Strength. They enjoy themselves pushing their little feet against their mummy's soft tummy while she changes them, or when they use the Strength in their arms to "take their distances" when in an adult's arms.

One way of understanding the nature of Original Strength is to reflect on the pleasure of detachment from others; not a genuine "separation", but rather the spatial, motor, physical sensation of pushing, Distancing others, Taking our Distances. We can push to Make space for ourselves (birth is the prototype of this sort of movement), in order to travel our own path, to keep others at a Distance, to taste the first effects of our Strength.

Often, when a newborn is tired of being "held" he starts using his Strength to release himself from his mother's grasp, happy to be set down in his crib, "free" to move as he wishes in space and calmly fall asleep in his own company.

Opening the foetal position

In groups of three or four. One person lies down on one side in the foetal position with his face towards the wall and the other two cover him with their bodies and with the help of a blanket. The person stays lying down for a while feeling protected, warm, and safe. After a while, when he has absorbed enough, he starts to feel the desire to open up and he starts to push gently with his feet and hands against the wall, pushing his back forcefully against the other two people, gently using his voice as well. Until he opens up completely and stretches out.

This experience gives Giovanna an old and reassuring sensation of softness and containment that pushes away all worry. Giovanna manages to make full use of the moment of protection and it calms her completely, as does the gentle movement of opening up.

This is not the case for Nadia who is unable to feel a reassuring and protective presence within her. She is overtaken by an infantile sensation of fear and preoccupation. Nadia will have to work on being held further so that she will be able to dissolve the old traces of this fear completely.

Gentle Strength

Continuing along the course of child development, we find another type of Strength, less archaic but still delicate and gentle: a Strength which does not yet consist in confronting others, but rather experiencing our own ability to move the objects and people around us. Gentle Strength, therefore, is when the child takes his cushion and pulls it towards himself, when he grasps the adult's finger and squeezes it, when he pulls his dummy out of his mouth with energy, when he hugs his favourite toy right up close and adjusts its position better within his arms.

Calm Strength (Strength)

Although it is often underestimated, Calmness plays a vital role in the expression of Strength. Calmness can help us reach our aims much more effectively than anger or agitation. When serenity is linked to determination, it transmits to others a far greater sense of security, of strong will, the need to proceed in a particular direction, and positivity of the decisions that have to be taken.

Luisa had tried to let her family understand that it was impossible for her to study if they were always walking into her room, turning on the television, turning on the vacuum cleaner, or asking her to do things. She used to get very angry and ended up shouting her protest in an explosive and choleric way. Her screams, however, never did any good except in the short term. Everything always went back to normal because she was not being truly incisive. She used to get agitated, or explode, but in the end she always ended up suffering the same old things, without rebelling, until the next fit of anger.

With therapy, the situation changed drastically. Luisa lost her temper much less, upholding her point of view instead with great firmness and determination. To her own surprise, she managed to obtain her family's respect and consideration.

When we use Calm Strength, we communicate an intense sense of conviction in the requests we make. The logic we use is clear to others: they see our proposals as extremely reasonable and they are inclined to say yes. We must not forget that anger and rage are the child's last resort. It is only when the child has failed to draw attention to his basic needs using Calm

Strength and tenderness that he will have to fall back on anger to capture his parents' attention. This is already a defeat, however. It means that he has already lost. His sensation is one of disappointment and pain at not having received a full and loving response.

Pushing with the arms

The patient lies down and pushes with first one arm, then the other, and then with both whilst the therapist provides an opposing force with his own arms.

Pulling with the arms

Lying down, the patient pulls the therapist's hand towards his face, in a gesture aimed at obtaining a "good" thing from the new parent. He does this first with one arm and then with the other Then the patient uses both arms, taking the therapist by the shoulders and pulling the therapist towards him with some force (the therapist resists the gesture so that the patient must fight to obtain what he wants), until the patient holds the therapist in a big hug and squeezes him tight.

Marzia finds that it is difficult, if not impossible, for her to push the other person away from her. She experiences a growing sense of anger: her hands have become cold, she is unable to access her strength. Despite her efforts, she is simply unable to push the other person away. Her strength, used to repress an old sense of anger, cannot yet be accessed to deal with this type of experience. She notices however that her breathing is not laboured as it was at the beginning of therapy. It is much better. She undoubtedly feels calmer than she did. On the other hand, pulling the therapist towards her gives her a real sense of pleasure: she feels that she can really take what she needs.

Marisa is by now at the end of her course of therapy, and she is calmly able both to defend her own space and push the other person away without experiencing unease or difficulty. Neither has she problems when it comes to drawing the other person towards her. There are no thoughts or sensations hampering her. She is not afraid of failing, or that she won't manage to use her strength. Her strength is present and she is aware of it. Her sensation is one of calm and confidence.

Open Strength (Strength)

Significant misunderstandings have accumulated within the field of Psychology and Psychotherapy on the subject of Strength.

There is no doubt that Strength is an indispensable component of life for all living things. This can be seen in the amount of time mammal young spend play fighting, developing their own Strength, and continually putting it to the test. It is precisely these experiences, so intense and diffuse, that can help us to understand what Strength really is. Open Strength can be used to free us from something that we do not like or which oppresses us, but it certainly does not have the function of attacking others.

Functions

First of all, Strength must not be confused with aggression (which we will be dealing with later). Strength lies in *demonstrating* what we are capable of to others, or *acting, taking the movement as far as it will go*, until they are satisfied. It does not lie in destruction. In fighting, we can experience the possibility of putting Strength into our movements and carrying them through to their conclusion, without holding back, without stopping them; but there is no need to let our Strength "explode" in exaggeration.

An example that can give a clear idea of Strength is the classic arm wrestling match: the two contenders apply their Strength to their arms and their hands without reserve, and they take the movement as far as it will go, until their opponent is forced to give in. Yet there is no aggression, there is no anger; there is no destructivity, just like when cubs fight.

What do cubs prepare for with their play fighting then? They also prepare to use their Strength to hit an adversary if indispensable (aggression); but for the most part, they try out their Strength so that they will be able to *show it to others clearly and openly*. However, as cubs grow older, they no longer have to even resort to fighting: what emanates from their whole persona to express Strength is enough to obtain the expected results. It is enough for them to make others feel that they are Strong rather than having to attack. Moreover, showing Strength requires no "nastiness": the tone of voice, body language, the self-assurance that the person puts across are enough; all of which is often underlined by a smile.

Therefore, Strength lies principally within the *muscles*, the *tone of voice*, *posture*, *movements*, a look, but also in being sure of our *convictions* and *values*, in the way that we *communicate them in words*, and in the fullness of our *rationality*.

Strength can, moreover, be externalised in a clear gesture of refusal: we can forgive, we can give the other person another chance; but, in the end, the things that we do not like at all, that really hurt us or that we really cannot stand any more need to be "thrown away", firmly and definitely. We cannot always save or conserve everything in our lives.

Alterations

Yet, what causes children's Strength to become twisted into violence? Why is it that other times it is completely lacking?

Children's Strength is almost always disapproved of and stopped by adults who cannot tolerate it, and who exert their own authority and rules without bringing their decisions into discussion. Violence towards children, both in its physical, explicit form and its more subtle and indirect form is still tragically present in the world. Moreover, violence does not allow for reactions of Strength on the part of the children. This is even more evident in the case of girls. Their Strength is mutilated, suffocated and continually demolished, sometimes directly, sometimes more subtly. Little girls must remain "composed", little girls do not fight, little girls should not play like tomboys, they should not raise their voices, and they should not hit each other. Deprived of most of their Strength, they end up being passive, victims or with a victim mentality.

On the contrary, little boys are allowed to express their Strength, but not towards adults or parents. Their anger (when they are forced to suffer the will of the adult) becomes grafted onto the private Strength of tenderness and sensitivity, pushing them towards violence: violence towards those who are weaker than them, towards strangers, towards girls. Furthermore, this violence is not stopped but rather encouraged, as something the family can be proud of, as a proof of virility. In this way, a closed circuit of violence is created, which perpetuates and feeds itself from generation to generation. Little boys who succumb to adults' criticism, aggression and strictness, and who do not immediately become able to express aggression towards others, suffer the same fate as little girls: they become timid and reserved, often full of fear, withdrawn into passive positions, with a pervasive sense of self-devaluation; but also with a sense of anger and rancour smouldering within them, which they are able to express only rarely, in indirect and transverse ways.

Yet, it is often due to the dynamics of Strength and its possible alterations that the misunderstanding that we were talking about has sprung up. For many years, especially within certain branches of psychotherapy, it has been maintained that in order for us to be happy we must express our anger openly, "attacking" others every time things did not go exactly as we would wish. It has been maintained that attacking at every possible opportunity was right, natural, and healthy.

In this way, emphasis has been placed on aggression rather than Strength, i.e. on something much more similar to violence. It was not unusual, in certain therapy groups, that members found themselves encouraged by the therapist of the group to attack every time there was the slightest dissent between participants. The important thing was to learn not to endure any more, whatever form it took. Shouting at the other person, pushing them away and showing all one's anger was considered to be the last word in "liberation".

Deep contact with the other person ended up falling completely by the wayside; the complexity of human relationships was often reduced to a simple *up-down* relationship: winning or losing. Sometimes, this drive to fight come what may was theorised as a vital part of child development. There were, for this reason, nursery schools where children were encouraged to attack any other child who invaded their personal space, rather than to play-fight joyously. This type of thought was bound not to lead to positive results and provide ammunition for a whole series of criticism, which went back to theorising on the necessity of a type of education based on control, prohibition, and strictness.

Furthermore, the prevalent psychological theories of this century had formed theories on the existence of an innate Instinct towards violence in Man: the only possibility was blocking, controlling, inhibiting, or exalting the destructive impulse.

All of this did nothing but deepen the rift separating children from the possibility of a healthy and harmonious development, from the possibility of using their Basic Experience of Strength rather than blocking it or unleashing it in the form of violence. Because true Strength is not inevitably and genetically polluted by violence and destructivity. On the contrary, it is one of the resources that, if preserved in their profound potential, can allow all human beings to act serenely but firmly in their surroundings, no longer accepting abuses or injustices and at the same time respecting others and life in all its expressions.

Therapy

Often the entire course of Strength, starting with its most archaic and Original form, has to be relived in therapy, a course that children should be able to practise and try out over and over again under adult's affectionate protection. We are only unable to appreciate children's Strength, mistaking it for aggression, if we ourselves have deep and old wounds. Since this is very often the case, it is very common that all these mechanisms leading to violence or passivity are put into action.

Pushing with the spine

In pairs. Lying face down on the mat, the first person pushes the other person (who is lying slightly across the patient) with his spine. The first person feels the sense of oppression and then starts to push, first getting on all fours, breathing, using his voice, pushing even further back, until he completely frees himself from the weight on his back with one last, decisive effort, using a full voice.

Sometimes the patient feels oppression at only the slightest pressure, other times the limit beyond which the pressure becomes intolerable is too high. Moreover, when the Strength is finally expressed, it doesn't always take the form of a decisive and open thrust, and it is not always completely carried through.

In the case of Laura, a woman who was normally inhibited in the use of her Strength, the thrust finally managed to come out, but it was accompanied by the unpleasant sensation of losing control, fear, and agitation. Laura is shaken, her head spins, and her voice trembles. She looks for refuge in the arms of the therapist in order to seek reassurance because this rebellious gesture is so new to her.

Juana, on the contrary, is used to using her Strength and physical structure to defend herself. Previously she was very fragile and skinny and her schoolmates used to take advantage of this to hit her easily, and she was unable even to get angry. The thrust with her back is powerful and open.

Rosamaria's hesitant movements during this experience are those of a little frightened girl. Her Strength is completely blocked by the fear that completely pervades her entire behaviour. She thinks that this may be due to her brother's birth when she was four years old, but the behaviour observed by the therapist pushes him to investigate further back in her development. As a matter of fact, Rosamaria suddenly remembers that at two years of age, she had been lost in the street and she had literally been paralysed with fear.

Changing Others (Moving)

The newborn is not passive when faced with the world around him. In actual fact, he has an incredible Strength in moving adults until they intervene in his favour. He has a communicative repertoire that is already well-developed, made up of ways of *crying* that move his parents at a deep, gut level: it is difficult to resist the pressing requests of a newborn. However, his *tender endearments*, his *smiles*, his *looks* have an irresistible claim on the emotivity of the adults around him. The tender, sweet, and slightly funny look of young ones has the basic aim of arousing kindliness and love in the adults of the species, dampening intentions of violent aggression. This aspect is a fundamental element in the defence and survival of young ones, and it is also a powerful means of drawing attention to their need for help and protection.

Human beings experience the possibility of considerably influencing the people around them right from the beginning of their lives, attracting them to their side, making them allies. This Experience should continue over the course of their existences were it not for the fact that (in many cases) what prevails is the completely opposite sensation. An unwelcoming environment, incapable of allowing itself to be moved and involved by the child's basic needs, ends up destroying his profound conviction that he can "rely" on adults. A hardened and rigid environment ends up communicating to the child the message that it is impossible for him to be a protagonist in his own life: after years and years of frustration the child convinces himself that trying to influence things is pointless, "nothing would change anyway".

A huge number of patients have already stratified this basic distrust within them. Recurrent phrases when talking about "difficult" parents are, for example: "they haven't understood anything in thirty years of life. If they haven't changed by now they're never going to!"

Yet, these same people, after a certain course of therapy, recount with surprise that their father (or mother) did not criticise them as they would normally have done, and that he (or she) actually looked at them with a clear expression of approval, decreasing their attitude of excessive anxiety towards them. They narrate that the last time they went to see their parents it was actually enjoyable, they talked to each other with interest, they found that they strangely agreed with each other. In reality, it is the patients who (sometimes without realising it) have recovered their ability to "Change

Others", until they cross perhaps the most difficult hurdle, that of Changing their parents or the most important figures from their childhood.

We must not, however, think that Changing Others means that they are modified profoundly or completely in their essential nature. Although therapy is basically an energy that acts like a "chain", influencing the people nearest to the patients as well as the patients themselves, these people will not be modified genuinely or completely. What happens is rather that the *relationship* between the patient and those closest to him changes, and that the latter change the way that they relate to the patient, this time genuinely and practically. Alternatively, better still; it is the patients who manage to change the way the people that are closest to them relate to them. It does not matter much that the patient's father continues to be strict towards his other children, or the mother continues to be excessively anxious towards a sister or her friend. The important thing is that he or she has changed towards the son or daughter in question, the one who has recovered the ability to Change Others during their course of therapy.

Changing Others is an exciting Experience, however, that allows us to perceive how easy it is to render situations malleable and flexible and turn them to our own advantage without forcing them or resorting to violence. Changing Others has nothing to do with deception, duress, or abuse. It is a joyous movement that dissolves closures and resistance and which gives others the pleasure of travelling along the same path as us, doing things together, proceeding in the same direction.

Obviously, not all relationships can be modified, and not all the results that we wish for can be attained, however, a remarkable number of situations can be Changed positively; a number of situations far beyond what we might normally expect.

Stopping the other person complaining

In pairs. One person starts obsessively complaining about the same things over and over again. The other person firmly but affectionately stops them.

When Francesca has to stop the other person complaining, she feels a huge sense of inadequacy. She becomes rigid, has difficulty breathing, she doesn't know what to do, and above all, she is insecure, deep-down, whether she is capable of stopping the other person or not. Initially, her attention is focussed almost exclusively on what she can say to calm the other person down, and she experiences a lot of difficulty because she doesn't know what she ought or ought not to say. Instead of being able to feel the need that underlies her partner's stream of complaints (her partner in this therapeutic experience, that is), she is seized by her *own* worry, which prevents her from finding the right way to reach the other person and stop him.

Then again, when she finally decides to stop worrying about what she should say, when she allows her breathing to become deep and calm, as she has learnt to do in therapy, she starts making real, concrete steps towards reaching the other person, using contact, moving towards the other person with her body, managing to feel his profound needs. By passing from words to body language everything suddenly becomes easier and she finally manages to feel how fragile the other person is in his anger, how vulnerable he is and how much he needs to be listened to and understood.

When Carlo plays the part of the person who is incessantly moaning, he finds it a new and pleasant experience: he feels checked in his fears and negativity, and he feels reassured, simply through the sensation that the other person is there for him, that he is near, and that he understands him. It is a seemingly simple and common experience, but it is rare for patients to go through it with emotive intensity and completeness. People are often only outwardly "there" for the other person: they seem to understand and help him, but in reality real contact, a real sharing experience is missing.

Aggressiveness

Aggressiveness undoubtedly has many points in common with Strength, but it is different in that that Strength is tends to be more focussed towards *other people*. The word "aggressiveness" comes from the Latin *ad-gredior* (assail, go towards), and is, therefore, essentially a movement towards other people: a decisive, strong movement. At times it is openly nasty, at times it is playful.

Functions

Aggressiveness, in all its forms, is not only made up of *movement*, but also *strength* and *muscle tone*, a state of *sympathetic* stimulation, a clear *awareness* of what we wish to obtain, a capacity for *imagination* and *forward planning* (although in a somewhat limited manner), a *feeling* of determination (at times dictated by anger and at other times linked to joy or ribaldry), and attaching a positive *value* to our own action.

As we gradually proceed over our development, the way in which we express Aggressiveness becomes more focussed, stronger physically, more directly expressed and declared, and at times more joyously.

Alterations

It is within this group of Basic Experiences (as we have seen occurring in the case of Strength) that the seed of violence can insinuate itself. Affectionate Aggressiveness can be stifled until it is practically absent in the fully grown adult; or it can become distorted and take the form of violence, losing playfulness, affection and softness.

Affectionate Aggressiveness (Joyous, Playful)

At the beginning, people who participate in our therapy groups are often unable to understand how there can be such a thing as *Affectionate, Joyous, or Playful Aggressiveness*. Toughened by the numerous aggressions we have experienced in our lives, we all too often forget the Joyousness attached to strength. If we think of puppies, though, or bear cubs, or fawns, then it is easy for us to understand the real nature of Affectionate Aggressiveness. There are numerous experiences of Affectionate Aggressiveness that can be offered (with the necessary specifications) during therapy and in group workshops in general.

When a mother teases and tickles her little daughter or son, strength plays a part, but this has nothing to do with being unpleasant or destructive. Children love testing their strength in play fights, even with adults. They love being "squashed" on the bed, thrown down like a sack of potatoes, being hit playfully, being pulled around and thrown in the air. They laugh heartily during this sort of game, without the slightest semblance of anger or destructive hate.

It is only when a child has had to suffer excessive clashes with the adult world, such as the tragedy of continual attacks and criticism, that he risks losing this fundamental Basic Experience, i.e. the capacity for Affectionate Aggressiveness. We lose the capacity of pulling another person towards us in a friendly way, our positions become unmovable, we reproach each other with hate, and we impose violent ultimatums. Then, when we arrive at this point, we become scared to use our strength because Aggression is mixed in with it. Strength therefore becomes extremely dangerous. It is contracted, repressed, and explosive. Yet the less we are able to express our Strength calmly and openly, the more we accumulate anger and bitterness, the more explosive and destructive our Aggressiveness becomes and is no longer kept under control.

The recovery of the Joy of fighting, exchanging opinions and criticism is one of the most important objectives to reach in therapy. Life becomes truly (and dangerously) tragic without the light heartedness of smiles and Joyous Aggressiveness.

Affectionate play fighting and tickling

Play fighting like animal cubs, with the help of tickling. Affectionate and playful fight between the patient and the therapist. The patient can try attacking the therapist.

Caterina clearly finds it difficult using aggressiveness in the context of a game. The strength that she uses quickly becomes disproportionate to the situation and she senses a strange feeling of confusion, as if she were unable to understand what she was supposed to do.

Marco never wants to give in to the other person, even though it is only a game. In his eyes, giving in has become too associated with fragility. It was very dangerous for him to allow himself to be fragile when he was little because it meant succumbing to his older brothers' continual attacks.

Lina has a whale of a time play fighting and tickling. At the end of her course of therapy, she no longer has problems with affectionate aggression, which is something she is very happy about.

Aggression

Aggression is a form of Aggressiveness that aims at striking out. For this reason, it should only be used in cases of real necessity, serious danger or to eliminate an enemy who in turns wants to attack or harm us. When altered, (with the same mechanisms that we have already seen at work in the case of Strength), Aggressiveness becomes gratuitous Violence, or continuous, subtle Violence. It becomes the Violence that is insinuating itself into our lives more and more through films, computer games, television; in towns and in our children's lives.

Authority

Authority (Standing, Confidence, Knowing our own Worth)

When talking about somebody we might say, by way of a compliment, that they have Standing, that they count, that they are an important person. This sense of Authority is sent out through a series of signals, which essentially belong to the sphere of non verbal communication. Authority can also be defined as solidity: someone who is firmly rooted, centred, who does not change their position too easily, who has a significant influence over others.

Functions

Standing with our *feet* well placed on the ground, with an erect and energetic *posture*, elastic and toned *muscles*, an open and frank *look*, with the *face* raised and an *expression* that demonstrates that we are quite proud of ourselves are all elements that make up the basis for Authority.

Confidence

Another way of describing these last nuances of Strength is to use the word Confidence. Confidence (and not arrogance) is the pleasant sensation of having made the right choices, of having acquired enough knowledge to deal with the question in hand, of having interpreted the situation in the right way. This does not mean having a religious-type faith in our own infallibility. On the contrary: someone who has a discreet amount of Confidence knows how easy it is to make mistakes; and they also know that making a mistake is no tragedy and that they can always correct their error or turn back on themselves, and that making mistakes are a vital part of the learning process.

Children should be taught at school that making mistakes is completely natural, essential even, if they are to make progress in their learning and development.

Confidence consists in not letting ourselves freeze up with indecision, in not thinking that every decision to be made may seriously condition our existence. It is a mistake to think that every step can be dramatically decisive. It is much better to try than to become completely immobilised. Stasis is not to be confused with prudence.

The corollary of all of this is in the sensations that accompany Confidence, decisive action and Authority, i.e. very enjoyable sensations that permit us to appreciate ourselves, know our full worth and be happy and satisfied with what we are doing.

Alterations

It is fairly predictable that Confidence and Authority can be undermined in children with constant criticism, disapproval, or by denigrating their capacities or actions. This does not mean that we have to pretend to appreciate every single thing they do, always say yes, or allow them to have or do whatever they want. On the contrary: children need guidance and help, although it should be affectionate and respect their efforts. Appreciating children's capacities and successes is a good way of consolidating their Confidence. So is underlining their capacities and successes before highlighting their errors. Children develop and grow through gratifications, which provide them with motivation and enthusiasm, not through frustration and delusions. Without this, they would end up being incapable of appreciating themselves.

Something lovely today

After an activity to loosen their control, the participants lie down on the mats, letting go and breathing deeply with their eyes closed. At this point, they are prompted to think about something lovely that they have at the moment, something they are proud of, that puts joy into their present lives. Look at it and "feel" it in all its details.

For the first time in her life, Melania has her very own house. Lia imagined a very simple scene: eating toast with her much loved nephew.

Lola works in the field of rehabilitation and it gives her great joy to see that one of her patients, who had been left completely paralysed in an accident, was showing signs of improvement. Romano's great joy was thinking of his son, how he is growing up, and the fact that their relationship is so good.

When Floriana thinks about her relationships with other people and the sorts of relationships she has now, she feels really content although her greatest joy is being able to dance.

Adriano imagined his girlfriend's smiling, tender face. There's a girl in Marcello's life as well. He really likes her and he feels that her ways really manage to open him up.

Marisa has a little granddaughter who always acts the clown and makes her laugh like she hadn't laughed in years. Melina had the clear image of her son (the youngest) running around the house laughing.

Most of the images recalled by the group are tied to simple, genuine, primary pleasures. Yet it is precisely these little and, at the same time, great moments of affection that fill people's lives with joy; as long as they are experienced, felt and valued as they deserve to be.

Three parts of the body

Everyone is lying down with their eyes closed. "Let's imagine that we are becoming smaller and smaller as we breathe. Smaller and smaller, even smaller. Now we can enter our big bodies lying there on the mat. We can enter our big bodies because we're tiny, and we are swept up into the blood flow straightaway and carried around. The blood is like a speeding torrent that pulls us along with it and takes us to whichever part of the body we want to visit, the first part of the body to attract us and that we want to visit. We stop in this part of our body and we note what it's like being inside, seeing it from within. What are the colours like? The forms? The consistency? What sensations and emotions do we feel finding ourselves inside the part of the body that immediately attracted us? Let's stay there a bit longer, and then we'll leave this part and let ourselves be carried about again by the flow of liquid, until we reach the part that's the complete opposite of where we were before. We stop. We explore it in our own time, this completely opposite part. We want to see what it's like, for us, being inside it, what sensations we feel. We see what it's like, whether it's dark or light, if it's pleasant to the touch, it it's colourful or not. What do we feel about this part? One more moment of contact before we leave it. Then we let go and we let ourselves be carried around by the flow of the blood; it's carrying us, dragging us along. We know that we have to leave this voyage through the body, but before we leave we want to visit just one more part: a part that we're curious about, that interests us, but that we hadn't thought of the last time. We stay inside this last part for a while. We notice whether being in this part is different from the previous parts. How does it strike us? We notice what it's like inside this part. We explore it a bit. We see its colours, its forms, and consistency. What are our feelings in this part of the body that interested us, before we leave our bodies? One last moment and then we leave".

Andreina is immediately transported to the *belly*. She is very maternal, and she has a habitual and incurable capacity for taking on other people's pain. In the opposite part, however, she is greeted with sensations of lost strength (she sees columns and ruins of ancient Greece under a harsh white light while she is there). This is the same strength that she is gradually rediscovering in therapy. The final part is the *breast* (an intensely feminine characteristic that acts as a call towards men). Over the following months, in effect, Andreina starts to rediscover her feminine vanity: she does her makeup differently, she changes her hairstyle, and she starts to dress with care. She discovers that men really do start to look at her.

Lory's habitual level is that of her rationality: she goes straight to her *brain*. Once there, however, she finds only a disturbing pitch black. Lory was extremely cold and formal at the beginning of her course of therapy. She used to experience difficulty during workshops that required emotional involvement or giving and receiving warmth with the others. The second part that she visits is the *heart* (finally). It is a new dimension (ignored for too long) that she finds particularly beautiful and welcoming. The point of force to be discovered and utilised is the *spine*: its renewed strength, its capacity to modify old suffering, creating new modalities (in her imagination, Lory walks along her vertebrae and goes and discovers the marrow within them).

Ezio found this journey inside himself absolutely wonderful: a world of colours and forms that he'd never have believed. His *throat* (his old skill as a talker, even talking too much at times) welcomes him at first with its colourful, slippery parts. His *chest* is his new strength in facing the world and other people directly and openly. What he really needs to rediscover, however, are his *eyes*. These are the third body that he visits and they are a lively, intense red. At the moment, Ezio still finds it difficult to establish concrete, tender eye contact with people. This means that he is still unable to 'get inside' people, beyond their outward appearance, without relying purely on logic. In reality, he has been thinking about having an eye operation to give renewed energy to his eyes, long fatigued by short-sightedness (the umpteenth proof of the correlation between the psyche and the soma).

Carolina also reveals a sclerotised habit of passively welcoming others going straight to her *belly*. The journey continues in her *brain*, cold, but sharp as a knife, indicating the recent recovery of the use of her intelligence, of the capacity to organise the local services where she works, finally being able to impose her point of view on the people who had forced her to remain isolated in her corner. For her, too, the last part to explore, a new source of strength, is a symbol of her sexuality, her *genitalia* (how many women there are, who have had both their intelligence and the capacity to express themselves using the full force of their femininity crushed!). Following this experience, Carolina (just like Andreina) will explore a new territory: that of a different relationship with the opposite sex.

Erica follows a different course however. She starts from her *womb*, although she does not feel too calm because it looks like part of an old abandoned factory, and then she reached the *throat* (which is an opposite, much neglected part), and which she imagines to be luminous, with soft, pleasant slides. Erica is winning back the capacity to talk to, and in front of, other people, using the full sociality of her voice. The third part that she chooses to visit before leaving her body is interesting: her *fingers*, rosy and pleasantly tepid. The new prospective that is opening in her life is that of being able to "poke her fingers in", touching situations, changing them and manipulating them (just as she does, then, with her hands). Above all, this capacity is manifesting itself in a soft and delicate way, rather than a hard, inflexible one.

Presence (Determination)

A further facet of strength that is very similar to the previous ones, although with slightly different characteristics, is that of a person's "Presence". Presence has more to do with form, with the way in which a person is perceived and the modalities of their interpersonal relationships.

In Italian, we also say that someone has a "good presence" when they are pleasant to look at. However, let us use the word "presence" to describe something more intense: the capacity to be there, to get oneself noticed, and to condition the relationships of the group. This is what we refer to when we say that an actor has a good "stage presence".

Functions

A person with Presence gets noticed even if they keep to themselves, but not because of their appearance, how they are dressed or the jewels they are wearing. What we notice, on the contrary, is the intensity of their *gaze*, the way they *move*, their *tone of voice*, their *posture,* and it is these elements that essentially determine a person's Presence. All of the above are basically outward manifestations of something that is within, something that involves the entire person, which is determined by a *symbolic* Function whereby the person attributes a positive value to himself, a series of *memories* confirming his Authority and a capacity to *project* themselves in the future, *planning* situations where they will meet with "success".

Alterations

Obviously, if a child has conserved profound nuclei of fear and self-devaluation within the Self, if he has not consolidated his Confidence and basic Authority, then he will not have Presence either. If an adult is gripped by doubts, insecurities and negativity about himself, then it is most unlikely that he will be able to transmit that indefinable sensation of personal "charisma" or "magnetism".

Naturally, the phenomenon of ostentatious over-Confidence or swaggering is just the other side of the same coin: it is a person's attempt to fill a hole by over-stretching the little confidence they do have, thereby losing credibility.

Assertiveness

Assertiveness (Self-Affirmation)

The capacity for Assertiveness is similar to that of Authority: it is the ability to create space for oneself and invite recognition. The only difference is that Assertiveness has more to do with reaching objectives, achieving one's goals, both in social and working life, as well as life as a couple.

Children are already a little older when they start to experience this form of relationship in a more structured way.

Functions

At the base of the capacity to be Assertive lies the feeling that when we are right, e are right, and that we cannot always passively suffer other people's decisions, that we cannot always conform to other people's opinions, that we can make the world listen to us and that we can explain our motives with our head held high. As suggested by the phrase itself *(head held high)*, it is the individual's whole *posture* that expresses Assertiveness: their *head* is held high and it allows them to look down on the world slightly, with pride. The *bearing* is erect and secure, the *eyes* shine, the *voice* is full, the *movements* and the *muscles* are relaxed whilst at the same time giving off a certain stateliness. The overall state is one of slight *excitement*.

Self-Assertion is linked to the capacity to carry out strong, decisive *movements*, and to assume attitudes that demonstrate a vivid sense of determination. Because these attitudes belong to the sphere of non-verbal communication in all its immediacy, they have a very intense effect on the interlocutor. We are impressed by an individual who is able to put themselves across with a firm, resonant voice, with decisive movements, energetic muscles, and a well-set posture. The most interesting thing, however, is that the activation of all these psycho-physical Functions positively influences the subject himself, actually making him "feel" more confident and decisive.

Let us not forget, however, that another of the most important Functions involved in Assertiveness is without doubt that of the whole series of *values* (the *symbolic* world) with which the subject perceives himself: a series of values that are genuinely positive, i.e. a good self-image based on his real capacities. The *imagination*, then, is also stimulated to make large and small-scale plans, undertake new paths and experiences, because the subject feels capable of carrying them out, and able to face obstacles and difficulties as well, certain that he can overcome them if they are within his reach.

Alterations

Whilst it is true that modern society stimulates Assertiveness and Self-Affirmation, it must however be said that this stimulation has been excessive and discordant, in the name of competitiveness, which has become almost our only reason to live. This Basic Experience therefore ends up becoming altered in its fundamental essence: Self-Affirmation becomes the will to show ourselves off at any price, to seek "popularity". The definition of the word "success" no longer means knowing that we go our job competently, with satisfaction and pleasure, or managing to carry out the plans that we set ourselves. Success is only considered as such if we manage to reach out to the public, if we become famous or well-known. Success has been confused, therefore, with popularity.

Today, we can already see a tendency towards this type of alteration in children: they try to be at the centre of attention at any cost, even if it means becoming quite a nuisance; or rather they insist that they are right even if they are proved wrong. If it is not harmonious, Self-Affirmation can become “impudence”, “arrogance”, or “presumption”. Once again, the polarity *assertiveness* ↔ *humility* should work fully and openly at both poles. Yet again, when this Basic Experience is dysfunctional, fixed at one or the other of the two poles, then neither can really work properly.

It is not just altered mechanisms in the social world that push children towards an alteration in their Assertiveness, but once again the root of the problem is to be found within the initial microcosm of the family. A child who is not sufficiently encouraged seeks other ways of gaining attention; if he only obtains it when he imposes himself, then he will be pushed to place himself increasingly at the centre of attention. He will be less and less disposed to question his affirmations, above all if he sees his parents doing the same thing.

Yet it can also occur, on the contrary, that he forgets how to maintain his position and values. This happens when the child has been criticised excessively, or if he has been constantly undervalued and undermined. As an adult, it is therefore unlikely that he will put himself forward for a post at work; he is unlikely to feel up to difficult tasks, or to assert himself proudly, with his “head held high”.

It is for precisely this reason that Assertiveness is a fundamental pillar of human development. An altered development of this Basic Experience of the Self constitutes one of the principle factors that lead people to the wild search for “success” and power, aiming at obtaining intense sensations that a “normal” life cannot offer them.

On the other hand, people who are completely unable to express Assertiveness end up accumulating a sense of hate and bitterness towards humanity in general. Whilst on the surface they have an almost excessively submissive demeanour, this facade hides a flame of hate nurtured within, which is expressed indirectly, following indirect and hidden paths to reach its target.

Our society is full of people who are sick with power or passive aggressiveness. Naturally, we all suffer a little from envy and jealousy. We all feel or have felt ourselves to be victims of some social injustice. Another aspect is when, instead of a frank and open Assertiveness, or a "flexible" Assertiveness put to the service of our desires, we constantly remonstrate with ourselves for what might have been. Naturally, as we have already pointed out, a society where everything is based on image, appearances, and popularity, where a person who is not successful is considered to be a loser, cannot facilitate a healthy functioning of this Basic Experience of the Self.

A Sequence using the hands

The group walks around the room. "While we walk around the room, we feel our hands. Our hands are wide open. They sweep and stretch out. We let our sensations flow down to our hands. The hands move around faster. We hit our hands together a little. Now our hands are irritated, they try to wring this horrible sensation out of themselves. They are annoyed, they sigh, and they throw away all the things we don't like. Our hands don't want any contact with the others. They are disgusted by clinging, false contacts. They try to avoid the other hands, and when they meet them, they push them away. Now they are tired and they stop to lean themselves against the wall. They start to feel the sensations of contact with other objects, and they explore their tactile sensations as if they had never done so before. We discover the world through our hands, and with our eyes closed, we discover the sensations in our fingers. First, the hands touch one another. First, the right hand touches the left one and holds it close. Then, vice versa, the left hand holds the other hand close. The hands give each other tenderness. Then they give us a little tenderness, touching our bodies calmly and affectionately. We need a little gentleness. For once in our lives, we give ourselves a little tenderness. We have a right to it. We are tired. We sink to the floor; we lie down, while our hands touch us tenderly. Then we let go completely. The hands touch the ground, and then they feel the tactile sensations as they move softly along the floor. They start feeling curious about the world around them. They want to feel other contacts and so they start pounding lightly on the floor, as if they were trying to call the others, as if they wanted to make themselves heard. They beat harder to make themselves heard, to express assertiveness. Then they start moving outwards, searching for other hands, so that they can be a bit assertive with the others as well, in the outside world. We move along the floor and we go to meet the other hands. At the beginning, the contact is simple and tranquil, almost without moving. Then the contact is more tender. Then it is a little more assertive. We take the other hand, and we let the other hand take ours. Once the contact is over, our hands stay on their own for a while; trying to relive the sensations they have just felt as fully as possible. (This sequence can be carried out entirely on the ground as well).

At first, Mina doesn't want her hands to be taken by the others because it gives her an unpleasant sensation of feeling trapped; but then she stops avoiding the contact and squeezes herself into the group of hands and lets herself be held and contained. Because of her difficulty in accessing this deep experience and the fact that she arrived at the workshop later than the others, Mina absorbs too little of the warmth and nourishment (which she needs much more than the others); and so she feels cold when she lets go, and her hands feel as if they had been anaesthetised.

Fabiana only manages to feel unpleasant sensations. The feeling that she will be unable to pull the hands towards her gives her sensations of impotence and mistrust. As a result, she feels unable to "dive" her hands in with the others to get warmth and protection. She even finds it difficult to recall the experience once the contact is over. She suffers tachycardia and nausea as she fantasizes about things she has lost forever.

A lot of the nuances of this sequences come easily to Giovanni; others are more difficult for him: such as pushing and pulling the other hands, because these (healthy and legitimate) actions were so condemned during his childhood as to be confused with "presumption", i.e. an arrogant, unpleasant modality.

Michela lingers for a long time over the pleasant feeling of her hands on her body, giving tenderness and consoling her; whilst in real life her consolation is given too often to others and rarely to herself. She is moved, and she cries softly. When she beats her hands on the floor to call for attention, the movement takes on a hint of anger. This anger is transformed into the desire to go to the others and get the contact she wants, instead of retaining anger for its own sake. When she stops at the end of the sequence to recall the sensations of a few minutes ago, the memories arrive clearly and precisely, particularly the sensation caused by one hand that invited her to let go and just be, until she drifts far away with her thoughts.

Felicia feels two specific desires linked to her hands: her left hand wanted to feel her heart beating (like an intimate contact with her affections); whilst the other hand, lying in the palm of her left hand, let her know that it didn't want to have to become active and have to keep battling on in life.

When Salvo met the other hands in the group, he felt them to be strong and firm like those of his father. This discovery filled him with the wish to let go and play together with the others.

Making Plans

Assertiveness is also connected the ability to evaluate real situations intelligently, discerning and choosing which is the right path for us, and it allows us to make Plans.

We should never lose our original capacity to make Plans, feed our desires, and become enthusiastic about their possible fulfilment. Enthusiasm and passion are cardinal aspects of Assertiveness.

Functions

Yet again, this form of behaviour cannot be considered as solely *cognitive.* It must derive, above all, from inner *sensations*, body sensations: both at the level of the *proprioception* of our posture and muscles and that of our innermost organs. Popular wisdom expresses this well: when we want to say that someone has a real passion, we say that they are moved by passion "from the gut", or that they are "on fire with anticipation", or that their excitement is "feverish". It is the whole body that moves towards an objective, it is "lit" (as if the body were burning) and participates at every level in a dream, a wish, or a Plan.

Perhaps it is precisely the lack of a full vitality at psychobiological level (the significance of which has been little recognised by post-industrial society) that is one of the reasons that young people today find it so hard to become really enthusiastic about ideas, ideals or a projects.

Planning to fulfil a desire

Lie down after "letting go" and breathe deeply. Formulate a concrete desire to put into action that evening or over the next few days: a little, concrete desire. Feel the desire, feel its strength. Feel the pleasure and the excitement without anxiety. Imagine the practical steps that you will have to take to make it come true.

Renato wishes to prolong the sensations that he has felt during this group work until night time, and he manages to imagine each step in detail: the moment when he will accompany his dinner with soft music and unhurried movements, a good book to read and in the end going to bed, enjoying the pleasure of lying down in bed and stretching before falling asleep. The numerous details and the clarity of the images that Renato recounts bear witness to the recovery of his capacity to plan (this is very different from "fantasising", which means getting carried away with one's imagination without picturing a way of making it come true, often poorly related to reality). This capacity finally allows him to set himself a goal and reach it in the way that best suits him.

Paolo, who started his therapy just short while ago, expresses the desire to make a journey to a distant place, but he doesn't know where to go or how to make his dream come true. We can say that Paolo has given voice to a fantasy, rather than the realisation of a desire.

A poor capacity to make plans makes it difficult to reach our objectives in many areas of life, and for this reason it contributes to a feeling of precariousness and insecurity.

Making Choices

Alterations: obsessive and ritual disorders

Obsessive disorders are on the increase today, as are anxiety disorders, anxiety, and panic attacks. It has therefore become more difficult to Make Choices serenely and tranquilly, given the lack of real certainties and concrete, intense sensations. What can we base our decisions on? Every Choice obviously has *pros* and *cons*: so what can we do to make sure we do not regret our decision or make mistakes?

The obsessive compulsive resolves this anxiety (a result of not having clear and concrete perceptions) with a series of rituals, repeated gestures, and a series of identical movements. In this way, he fulfils four objectives at the same time.

First of all, rituals represent a way of trying to ensure that the subject makes no mistakes whilst performing a given action. If I go and check that the front door is locked ten times, the probability that I will leave the door open by mistake will be significantly diminished.

Secondly, the repetitive mechanism serves to cover the vacuum of physical sensations and perceptions. It is as if the musicians at a concert, in the absence of a set piece, decided to play whatever music came into each of their heads, even if the result were a cacophony: they would rather play anything so as to avoid facing the silence in the concert hall and admit to a complete failure.

Essentially, it is the origin itself of these rituals that can provide us with the third key to understanding their use. Rituals are "normal" during childhood, i.e. when children want to hear the same story over and over again, or when they have to have a kiss goodnight every night, or when they have to have the same doll on their pillow beside them every time. What reassures them is finding that which is "known" once again. What they want is something they know very well, which wraps them up in its warm and tranquillising familiarity. It is for this reason that little boys and girls want to rediscover situations with which they are already familiar and delve into them many times. Naturally, if this reassurance (which they normally need while they are little) is insufficient, falling back on the same object, the same gesture, or the very same pattern of behaviour becomes indispensable. Since it never seems enough, it requires continual repetition, becoming an obsession.

On the other hand, rituals have a magical significance in the life of the child and later, of the adolescent. The rapid growth at that age and the innumerable, unexpected changes force adolescents to have to deal with situations that are far more complex than they have previously had to deal with during their childhood. It becomes very difficult to keep the situation under control. It is hard to manage a grown up body that suddenly puts the adolescent almost on a par with adults, changing the equilibrium of his relationships, as well as those with the opposite sex. It is much easier then to fall back on "short cuts", or actions that skip all logical steps. "If I don't tread on the cracks in the pavement I'll definitely pass the exam". "If the coin spins more than twice before it hits the floor things with my friends will go well". Obsessive rituals are also reassuring because they give back the illusion of being able to rule the world that the individual desperately needs, having lost *contact* with himself, with his own sensations and with those arriving from the outside world.

Lastly, rituals take the place of the "laws of functioning" that the child has not been helped to learn, i.e. laws governing social relations, relations with other people, and laws relating to the complexity of real life. If these laws (which are indispensable for life) are lacking, given the difficulty involved in gradually finding them out and learning them on his own, the child will be forced to create them for himself, hence rituals. Rituals are laws that do not correspond to a real relationship with the surrounding world; they do not have the same elasticity as the laws governing social behaviour. For this reason, they have to be followed at all costs, obsessively, otherwise there will be chaos, anxiety, and the person will feel lost.

Let us return to the fundamental question of how to Make Choices with serenity: the answers come, once again, from the world of children.

We have already underlined the fact that Making Choices should not be an operation that is carried out at random, but rather one that is based on the clear and intense presence of psycho-physical *sensations*. Being able to "feel" whether the other person is basically a positive, good person, whether they are well disposed towards us and whether they will be supportive towards us, allows us to avoid most of the mistakes that we generally complain about. *Feeling* where we are, clearly *perceiving* our moods and noticing the atmosphere around us are all extremely useful for Making a Choice that is not harmful. This is also the case with a full capacity for *forward planning*, predicting given situations and preparing the most functional line of action or behaviour for our wishes or objectives and extrapolating all the relative consequences.

We must not forget, however, that making mistakes is absolutely normal. It is not an irreparable disaster. There is no drama. We learn precisely because we make mistakes: mistakes are therefore functional for the development of the individual and for success (in the sense of succeeding in carrying out activities undertaken). Young people would have fewer problems if we emphasised the positive nature of making mistakes.

Thirdly, there are no such things as absolute errors. That is to say that in most daily situations, many of the possible choices have their own advantages. Buying a plain sweater instead of a stripy one is not likely to cause grave problems for our existence. The important thing is knowing how to appreciate and value the positive elements of our Choice, which has nothing whatsoever to do with the bigoted and self-denying idea of having to "make do". It is more to do with the vital capacity to enjoy the minutiae of life, even if they are not considered to be "exceptional" from the point of view of the consumer society.

On the other hand, if we come to the conclusion that our Choice really was mistaken and damaging, in most cases we can turn back on our decision and try new solutions. Obviously, not everything will be exactly the way it was before we first made our choice, but it is rare that any modifications will have been such that they have completely distorted the meaning of our lives or that they prevent us from making further Choices. By and large, the Choices that we make are rarely irreversible; rather they offer us further opportunities of branching off or of changing direction.

Lastly, we must recognise the fact that excessive control over all our Choices does not always prove to be useful. Most of the positive events that happen in our lives come from a completely unexpected direction, purely by chance, and their results go well beyond what we would have been able to obtain had we tried to make them come about deliberately. Letting things "happen" every so often, without making as much effort, is healthy and sometimes opens up unexpected possibilities. This does not mean embracing fatalistic theories. Rather it implies first of all that we understand that our surroundings cannot be moved solely using our will and rationality, but also, above all, by using the "gut", i.e. using the deepest states of functioning which, if positive, can communicate with the outside world much more effectively than words can, to bring about events in our favour. Secondly, it means remembering that it is not just us that move the world, but also the world that moves us.

Negativity

Anger

Experiences of confrontation and contrast with others are not to be considered less important than those of love and contact. Children feel a strong need to argue with others when necessary, testing their Anger and strength when the need arises. If we have given more space in this book to the more "positive" kind of Experiences, and if we do so in therapy, this is mainly due to the fact that the alterations that have intervened in the patients' lives mainly regard deficiencies in these Experiences.

If an individual has an altered and neurotic life, all too often there is no real reason for him to express Anger, hate, and unpleasantness at that moment. These expressions are just old automatic reactions that prevail, suffocating any other ways of relating to people. In this way, the most suitable reactions to the circumstances remain buried under numerous layers of Negativity.

Functions

Anger and hate leave traces in the entire organism, and not just on the *emotive* plane. At the level of the *neuro-endocrine apparatus*, neurohumors are released, such as adrenaline and norepinephrine, or cortisoids released by the adrenal gland. The *sympathetic nervous system* is intensely activated, the *breathing* is shallow and suppressed, the *heartbeat* is accelerated, the arterial *pressure* increases, and the blood is drawn to the brain and the internal organs. The *rationality* is obscured by *violent emotive reactions* and the individual's *fantasies* at that moment are acutely destructive. The *movements* are intense, but also brusque and hard. The whole *posture* is ready to attack, and the *face* also expresses the mood of Anger with great intensity. The *voice* is extremely loud and the *muscle tone* is spasmodically ready for combat.

Alterations

Whilst this general state of the organism lasts a short time in the case of healthy functioning, and is activated only when there is an absolute necessity, the reactions described above can become chronic, primed to be set off continually and automatically, regardless of the external situation. Little is required to set off the entire mechanism, in a repetitive short circuit. This means that all too often Anger and hate are reactions that are completely unsuitable, mistaken. It is not even true that they are that as "cathartic" as is often stated. When it comes down to it, Anger and hate are experiences that procure pain and not happiness, which we ought only to call on in "desperate times", in order to defend ourselves from attack, situations of real danger or from destructive enemies. In such emotional states, the organism undergoes biochemical modifications that are neither pleasant nor completely "healthy". The theory that "releasing" Anger and negativity is beneficial and therapeutic for its own sake has been completely overtaken now. What normally happens, conversely, is that when these emotive expressions emerge, they leave a painful trace, a sense of unease that leaves us feeling upset and disturbed, unless we have become hardened and we let the emotions slide off us with cold detachment.

This does not mean that expressions of Anger and hate should necessarily be considered as "tragic" events that are always destructive. Children quickly become Angry when they sense incomprehension and insensitivity in adults, but the situation reverses just as easily. They can have moments of intense hate, when they genuinely wish that their parents would disappear, but they forgive them straight afterwards and return to the pleasure of contact and tenderness.

The continual expression of Anger indicates an altered general state of the Self, which can easily lead over the long term to a serious risk of even quite severe illnesses. On the other hand, an inability to express negativity when the occasion calls for it is undoubtedly damaging in life. Children learn to be afraid of their Anger, even if it is just and righteous, when their Angry reaction is continually disapproved of, and they are made to feel guilty. In fact, they often have to choose between the Angry reaction and the possibility of keeping their parents' affection. Because affection is vital at that age, they end up swallowing their Anger, suppressing it, burying it. If Anger is suppressed, it accumulates and becomes "bitterness", and as such, it persists for a long time within the organism and colours every relationship negatively, even though it is hidden.

Bitterness hatches below an apparent tranquillity, undermining the individual's basic trust in relationships, destroying the possibility of affection and love. It re-emerges every so often in the form of violent and (this time) destructive explosions. People end up fearing their own exasperated outbursts and they tend to suppress their Anger even more, feeding the closed circuit of bitterness.

Therapy

During therapy, we work towards the recovery of a type of Anger that is open and direct rather than destructive, similar in many respects to children's quick and fleeting fits of Rage. In this way, we soon discover that our Anger is neither devastating nor unlimited: it is easily expressed and is soon over. Not only that, but rage can be followed by serenity and tenderness. However, the most recent research has shown how important it is that we primarily use our calm strength, playful strength, and gentle strength in these cases, because these Experiences and capacities construct relationships that are more open and direct. They obtain much more effective results with less effort than Anger, and they can help to dissolve Anger that has built up or been repressed.

Hate

Thanks to therapy, Hate, just like anger, can lose the connotation of destructiveness that it is all too often associated with. Hate is a completely natural reaction, and can even be turned towards the people we love the most. It can be extremely intense, but it is normally brief and fleeting: the desire, for a moment, that the other person really would disappear from our lives. Children often go as far as saying "I wish you were dead!" but they do not wish that this were actually true because they have absolutely no wish to live their lives without the loved one in question.

Although Hate for an enemy is of a very different nature to the above form, it also has a legitimate basis, but only when it causes us to act, defend ourselves or attack, to avoid the other person destroying us. It is a biological inheritance that allows us to safeguard our own lives, allowing us to take action to this effect. However if Hate, like anger, does not lead to direct and open action, or, if due to our fear, it gets exaggeratedly suppressed and mulled over within the Self, it becomes profoundly altered, losing its original, useful meaning. In this way, it ends up destroying not our enemy but ourselves (with its psychobiological mechanisms), permeating our existence with a continuous background of malice, discontentment, and unease.

Being Provoked

Reawakening the Experience of Provocation within patients is a chapter in therapy that constitutes the basis for the recovery of open, healthy anger and hate. Provocation, in particular, forces the subject to act, setting off immediate reactions, which tend to go beyond the patient's exaggerated self control, creating immediate small-scale explosions. These explosions reawaken old sensations with instant immediacy, bringing back sane, healthy reactions. When the patient's reaction is this immediate, malice is almost always absent. When hate and anger have been deprived of their load of malice, they go back to being concrete, direct and open expressions that are in no way destructive at all.

Autonomy

We come to the last stage in this journey, that of Autonomy. Autonomy means *feeling good in our own company*, even when others are near. If someone is autonomous, it means that they do not necessarily need others. Autonomy is strictly tied to the Basic Experience of authority, but it is oriented more towards the *relational* side, it is more closely tied to our relationship with others, whereas authority has more to do with our relationship with ourselves and how we feel inside. Autonomy can be experienced in the simple form of Separation or as a movement that is focussed more directly, in contrast with another person's choices.

In any case, Autonomy is not a late conquest during childhood. On the contrary, it is present right from the beginning. Naturally, at the beginning

Autonomy takes a very simple form: staying in our cot in peace with ourselves. It means having our own thoughts and images beyond the images that our parents offer us as children.

Separation

Separation must also be seen from the *Functional* perspective, i.e. as one pole of the polarity *being contained* (the first Basic Experience of the Self examined in this chapter) ↔ *separation*, or the polarity *fusion* ↔ *separation*. Moreover, as with every other polarity, it is unlikely that a child will be able to accept *detachment* (one of the poles) if he has not experienced profound contact, being inside, *being nourished* (the other pole) fully and satisfactorily.

We are talking about a dynamic rather than a temporal polarity. That is to say that within this model it is no longer possible for us to think of a baby *first* being in a state of fusion with his mother and *then* separating himself, seeing himself as an individual for the first time. Both poles are *coexistent* right from the beginning (obviously in relation to the modalities present at each stage of development). A newborn baby feels Autonomous and Separated from his mother when he enters into contact with a different adult who holds him well; or when he enjoys contact with himself and takes delight in being on his own in his cot in the company of the fantastic world of his internal movements, his breathing, tactile sensations in his mouth and the rest of his body, and fascinating kinaesthetic sensations.

Autonomy must not, however, be confused with *independence*. Newborn babies depend on their parents' care in order to eat, move, and live. They do not know how to manage on their own in life, and therefore they are not independent of the world of adults, but they are Autonomous and Separate, in that they are content in the moments when their parents are not there, and they are Separated from the manifestations of affection, words and contact that adults address to them. Newborn children know how to procure pleasant sensations on their own.

Our theoretical model allows us to think of Separation in terms of identity either. Babies already possess their own identity (in part), which they will continue to develop their entire lives. It is not a result of Separating themselves from their parents, or rebelling "against" them or anything else. Newborn babies do not need individuation because they are already a complete individual.

This way of interpreting child development dispenses with another belief that has accompanied certain currents of thought for years, i.e. the idea that human beings aim to return to a *lost paradise* their whole lives, trying to rediscover the peace of *total fusion* with their mother, the primordial and idyllic condition of non individualisation and non autonomy present in the mother's womb.

Today we know that this is not the case, and that even in the mother's womb (at least during the last phases of pregnancy) the child perceives himself, consoles himself and obtains pleasure for himself. In short, he is already a complete individual and is already Autonomous in certain aspects before he is born, let alone after his birth. Consequently, Autonomy and fusion are present from the beginning and they are in no way opposites. Rather, the greater the fusion, the greater the Separation and vice versa.

Alterations

Logically, the Experience of Separation and Autonomy may be hindered during the course of the child's development. If the child is constantly considered to be incapable or corrected continually, or, conversely, if he is not left to learn on his own and find his own way of resolving problems and overcoming obstacles, his Autonomy will wind up being seriously compromised. Notable fears will insinuate themselves within the child's Autonomy, polluting it and paralysing the child.

How many times do we hear of parents who help their children do their homework, until they become completely incapable of studying if there is not an adult nearby, not taking into account the negative consequences that this will have on their capacity to find their own study method and their own path?

A consequence of the opposite polarity is the child's incapacity to trust other people. When Autonomy has become the only way of surviving, when a child has had to do everything for himself from a very early age, then it is unlikely that he will be able to give his trust to another person. This forced independence does not, however, equal a full and complete Autonomy. The pressure of having to do everything on our own has a heavy price in terms of health and overall psycho-physiological equilibrium. Not only that, but it is in precisely these cases that the individual unconsciously seeks, deep down, to live in a state of dependence; the same state that he had not experienced sufficiently as a child. Sooner or later he ends up giving in all at once, without being fully aware of it; often with the wrong person: someone who is either unable or unwilling to take responsibility for another person. At this point, disappointments are inevitable, and often push the subject to be Autonomous at all costs, as if they had witnessed the last in a long series of proofs that confirm that trusting others is simply not possible.

Often people maintain the conviction that they should avoid getting their hopes up. Trusting others and letting themselves go always leads to trouble and they always end up being fooled! Better to stay on their own, never showing fragility, weakness or showing a sign that they need others. In fact, opening up and trusting ourselves to the right people is never dangerous, there is absolutely no risk. If anything we are enriched, we find strength and hope in life.

This is the same reason why a well-guided course of therapy carries no risk of leading to chronic dependence. The more profound the phase of containment, nourishment and contact, the easier it will be for the patient to detach themselves from the therapist and to feel that the course of therapy has really come to an end. Still it may not occur that the moment of "detachment" necessarily coincides with the "end" of any form of relations between the two. We can assert with serenity and authority that the relationship can continue positively even after the therapy has ended (if both parties wish it and if there is the possibility) in the form of friendship, collaboration and affection, due in particular to the profound contact that has been established between the two people.

Opposition

Opposing others is one of the manifestations of Autonomy, i.e. contrasting something that we do not like or want that the other person wants. However, it must be restated that Opposition is not the movement that *underlies* Autonomy and separation. It is not necessary to pass through a stage of Opposition before we can arrive at Autonomy. Autonomy, rather than being *against* something or someone, is *side by side* with something or someone. We do not become adults and go through adolescence *despite* our parents, but rather *with* their affection. It is not necessary for us to be *against* our children to make them grow up. On the contrary: a profound closeness will help them to search positively for their own path in life. A child that has been deeply loved and understood has no need to affirm their independence with rebellion and aggression, nor with behaviour that is excessively in Opposition to that of his family.

The newborn, furthermore, already knows how to Oppose his mother when she wants to give him milk and he is already full, or when he does not wish to be held and wants to lie down in his cot, or when he does not want to be played with and just wants to be rocked gently. His Opposition is unmistakeable. Opposition is a Basic Experience that helps us to understand each other, that prevents confusion and which allows us to express and sustain our wishes needs and ideas.

Alterations

Opposition is not normally linked to hostility. I resist you but I still care about you, unless you carry on forcing my limits. If a child is forced, Opposition loses its efficacy and he will continue to associate it with anger, hate, and bitterness. It will therefore be very hard for him to use Opposition in his adult life because it would mean releasing all his other negative and destructive feelings. Opposition is not destructive in itself, but what is destructive is the accumulation of negativity that has become mixed up with it. This prevents little ones from expressing their capacity for Opposition serenely without running the risk of losing their parents' affection, esteem, and love. However, if the subject becomes blocked in the excessive polarity of Opposition it can lead to deficiencies in this self-same Basic Experience. The only difference is that the child is driven to Oppose others constantly because this has proved to be the only way in which he can win himself a little space within the family, to be noticed and to receive attention. Once again, this continual Opposition is not full, real or satisfying Autonomy, but rather it is a manifestation of all the insecurity and need for help that the child has inevitably had to suppress.

Once again Functional Psychology demonstrates how the Polarities are the very essence of vital functioning, and how both extremes of the Polarity must be present and full within the subject's life, given that they are not antithetic at all, but rather complementary. If both extremes are fully developed, they can guarantee us equilibrium, harmony, and vitality.

Opposing others using percussion instruments

In a circle: one person sits in the centre. Another person in the group faces him and opposes him. We oppose each other using one of the percussion instruments in the centre of the circle. There are not just traditional percussion instruments; there are also makeshift, homemade ones. We oppose each other by inventing our own rhythm and trying to make the others follow our rhythm. This is not a competition to see who can make the most noise; it is more of a tribal rhythm.

Emilio would like to manage to shake up the other members of the group; he would like them to perceive his presence, and the fact that he's there, because he's felt left out too often in his life. To make this dream come true, he decides to do something different and gathers all the other people's instruments in a box and he shakes the whole thing vigorously, using a lot of strength and making a lot of noise.

Anna chooses to express herself with the lively vibrations of jingling, tinkling instruments, to indicate the state of joy that she has finally reached in her course of therapy. Roberta, on the other hand, expresses her sweetness with the soft and persuasive sound of the wooden sticks.

Chapter 6

Functional Development in the various Districts of the Body

Functional development in children

At this point, we will be examining the Functional development of the child District by District within the body. We will be tracking child development during the important phases of his growth, exploring the child's profound functioning on all planes of the Self (not just the cognitive or emotive planes), and above all we will be paying particular attention to the various parts of the body that the child uses to experience the world around him.

This work will not be concentrating too heavily on the process of neuropsychological maturation during the various phases of development, or the many psycho-physiological Functions of the human being. These areas have already been covered more than adequately in the relevant literature. Rather, this work aims to discover how children interact with their surroundings through every part of the Self and the body.

When talking about the child's body, then, we do not mean an analysis of the history of his muscle development, nor growth in height, hormonal modifications or the modification of the skeleton. We wish instead to shed light on how the various parts of the body *participate* in the development of the human being's basic functional processes, i.e., that which is at the root of the individual's actions, behaviour patterns, thoughts, and fantasies.

To be more precise, we wish to look at where the Basic Experiences are *stratified* within the various *Body Districts*, and how these Districts work together as the child crosses the most important steps in his development.

Until not long ago, some currents of thought in psychology held that certain parts of the body were linked to a single emotion (today, we would say a Basic Experience instead of one single emotion). This over-simplistic view went so far as to insist that "control" was in the neck, a sense of being "rooted in reality" lay in the legs, "rigidity" was in the back and "affectivity" was in the chest.

Other, more traditional, currents of thought took only certain areas of the body into consideration, giving each one a central and exclusive role at each of the various stages of the development and maturation of the libido. Theories that claimed the absolute existence of an "oral" phase and an "anal" phase became very diffuse, hypothesising that the child lived and experienced the world only *partially* during the various phases, in a non-integrated and immature way. The parts of the body ended up assuming above all a symbolic or metaphoric value. The oral phase, for example, was characterised by the idea of absorption, or taking in, introjecting: not just milk but also the good breast, the mother, other people.

Today, we know that the situation is different. The state of affairs is a lot more complex and articulated, and it cannot be examined from a purely symbolic and metaphorical point of view. Today we examine the child's real, concrete functioning as a whole, considering the union of the body and the mind. Indeed, it is the child's *whole* body that is called into play, time after time, in the same experience, in a given phase of his development. The experience is not merely "physical" however. On the contrary: it is always *global* or whole. In short, each experience is always psychophysical. The word *body* is used in this text merely to exemplify something that is already an immediate part of our knowledge base and our modality of perception.

The child therefore senses each Basic Experience through every part of his body, through every District. All of the Body Districts have "memories" of Strength, Control, Tenderness, and Relaxation. Naturally, each of them participates in their own specific way, with the modality that is specific to that age group. However, it is impossible to talk about Tenderness as being contained solely in the belly or the face: Tenderness is perceived and experienced by the child in all the areas of the body (although obviously to a greater and a lesser extent). That means the spine as well, despite its prevalently skeletal structure, and the legs, which do not merely have the purpose of keeping us standing up, and the head, which does more than just think.

In the same way, we cannot say that a given phase in development is characterised by the "supremacy" of one part of the body or one Function; and that only later will the individual's drives and Functions reach full integration and maturity.

All of the Functions are already present, as we have already seen, right from birth, and they are closely interconnected. They are *integrated* right from the very beginning. That is not to say that each of the Functions does not follow its own line of development or that it does not become more complex over time, taking on ever more varied and numerous nuances. What it means is that little children are not *incomplete*, there is no *immaturity* and there are no *jumps* in the child's functioning over time. On the contrary: there is a fundamental *continuity* in child development. A child is a *whole*, *complete* person right from the start, who gradually utilises *pre-existing, integrated* capacities in different situations and ever newer contexts; learning how to consolidate them and render them more flexible, in order to interact satisfyingly and successfully in the most disparate realities and to learn the rules of life.

Child Development, District by District

Analysing Development in each of the various Body Districts, one at a time, allows us to better understand these more recent points of view. Moreover, it allows us to deal with the theme of the *complexity* of Functional Development in a fairly simple way.

For the purposes of explanation, this text talks about Districts, but we must not think about them in isolation from one another. Human Beings must always be considered as an integrated whole. Despite this, referring to one District at a time helps us from a didactic point of view. It allows us to trace the individual's case history and to follow a single line of thought, highlighting more clearly what happens in each part of the body as we go through life, and what Basic Experiences the child is going through and consolidating with that part of the body.

The course of Functional Development can also be traced using two other criteria: either by tracking the Basic Experiences or using a strictly chronological order. The last chapter dealt with the reconstruction of child development according to the Basic Experiences. The chronological order can easily be deduced both from the reconstruction of child development by Districts and through that of the Basic Experiences, by referring to the age of the child. It has not been included in this book simply to avoid the risk of the reader having to jump back and forth between one District and another, from one Basic Experience and another.

The Districts

I have used the term District because I did not wish to refer to a single part of the body, fragmenting the individual's functioning still further. The District is rather a group of parts, zones, muscles, bone structures, tissues, nerve endings, movements, receptors, internal sensations: all linked with one another by one of their specificities. This specificity refers both to where the District is located within the body (the upper or lower body, behind or in front) and the way they function (visual perception, movement within space, grasping objects and relating to the surrounding world, digesting and metabolising and skeletal support).

Stratification within the Districts

We will report the most significant Basic Experiences that the child experiences through each District during the various phases of his development. In actual fact, each District lives the Experience in question "in its own way", participating with the potentialities and characteristics.

As the child gradually develops the effects of the various Basic Experiences, they accumulate within that District as experience, as a peripheral trace that remains over time. We can say that the effects and feelings of all the various Experiences are "stratified" in every single District, even though the word "stratification" does not do full justice to the process' complex nature in reality. All these traces are in fact present within that District *simultaneously*, bearing witness to the individual's relational experiences as a child; or at least this should be if the process has followed the natural, physiological course of growth.

This signifies, in a *practical* sense, that if the District in question is touched, moved, held, caressed, or squeezed, the individual *relives all the various episodes* in the childhood Basic Experiences of the Self each time. *All* the Experiences are potentially present within the individual. His whole body is alive and vital, participating *concurrently* in that given Experience; or rather, what has now become a consolidated Basic Capacity. Each District makes its own characteristic, specific contribution.

If, however, during development, the Experiences have not been undergone in a full, positive, open way; if they have not been helped and encouraged by adults, then the traces that are deposited will not be harmoniously connected to *all* the other Basic Experiences, but rather to the *alterations* that they have suffered and the distortions that they have formed. This means that when we touch or move a certain District, the first thing to emerge will be the *old traces* of the alterations that have become crystallised within that District, taking it over. The traces of these alterations remain near the surface and cover the deeper, more positive traces, hiding them deep down. As a result, the feelings that that type of touch or that Experience should recall do not emerge.

In one case, caressing the head of one patient produced an inescapable, dramatic sense of oppression, a reaction of intolerance. In another, lifting the patient's legs gave them an unbearable sadness and a frightening sense of fragility. One woman who attended a therapy group found that her spine always communicated a sense of danger and possible menace to her, even if the hands of the therapist were touching her to reassure her. For one patient, the legs, when massaged, were an unfailing source of anger and rage.

An individual should be able to have the *whole range* of sensations, feelings, and traces that that District has passed through during its development at their disposition. What happens instead is that the *alterations* grow like a tumour, until they have a predominant presence, suppressing the other traces.

Only the patient and gradual recovery of the suppressed traces, as well as any lacking or deficient Basic Experiences, will allow the individual to have access to functional processes that are once more full and varied, and modalities of interaction that are once more suited to the real situation.

Description of the Basic Experiences in the various Districts

The Districts that have been chosen for Functional development are those that cover a central role in child development, as well as in our personal experience in life.

For each of them, we have cited (with capital letters, in italic) the most important *Basic Experiences* that that particular District experiences, and to which it contributes with its own particular characteristics. The *age* of the child that the particular Basic Experience can be dated back to within that precise District is also cited (again in italic). The ages are obviously *approximate*, and they should only be used as a guideline: both because they vary from subject to subject, and because they can never be completely exact.

The head

The head has an extremely rich history of emotions and experience. It covers a fundamental role in the developmental history of the child even prior to birth. The individual essentially feels more *present* and alive in the head than in other parts of the body: the eyes are positioned in the head, and the impression that each of us has is that our Ego is looking out at the world from there, from "behind our eyes".

All too often, the head has been linked solely to Functions of a Cognitive nature, to mental Functions (erroneously considered to be the most important ones), and to so-called "superior" Functions. As we shall see, the history of the head is instead intensely characterised by experiences that are much more "emotive", as well as much more diversified and complex than we have normally been led to believe.

The crown

One of the most archaic Basic Experiences, already present in the *mother's womb*, can be traced to the feelings present in the top of the head: *Protection*. The head is continually in contact with the wall of the uterus, especially in the later months of pregnancy, in a condition that is without doubt one of total safety. Even after birth, however, the head seeks out reassuring and protective contact. Children love having their head stroked gently, and this form of contact has an almost hypnotic effect on newborns.

When a child is held lovingly in the arms of an adult, the greatest part of the contact is through the head: either curled up in the adult's lap or nestled in the crook of the arm, and an intense feeling of safety and protection is transmitted to it. Common Experience tells us that other mammals share this feeling of Protection with Man: dogs and cats stop, entranced, when a hand caresses their head.

Many parents have been able to observe that very small children often search out an angle in their little bed where they can nuzzle their head against a cushion or the pads on the walls of the cot. Later, children often hide their head under the covers to feel safe from "dangers" lurking in the dark. A hand on the head conventionally represents a gesture of protection in adults, too (unless negative feelings have prevailed in the stratification of emotions in the crown).

Tenderness is also present from the *beginning* in the history of the crown. A gentle caress is one of the most intense and touching gestures of tenderness that a newborn can receive, quite independently of the feeling of Protection described above.

Opening up to the World is also a *very archaic* sensation, and it corresponds to the specific event of our birth. The child makes way for itself, pushing with the head and he finally comes out into the world, opening himself up to a life rich with new stimuli and sensations. However, opening up to the world is not just a characteristic of birth, it remains afterwards too. It means making space for oneself, exploring, moving towards other places, and getting out of bed every morning with a bounce of vitality.

Another facet of the Basic Experience of Protection, experienced by the child at length during his first years of life, is *Being Held.* Every time that a child is lying in an adult's arms or sitting on a parent's lap, he feels the support, he can let go of his body and feel held; he feels the solidity of something that is holding him and preventing him from falling. The head is the principle protagonist in Being Held, because adults are very careful to support the baby's head seeing that he is unable to support it himself.

When a baby *Throws himself Backwards* with his head whilst in his mother's arms, sure that she will catch him and support him, the Basic Experience that he is going through is that of *Loosening Control* together with that of *Abandoning Ourselves.* This is a fundamental stage that begins at around *5–6 months of age*, and it is important because it contributes to stable construction of a sense of *Trust.* Later on in life, if this Basic Experience has been positive, the individual will be able to Throw himself into situations without knowing exactly where they will lead, or what will happen, now and again savouring the feeling of not having a precise objective, enjoying the fun of letting events lead him where they will.

It is this aspect, that of not seeing where events will lead, throwing oneself backwards, and the necessary presence of another person, that differentiates the latter Experience from another, apparently similar Experience: that of *Throwing Ourselves in Head First.* Throwing ourselves in headfirst denotes a clearly focussed movement with a precise objective, with energy and decision. A child already throws himself on his favourite toy at around *10–12 months of age.* Even as adults, as the phrase itself says, we "dive *head*first" into a new project, a new love affair, into a hobby or a passion, without reserve. The Basic Experiences that this touches are *Making Choices, Energy, Vitality,* and *Impetus.* Obviously, when this movement works well, there will not be the risk that the individual can fall in the wrong place and hurt himself because passion and Impetus are linked, as we said, to a good capacity to Make Choices.

During growth, each child experiences the exciting sensation of noticing how much he has grown in height; and he does so by measuring precisely *the height of the crown of his head* (sometimes leaving a pencil mark on a wall or a special ruler). "How tall am I?" is the question that a child of at least *4–5 years of age* asks, expressing the pleasure of growing, linking this to feeling his own *Authority,* his *Weight* as he grows, changing his relationship with other people. In this natural need of his for expansion, the growth of his body is perceived as one of the ways in which he feels *Appreciated,* as well as feeling that he is *Seen* more than before.

However, we must consider that a baby at around *one year old* already has fun *Lowering himself* and then *Rising up* suddenly on tiptoe up to the edge of his cot or playpen in order to be able to see the surroundings from a higher angle. We must not forget that a child's *"point of view"* is always that of looking up at the world from below, as if an adult were to find themselves in a world of giants, with giant furniture and giant objects. It is therefore natural that he should enjoy the sensation of suddenly becoming taller, looking at the world less and less from below and acquiring a *Different Perspective.*

If the pleasure of growing is not sustained and solicited by adults, it can gradually turn into the *Fear of Growing,* which, unfortunately, we often encounter in children of over *6–7 years of age* who refuse to abandon (or who once more adopt) the actions and the way of talking, eating and moving of very little children. Sometimes this fear can become a bona fide fear of becoming an adult.

A further nuance of the child's relationship with their stature comes into play when children *jump, hurling themselves as high as they can.* At the beginning, at *2–3 years of age*, the child jumps on his bed, with the pleasure of jumping as high as possible, surpassing the limit of his own head; and then, later, he does the same in all games that involve jumping, together with the component of pure pleasure and excitement transmitted to him by *Play* and *Impetus.*

The first impulse relating to *Opening up to the World* later becomes *Making Space for Ourselves* (at over *5–6 years of age*), and then it evolves still further, becoming the capacity to go out into the world and deal with situations using *Strength* and *Determination.*

Determination, which is crucial if we are to reach our goals or carry out projects, can become altered negatively, becoming *Stubbornness*, i.e. carrying on inexorably on our own path, "head down", without adequately evaluating or modifying what we want to achieve *(5 years and over).*

The crown of the head does not always conserve positive sensations. In patients who come to therapy, we sometimes find that one of the first traces that manifests itself, in the most superficial part of the stratified "memory", is an unpleasant reaction to an exaggerated touch of control *(Being Stopped)*: above all when the child starts to be too autonomous and enterprising *(5–6 years).* The adult's hand is placed on the top of the child's head almost as if stopping the child's growth, as if to say "you're young, what do you know *(Devaluation)*? Stop what you're doing and keep to your place." When this experience becomes even more negative, the child develops a feeling of *Being Put Down and Oppressed.*

Several patients could not bear even the slightest caress to their heads. They reacted with anger and irritation, sometimes even a violent sensation of oppression, because they were unable to perceive the tender and affectionate gesture for what it really was.

The forehead

Although similar to the feelings experienced by the crown, the experiences belonging to the forehead have particular nuances and characteristics of their own. Even though the forehead is a small part of the head, it remains, however, a meeting point for facial expressions, touch, and contact: we place our hands on our forehead extremely frequently (often without exactly intending to).

It is common to see a newborn baby try to rub his forehead affectionately against his parent's neck or shoulder, when held in a parent's arms or held standing up on an adult's lap with his thorax against the adult's chest. This is a first, archaic *Contact*, with no aim other than contact for its own sake. It is also a first, archaic experience of *Leaning on others*. We can also glimpse a need to snuggle up, to settle themselves in order to be able to enjoy the Contact completely.

If we move closer to another person and we go as far as to touch them *forehead to forehead*, it means entering into their intimate, private space, overcoming the distances established in the rules governing normal social relationships. Entering into another person's private space immediately provokes a condition of vigilance, which can develop in one of two ways: the individual either rejects the invasion, or else he will accept the other person, sharing feelings of enormous closeness, warmth and profound intimacy. Intimate, private space is delineated by a limit, beyond which it becomes impossible to keep a watch over the other person's movements with our eyes. For this reason, we either prevent the other person from entering into this space, or we accept the other person trustingly, modifying the way we perceive them: from visual watchfulness at a distance to a form of contact that is made up of tactile sensations, smells and warmth.

The forehead is an area that makes an increase in temperature evident straightaway; both when the individual has a fever, or when there is an imbalance and the upper body is overloaded. However, it is also the part that most experiences a sense of *Relief* when cooled. When a parent passes their hand on the child's forehead, it produces a sense of relief and serenity. The child gives himself a sense of relief and serenity by *placing his own hand on his forehead* and on his face (at around *6–7 months*).

A newborn baby's face is an incredible site for movements and expressions that change suddenly, but also openly and clearly, hiding nothing. When the forehead and the eyebrows move upwards, what he is manifesting is *Amazement*, a faculty that the newborn already possesses at just a *few months old*. Just as he already possesses and experiences waves of *Worry* which are painted on his face when he wrinkles or furrows his brow. As an adult, the wrinkles that form there will be called "worry lines", a name that harps back to precisely this phenomenon.

After the child has already learnt to walk, when relationships of "strength" with his surroundings start to play a part in his life, holding his head high (at around *5–6 years of age*) becomes an important feeling of *Pride* and *Assertiveness.* Walking with our *"head up"* and knowing how to *"face up to"*, others are common expressions that denote that we are not afraid of other people, that we do not have to lower our eyes, rather we can raise them as a sign of open challenge to the other person, a sign of not having anything to be ashamed of. Facing up to Others does not mean being unpleasant, it means being confident, sure of ourselves. It means we are willing to measure ourselves with others and we need not to have to put up with things that are imposed on us.

On the other hand, lowering our head gives the impression of *(at 6–7 years old)* the presence of a *Defeat*, lowering our eyes, not being able to Face up to difficult situations or other people. It reveals a state of *Sullenness* that can at times run very deep, especially as the child gets older.

Yet there is a further trace, when the brow is lowered, that is not negative: it is a way of not being distracted by looking around, concentrating, and gathering our thoughts to be able to *Reflect* better *(5–6 years).* Sometimes the hand is placed on the forehead as if to help us to think, to help this pause in which we gather our thoughts to help us to act more decisively afterwards.

The eyes

The eyes have always been considered to be the "windows of the soul". They are one of the most important ways we have of communicating with others, expressing ourselves and transmitting our feelings; but they are also our means of looking at the world, understanding it and keeping track of it. The eyes transmit the most varied and meaningful images, but they start to do so only after birth. They represent a resource that widens the horizon of our sensations and pleasure when we pass from the enclosure in our mother's womb to the vast, multiform, and multicoloured outside world.

Contrary to what was thought a few years ago, we now know that the newborn child can see right from the beginning. He can distinguish colours and forms to the point that he already expresses his very own preferences.

A recent experiment has demonstrated that the newborn is even sensitive to “beauty”, reacting positively to harmonious faces with a pleasant shape and negatively to frowning faces that are distorted or disharmonious.

Even if sight is not the only tool that the child uses to “take possession” of the world around him (because touch, smell, taste, sounds and internal body sensations are absolutely not to be ignored), it is, however, one of the most important ones, because it is using precisely this tool that the child learns, intentionally *Imitating* adults *(5–6 months)*. It is also through his sense of Sight that the child *Absorbs* the mechanisms of the world around him *(3–4 months)*. The Function of Absorbing is of an incomparable importance, given that the sensations that are absorbed are then impressed within him, leaving intense traces within the various levels of the Self.

Right *from the beginning*, the eyes are capable of transmitting a profound sense of *Relaxation/Loosening of Control*, when they *half close*, gently, without effort. The eyelids are lowered to “half mast”, sometimes even before the child falls asleep, or after having been breastfed until full, as a profound sign of *Letting Go.*

If, on the contrary, the eyes are *tightly closed*, then the muscles are in action. If we see someone with their eyes tightly shut, then we can be sure that they are not in a state of abandonment, but rather quite an intense state of activation.

Closing our eyes whilst awake generally represents a desire to shut out the outside world, an *Opposition*, a wish for *Separation*, or a moment of *Closure* that can also be associated with *Anger*. The newborn starts to live this Experience in a more direct and conscious way after the *4th–5th month.*

Sometimes, when patients who are lying on the couch are invited to completely “let go”, they instead keep their eyes open and alert, because of the presence of an excessive *Control* that they are unable to loosen. Other times, the eyelids close but they are subject to continuous fluttering, i.e. continuous, tiny **movements** whereby the eyelid opens and closes continuously in rapid succession. The eyelids tend to open, and the subject’s will automatically closes them, in a sort of “battle” between Control and Letting Go.

Right from a very young age, (from the *first few months of life*), the eyes exert a continual *Vigilance* of what is going on around the baby. Very soon *(2–3 months)*, the child starts to follow everything that enters into his field of vision intentionally *(Control)*. The phrase “keep your eyes peeled” refers to just this state of alert.

However, following our surroundings with our eyes well open does not just imply a pure state of Control. It also implies something else: i.e. curiosity, discovery, and wonderment *(Sensations, Amazement)*. In this case, the eyes "dilate", they *open wide* in amazement, in the joyous surprise of discovering objects, people, colours, the pleasure of seeing new things and returning to known objects of which the child has become fond. This takes place from the *first months* of life. Later *(3 years)*, Amazement can take on a nuance of *Incredulity* through the eyes, as the eyebrows assume an inclination characteristic of perplexity and silent questioning.

There in another important motivation that induces us to open our eyes completely: the presence of a sudden danger. Our eyes open wide to allow us the widest field of vision possible allows us a much more intense, and even spasmodic, Control so that nothing escapes our attention. Opening our eyes wide indicates *Fear*, or even *Terror*. The frightened look of a newborn when suffering a sudden colic (from *the 2nd–3rd month onwards*): he feels something strange and painful within his own body.

Many writers use the words **moist** and **shining eyes** to indicate that a character has a vivid, active, and fundamentally earnest expression. Today we know that a condition of vagotonia, or profound serenity, moistens the eyes; *Tenderness* makes the *eyes soft and watery*. In the phrase "shining eyes", it almost seems as if the emotion of sweetness can reach and surround the other person almost "physically": it is something that we perceive at a concrete level. An intentionally *Tender* expression is present in the newborn right from the *first months of life*: it is the gaze that he uses, for example, to enter into contact with his mother when she is breast feeding him.

Sadness can also moisten the eyes, but the facial expression that accompanies the look is much darker with respect to the "luminosity" that pierces Tenderness. On the other hand, there is little to wonder at if there are similarities between the two emotional states: we must not forget that Sadness has a large component of Tenderness towards ourselves, which has nothing to do with despair.

Some people can be described as having *"laughing eyes"*. In reality, these people have an unusual light in their eyes. This light expresses *Joy*. When children are well, their eyes burst with Happiness. This can be observed in a newborn of *2–3 months*: the eyes smile, and with them, the entire face.

A person's eyes can express a *Vivacity* and intensity that indicate a general state of vitality even when they are not happy. Often, however, people lose this vivid expression over the course of life's vicissitudes and the eyes become "dull", opaque, as if they were without life or energy.

When we are too worried, our eyes lose their vital dynamism and the eyebrows and forehead take on a corrugated appearance. In *very young babies,* (up to a *few months old*) the eyes are *hidden* by the wrinkles of the eyebrows and eyelids, as if to *Protect themselves* from indiscrete looks by others. Later, a wrinkled brow comes to reflect a genuine sense of *Worry*.

Whilst Opposition and Anger are generally expressed with the eyes tight shut (a "blind" rage), *Hate* is also expressed with the eyes wide open, but this time the expression is hard, stone cold, and focussed on a precise person. Children attain this "nasty" expression at around *7–8 months old* because at this stage the child starts to feel a sudden (although brief and temporary) urge to destroy the person who has made him angry.

Strength also starts to be expressed facially at around *the same period.* The eyes express Strength and *Determination.* They turn towards the other person without hesitation, holding the other person's gaze in an intense challenge, and they channel all their energies into their vision.

If we want to stop a child doing something forbidden, we do not have to shout at them, run after them or physically check them: often just a look is enough, as long as it expresses Strength, intensely and decisively. It is a well-known fact that there are a whole series of laws and social hierarchies among mammals that are based on looks. If we stare at a dog at length, with Strength, he will not be able to sustain our gaze: he will lower it and he will calmly submit himself to our will. On the other hand, gorillas see a direct stare as a dangerous threat to their social standing.

For our attention to be affective, it does not necessarily have to be spasmodic and exaggeratedly vigilant and concentrated. There is a type of attention that is called *Relaxed Attention.* Our eyes are not concentrated on the thing that we have to control. Our gaze is not is not fixed and hardened. Instead, it casually moves around us, resting gently at several points in our field of vision, without anxiety or fear. We can drive a car watching the road with Relaxed Attention: our driving will be much safer and effective than if we were watching the road spasmodically, worried about a possible sudden skid, another car that might run into us or an unexpected obstacle.

When we drive with Relaxed Attention, we can cover large distances almost without realising it; and what's more, we will have had a much greater capacity to deal with unexpected problems because our gaze will have swept calmly around our **entire** field of vision without stopping in a hardened and restricted way on only a few certain details or sectors. This can be demonstrated: with a relaxed gaze we are much more able to notice what is going on at the edges of our field of vision, even if the images are not in focus as they would be in the central part of the fovea.

Children are well aware of this type of Relaxed Attention when, calmly and serenely, (at *3–4 months old*) they lie in their parents' arms or in their crib, letting their gaze sweep softly all around them, without any precise direction and without concentrating on anything in particular.

The eyes also allow us a pause in our Attention, whether it is Relaxed, or rigid, when they "stop" looking even though they are open. In older children, *(2–3 years)* the eyes acquit this Function of *Loosening Control/Relaxation*, getting lost in the distance. The ocular muscles completely let go for a short time; the two axes of the individual's gaze become parallel and he stares off into infinity, he no longer focuses on anything, the eyes do not adjust their focus and they do not concentrate on the objects that they encounter. We actually see double, because each eye sees the objects independently. There are printed images that are designed in such a way that we can only see their 3-D content if we let our gaze wander off into infinity. In these pauses for Relaxation, the child stops, he starts *"daydreaming"*, his thoughts float and his attention stops for a minute: this has a regenerative effect, as if the child "switched off" for a moment.

The mouth

The history of the mouth is one rich with sensations, expressions, emotional nuances, relationships with the world and the people around us.

One of the *oldest* experiences is that of *Letting Go*: the mouth half opens softly when the newborn relaxes after having been breastfed, or when he is daydreaming in his cot, full up and a little bewildered; or when he is letting himself drift off to sleep. When we Let Go, the mouth is never closed because the muscles are loosened, the jaw slightly open. A mouth that is tightly shut indicates that the jaw muscles are in action and that the individual is tense.

Taking and *Filling oneself* through the mouth are also experiences that originate *from birth*: suckling the mother's breast.

Just as opening the mouth is a sign that the newborn wants to be filled, closing the mouth is the *oldest* signal for *Refusal*, together with the lateral rotational or upwards movement of the head to move the mouth away from the breast, the bottle or the spoon. Shaking our heads to say "no" originates in this very form of Refusal in newborn children, and it is for this reason that it is universally understood among many, very different cultures.

Later in the life of the child *(a few months old)*, Refusal using the mouth assumes more conscious and active connotations, almost stating *Opposition*. Later still (at *2–3 years of age*), this can become authentic *Obstinacy*. The mouth shuts tightly against the mouthful offered by the adult; but it also opens to speak and explain reasonably what the child is thinking.

The mouth, then, performs another important Function in the vital exchange with the world: *Letting Out*. The *newborn* already regurgitates milk when he has taken too much, when it sits heavily on his stomach or when he has too much acid in his stomach. But right from birth he also Lets sounds Out of his mouth, which manifest his moods: pleasure, need, suffering. In these two archaic experiences lie the roots of two major Functions of the mouth: that of *Throwing Out* what is not good, and that of *Expressing* subjective sensations to the surrounding world.

Throwing Out can evolve into the Spitting out of everything that is negative, this time with more intentional connotations, and a more direct focus against the other person. At *three years old*, this can become an authentic *Contempt*. Disgust is expressed with a contortion of the mouth similar to that caused when we have tasted something really unpleasant, with a ritualised gesture and a hint at vomiting and spitting.

Children smile *very early on* in their lives: the mouth, in this way, expresses an experience of *Happiness*, and it opens even more in laughter, when there is a burst of genuine *Merriment* (from around *3–4 months onwards*).

Very early indeed, the mouth assumes the soft expression of *Tenderness*. It is slightly open, but this openness has nothing to do with repose or Letting Go, rather this expression is typical of contact with the mother, with her skin, her taste.

Disappointments are also printed on the child's face when the corners of the mouth are turned down, expressing bitterness. At first, this is due to real Disappointments, and then later, as the child grows *(8–9 months)*, due to imagined Disappointments (or perplexities).

The child's initial indistinct and transitory discontentment, at *10–12 months old*, is increasingly associated with the latter. The child becomes increasingly *Bitter* and *sulks* more and more, indicating that the child does not easily forget his animosity and disapproval.

Genuine *Anger* is shown, on the other hand, by a half-open mouth with gritted teeth, as if threatening the other person, as if to indicate that the individual is ready to attack and bite *(3–4 years)*. If the Anger is buried, it becomes *suppressed Rancour*, and at that point it only appears in the permanent contraction of the jaw, and in the expression of the mouth, which becomes very thin, almost to the point where it disappears. The mouth takes on an expression that is *hard* as stone and seemingly inscrutable. What it is, is in fact a contrived *"refusal to smile"*, i.e. the mouth is straight, clearly demonstrating that there is absolutely no chance of curving into a smile, which would communicate, on the contrary, affinity, tenderness, and friendship.

Open *Aggressiveness* lies, on the other hand, in activity: a shouting voice and words aimed to hurt. The voice can also express stronger feelings of Opposition and Anger, and it can directly express *Rage*. For the same reason, if Rage and Aggressiveness are continually suppressed in children, then the voice can be restrained, suffocated, almost as if it had been "swallowed", and lose its characteristic sonority, as well as its capacity to express emotions and feelings in a vibrant and open way.

The Shoulders

When the newborn is being bathed, the adult holds him around the shoulders, using a very firm grasp of the arm and hand. The child's neck, back and shoulders rest on the adult's arm whilst the hand grasps the other shoulder. The child feels that he is held safely and he lets himself go to the pleasure of being immersed in water.

Being Held is therefore one of the oldest, but also the most habitual, experiences that are stratified within the shoulders over their long history. Indeed, every time that the child is lifted from his cot or his pram, then once again it is the shoulders that are grasped firmly in the adult's hands. The child can therefore Be Held by the shoulders, but he can also *Be Taken Up* by the shoulders, which the child experiences in a slightly different way, with slightly different sensations. Whilst Being Held has more protective connotations, Being Taken Up implies more the joyous sensation of being lifted up to be held in the arms of the adult, being pulled closer to the parent.

Much later (at around *5–6 years of age*), this experience can evolve into an authentic sensation of *Being Suppressed.* Parents hold their children by the shoulders to "stop them" when they have gone over the top, to make them understand that they have to listen. A slight tug on the shoulders recalls the child to a state of attention and serves to stop a short circuit of tantrums, complaints, and excessive opposition.

On the other hand, shaking or shrugging his shoulders can be a signal of *Opposition* in the child, as if shrugging off the adult's grasp *(6–7 years of age).* In this instance, there is not only movement but also a type of intensity, a certain Strength behind it.

Shaking one's shoulders as a sign of Opposition, or quite simply to demonstrate that the child "doesn't agree" comes from a much more archaic and simple movement *(3–4 years)*: that of twisting the body and shoulders, more to "avoid" the adult's grip, rather than actually free himself from it, to remove themselves from the adult's will. Once again, the shoulders express the most complete form of *Rejection.* This happens when the child turns his back on the other person, completely turning round to express opposition.

At around *4–5 years of age*, young children learn how to *shrug* their shoulders to express *Doubts* and perplexities. They also do so to imply that what happened is not their responsibility, as if to say, "it's nothing to do with me". This movement is intentional and conscious, but its origin lies in a similar movement, this time uncontrolled and subconscious: that of *raising the shoulders* to hide our head between them, to avoid being seen, to *Disappear (3–4 years of age).* When children feel uncomfortable in a particular situation, they are ashamed, or they are not used to strangers, then they tend to try to make themselves as invisible as possible. They almost draw themselves into a "shell", raising their shoulders to hide themselves.

The shoulders can express Strength, but they can also express a Loss of Heart. Straight, rather than drooping shoulders transmit energy and an evident impression of *Strength and Force.* This expression becomes complete and explicit after *2–3 years of age.* Strength is actually transmitted externally through the shoulders, because it is the *shoulders* that impart strength to the movement of the arms. Pushing, striking, and pulling are all arm movements that start from the shoulder in order to have enough Strength.

On the other hand, *Bearing Weight* is more a form of strength based on *Resistance*, on the capacity to sustain, which ought only to appear in late child childhood *(10–11 years)*, but which is all too often a precocious attitude that children are forced to adopt when there is no-one in their life capable or willing to carry all the weight and responsibility so that they don't have to.

Many patients exhibit this Strength of Resistance more than active Strength, which would allow them to actually change the situations they are faced with. They put up with everything; they "bear the weight of the world on their shoulders".

Shoulders which can no longer bear to "carry weight" *Sag*, they droop downwards, as if to indicate that they no longer have the strength to carry others, to endure, to carry on as before (at around *7–8 years of age*). There is a very eloquent phrase that Italians use to indicate *Loss of Heart*, fatigue and admitting defeat, they say "my arms just fell": a clear reference to this phenomenon.

Raising the shoulders, holding them up, and therefore "holding ourselves up", is a way of gathering our energy, producing a pleasant level of excitement, as well as feeling more alert and attentive. Children already show this characteristic at *4–5 years of age*. The capacity to *Mobilise towards the upper body* is useful for *"gearing ourselves up"*. However, this same action can become excessive and chronic. It may become an exaggerated development of the "higher", intellectual capacities, and a state of alertness, which soon becomes a laborious and stressful state of control.

Just as there are situations in which children hide their heads by raising their shoulders, there are others in which they tend to close their chest and themselves by *curving their shoulders forwards*. This movement is the opposite of when we open up with our shoulders thrown back and our chests open. The movement in question is an expression of *Withdrawal*, of an, at times, excessive modesty, and it appears on the scene for the first time from *6–7 years* onwards.

This attitude can also be observed in girls who are developing breasts. If they are not given adequate support at this delicate stage of puberty, they may feel uncomfortable and embarrassed about their development.

When the shoulders are held back, straight (further back than the expression of Strength), they represent the opposite of Withdrawal, i.e. *Overconfidence*. They display the wish to face the world, show their worth, indicating that they are not afraid, from as early as *4–5 years of age*. It is no surprise that this attitude is typical of the military world.

However, the shoulders can also suppress Strength and Overconfidence, becoming hardened and immobile. In so doing, the child avoids letting out their anger, striking out, entering into conflict, or pushing. *Suppressed anger* is stratified in the muscles of the shoulders and the back in the form of a "trace", as if someone were restraining all the child's aggressive impulses from behind, as if a person were holding the child and checking him. In reality, it is the child himself. He learns to repress his aggressive feelings and movements *(9–10 years)* despite himself, because he feels his anger is too strong, it is censured by adults, it is considered to be "bad" and destructive.

Once again, if the child's functional processes are blocked and altered by his surroundings, then these alterations will be deeply carved into his body and his life.

The Arms and Hands

The arms and hands are the part of the body that we most use to enter into active contact with others, to alter relationships, to express affection or negativity without the mediation of language, to get closer to others, to move them away, to hold them, caress them or even to hit them. They are also the part of the body that we most use to grasp objects, discover, feel, manipulate, and alter our surroundings. Consequently, they perform a central role in that part of the child's relationship with his surroundings that is conscious and intentional; and as such, they take on importance later in the child's development.

However, the story of the arms and hands starts very early on, with the experience of *Contact*: the serene, tender Contact that the newborn experiences when he moves his arms in the direction of his mother to touch her face, or her breasts while she is feeding him.

Much later, (at *2–3 years of age*) this archaic form of Contact becomes *Being With*, being together: holding hands, or walking or sitting arm in arm with our parents, our sibling or our first nursery school friends. Contact with our arms and hands symbolises an important "tie", feelings of *Closeness*, *Alliance* and love, which preserve this evocative power all our lives. In numerous primitive peoples, deep attachments were sealed with rituals uniting the wrists (at times even letting blood to form an even deeper bond).

One of the first, archaic movements of the arms (in the *first* months) is simply an expression of pure *Pleasure*. Lying in his cot or in his mother's arms, the newborn lets his *hands wander* around him with no particular aim, for the Pleasure of moving them, to explore their movement, and to perceive the agreeable sensations that this produces.

Almost at *the same age*, this form of manual exploration takes on another connotation: that of *touching*, seeing what's going on around them, sensing different tactile sensations and discovering objects and people. Stretching out the arms and hands becomes a gesture of discovery, of *Curiosity* towards the world around them. The gesture becomes conscious and directed, even though not yet fully or completely.

The first aggressive movements start very early on. The child already uses his arms and hands to *push* the adult away when he is in their arms, to *Distance* himself and to make room, at *6–7 months* old. This is not a movement of Opposition or Anger, but simply one of *Original Strength*, or *Gentle Strength*, aimed at opening up the world and making room for himself. Aside from pushing away his mother, the child may move his arms around in the space surrounding his body, as if stretching. By doing this, the child is *Opening himself*, taking possession of the world around him. This starts at *5–6 months old.*

Gentle Strength is also expressed when the child *Takes*: grasping objects *(3–4 months old)* or Taking people, drawing them in towards him or cuddling them. Before the child Takes, however, he *Stretches forwards*, with excitement and happiness, towards the object or person he desires: to take them, but also to be taken up into their arms.

Later (at *a year an a half*), we see the first signs of *Assertiveness*: the child uses his hands and arms to hit a surface, his legs or his hands, with a fair amount of strength and determination. In this case, the child isn't really demonstrating anger or aggression towards the other person, but rather the necessity to assert himself, as is the case when we find ourselves saying things like, "That's the way it is" or "I know when I'm right!"

Lastly, at *(2–3 years of age)* we develop genuine *Strength*. The Strength in question is not a bad or destructive Strength, however, but rather a *calm Strength*. Strength manifests itself in the firmness of the muscles in the arms and hands, in movements where the child asserts himself over others, where he grasps objects or people, and where he pushes people or objects away from himself or his life.

Intentionally *hitting* in order to *Attack* also starts at around *2 years of age.* This can take the form of a slap (more affectionate) or a punch (a harder and angrier manifestation). The child can hit out in cold blood and with precision, or in spite; or he can lash out randomly, in all directions at once, giving in completely to his sensations and emotions, without control.

A hand can offer Friendship or it can Threaten. An *open hand*, palm upwards is an unmistakeable sign, even for animals, of *Peace*, non-belligerence and friendly contact. The roots of this "movement" lie in the more archaic movement of seeking Contact, but its intentional use as a sign of Peace appears at around *5–6 years old.* The palm is turned upwards to indicate that there is no intention to hit (it is impossible to aim a slap or a punch from below). The open palm also shows that we are not holding a weapon, and invites the other person to place their hand, or their muzzle, in the case of an animal, in ours, for a tender and friendly contact.

On the other hand, a *closed fist*, which children learn to brandish at around *4–5 years old,* is clearly a sign of *Threat*, a gesture that reproduces the act of aggression. The act of aggression can in fact be carried out using the hand the fist, or with a weapon that the fist represents (such as a club or another object).

However, the closed fist is in fact a much older gesture *(2–3 years)* that the child uses when seized by a wave of *Anger*. It is not yet a threat as such, but rather a movement that expresses the wish to attack the adult, but which instead becomes a form of suppression. The fists, in this case, are pointed towards the floor and the child shakes them in impotent rage.

When we feel that we have lost, that we cannot make it, the *arms* collapse downwards as a sign of *Resignation (5–6 years old).* This is a form of Letting Go, of halting a state of activation, but it is not serene. The arms fall downwards, inert and without energy. We stop making any effort; it is no use anyway. Children normally experience this state when they perceive that there is really nothing to be done. Their vital energy does not allow them to admit defeat easily. However, it can occur that discouragement takes the upper hand over children's natural Assertiveness, Strength, and energy. In this case, the arms lose muscle tone. They flop downwards, giving up.

The legs

Some of the experiences and movements of the legs are similar to those of the arms, and some are different. However, these movements are always characterised by the fact that they are less intentional, less directed, and less linked to the regulation of emotional and social relations.

The history of the legs starts with the soft, gentle, and protective experience of *Being Held* (from the *first months of life*). The newborn is supported not just beneath his head, but also his legs. When the baby is changed, refreshed, and cleaned, his little legs are raised and Held. A lot of *Tenderness* always emerges when we hold a person's legs. If a patient has negative feelings about the therapist holding his legs, then this means that something critical and difficult happened in his life *before the age of two.*

An *aimless movement of the legs*, i.e. moving them around in different directions whilst lying in the crib, exploring, and letting them wander, appears very precociously in the life of the child *(the first few months).* Part of it is the pure and simple *Pleasure* of movement, and part of it is *Curiosity* towards meeting with and feeling everything around us. At times, the movement of the legs is frenetic, fast, and *Happy*: the child laughs and beats their legs on the walls of his crib *(4–5 months).*

This may sound strange, but the legs are one of the parts of the body where we most experience feelings of *Intimacy* with ourselves *(1–2 years).* When the child lies on his back or on his side, with his legs *curled up* to one side or towards his chest, he experiences a feeling of being in his own company, with his own feelings and emotions. This position becomes a frequent expression in little girls and boys who have relational difficulties or who suffer from intense shyness. In group therapy sessions, there are sometimes adults who usually sit with their legs curled up in front of them, hugging them tightly with their arms.

We can trace the development of Strength in successive and gradual phases in the legs, just like we did with the arms. The child starts his first movements of *Gentle Strength* with *Original Strength* (at *3–4 months*), pushing against his mother's belly with his legs while she is changing him. This is not Opposition, it is not aimed at pushing his mother away: it is a joyous and tender movement (even if there is already a bit of Strength), not specifically directed against his mother. There is a movement of pleasure in *clearing space* ahead of him, opening up space in the world around him.

This first pushing movement becomes *Going*, *Walking*, moving from one place to another (from *2 years and upwards*). If a patient has an attack during therapy whereby his legs collapse from under him, then we know that this is a very old trace, going back to before he was 2 years old.

As his Strength grows, the child uses it to start *Standing Up* on his feet *(at a year and a half old)* using the same pushing capacity that he has been developing. He learns to take his first few steps, although wobbly and uncertain (at *2 years*), with the emotion of being able to *Go*, of being able to move around in space as he wishes.

Lastly, full *Strength* appears in the child at *3 years*: in the ability to *Stand Squarely on his Legs*, in the ability to *Push away* what he doesn't like, in being able to rely on his own legs every time he needs to *Move*. When a patient desperately tries to grasp the floor with his feet rather than standing squarely on his legs, it indicates that something did not go well at that age.

Another experience that comes as a result of that initial Strength, that first Pushing, is the child's discovery that he can *raise* and *lower himself* on his legs; i.e. standing in his cot and holding on to the bars *(10 months)*. The child discovers, with joy and *Amazement* that he can *Alter his Viewpoint* at will. When he lowers himself, objects disappear behind the railing, table, or chair, but when he pushes himself upwards with his legs, he discovers that his view widens considerably. He discovers the pleasure of discovering objects that he had not yet seen, or the same objects from a different angle, from higher up.

This up and down motion constitutes the basis for a later development in the movement of *Joy*: i.e. the fun of *Jumping* up and down, experiencing an upward surge and the feeling of "flying" *(3–4 years of age)*.

Walking also has several phases in its development, each of which has very different emotive connotations: *Running*, reaching considerable speeds, springing unexpectedly, and speeding up suddenly. The child reaches this stage through a series of stages, first of which is the *Crawling* stage, which at times is very fast indeed, with no aim other than to enjoy the speed itself. Later, *(5–6 years)* the child will reach higher speeds on foot as well, again with no other aim than the sheer pleasure of going fast. Apart from the fact that running allows the child to develop Strength and Power, as well as future sporting activities, springing and accelerating, represent the expression of *Joy* itself. They represent a "wave" of *Happiness*: little explosions of contentment.

Many people have tired and tense legs. They are, in fact, a genuine "deposit" for irritability, negative feelings, and stress, right from an early age.

We start with sensations of *Angriness*, with *Tantrums*, where the legs move restlessly, sometimes even frenetically. This movement is very different from babies' first casual exploring movement: it arises from frustration, irritation, and intolerance *(2 years old)*.

There is, on the other hand, an experience that originates and develops from the basis of Original Strength, and that is when children *Dig their Heels in (3–4 years)*. The child plants his feet firmly on the ground, pushing with his heels, as if refusing to move a single step. In this Pushing and Digging in his Heels, the child is sending out a strong message of disagreement, the refusal to move or carry out a particular action.

Digging in our Heels can become a bona fide *Opposition* towards the adult. Not only that, but it can also become *Stubbornness*: always saying "no!" never wanting to change opinion, a more exaggerated, closed and inflexible form of "digging their heels in" *(4–5 years)*.

The first experiences of Strength, of a serene and peaceful Pushing become *Moving Away* from others in a clear, direct, and intentional way *(2 years)*. As the child's Strength grows, it can be united with Anger and the legs can be used to *Hit (4 years)*, kicking others, defending himself or to attack others without reserve, either with the toes or with the arch of the foot. Children do this with determination and effectiveness.

The back

The back is perhaps the part of the body with the longest and most complex history. The back is extremely sensitive, with a marked capacity to absorb a wide and very varied range of experiences, even though it is an area of the body that is mostly made up of bone.

The spine plays a role of primary importance in mammals, too. Dogs and cats very much love having their back stroked; but beware of stroking a cat the wrong way, from the tail towards the head: it will arch its back and become angry because this is a movement that "charges" rather than pleasantly relaxing it. Bears often rub their backs on tree trunks with evident satisfaction. Cubs readily curl themselves up with their back against their mother, in contact with a warm and welcoming surface.

One of the most archaic experiences deposited in the back, therefore, is precisely this feeling of *Being Contained.* Right from inside the *mother's womb*, the spine experiences the sensation of being welcomed, cocooned and protected. Later, too, there are many situations in which the child feels pleasantly Contained: in his parent's arms, curled up under his mother or in his bed.

It is the back that experiences sensations of contact the most during the first years of life. The child lies on its back for many hours a day, and when it is held in an adult's arms it is for the most part lying on its back. For this reason, *Being Held*, *Support*, and *Just Being* (lying in the crib without doing anything other than enjoying the repose, doing nothing) are all experiences belonging to the *very first months.*

Being Lifted Up is also a very *archaic* experience of the spine, because when a child is picked up the adult grasps him by the back. Being Lifted Up has a more joyous connotation than just Being Held, however, because the child feels himself raised into the air, he sees his mother or father's face zooming towards him in the anticipation of being held in their arms.

If a baby is Held correctly then he will be able to *Trust himself to* the adult without fear. A comfortable sensation of *Trust* will develop in the spine: a sensation of being able to abandon himself to the adult's hands. This sensation becomes more present and conscious at around *4–5 months.* It is thanks to this Trust that the child can allow himself to play the game of *Throwing himself backwards* blindly *(5–6 months)*, without even looking where he will fall, safe in the knowledge that his parents will catch him, confident that he can come to no harm.

This sense of security can be undermined if the child's back does not feel adequately supported in the adult's arms, making the child feel that there is a risk he may fall. In this case, *Fear* starts to embed itself in the child's spine: a feeling that he might *"fall"* backwards, a sense of emptiness behind him *(3–4 months).* The vague threat of *Impending danger* that many people sense behind their backs is a direct derivation from this first danger. Little by little, this negative experience can intensify during the infant's childhood if he is subject to reprimands, fits of anger or the threat of being smacked. This can lead to a bona fide sensation of the possibility of *Being Attacked from Behind* (at around *1 to 1 and a half years of age*). Many patients report having had the same nightmare when they were small (or even as grown-ups) where they have to escape because they are about to be attacked from behind.

There are other negative experiences that can be deposited in the muscles of the back, besides Fear and Threat. A child may start to accumulate *Anger* in his back muscles. The child may feel Anger towards adults if his basic needs are not sufficiently respected and looked after *(1 year old)*. Many animals also demonstrate Anger through their backs: if a cat arches its back with its fur standing on end, it is a clear warning signal.

The experience of *Anger* in the child's back does not necessarily remain open and free. Indeed, if the expression of this Anger has been obstructed by adults, then it may become *Suppressed* and compacted, as if it were frozen. We can *Endure* ill treatment, attacks, and exasperation from others through our backs. Children's backs often have to bear criticism and negativity, and they get through this experience of Enduring by curving their shoulders, just as they would do to defend themselves from real, physical blows *(4–5 years)*.

As a result of this Endurance, a child may develop a sense of *Oppression (7–8 years)*, which many backs preserve throughout their adult lives. Often, the traces of this experience are so strong that as soon as a hand is placed on the individual's back, he feels an immediate sense of Oppression.

However, the spine is, above all, a reservoir for positive experiences. *Just after the child is born*, the child feels the clear sensation of *Pleasure* as his back is touched and *caressed*. Baby-massage, developed by Eva Reich and further refined by our School, has never failed to surprise those who put it into practise. Newborn babies show huge pleasure, reacting with an unforeseen level of tranquillity and sensuality.

Tenderness is also a typical sensation of the back, even though it does not have "soft" parts like the belly does. The back is the seat of hugely intense shivers and currents of feeling, and it is the back that most feels Tender Contact, after the face and hands.

The back, however, is also the seat of Strength and muscle power. It contains our capacity to react and assert ourselves. There is one back movement that expresses all of this: that of *Throwing off* Oppression, shaking off negative feelings, freeing ourselves of the imaginary chains that bind us. We do this by suddenly throwing back our shoulders, straightening the spine, and opening ourselves up completely *(8–9 years of age)*.

The Belly

Unlike the back, the belly is the soft part of our bodies. In some ways, it is an intimate part: delicate and vulnerable. However, we discover once again that the experiences stored in this part of the body are not simply those related to soft, tender feelings. In each part of our bodies, a wide and multiform variety of experiences and emotions is stratified.

The most *archaic* experience of the belly is that of *Contact.* When a newborn baby is lying face down on his mother's belly, it is intense, Tender Contact that he is experiencing.

Naturally, this is also a first step towards *Sensing* ourselves, perceiving our own belly, with its internal movements, in intimate contact with our mother. It is only later that the child will learn to make *Contact with himself* on his own, by touching his belly with his hands. He will learn to listen to his internal Sensations, with his hands resting on his belly *(8–10 months).*

Right from the *first months of life*, the belly communicates something very important to the child: that of being *Full.* A full stomach, well visible in a newborn baby after being breast-fed, reassures the child, calming his desire to eat and producing a pleasant sense of relaxation. Eating problems are notoriously connected to alterations in the mechanism of Satiety, among other things.

Another problem associated with eating is when sudden *Pains*, colics, and diarrhoea frighten the newborn *(2–3 months).* Apart from the pain (which is not exactly pleasant), it is the sensation of *Dissolving* that frightens the child. The newborn feels that his insides are being sucked downwards, that he is becoming liquid, and that something is travelling through him without him being able to stop it, almost as if he were losing himself.

Later on *(6–7 months)*, the child will find that *lying face down* will be a completely natural way of *Protecting himself*, of keeping his most vulnerable parts safe, beneath the "shield" of his back. Many people continue to sleep face downward even as adults; some are even unable to get to sleep unless they adopt this position.

Together with Contact, one of the most central experiences of the belly during the *first months* is that of *Tenderness.* The belly has always been a symbol of softness, warmth, affection, and *Love.* It is only in recent times perhaps that a round tummy is seen as a negative attribute and fashion dictates that it should disappear completely. Until recently, though, soft "curves" in the belly were very much appreciated, and they expressed a pleasant sense of promise. Stroking the tummy is a very intimate gesture, full of Love and Tenderness. Stroking a child's belly will immediately calm him down.

The positive experiences relating to the belly do not end here. It is with our bellies that we perceive pleasant sensations of profound *Well-being* (from *5–6 months* onwards). This is not so much to do with feeling Full up as it is to do with what we feel when we are in a "state of grace", in which the entire organism is genuinely glowing.

The belly is also the seat of *Openness*. Lying *"face upwards"* means enjoying doing nothing, being *Idle*. The individual is not closed, but rather open to whatever or whoever might cross his path *(1–2 years)*. An open belly is only possible if the child has learnt to be calm and has a good level of contact with himself.

"Sticking one's belly out", on the other hand, is an open demonstration of *Confidence (4 years)*. By walking about showing his belly, the child is almost showing that he doesn't care what other people think, showing off his sense of well-being to everyone else, enjoying his own sense of fullness. In some cultures, a full belly is nothing to be ashamed of; rather it denotes pride, or a "show-off" attitude (especially in the men). It is seen as indicating economic well being and prosperity, not to mention social weight and power.

The other side of the coin is that a tummy that is *"held in"* is a sign that the individual is *Suppressing* their emotions, and above all trying to control their *Fear*. The individual holds his breath, the diaphragm is contracted: this is what sucks the belly inwards *(2 years of age)*. On the other hand, the sensation and effects of Fear are not new to the stomach. The child had already experienced colics, and that frightening sensation of dissolving and liquefying beyond his control. Fear reappears in the belly with the same characteristics. It is no coincidence that fear is associated with sudden bowel movement, or that the more colourful phrases associated with fear describe precisely this effect.

There are other occasions in which the belly is not soft. At times it hardens, when the individual is trying to *Work himself up* to doing something. This is indispensable in certain situations (from *5–6 years onwards*), and is a way of being strong, whatever happens. The belly is also, therefore, a source of Strength, but in this case, the strength is more passive, less active.

Anger can also involve the District of the belly, but what the child actually feels in his belly is not the genuine sensation of Anger, but rather its effects, in the form of intense sympathetic contractions at first, followed by parasympathetic ones (from *2–3 years* onwards). Once again, the symptoms are colics and diarrhoea, this time as a result of Anger. These effects are not immediate, rather they follow on when the Anger is over and it has been "digested", when the body lets go following the strong contractions described above.

Another negative sensation that we feel in our stomachs is when we have eaten too much. The sensation of being Full goes from being a pleasant sensation to being a condition of *Swollenness* and discomfort. The belly is *Upset* from too much food and is unable to break it up and digest it. This does not happen in newborns because the self-regulatory capacity is most certainly still intact. Later, however, *(2–3 years)* the impulse to eat can become separated from physiological hunger and the child is pushed to continually fill up with food. This can be because parents are obsessed with the idea that the child must eat enough, or as a substitute for other basic needs which are unfulfilled. As an adult, the individual will preserve this sensation of having an upset stomach when he has too many *Worries*, or when he is forced to "swallow down" too many things that "lie heavy on the stomach".

The belly is a "cavity" which can *Contain* not just food, but also *love* for other people. We experience love for others, in all its forms, in our bellies. We ideally take others into our bellies. Children are not ready for this Containment until at least *6 years of age*. Much later, in the girls, this capacity will be transformed into the desire and capacity for maternity: the ability to actually grow and carry a new life inside them.

Pedagogical indications

One of the advantages of a Functional analysis of Child Development within the various Districts (as indeed of a Functional analysis of Child Development in terms of the Basic Experiences of the Self) is the possibility of obtaining valid and detailed *pedagogical indications* that are, at the same time, simple and practical.

Today's parents have a lot of doubts and confusion about how to raise their children well, and how to avoid negative situations. They always ask countless questions about problems of every type and on each and every aspect of both their own and their children's behaviour. We can clearly see that there is a considerable amount of confusion – and their parents just do not know what path to take.

The answers provided by society are not much help. On the one hand, people continue to repeat clichés that are not valid. On the other, television shows and magazines offer conflicting viewpoints on the subject, which only serve to prolong the confusion: everyone feels himself to be a "Psychologist", at least in part. Moreover, several scholars suggest that parents should just follow their instincts and inner feelings, without taking into consideration the fact that parents have all too often lost contact with children's real needs. Lastly, within the field of "Psychology" itself (and especially that of child psychology), psychologists have insisted on the *relativity* of the various thoughts and theories for too long: almost as if everyone can say their piece without there being any need for a solid, verified and up-to-date scientific basis for their affirmations.

At this point, on the contrary, it must be repeated that human functioning is scientifically determined. It cannot simply be left to common sense, or popular beliefs, or to personal intuition. Nor can it be left to obsolete theories. If we want children to be able to function fully and positively, if we want them not to have to face a life of alterations and suffering, then we must choose a *precise course* for them. Their development must be encouraged to follow a specific path. Today's body of knowledge is sufficient (even though it still has to be widened) to provide us with an exhaustive set of correct *pedagogical indications.*

We are not talking about a meticulous rulebook with thousands of different rules for the thousands of different situations in every day life. We do not have to *learn* thousands of different ways of behaving (as newspapers and magazines seem to suggest). There would be no point. If, on the other hand, (as Functional thought suggests) we look at the individual's *underlying functions*, then we can easily delineate the *general lines* along which we should proceed, the fundamental principles, the clear and concrete paths upon which we should base a good relationship with our children, as well as their education. Once these general outlines are in place, then it becomes easy to derive specific and detailed indications, as and when the situation requires it.

It is with these objectives that the theory of Child Development according to District has been developed. The aim is to provide a specific contribution to the formulation of a general, correct, effective, and complete pedagogical system.

Applying the theory to psychotherapy

Therapeutic indications

If a person is healthy, then we should find that each District conserves all the Basic Experiences and feelings described above, intact. To give an example, in examining the individual's legs, we should be able to find the Tenderness of Being Held, the Strength of Standing on his Own Two Feet, the Joy of Leaping and Running, Opposition and Anger, the Strength to Lash out and Move Away.

What is it that we really find in adults, though? What might we observe in a patient coming to us for help?

By tracing the individual's Development, District by District, we are able to verify what Experiences really are available and present in the patient's legs. We are also able to establish which of the Experiences and feelings are ready to emerge in relation to the real situation around them (whether or not Tenderness emerges when the legs are held, whether the patient experiences pleasure at Pushing with Gentle Original Strength, whether the patient is able to Run with Joy and Happiness, as well as feeling well planted on his feet). We can note that some of these Experiences are no longer available whilst others are. We may also observe that certain Experiences have a tendency to emerge at all times, regardless of the real situation: a lot of Anger, Fear, exaggerated Opposition or continuously Digging their Heels in.

To recap, therefore: certain traces are present to a normal degree and they emerge in a congruent manner when the therapist provides the correct stimulus to the legs (holding them, massaging them, squeezing them strongly, pushing hard against them, making them push or provoking them). Other traces have, on the other hand, become dominant, altered, or chronic, becoming stereotyped. These tend to be evident at all times, and at the same time, the traces, which are no longer available, have become suppressed. They are present only at a very deep level, buried beneath layers of negativity created by other altered experiences.

All of these indicators provide us with a very clear idea of what to do doing the course of therapy, what aspects it will be important to work on (sooner or later, depending on the program of therapy for that particular patient).

If we find that the legs are full of Anger, then we know that our course of therapy will have to deal with the problem of Strength and Anger. The patient's Anger has in fact become inflamed, becoming compressed and suppressed. The Anger is still present, but in an altered, pathological form.

If Tenderness is absent, we will have to fish it up from the depths sooner or later, patiently and gradually reconstructing it, after having removed the negativity that was above it.

"Crisis points" during therapy

Observing whether determined Basic Experiences are present in the various Districts furnishes us with precious clues about the patient's life during the period of their development as a child and as an adolescent.

However, there is yet another way of using this form of analysis according to Districts, which can help us to reconstruct the underlying knots and *central episodes*, which have brought the patient to their present state.

It can occur during a sitting that the patient finds himself immersed all at once in old feelings and sensations, without the filter of "memories" to keep him at a certain distance: as if the old situation were once again present, here and now.

During these situations (which we define as *crises* in the sense that they are crucial, "extreme" in some way), very precise sensations, dramatic moments, and intense feelings can re-emerge: things that have conditioned the individual's life, or which have determined his choices. This does not necessarily imply a return to one, *single* traumatic event in the patient's life. Rather, what tends to happen is that the individual returns to situations that characterised a whole period in his childhood or adolescence, such the vague fear of being abandoned, impotent anger, sensations of emptiness, discouragements, feelings of uselessness or excessive worrying.

It is as if the patient were returning to a point where a chain of negative experiences presumably started, which have since led to the present pathologies and dysfunctions.

During these *crises*, patients overcome with the same fear as in the past, the same anger or the same anxiety. Reactions can include becoming tense, shouting, growing silent, crying, or becoming completely immobilized with terror. The patient relives all of this with the exact same *modalities* as they did in the past, which *are precisely linked to his Functional Development*, and to the periods in which the Basic Experiences present themselves in the various districts.

Thanks, therefore, to an analysis of Functional Development according to the various Districts, we can identify the period in the patient's life when something serious happened. We can establish, with a fair amount of precision, the patient's age when they first experienced the feelings present in these *crises*: sobbing tears, moving the legs chaotically, a feeble voice, eyes tight shut, head lowered, crawling like a baby, fragility in the legs, and so on.

Even if we do not know the patient's history or anamnesis (as can happen, for example, with intensive, short term therapy groups), we can Functionally identify to what period their *crises* refer to. If we ask the person what happened to them at around that age, patients refer specific difficult, painful, or traumatic events that occurred in precisely that period.

Other times, the patient is unable to respond to the therapist's question because they do not remember that era. However, these patients almost always return to the next therapy session having discovered to their surprise that traumatic events really did happen in that period, after having asked relatives what had gone on in at that time.

How do we reconstruct the period that the *crises* refer to? What are the elements that we may observe during these "regressions", so intense and crucial to patients?

There are an enormous number of Functional elements that can be examined and taken into consideration, given that they are linked to all the various levels of the Self. We have used these elements to trace an outline of the processes involved in child development, at both a wider level and a more specific one, in terms of reconstructing the patient's individual history.

At this point, it may be useful to bring all the most common elements presented by patients together in one brief list. These are the elements that allow us to form an idea of the patient's age, or the period in his life that these resurfaced feelings belong to.

- *The voice:* is the patient's voice feeble and thin like that of a baby before it is 1½ years of age? Is it more open but still high and "piping" (2–6 years)? Is the patient's voice on the contrary intense and strong, more assertive, like an older child? If the patient shouts, is his shout full and open or merely hinted at?
- *Crying:* does the patient cry like a newborn, desperately and without warning, almost without being able to breathe; or does he cry in a calmer and more controlled way, like an older child?
- *The patient's use of language, level of schooling:* does the patient's vocabulary correspond to that of a child before the start of school (6 years), a very young child, a child after the beginning of school, or a child much later still?
- *Leg movements:* do the patient's leg movements indicate opposition, as with an older child, or are they more chaotic, like those of a newborn; exploring the world around him, expressing anger in a tantrum or kicking his legs with irritation.
- *Strength in the legs:* does the patient have strength in his legs? If so, how much? How are the legs used: for defence, to attack or merely to explore?
- *Arm movements:* are the patient's arm movements calm, aimless and chaotic, angry or assertive, or rather aimed at lashing out and injuring?
- *Body movements:* does the patient tend to throw himself backwards in an uncontrolled gesture, typical of babies at 5–6 months? Does he tend to throw himself forwards? Are the patient's movements rigid or relaxed, erect or limp?
- *The position of the head:* is the head supported or does it hang like that of a baby at just a few months old? Does the patient hold his head high, capable of "facing" difficulties, or low, as a sign of gloomy obstinacy (present only after 5 years of age)?
- *Standing or not:* does the patient tend to stay on his feet or does he tend to kneel? Does he tend to go down on all fours? Does he tend to lie down?
- *The eyes:* does the patient seek direct eye contact or does he find it difficult, averting his eyes? Do the patient's eyes wander off into the distance, daydreaming, relaxed?

- *Perception:* is the patient fully able to perceive the reality of the people around him (is he "decentred") or is he only centred on himself? Is the patient able to perceive the therapist or is there no contact at all?
- *Fear:* is the patient's fear vague, panicky, more archaic, or is it directed at something more specific, characteristic of a later age? Is the patient afraid of growing up (7 years and upwards)?
- *Anger:* is the patient's anger generic, archaic or is it more focussed, as we find in more adult phases? Does the patient feel hate towards others?

During these *crises*, the most significant elements strike one almost immediately. Even if the precise period cannot be determined, what emerges is always clear and intense. A reconstruction of the exact period and of the crucial episodes in a patient's life can come later. What is important is that the therapist understands what is happening, takes mental note, and creates some kind of link, or bridge, between what happened in the past and the patient's present difficulties.

The most important thing, however, is that the therapist intervene immediately, so that the patient is not left to deal with the old drama, the old "black hole", on his own yet again. It is important to take a *new direction* straight away: a new phase in the patient's development which will put the patient back in action and branch off into new, positive, turnings; using the crucial moment in the past as a starting point for a new beginning.

Chapter 7

Integrated Functional Psychotherapy

The therapeutic process

The most recent research into psychotherapy places a marked emphasis on understanding *what it is that the psychotherapist really causes to happen* during a therapy session; regardless of the specific technique used, or the wider, more generalised aims of the therapy.

Fig. 1. *Different levels within Psychotherapy*

Overall objectives

- ❑ Expansion of the Self, Reinforcing the Ego, Rebalancing, Curing the symptoms.

Therapeutic process

- ❑ What really happens during therapy

Techniques

- ❑ Interpreting transference, looking for new strategies, making paradoxical prescriptions, massage, getting the patient to speak to his "double", getting the patient to breathe correctly, helping the patient to be aware of his sensations "here and now"…

Instead of concentrating on the *results* of treatment, this research centres on the psychotherapeutic *process*, around what really happens. This pushes the central part of fig. 1 into the foreground, which is halfway between a more detailed description of the precise techniques used and the more general level of the overall objectives of the course of therapy.

Interpreting transference in the patient/therapist relationship, finding new strategies, using paradoxical prescriptions, massaging, getting the patient to breathe correctly, using guided visualisation, getting the patient to talk to "another person" who is not there, or creating a dialogue between different parts of the patient are just some of the *tools* used during therapy. Yet, what is it that is really happening between the patient and the therapist? What is it that is being established, and how does this bring about real change?

On the other hand, when we say that therapy consists in helping the patient's dynamics, bringing subconscious thoughts to the level of consciousness, reinforcing the Ego and developing the patient's capacities, we are still at too general a level. These aspects are the basic objectives of a course of psychotherapy, rather than methods for carrying it out.

Besides the techniques used during therapy and the overall objectives, what is most interesting is trying to reach an understanding of exactly *what is being put into play* in the relationship between the patient and the therapist at a given moment during therapy. What are the real "modalities of therapeutic intervention" in force during the different phases and moments of a course of therapy? What does the therapist really set off by choosing to intervene in one way or another, with the way he interacts with the patient, the way he talks, whether or not he remains silent, the way he moves, his touch, his facial expressions?

The study of process offers perspectives of profound interest and relevance for the future of psychotherapy, as well that of care giving in general. It is precisely by understanding what really occurs in therapy that we can improve the process itself, making it more effective, and as short and painless as possible, pleasant even. Not only that, *a wider discussion on process could help to open up a channel of communication and interaction, a sort of common ground, between the many theoretical models that exist, over and above the specificity of the different techniques.*

It is very probable that the result of so-called "equipotentiality" within the field of psychotherapy (i.e. the fact that all the various methods of psychotherapy seem to produce more or less the same results with regards to effectiveness) could be explained using the same method. Several scholars have chosen to consider what has been called the "K-factor", linked to the personality of the individual therapist, as being unconnected to the psychotherapeutic technique or model being applied. However, it is much more probable that any therapists, from whichever school of thought, that are "sufficiently competent" end up adopting, during a given phase of therapy, the same therapeutic modality (that of *welcoming*, for example, or of *containing*, *nourishing* or becoming a *new parent figure*) independent of the particular verbal or non-verbal technique employed within their specific approach.

To conclude, a thorough knowledge of this middle level, the level of *therapeutic modality*, would allow us to significantly improve the effects of treatment, because it would allow us to unite the various techniques and to find out which of them best support and improve the various forms of therapeutic intervention.

Integrated intervention on all levels of the Self

At this point, it is well to stipulate once again that Functional psychotherapy is not characterised by direct intervention at a physical level (as is often mistakenly thought), but rather for its singular and original theorisation of the mind-body relationship.

Over the course of years of practise in psychotherapy, I began to discover that direct intervention at a physical level did not merely represent a sort of "acting out", as had previously been thought, nor did it represent an escape into physical action, impeding the *elaboration* of patients' experiences and the gradual reclamation of what emerged. On the contrary: it was often the work on the body that permitted us to access all levels and emotions, and parts of the patient that were buried deep-down, that would never otherwise have been allowed to emerge.

The phenomena that I witnessed, as I went on with this type of practice, were extremely intense, and often brought back very archaic moments in the patients' lives (infantile facial expressions, a feeble voice, the tears of a tiny child, infantile involuntary movements, variations in body temperature, memories, images and so on). What emerged in just a few minutes of Functional psychotherapy was often much more intense than what would have emerged over a lengthy course of solely verbal therapy.

Little by little, however, through my research over the last twenty years, I realised that it was not the treatment of the patient's body that caused such surprising results, as a specific type of therapist-patient relationship: a relationship that went well beyond the traditional, habitual detachment, becoming an emotive relationship, reliving old affective relationships with great intensity. What was it, then, that caused this intensity?

The most probable hypothesis is that it derives from the fact that the method managed to enter into the patient's deepest nuclei through *many different Functional levels* and elements of the Self, rather than just through speech or free association. In this way, the therapist almost immediately manages to penetrate below the level of the patient's rational control, beyond his surface structures, beyond his "defences" and his "resistance"[1], right down to the level of his deepest, primary needs, which, if they have been left unsatisfied, have led to the gradual alteration of the Self. This means being able to get right to the root of problems, right back to the crossroads where well-being first turned into distress, right back to the levels where the most important processes linked to the patient's illness or distress first originated, and where they continue to be active.

Another thing that characterises this sort of *integrated* therapy is its methodological approach during therapy itself. This does not just consist in "moving the body" and then analysing the feelings that emerge in the classic psychoanalytical, cognitive, or systemic way, as some schools have actually tried to put into practise. Functional therapy intervenes directly on all levels of the Self, and changes must, and do, come about all of these levels. The result that we are aiming for is not merely that of re-elaborating experiences, gaining insight on past events, symbolisation, or rendering patients able to think about and communicate past painful experiences. What interests us is that there is a *decisive, real change* in *all* the altered Functions, not just the more 'mental' ones. Recovering the ability "embrace" is, in the end, exactly that: *the capacity to embrace* in the most practical sense of the word. A sense of physiological well being has an intrinsic value on its own, not just because of the way the patient represents this state to himself at a symbolic

1 The concept of "resistance" becomes completely redundant if we manage to forge a direct connection with the individual's deepest needs. Any resistance to therapy disappears thanks to the multidimensional nature of the therapeutic process.

level. The physical relaxation of muscle tension is positive precisely because it really does undo the knot of anxiety and vigilance that was making the patient suffer, and often words are superfluous, adding nothing to the process.

Fig. 2. *The different levels in a course of integrated Functional Psychotherapy*

Overall objectives

- The re-harmonisation of the Functions, the mobilisation of the Functions, restoring their integration, the recovery of the Basic Experiences of the Self

Practical Objectives

- The reconstruction of the individual's basic functional processes → Functions → The Basic Experiences of the Self

Techniques used

- Methods must be calibrated, refined and adapted in order to render them suitable for the reconstruction of the individual's basic functional processes
- Methods must be multidimensional, on all levels of the Self

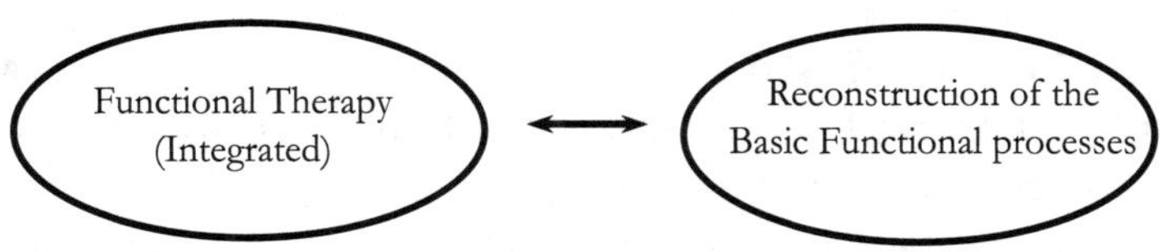

Obviously, change will also come about on the symbolic plane, and the patient's ability to talk about the painful or joyous moments in their lives will be reopened. However, this occurs as one of the *many* effects caused by the therapist's simultaneous intervention on the patient's capacity to "embrace"; i.e. on his muscle tension, anxiety, as well as on the corresponding representations on the cognitive/symbolic plane. Symbolic elaboration is not, therefore, the main objective in therapy. It is one of many objectives: just one Function among many. What we expect, as our final aim, is the overall re-balancing of the Self. This means the *mobilisation* of all the various

Functions, their *re-harmonisation*, and the recovery of their original *integration* within the reconstructed Basic Experiences.

Mobilisation consists in dispelling the patient's stereotypies and restoring full amplitude of the wavelike movement of the Functions as they range between one polarity and another, allowing them to use the nuance best suited to the situation in hand. Sadness must be allowed to exist to its fullest extent, but so, also, should happiness. Strength is as important as fragility, being tough is as important as being tender, vigilance is as important as relaxation, speed is as important as the capacity to be slow.

Re-harmonising the Self allows us to rebalance any possible disparities among the Functions, reducing those that are swollen and overflowing, and re-activating those that have not been sufficiently developed.

Lastly, integration makes it possible for us to restore people's lost unity. They will be able to live experiences using their whole being, with all the Functions, congruent to each other, all working in the same direction: a joyous Experience accompanied by the emotion of joy (and not fear); memories of other joyous moments in the past; the physical excitement of joy (and not anxiety, colics, or other somatic reactions); joyous muscle tone, movements and postures; a joyful voice, the awareness of joy and the ability to express joyful words.

In order to obtain these results, to arrive at deep, stable change, it has proved necessary to intervene on *all* psycho-physical levels (though not always right from the beginning). This is because the altered Functions are often closed in a kind of "short circuit", i.e. they continue to remain altered and to present themselves in a stereotyped and repetitive way, despite changes brought about on different planes of the Self. Realising that I breathe badly will not modify the way I breathe. A deep fear will not go away if I continue to suffer from sweaty palms and an accelerated heartbeat. We cannot consider treatment as complete if other alterations continue to be evident on some or other level of the Self. The Functions on this level may not return to normal on their own. On the contrary: they often end up retroacting on the remaining Functions, re-establishing the patient's original difficulty or pathology as before. Laboured breathing will inevitably bring back unacceptable levels of anxiety. A tendency to suffer from frightening fantasies will end up lending a sense of tragedy to the patient's whole life. A contracted posture will bring back closure, in terms of both the patient's emotivity and their ability to relate to others.

This sort of clinical experience and its theoretical correlations used to create huge difficulties for former, "pyramidal" conceptions of the mind-body relationship, which placed all that is symbolic, mental or elaborative at the top of the human organism, capable of controlling the individual's entire functioning from above.

Today, however, we have gradually reached a more "circular" conception in which all planes of the Self, all the psycho-physical Functions, contribute in equal measure to the Functioning of the individual. All the Functions are *equally important* to life and for the development of the individual. No Function is secondary and no Function can therefore be neglected, either during the delicate phase of growing up, adult life, or any given type of therapeutic treatment or help.

Moreover (as we have already seen with regards to the latest findings on early infancy), all the Functions are profoundly integrated right from the beginning. The child is innately able to go through the Basic Experiences of the Self and consolidate the heritage of capacities that will allow him to face life successfully.

However, it has taken a long time to arrive at the full, articulated, and complex theory of the Functions as it is today. It started with intense experimentation, as well as ceaseless delving into our creativity, involving different levels: the voice, movements, massage, breathing, peristalsis, music, dance, and artistic expression. There have been huge changes and adjustments along the way.

For example, we can no longer affirm today that the body is "truth", that the body has an inherent, autogenous capacity to be healthy, that movement alone is enough to allow us to find ourselves, and the road to recovery. The body can suffer from alterations, just as thoughts and fantasies can, in the way it moves, its postures, muscle tone, and the balance of the autonomic nervous system. Why continue to refer to the body and the mind as if they were two separate things?

The contribution made by the various clinical approaches that have emerged over the years in the field of psychology has also been vital to these discoveries, being differing, but also complimentary points of view on human functioning. However, it is also vital that we put aside any conceptions within these approaches that have proved to be inexact or which no longer correspond to the advancement of knowledge.

To give an example: practises which concentrate on "releasing" emotions that are excessively dominant in the patients' lives, on "letting it all out", or techniques aimed at "unblocking the body" by moving it just for the sake of moving it, have revealed themselves to be obsolete from a scientific point of view.

Apart from the occasional leap backwards or closure, the entire history of psychotherapy can essentially be seen as a continual growth towards intervention with ever greater potential: in terms of diagnosis, the planning of a course of therapy, care and prevention, as well as in terms of helping the individual or society to develop their innate capacities.

Functional Psychology has arisen, therefore, from the need to overcome the barriers between the various therapeutic models, towards a genuinely *multidimensional* vision. Here, the individual is seen as a whole, no longer divided by the old psyche-soma dichotomy. This concept of wholeness is not just a general principle however, neither is it a vague and implicit assumption. In actual fact, the concepts of psyche and soma are extremely imprecise and cloudy as terms. After all, is anger mental or physical?

Once we overcame this dichotomy, it actually became necessary to stop using the terms *body* and *mind*. Equally, it became necessary to overcome the limited vision whereby the mind alone (or a few of its aspects) is seen as being capable of governing the whole of human existence: we could no longer afford to forget about the deeper levels which regulate the equilibrium of human functioning in all its complexity. Nor could we allow ourselves to be trapped by other partial conceptions which claimed that deep change could only be brought about through "physicality", or by working on subjects' family relationships, or by altering their behaviour, or again, only by changing certain "parts" of the person, or their vital energy.

On the one hand, therefore, a conception of the Self was emerging that was not solely limited to the subjects' feelings, or experiences, or to the "representations" of the conscience, but rather which embraced all the individual's levels of functioning. It was not to do with imagining a sort of material "structure" or substrate underlying all human phenomena. Rather, it had to do with the capacity of the human-system for *organisation*.

On the other hand, it was necessary to identify, in order to determine the precise techniques to use in therapy, what therapists should look at, what they should then work on, since the "mind and body" concept had been abandoned.

The concept of the *Functions* answered both of these requirements. The Functions allow us to talk about the complexity of the human organism without, however, falling into the difficulty of impotently describing every single aspect of its functioning. They allow us to apply complex thought without abandoning the possibility of intervening at a practical level.

The Functions are not "things" or structures. They are levels of organisation. When we refer to "movement", we are not simply talking about the head, arms, or another part of the body, but the *way* in which the person moves as a whole. There are children whose movements have already lost their fluidity, and who have only developed the capacity to move in a brusque manner, or make sudden movements. Other children are continuously speeded up, hyperactive, and others still are lazy and slow. These modalities of movement are to be found in all parts of the body. A chronically hyperactive child (or one at the opposite end of the scale, one who tends towards immobility) cannot choose another way of moving, in that the "movement" function has become altered, and its movements are no longer connected to the situation in hand or the child's will.

In the same way, all the other Functions are not merely pieces or parts of the individual, either. In fact they are modalities of "organisation" of his overall functioning, e.g. anger doesn't just reside in the arms or the jaw; the sympathetic activation involves all organs that are connected to the autonomic nervous system; memories don't just belong to the central nervous system, they are reflected in every part of the body (peripheral memory).

The most significant epistemological change that has come about as a result of adopting the concept of the Functions has been that of overcoming the idea of dividing the individual into "parts". Parts, by their very nature, are set in opposition to one another: they cannot but fragment and divide the individual. This new way of looking at things sees living organisms not as systems of parts, but as different organisations of the Functions. Parts just represent pieces of the individual. It does not make much sense just looking after a person's heart, or their stomach, or their mind. It has actually been proven that when a person is ill, the whole organism is ill, not just one part.

The Functions are not just "pieces" of the individual. On the contrary, we can find the whole individual in its entirety within each Function. Emotions, movements, postures, sensations, and fantasies are not something limited and partial. They do not correspond to parts of the individual. It is the whole individual to express himself through them. The Functions are not set against each other. On the contrary: the greater their integration, the more the individual will enjoy good health, completeness and well-being.

The Basic Functional processes

Fig. 3. *The Basic Functional processes*

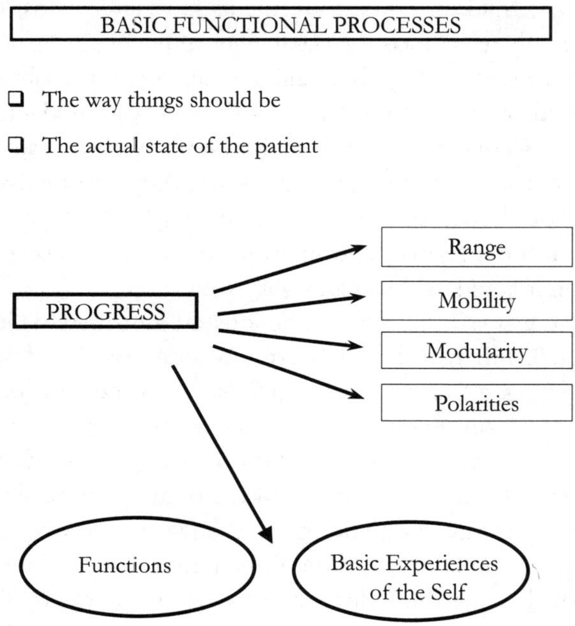

On the other hand, the Functions, as we have identified and described them, allow us to detach ourselves from specific events and situations. If a Function is altered, its alteration will be evident in any situation the individual faces. Similarly, if a Function has full mobility, this will come out in every situation. Functional Psychology operates at the very roots of behaviour patterns or experiences, however different they may be, modifying the human organism's underlying functional processes, which are the origin of every action, i.e. both the Functions and the Basic Experiences of the Self. As fig. 3 shows, we can modify these innermost functional processes by analysing the way they move over time, together with a sound knowledge of what their progress should be, and how this has, on the contrary, become altered.

Diagnosis, planning, and process in therapy

In Functional therapy, diagnosis takes the form of a well-articulated and multidimensional overview of the Self in all its aspects: an analysis of all the Functions of the Self, their level of mobility and any alterations that may have occurred. A diagnosis of this type means that we are no longer subject to the imperfections and inadequacies inherent in older, "typological" forms of diagnosis. In clinical practise, no-one has actually managed to find a patient who corresponds completely to a *pure type* (i.e. there is no such thing as an "oral" type patient, or a pure "narcissist"), but merely a mixture of different typologies. For this reason, the corresponding indications for therapy often reveal themselves to be useless.

On the other hand, diagnoses centred on the individual and his functioning provide us with operational indications which have been calibrated to the individual's exact needs, and which are therefore more effective.

Functional therapy actually allows us to create a concrete *program of therapy*. A plan of this sort is unusually precise in that it is based on, and closely follows, indications which are derived directly from the patient's individual diagnosis, planning how and where to intervene in a much more detailed way.

However, another point of significant importance is the discovery that the therapist cannot intervene on all of the different levels at the same time. On the contrary, each intervention must be made in its own time, following different phases, depending on the circumstances and the alterations, disharmonies and disconnections present within the Functions, and in the history of the subject. Therapy therefore *evolves over time,* becoming an authentic journey, made up of different phases, which are each clearly differentiated, each following on from the next. These phases differ both in terms of what is happening in the patient-therapist relationship and also in terms of the "modalities of therapy" undertaken by the therapist in the journey towards a positive conclusion[2]. Profound effects are produced during this process, touching several planes and Functions of the Self (once again, multidimensionally). Among others, intense modifications can also noticeably be brought about at a deeper, biological level, such as the rebal-

2 See Chapter 9 of this book.

ancing of the endocrine system, the normalisation of the body's neuro-transmitters or a renewed capacity for the osmotic exchange of liquids.

Objectives, factors of change

Given the above, it follows that traditional concepts regarding *factors of change* are no longer sufficient. We can no longer define the sole underlying aim of therapy as being that of rendering the subconscious conscious, or gaining insight, resolving conflicts between *psychic instances*, or setting off the process of symbolic elaboration, reinforcing the ego and rendering the subject able to tolerate his own anxieties, or rebalancing the levels of power within the family, modifying cognitive strategies and patterns, establishing a dialogue between different parts of the individual or "letting out" the emotions. We can no longer talk generically of unblocking "rings" in the body, loosening the individual's "muscle armour", eliminating tension, moving and freeing the body or unleashing energy.

Functional psychotherapy has established the necessity of *retransforming* all the Functions that have become altered. Just moving the body "for the sake of it", on the contrary, can lead to a worsening of the patient's pathology. If it does not actually worsen the patient's condition, then in most cases it is insufficient to produce significant or lasting effects.

As a result, we have moved more and more in the direction of a "series of assessment criteria" regarding both emotions and awareness, posture and movements, breathing and muscle tone, the voice and facial expressions, the autonomic nervous system and the symbolic world.

In the attempt to reach a *complex* and *integrated* conception of psychotherapy, emphasis will, on the contrary, be placed on rebalancing the Self *as a whole*, *remobilising* all the Functional levels and reconstructing their *integration*. Recreating a deep integration among the various Functions of the Self means helping them react in a way that is appropriate for the circumstances, and helping them all to work in the same direction, i.e. rejoicing in positive experiences, facing obstacles with confidence, relaxing tension and vigilance when they are not necessary, leaning on others when it is appropriate in order to recover lost energy, being able to "take" a person and bringing them around to our side of things.

However, the Functions must also be able to lose their rigidity and reacquire a good level of *mobility*. An individual must be able to move freely between opposite polarities according to the requirements of the situation around him. He must be able to express anger, and yet also be able to feel real, deep calm. He must be able to feel his own strength to the full (calm, not agitated strength), but also experience and enjoy his own fragility, and his capacity for both joy and sadness, both rationality and creativity must be fully open. The individual must be in control, but he must also have the capacity to relax, he must be able to activate the "fight or flight" (sympathetic) response but he must equally be able to activate the "rest and digest" (parasympathetic) response. The subject must have at his disposal both his memory and his imagination for the future; he must be capable of being both tough and tender, fast and slow and making both small and expansive movements.

Together with mobility, a course of therapy must also re-harmonise the Functions of the Self. Those that are most stifled must be allowed to rise to the surface, the ones that are closed must be reopened, the most intrusive ones must be reduced, and the most underdeveloped Functions must be given more space.

The Functions, and their alterations, can provide us with practical and detailed guidelines as to how to intervene at a therapeutic level. We are not talking about producing "sensational" events such as outbursts, screaming, shouting or crying. This means, for the greater part of therapy, working patiently to sew together the torn fabric of the Self, in order to reconstruct, with great love, its continuity, and to restore mobility to the Functions that have become closed or blocked, disconnected or cramped. The time of experiential group therapy sessions aimed at producing huge "emotional releases", apparent "hysterical" cures, and the discoveries of the "world of the imagination" has thankfully come to an end. In order to obtain stable, meaningful results, rather than superficial and apparent ones, it is necessary for the therapist to work with great patience, precision, and involvement.

The relationship

The relationship between the therapist and the patient remains, however, the basic fulcrum upon which the process of change is based. In *integrated* therapy, this relationship is seen as being on all planes on which relationships are normally based, i.e. cognitive, emotive, motor, postural and physical planes. In integrated psychotherapy, therefore, all channels of communication are taken into consideration (see fig. 4).

We can say, therefore, that in a therapeutic process that moves on all levels, the therapist cannot possibly be *distant* from the patient. On the contrary, he or she is *deeply involved*, because it is impossible to fake an affectionate relationship or completely hide our own negative reactions in a context whereby facial expressions, physical contact, looking into one another's eyes, and perceptive sensations at all levels are involved.

In integrated therapy, the therapist really is a *new parent*, a *positive* parent. He represents an authentic second chance for the patient. Thanks to this "new parent", the patient will be able to reconstruct the deep experiences that have become closed or altered over the course of his life.

Being a "new parent" means that the relationship must be full and complete, rather than limited to just a few aspects. This means that the functions traditionally carried out by the therapist are now no longer sufficient if taken singly. Empathy, on its own, is no longer enough, nor is it any longer enough to serve as a *mirror*. It is not enough just to *guarantee the setting* as a safe place where the patient can rediscover parts of himself that are lost or hidden. Similarly, it is not enough just to limit ourselves to interpreting transference or analysing countertransference. In integrated therapy, the therapist goes beyond merely tolerating the patient's fears and negativity, beyond the search for new strategies, beyond permitting emotional abreactions.

The therapist does not just perform one of these roles; he performs all of them, and much more. It is the therapist's capacity to love (in the full, genuine sense of the word) and his ability to be a "good parent" that will allow the patient to retrace the old roads that led to his present difficulty, but in a completely different way. This totality may seem a utopia, but if in fact we work on all levels of the Self, it is easier to establish than one might think. It is easier than a false interest or a forced and unnatural empathy.

Fig. 4. *The patient-therapist relationship in integrated therapy*

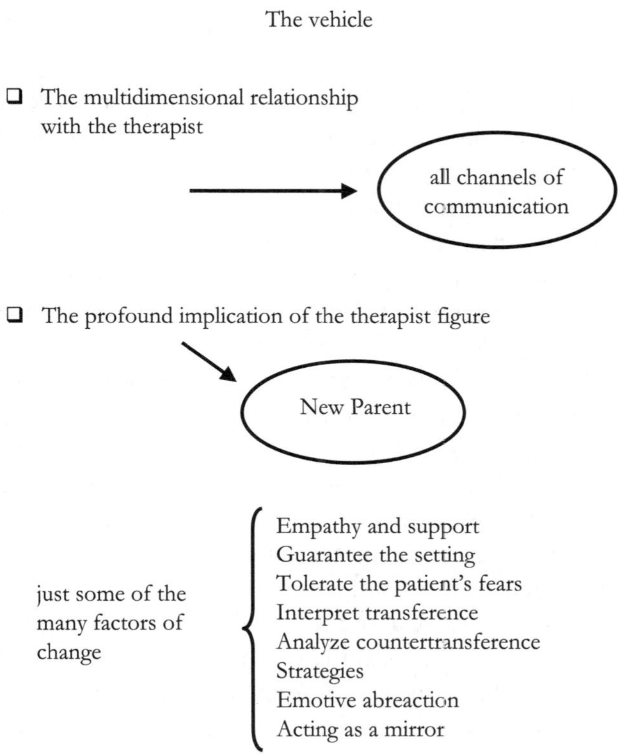

It is by intervening on all levels of the Self, by holding the patient in our hands, that we can become fully aware of how fragile he is below the surface, how much he needs our help. As a result, all the negative sensations that can arise at more imagined or verbal levels, or at more adult phases in the relationship, melt away without effort, and it is not difficult for the therapist to draw the patient in towards him and be a different parent to him. What is more, as an expert, he is able to be a better, more capable parent, because he is able to understand what to do to fill the patient's emptiness and how to do so.

Evaluating the therapeutic process, "standard phases and events"

Despite the fact that this discipline is a very recent one, it is taking on an ever more fundamental importance within the psychotherapy sector, and not just because it allows us to ascertain whether or not a given treatment has produced noticeable *results*. Studying techniques of evaluation implies, in its most advanced sense, the study of the most meaningful effects produced during treatment, and therefore the study of the therapeutic process itself[3]. This therefore allows us to focus on the way a course of therapy progresses, as a journey, as a process of evolution.

As we have already seen, this method reveals the existence of real *phases* during therapy[4], each one following on from the last. The way therapy is carried out changes significantly from one stage to another. The modalities with which the relationship unfolds also change from one stage to another (for example in the level of the patient's dependence) and the modalities of intervention must likewise change at the same rate if we are to avoid the risk of getting stuck in former phases.

Furthermore, research carried out using Functional methods has allowed us to take a further step towards understanding therapy itself. The therapeutic process has been shown to be punctuated by *specific events* that present themselves *regularly* in all courses of treatment, regardless of who the patient and the therapist are. These are the result of the process of change itself, rather than the specific circumstances of the clinical case in hand[5]. What therapist has failed to notice that at the beginning patients talk almost exclusively about the events that characterise their everyday lives and then, at a certain point they start to turn their attention to what is happening in therapy and the relationship with the therapist himself? What therapist has failed to notice, moreover, that for a long time the patient does not notice his external appearance at all, and that a patient is only able to perceive the therapist as he really is, as a real person, at a very advanced stage of therapy: whether he's tired, calm, unhappy or worried?

In figure 5, we present a possible list of such "standard events".

3 See Di Nuovo S. (1998), Rispoli L. (1998a).

4 See Chapter 9 of this book.

5 See Basch M. F. (1988), Luborsky L., Crits-Christoph P. (1990), Rispoli L. (1998a).

Fig. 5. *Standard events or phases in the therapeutic process*

STANDARD PHASES/EVENTS IN THE THERAPEUTIC PROCESS		
Improvement	(I)	The first decisive, clear improvement in symptoms.
Deterioration	(D)	Intense deterioration of initial symptoms, patient responds dramatically.
Return of an old symptom	(OS)	Reappearance of a symptom which had already arisen in the patient's past (childhood or adolescence).
Rapid alternation	(I/D)	Rapid alternation between improvement and deterioration between one sitting and another.
Symptom arises during therapy	(ST)	A new symptom arises, completely different from the symptoms that led the patient to seek therapy.
Entry in therapy	(ET)	The patient sees the therapist as an interlocutor. he pays attention to the way therapy is progressing. patient may dream about the therapeutic situation.
Real perception of therapist	(PT)	The patient perceives the therapist as a person, noticing his expressions and moods.
Loosening control, letting go	(LC)	Outside the setting, the patient reports signs such as vertigo, forgetfulness, confusion, mistakes, etc.
Deep release	(R)	When "letting go", within therapy, there is no longer any trace of attention or control; the body enters the parasympathetic state with no trace of sympathetic activation.
Patient completely abandons himself to T (patient taken up by T)	(AT)	In the therapist's arms, the patient lives through the experience of "abandoning oneself to" and that of allowing himself to be "taken up".
Sensation from childhood	(SC)	Emergence of archaic feelings, not perceived as such by the patient, who instead perceives them as belonging to the present.
Appearance of dysfunctions	(AD)	The patient becomes conscious of his own dysfunctions with a new level of awareness.
Sensations similar to symptoms	(SS)	During therapy, sensations are produced that are similar to the initial symptoms, following intense work on the patient's physiology. however, these no longer carry the same negative value for the patient that they once did.
Intense beneficial effects	(B)	The patient experiences situations of intense wellbeing both within and outside the therapeutic environment.

Complete inversion of stereotyped functions	(IF)	Therapy has opened up the possibility of new ways of functioning. the patient swings (for a short time) to the opposite polarities in those functions which have until now been limited or stereotyped.
Changes, profound modifications	(PC)	Profound modifications in functional processes (but not inversion).
Recovery of capacities	(R)	Recovery and development of life potential.

Through these "standard events", we have been able to get closer and closer to the profound meaning of every process of change, and to what really happens as a course of therapy progresses. Furthermore, these *standard events* help us to give a concrete structure to the concept of "phases of therapy". They also allow us to see whether therapy is proceeding as it should or whether it is losing ground, because certain regularly occurring events arise chiefly during the initial phases of therapy, certain ones only during the intermediate phases, others only in the more advanced stages, and still more only in the final phases of treatment[6].

One of the "standard events" consists in a *complete inversion of the individual's characteristic ways of functioning.* People who never dream start to do so; people who dreamed a lot stop doing so; those who slept a lot sleep less; people who urinate rarely start doing so copiously; people who never get angry find that they cannot stop losing their temper.

Another extremely characteristic phase is that of reliving very early sensations that are identical to sensations experienced at a given stage during childhood or adolescence, but perceived as belonging to the present. They represent a sort of voyage into the past.

There are another series of important *standard events/phases, which* regard transference, the present patient-therapist relationship, the flow of the patient's emotions, and the progression of symptoms. Of the latter phases, one of the most interesting is that of the return, in all therapeutic treatments, of old symptoms from the patient's childhood or adolescence. This time, however, the old symptom is much less virulent and is of shorter duration than when it first appeared. The interest lies in the fact that this event (which repeats itself in all clinical cases and which can therefore be considered to be a characteristic of the therapeutic process) allows us to

6 Research on the standard phases linked to the phases of therapy has already been underway for some years, conducted by the author of the present volume, Results will be made public in a future publication.

glimpse the possibility of getting right down to, and touching, the "root" of the subjects' problems, the original source of their imbalances and the first external, evident manifestations of such alterations (i.e. the symptoms). This would lead us to presume, therefore, that for a course of psychotherapy to be effective, it must be able to modify the subject's deepest functional processes, at exactly the point where the first "crossroads" was created, when the organism took the road that was to lead to its present difficulties and illness. A course of therapy can and must reach these archaic functional processes, and it must do so *on all the levels* that are affected by them: biological, physiological, motor and conceptual levels.

Another advantage gained by evaluating the therapeutic process in this way lies, lastly, in the fact that it is now possible to continuously "readjust" the objectives of therapy (and therefore of the tools of evaluation themselves), and also, more importantly, to readjust the "modalities of intervention in therapy" and the methods used to make the therapist's intervention as intense and as incisive as possible.

Evaluation also allows us to verify the results of therapy and ascertain their real efficacy in relation to the proposed objectives. By objectives, we do not mean the simple resolution of symptoms but rather a genuine restructuring of the individual's deep functioning, on all levels of the Self. To this aim, we have elaborated and developed an assessment protocol that monitors the different levels of the Self. This protocol is made up of 16 points, some of which are based on direct questions to the patient, others on direct observation carried out by the therapist while the patient carries out specific movements, breathing exercises and imagination work.

Fig. 6 shows the results of research carried out using the assessment protocol, which was completed at the beginning and the end of therapy (and in some cases halfway through the course of therapy). The protocol gives an overall score each time it is completed, with a minimum of 16 in the case of maximum alteration, and a maximum of 64 points for a full and complete functioning. For ease of reading, the total values in the graph have been divided by 4.

Fig. 6. *Assessment of the results of Functional Psychotherapy*

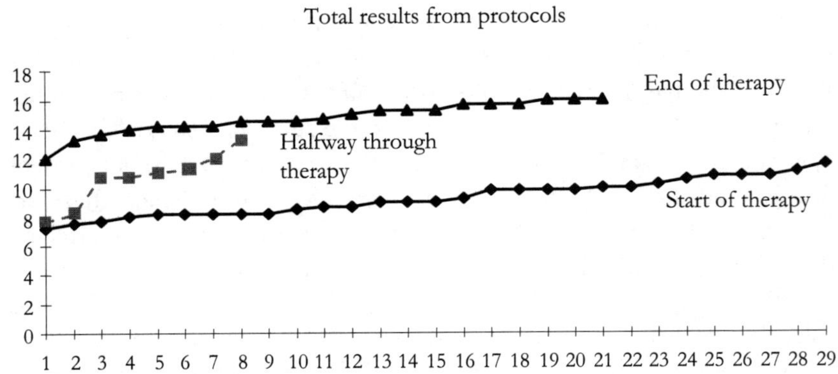

The phases of the therapeutic process and the "modalities of therapeutic intervention"

We have already talked about the importance of investigating what really happens in therapy, understanding what the therapist sets in motion by his actions (or his inaction). I have always considered this as being the most important level on which to carry out analysis if we are to understand how to provide help and bring about change. This must, certainly, involve a degree of creativity, but it must also be markedly scientific. What we are looking to do, for example, is to help the patient in the most effective, but also the most rapid, way possible. What the therapist really sets off in therapy, i.e. the "modalities of therapy" (as I have defined them) represent an intermediate level between the "highest" level; or the overall aims of the course of psychotherapy (such as helping the subject to develop, reinforcing the personality, improving the patient's quality of life, letting out the emotions and so on) and the more detailed, "minor" level of what techniques are adopted (interpretation, massage, directives, advice, free association). This halfway level therefore *transcends* both the purely technical level and also, in part, differences in the model or approach of psychotherapy used.

This is not to say that the technical level is unimportant, rather that by ascertaining precisely what effects need to be produced, *and at what exact point in therapy they need to occur*, the techniques used can be improved, perfected, and new ones can even be invented. If we have a clear and demonstrable idea of the processes underlying therapy, and of how change is brought about, then we can plan the techniques that we need to bring about the changes we desire to produce in the best and most efficient way possible.

The figure below shows a possible hypothesis about the course of the *therapeutic process* through the different *modalities of therapy* that the therapist puts into action.

Fig. 7. *The therapeutic process and its phases. Modalities of therapeutic intervention*

Short courses of therapy	WELCOME	Understanding – Listening
	FIRST HELP	Diminishing the symptoms
	DEEP RELEASE	
Control	BRINGING DYSFUNCTIONS TO LIGHT	Sensations
	EMOTIVE EXPRESSION	First signs of reconnection and mobilisation
	OLD PARENT	Early sensations
Present perceptions	NEW PARENT	Nourishment – Abandoning oneself to others – The earliest Basic Experiences of the Self
	SEPARATING OLD PARENT FIGURE FROM NEW PARENT	
	SEPARATING PARENT FIGURE FROM FIGURE OF THERAPIST	
Autonomy, Capacities	RECOVERING THE MORE ACTIVE B.E.S.'s	
	CONTINUITY OF THE RELATIONSHIP	Positive Experiences of the Self
	REINFORCEMENT	Functions – Expression – Advice Reinforcing experiences external to the setting

The idea is that, regardless of theoretical differences, the different ways each model progresses within the therapeutic process or which techniques are used, every course of therapy should more or less go through these phases in order for it to have a positive outcome. Indeed, good therapists very probably do instinctively follow this course (obviously each one in his own way) already.

The hypothesis described here reveals very distinct "phases". As we can clearly see, the central part, the most important and meaningful of the above phases, is made up of the reconstruction of the Basic Experiences of the Self.

Proceeding with a more detailed analysis, we can see that the initial phases of therapy are aimed at welcoming the individual as a whole, with all of his qualities and dysfunctions. It is the first time that the subject has felt that he is really being seen for what he is, deep down, completely, beyond his more superficial behaviour patterns – even his most hidden fragilities or tenderness. This represents a crucial passage if the patient is to be able to abandon himself completely to the therapist.

Later, in all probability, in order for therapy to proceed positively, the therapist will have to help the patient relieve his difficulties or his most pressing symptoms (first help), dealing with these more or less directly or specifically, as the circumstances demand. It is probable that every good therapist does this, regardless of the theoretical model he adheres to.

It is now fairly clear that, after this phase, the individual must loosen his control and vigilance and completely let go, if therapy is to proceed to a deeper level, below the most superficial or cognitive levels of functioning.

The improvements brought about in the initial three phases of therapy are really astonishing, and they come about in a very short space of time. We can therefore advance the hypothesis that "intensive" courses of therapy are specialised in maximising the efficacy of precisely these three phases. When therapy then starts to work at greater depth, the most hidden and buried sensations start to rise to the surface and the patient becomes consciously aware of the dysfunctions that exist on various levels.

At this point, we start to solicit and examine the patient's different capacities for emotive expression, the potential for relation on multiple planes; and we discover what works and what does not. At the same time, however, we start on the primary phase of mobilisation; mobilising repressed anger, buried sorrow, faded joys, and strengths of which the patient had never been aware.

After this, the therapist must work more intensely, and with more precision, to reduce the patient's tight, excessive self-control. This causes the patient's more remote feelings and experiences to overflow with great spontaneity. The therapist is associated even more clearly with the old parent.

This is the beginning of the most important phase in the therapeutic process: the reconstruction of the most nourishing and archaic Basic Experiences. This will be a long, full phase, the length and fullness of which increase in direct proportion to the extent of the deficiencies present.

The old traces and negative sensations are gradually replaced with sensations and perceptions belonging to the present, provided in ample measure by the *therapist/new parent/ good parent.* In this phase, the patient is *like a baby* in that he is receiving, absorbing and being nourished.

For this to happen, however, the patient's old fantasies and sensations must be divided ever more distinctly from what the patient is feeling in therapy at present; i.e. the therapist's affectionate tone of voice, calming gestures, an enveloping look, a reassuring touch. These new sensations must root themselves deeply in the patient's Self if they are to remain in the long term.

Therapy must then proceed even further, in order to transfer the improvements reached during therapy to the outside world, in the patient's everyday life.

It is crucial for the patient to realise that the therapist is not his old parent but a new possibility of reconstructing experiences that are very different from those of the past. However, he must also realise that the improvements he is experiencing are not so much due to the new parent, as to the fact that he is attaining new sensations and capacities himself. He inherently possesses them. They are not given to him by the other person. With the same aim, we start on the reconstruction of the *continuity of positive experiences of the Self*, i.e. the continued positivity of the affective relationship with the therapist (and with others in general) regardless of physical distance, daily disputes, or fleeting upsets.

This is the moment when we must reconstruct the more active Basic Experiences such as Strength, affectionate aggressiveness, giving, drawing others to us, opposition and separation.

The result of all these phases is the recovery of the patient's independence and capability. The therapeutic process must lead to stable, durable results. We ought, therefore, to make sure that all of the Basic Experiences are sufficiently replete, before we end the course of therapy. The relationship is now more personal, more like the relationship between friends than one between parent and child, and the patient's last residual deficiencies and alterations dissolve with advice, encouragement, and comparisons. At this point, he will be able to open himself up to new experiences, putting his newly rediscovered capacities to the test and diving into the great river of existence.

Modalities of therapy and factors of change

In the following figure (fig. 8), we have sought to examine the therapeutic process by linking the various phases to the different *factors of change* that have been gradually brought into focus by the various theoretical models as they developed, grew and became an established part of the history of psychotherapy.

Fig. 8. *Factors of change and integrated therapy*

FACTORS OF CHANGE DEVELOPED OVER THE YEARS IN PSYCHOTHERAPY	*PHASES IN INTEGRATED THERAPY*	*FACTORS OF CHANGE IN TERMS OF FUNCTIONAL PROCESSES WITHIN INTEGRATED THERAPY (Functions and Basic Experiences)*
Guaranteeing the Setting	*Vary it over the various phases*	
Welcome	*1st Phase*	Start to use some of the B.E.S.'s
Alleviating the symptoms	*2nd Phase*	Open and modify some of the Functions
Bringing dysfunctions to light	*3rd Phase*	Explore the Functions: Emotions (and Movement)
Explore painful emotions and memories Help patient to verbalise them, symbolise them and elaborate them	*3rd Phase*	Explore B.E.S. Modify Functions: Cognitive-Symbolic (in part)
Awareness of the positive and the negative. Gain awareness. Memories. Emotions. Self representations	*3rd Phase and 4th Phase*	Explore some of the Functions and B.E.S.'s Modify Functions: Cognitive-Symbolic
Help the patient to gain an awareness of the way he moves	*3rd Phase and 4th Phase*	Explore all the Functions and several B.E.S.'s

Postures. All patient's ways of functioning		Modify Functions: Cognitive-Symbolic
Conflict between the "parts". Accepting negative parts	*3rd Phase*	Explore the Functions: Emotive plane and some B.E.S.'s Modify Functions: Cognitive-Symbolic
Letting out emotions and releasing movement	*3rd Phase*	Explore the Functions: Emotive and Motor planes Going back over stereotypies or parts of Polarities
Representing pieces or parts of the self	*3rd Phase and 4th Phase*	Explore the Functions: Emotive, Motor, Cognitive-Symbolic and memories Explore certain B.E.S.'s Modify Functions: Cognitive-Symbolic plane
Reinforce the Ego Tolerate Anxieties and hurt	*5th Phase (active B.E.S.'s)*	Reinforce Control and Will Recover only specific B.E.S.'s or certain extremities of the Polarities
Recover a sense of reality	*5th Phase*	Modify the Functions: External Perceptions
Recover inner Groups	*6th Phase*	Recover B.E.S. of Positive Continuity Modify Functions: Memories, Awareness
Self-Expression, Art	*7th Phase*	Explore certain B.E.S.'s Explore Functions: Imaginative, Symbolic, Motor

The first thing we asked ourselves was whether it was possible to find the most well-known factors of change in *complex and integrated* therapy (as we have illustrated in our description of Functional thought). As we can see from the table, all the most well-known factors of change (or, as we could also call them, the concrete objectives set by the therapist, or the desired effects of therapy) can be encountered in this or that phase of an integrated form of therapy.

This reinforces our cardinal concept, i.e. that, in the light of the most recent knowledge, it is no longer enough just to set partial objectives or to utilise modalities of intervention that regard *merely a few aspects* of human functioning. We can therefore no longer accept as being sufficient a course of therapy which sets itself the principle goal of merely welcoming the patient, or alleviating symptoms, or helping the patient to express himself, or making the patient aware of what was previously subconscious, or even to release the emotions, unblock the districts of the body, or put different parts of the body in contact with each other, to find new strategies, to recover inner groups, to tolerate anxieties, or to allow the patient to verbalise his suppressed pain, or to mentalise or to elaborate.

In the first column, we have put these differing objectives (or factors of change) in an order that is as close as possible to the phases of the therapeutic process. In the second column, we have identified which phase each differing factor of change could be related to. In the third column, we have described (albeit briefly) the relative factors of change in the practical and multidimensional terminology used by the Functional School, i.e. in terms of the Functions of the Self and the Basic Experiences of the Self (B.E.S.'s).

As we can see, an integrated course of therapy by phases actually uses almost all of the factors of change and objectives that the various models of psychotherapy have brought to light over the years. The only difference is that instead of remaining constant throughout the whole course of therapy, these factors change phase by phase.

All this helps us to focus even better on *what really occurs* during a course of psychotherapy, regardless of its theoretical basis, differences between models or the terminology used. It allows us to capture the basic essence of interaction in the various therapeutic approaches, allowing us to finally integrate the theories, as well as the theories of technique. In other words, we can better understand which forms of therapeutic intervention most act on what Functions as therapy progresses, what this intervention is based on at a practical level, and, in the final analysis, which factor of change rebuilds what Basic Experience. In the end, every form of therapeutic intervention, whether old or new, can be traced back to one of the individual's underlying functional processes, and therefore to a precise moment in their development, and to certain specific Basic Experiences. Once we have completed this analysis, it becomes possible not only to understand how the therapeutic process works, but also to better it, by improving and refining aims, factors of change, and the techniques relative to them.

Methodology and Techniques

Approaching Functional techniques

I developed most of the techniques of Functional therapy (as is normally the case) over many years of clinical practise, and this bank of techniques has been continually updated as the underlying theory of reference was re-elaborated. Theory and practise supported each other, and brought me closer and closer to a new, innovative, and more advanced vision of man's functioning and how to improve it.

Gradually, I passed from the development of techniques relating to the various "districts of the body" (I had already theorised the stratification of experiences and emotions in the various districts), to techniques aimed at remobilising and reintegrating the Functions of the Self. Finally, more recently, I arrived at methods that were capable of recreating and reconstructing the Basic Experiences of the Self.

Along the way, as each of the central points of Functional thought became apparent, the techniques to use in therapy became defined increasingly clearly. The techniques were developed initially along vague lines, but they have become ever more precise regarding all aspects of psychotherapy: the effects the techniques bring about, their use, and the goals to be reached. Concurrently, the techniques became more precise, as it became clearer what results they could and should produce. We started out feeling our way, uncertainly, with the first mind-body theories, and then we moved in the direction of a complex, articulated, and at the same time well-defined, system of methods, capable of describing the flow of the therapeutic process itself.

In this way, from generic techniques aimed at relaxing the body or regaining awareness, or even randomly mobilising the emotions, we reached the ability to reconstruct fundamental life capacities that have been lost, and recover elements that had become altered or which had ceased to function. In other words, we became able to reconstruct Basic Experiences that had not had a sufficiently positive outcome in patients, reconstruct them, and give them outcomes that were different from what they had been in the past.

Techniques relating to the Basic Experiences of the Self

The techniques used today in Functional Psychotherapy are the ones that I have developed and modified by degrees (with the help of other colleagues) until they reached their present form. Of the 500 and more different techniques that we now use, only a few come from a different source: from Gestalt psychotherapy, or from encounter groups or from the vegetotherapy of the 1970's. Almost all of them, then, are the result of daily practise, and it is through daily practise that they have been gradually refined.

Our main efforts over recent years (on the basis of the cases cited in chapter 5) have focussed on the complete re-elaboration and fine-tuning of the techniques created and used up till now, linking each one with precision to a specific Basic Experience of the Self. This process has brought Functional thought to a higher level, which has allowed us to "purify" the techniques themselves, and render them more effective, thanks to the fact that the objectives had been identified in all their details. What we have done, in effect, is to construct a complete and systematic *theory of technique.*

All of this has ended up making the tools of therapy wider ranging and more complex, but at the same time clearer, more comprehensible, and also easier to use.

Using the techniques

All recent developments in Functional thought work towards increasing the efficiency of therapeutic intervention, reducing the duration of treatment, and creating methods of treatment that are gentler, less invasive, less painful and at the same time more profound. The other side of the coin, however, is that in order to obtain these results, we must be increasingly rigorous when it comes to the way in which these techniques are employed.

The level of precision is increasing, together with the need to remove anything from the techniques that might risk evoking Experiences that are very dissimilar from the ones we wish to reconstruct. Precision had already been an issue in Functional thought for a long time, with regards to the mobilisation of the Functions. This concept has now been extended, quite rightly, to the techniques relative to the reconstruction of the Basic Experiences of the Self.

The concept becomes clearer if we use an example, such as a "simple" technique like using our arms to hit the mat using "Calm Strength". It is clear that this movement must be a movement of Strength, without being either convulsive or frenetic, with a full, open voice that must not be associated with anger. Breathing must be diaphragmatic. It must produce power, not anxiety, and muscle tone must create the sensation of energy rather than weakness. This all seems obvious and easy, but for many patients it is extremely difficult to get even remotely close to the completeness of *Calm Strength*, because anger, fear, fragility, immobility or anxiety have insinuated themselves into the experience, polluting it.

When it comes to group sequences, made up of various "movements", things begin to seem less obvious, although the concept is the same. If we want to access the experience of *Leaning on others* completely, we must lead the participants to this exact experience gradually, helping them as much as possible to reach the real state of *Leaning on someone* for its own sake and nothing else. We must therefore get rid of the obstacles between the group and this objective, aiding their movement towards the experience in question. The way the group is led, the words used, the therapist's tone of voice and the sequence of actions carried out must lead the participants exactly where we want them to go. In the examples of *Leaning on others*, the group will be asked (depending on the obstacles that make it difficult for them to Lean on others) to pass through different stages:

1. not wanting to be in contact with anybody;
2. the desire to be on their own;
3. real distaste and irritation at the thought of touching others;
4. we will then get the participants to move around the room emphasising their desire to be in their own company, without having to answer to anyone about what they choose to do;
5. we will suggest that they avoid contact, so as to avoid irritation;
6. we will suggest that they continue on their way, making space for themselves among the others, using their shoulders to gently push away the other shoulders that they happen to meet. This will allow them to loosen any negativity that is still present regarding contact with others (or at least significantly reduce it), allowing them to approach the Experience of Leaning on Others more fully and will greater ease;
7. then we will gradually place more emphasis on tiredness, on the desire to rest, on the fact that we often have to carry a lot on our shoulders

in life, and that we have a right to leave this weight for a while, at least this once;

8. so, when brushing past someone else in the group shoulder to shoulder, we will suggest that the participants stop to take in a little of the contact, Leaning on the other person just slightly, and then to place just a tiny part of their load on the other person's shoulder, Leaning on someone else just a little in their lives. We will also ask them not to do anything else, leaving their arms hanging downwards, without having to communicate anything in particular to the others, without having to be active. We suggest that they Lean just a little, without falling on top of the others – Leaning lightly;
9. finally, we will suggest that they try Leaning their weight in different ways, a little bit more this time, to that their heads find something to lean on this time as well. We will get the participants to feel all of this making each of them lean on more than one person, to explore different, and perhaps better, possibilities;
10. at the end, we will create the possibility of Leaning more solidly, leading the group together towards the centre of the room, getting everyone to Lean their weight even better, giving them the sense of being one big *organism*, which welcomes each of them with a feeling of serenity and calm, helping them to feel close to one another and rediscover the tranquillity and pleasure of Leaning on Others.

The therapist must not neglect to make sure that the participants breathe correctly, helping them to "let go", calming them down, so that the sensations can flow freely. The Experience must be as pleasant as possible, as well as being as close as possible to the exact Basic Experience of Leaning on Others. All of this must be done without making the sequence last too long, or it would tire the group too much.

These considerations must guide us when we wish to construct or perfect a "group sequence". Obviously, the job of perfecting the techniques never stops. It must be continuous. All techniques can and must be perfected as we gain more knowledge of the way therapy and human beings work, hand in hand with our experience of clinical practise. This process of improvement must, however, aim towards a greater streamlining of the techniques, rendering them ever more pertinent, simple and effective. We must avoid the temptation to cram in more and more elements, complicating them, contaminating them with other Experiences.

Similar considerations must be made concerning the invention of new techniques and sequences. It is all too easy to fall into the trap of mixing different sequences together to form new, multiple combinations, or adding new pieces to a sequence, or removing parts that are, on the contrary, essential for reaching that particular Basic Experience of the Self. The risk is actually that of making the techniques that already exist less effective, or of creating new ones that are not new at all and which are, in fact, less suited to the reconstruction of a given Functional process.

Creativity and inventiveness are undoubtedly an essential part of therapy, but this does not mean improvising on the spur of the moment, or being creative for the fun of it. Techniques must actually be consolidated a little at a time, gaining strength gradually as they are applied and their effects verified. If we change these techniques, or substitute them with others, our actions must be the fruit of profound work at a theoretical level. Even when there are innovations, these must serve to improve existing methodologies, and they must therefore be based on rigorous testing as to how they really help us to reach the heart of a particular Basic Experience alone and none other.

The therapist's creativity lies in choosing and using the right technique for every situation, and also in executing them paying attention to every little detail (voice, words, tone, pauses, music, lighting...), more than in the creation of new techniques, much as an actor's creativity lies in interpreting existing texts, or a painter's lies in finding the right combination of colours.

The heritage of techniques and methods must be consolidated, rather than rendered confusingly unfocussed or disorganised. Whilst gathering together the work of years of experience and the techniques created, I have myself weeded out a lot, eliminating what appeared not to be useful, repetitions, or hybrid, confused "variations" of many group sequences which I had thought to be new possibilities but which had not been particularly effective in reality. In so doing, I have sought to consolidate a methodological heritage which gives Functional theory the richness of a complete therapeutic model, but which also constitutes the backbone of its success at a practical level.

Interpreting patients' experience

Functional therapy's theoretical and practical system, as it has been defined and organised, also provides us with a clearer understanding of patient's feelings and reactions to the techniques that we offer them. The same group sequence can be experienced differently by each patient, because of their different histories and their different paths through life.

However, if the techniques are effective and *focussed*, helping the patient to reach the very heart of a Basic Experience, then we will know how to manage any difficulties that we meet along the way with greater simplicity-situations that seem complicated at first sight, but which turn out to be merely complex. They are complex simply because there are numerous Basic Experiences that need to be reconstructed in therapy.

As we have seen, the basic knots that need to be unravelled are similar for many patients, regardless of differences in their personal histories. Either a person is able to live a Basic Experience fully, because they have conserved it (or it has already been recovered) or not. If they are not, then the ways in which people react may well differ, but always in relations to what it was that polluted that particular Basic Experience. Moreover, the traces left by the past in the various Functional levels are always more or less the same ones: alterations in muscle tone, in the way of moving, in fantasies, in the patient's symbolism, habitual postures, voice, breathing, alterations in the functioning of the autonomic nervous system. If a person finds it hard to "let go", he will find it hard to let go whatever the situation, whether it be diving head first into a swimming pool, letting loose at a party, dancing wildly or making love without thinking. The specific circumstances are no longer important if we deal with what underlies these difficulties, i.e. the Basic Experience.

Therefore, along general lines, we can say that if a Basic Experience is open and accessible, then everyone will experience a given situation in more or less the same way. "Being Held" sets off very similar emotions in every human being: a sense of security, protection, warmth, and tranquillity. Obviously, the nuances can be different according to each person's characteristics and experience, but the central nucleus of their feelings is more or less the same because it is directly linked to the particular Basic Experience that they are living. Let us not forget that intervening on a Basic Experience means intervening "at the root" – regardless of specific behaviour or situations. It means acting on the individual's deepest functioning.

If, on the other hand, the patient's feelings differ considerably from the sensations that are characteristic for that Basic Experience, then it means that there are altered functional processes, or other Basic Experiences mixed up with the one that we are currently working on. Anger can insinuate itself into Calm Strength and upset its functioning; "Letting Go" can get mixed up with sadness and solitude; the Experience of Being Held can become difficult if we keep worrying about the person holding us.

We must not therefore get lost in the meanders of individual experiences. Naturally, we must welcome them, but we must not stop at a passive acceptance that everyone experiences a given therapeutic technique in their own way because "that's just the way they are", and that beyond this there is nothing to be said or done. The important thing is to link these reactions to the patient's past, to the other Basic Experiences, and the other Functional processes that have insinuated themselves and become confused with the Basic Experience in question.

If Letting Go does not function, it means that something has become altered over time. That is what counts. The problems that arise are more or less the same for everyone: fear associated with Letting Go, negative feeling when Letting Go, Rigid Control preventing this Experience, or not having been Held enough.

By referring to the Basic Experiences of the Self, we can clearly see what Experiences are presently accessible to the individual, which of them have become consolidated capacities or the negative conditions that have impeded or altered them in the patient's past. At this point it becomes very clear what we must do for each person and what direction we must move in.

At times it is also possible to reconstruct exactly what happened in the past, highlighting a *recurring theme* which carries through to the patient's present conditions, connecting the characteristics of the patient's present baggage of Basic Experiences with his past experiences. However, it is not always possible to reconstruct the patient's past with certainty, i.e. finding the specific events and episodes that have prevented the full unfolding of the Basic Experiences. However, this by no means prejudices the process of change. The important thing is to succeed in recovering and reconstructing the capacities connected to the deficient Basic Experiences, helping the individual to regain a full range of behaviour patterns and potentialities that will allow him to face any situation, enjoy life, and live it intensely and with pleasure.

An integrated model of psychotherapy

Premise

At this point, it is easier for us to picture the direction that therapy may take or that it is already taking. It has emerged that it no longer makes sense to consider merely "fragments" of therapy or single, limited techniques (and this will become clearer and clearer as time goes on). We must make sure, however, that we do not put techniques together simplistically. We must combine them within the general framework of an overall view, a theoretical model and a theory of technique.

If we do not do this, we run the risk of mistakenly confusing the techniques for the process, when in reality the therapeutic process is something much more complex, of which the techniques are merely an expression. This becomes even more clear if we consider that today we are moving towards overcoming the confines that exist between existing therapeutic approaches to create an interconnected and unified picture of psychotherapy, as well as the relationship between helper and patient in general.

It no longer makes much sense to leave the contributions that each approach has made to our knowledge of human functioning, and the techniques discovered for restoring it to full health, in their separate "compartments". However, this does not mean that we must cut out and paste together lots of different techniques and bits of theory. What we need, on the contrary, is to build a new theory from scratch, together with a theory of technique, both of which must be *integrated*, within a *multidimensional* vision, in which we consider all the levels of functioning of the Self and all the points of view and sectors that have been gradually brought into focus by the various models of psychotherapy.

Integrated psychotherapy is not a scientific heresy. Nor is it a utopia. Rather, it is a reality that each reform in thought has helped to create, one of which is Functional thought, which has allowed us to look at the human organism as a unified whole, whilst at the same time improving operability, precision and depth.

Angela: a case history

This subsection aims to represent a cross-section of an *integrated* course of therapy: a "phase" in therapy undergone by a patient that we will call Angela.

Angela, a patient of mine, is a 34 year old woman who has been suffering from panic attacks for a few years, especially when she goes through tunnels on cars or coaches, when she has to go on a ferry or a plane, or when she is in lifts [elevators]. In crowded places, she feels like she is going to suffocate. Her life has become difficult, tiring, and sad, with continual thoughts, broodings, and recriminations that have become real obsessions.

The phase in therapy described below is centred on the recovery of *Strength* in Angela's life, which existed only at a very early age (as the capacity to intervene calmly, openly and directly on her surroundings), and which has now become suffocated by anger and a sense of impotence.

The example below shows just one of the numerous objectives that we can pursue in therapy; just one of the Basic Experiences that must be recovered and rebuilt in order to recover stable, concrete capacities.

The story unfolds to show, in the most practical way possible, which *techniques* and which *modalities of therapy* are used in Functional therapy (one of the first attempts at creating an integrated form of psychotherapy). Only an all-encompassing theory can give rise to a complex and articulated theory of technique, whereby the many techniques are integrated with one another around precise objectives and are remodelled according to an overall theory of reference.

The numbers in the text have been added to draw attention, together with the italics, to the various types of *techniques* and *modalities of therapy* put into action as we go along.

Phase in an integrated course of therapy

When she sees her brother, Angela is tense and worried. She needs to resolve a dispute that has been undermining their relationship for a while regarding who has to look after their mother, how to help her, what to do. Angela feels that Sergio has not helped her at all. On the contrary, all he has done has been to criticise her and oppose her.

Yet, as always, when it comes to what she should say and how to say it, Angela feels awkward and closed. She finds it really difficult to express her Strength. Her throat is contracted and her voice comes out sounding false and shaky; her breathing is laboured. Instead of Strength, what comes out is a stifled, impotent anger.

We talk about this in therapy. Angela tells me about an episode with her brother, and the malaise that prevents her from being able to face up to him calmly and with determination.

For the first time, she finally becomes fully aware of her difficulty: the fact that when she tries to express Strength she runs into other, early emotions that are mixed in with it, polluting her Strength, preventing her from using it and making her incapable of resolving her relationships with others satisfactorily.

This *full realisation* (awareness, 1a) is a factor of change (although this is not yet sufficient), and is clearly an element that has arisen in therapy. There have been moments during her therapy session where she needed to express Strength and she was not able to. The therapist had asked Angela to *hit the mat decisively, using her Strength* (1b), and it had already become clear that she was lacking a real *movement of Strength* (1c) towards the outside world. *The therapist made this element more evident* (1d), but he also *increased her sensitivity* (1e), getting her used to *reopening her breathing* (1f) and *perceiving the sensations deep within her body* (1g), *getting her to talk about them* (1h) after each exercise using the body.

Angela *talks during therapy* (elaborate, mentalize, 2a) about the situation with her brother and the way things are going, and she becomes more and more aware of the old traces and the old sensations that have got mixed up with her Strength, disturbing it.

However, the fact that she has realised this, and can talk about it with the therapist, is not enough to resolve Angela's problem. It is not enough merely to *gain awareness* (1) of the way she functions, nor is it enough for the therapist to *give suggestions and provide help to understand what new strategies of behaviour she can put into action* (2b). It is not sufficient for Angela to know she makes cognitive "generalisations" and for her to *decide* (2c) that she wants to get rid of them.

Angela has, however, shown *moments of anger, even during a therapy session, even at times with the therapist* (transference, 3a), and she feels that she is not receiving real help for the umpteenth time in her life. She feels that nothing will change, that deep down the therapist does not really care about how she feels, about how much she is suffering, about the fact that therapy is not going at all well.

However, given that the therapist makes the patient feel that *he is there for her* (3b) with his genuine understanding, the *way he looks at her* (3c), his *tone of voice* (3d), the *touch of his hands* (3e) and his *words of welcome* (3f), Angela will soon feel that the origins of her negative feelings lie in remote events of the past, and that in reality her feelings are aimed at these events in her life, and not her current relationship with the therapist.

This is less a case of *analysing transference* (3g), and more one of correctly tracing these feelings back to their original source. The therapist *connects this anger to past events* (3h) in Angela's life with great clarity. The *negative transference melts away* (3i) and the positive feelings that underlie the relationship with the therapist soon come to the fore.

Yet again, however, *resolving the transference* (3i) is not sufficient to bring about a permanent change in Angela's condition. How should we proceed then?

Of course, we could *"release" some of the old anger* (releasing/ letting out the emotions, 4a) that Angela has accumulated over time. We do work a little on this in therapy. Angela can *simulate a conversation with old and new figures in her life* (4b) as if they were there in front of her, chiding them quite bitterly, with negative words, eloquently angry movements and reproving facial expressions.

However, even this *release* (4) cannot resolve the situation: accumulated anger can never be completely released. It always reproduces itself. This because the functional processes connected to it have become altered of closed in a short circuit (breathing, postures, tone of voice, inner images).

All of this must therefore be modified. We must modify her Strength in an "integrated" way, recommencing our journey from a moment "before" the alterations set in, this time taking the right road.

The therapist *notes his own sense of discomfort* (countertransference, 5a), a *painful sensation in the pit of his stomach* (5b) that he is very familiar with, because he often had to deal with it during his own therapy: a sensation connected to his own, old sense of impotence. *Becoming aware* of this, and *going back to old memories* (5c) will help him to tune in to Angela's suffering even better, to really feel where she is right now. This will help him to get through to her more easily, and stay with her. *Countertransference that has been widened to multiple planes of functioning* (5a) is an important therapeutic tool.

Physical contact, touching the patient with his hands (deep contact, good-parent, 6a) also allows the therapist to feel Angela's fragility, going beyond appearances. Deep down, Angela is just a little girl who needs help. Her anger *does not produce resentment* in me (6b). It does not sadden me, nor does it hinder me.

Using countertransference (5) and *perceiving the other person on many levels* (6c) are the two pillars that permit the therapist *not to react* (6d) to the patient's behaviour, *not to lapse into an automatic response* (6c). Instead, he can take new paths and directions that are different from the ones that the patient had experienced in her old relationships with key adult figures, and which had been reconfirmed in her relationships as an adult. The therapist is a "new parent" (6f), a second chance for Angela; he is a "good" parent (6f) who doesn't react like her real parents reacted, and nor does he react life people automatically *react*, even now, to Angela's devious, hidden anger.

At this point, Angela also works in her *memories* (reconstructing the past, 7a). She talks about this complete inability to express Strength when she was a girl, and about the fact that her older brother suppressed and stopped it. Her memories have now become *enriched with detail* (7b) compared to the beginning of therapy, but also *full of emotions* (7c). Moreover, where Angela's emotions are not yet open, the therapist expresses them for her, *with her "auxiliary Self"* (7d), i.e. using his own *emotional reactions* (7e) to Angela's past situation, using a *suitable tone of voice* (7f), together with *eye contact* (7g), a *gesture* (7h) and an *encouraging touch* (7i). Angela's *sadness resurfaces* (7l) when she thinks about the little girl that she used to be. Her pain about the way the events in her life unfolded finally comes out, but this time the pain and the sadness are open. A soft weeping (7m) accompanies this, which the therapist, or "good parent" can welcome and console.

Yet not even this cathartic release of painful emotions, on its own or in conjunction with the previous phases, can be sufficient for profound, complete change; as was the case with the abreaction of her anger. The therapeutic process can offer still more.

Angela talks in therapy about *dreams that she has been having lately* (her innermost level, 8a) about crashing into another car whilst driving or an argument with a colleague from the hospital where she works. Angela and the therapist examine the dreams together, and *the therapist highlights that her Strength is beginning to come out* (8b) (new element), but that it is still too contaminated with anger (old element).

We work on *breathing* (BES Wellbeing, 9a) in order to *increase the level of pleasant sensations* (9b) and *consolidate wellbeing* (9c), going beyond the old encapsulated traces that produce unhappiness and suffering. *Massages* (9d) also finally help Angela to find moments of relaxed calm, diffused pleasantness, and quiet wellbeing. Because of this, her open, calm Strength will really be able to emerge. Only genuine wellbeing can provide a real basis, the foundations for her Strength.

Another element that can serve as a source for calm Strength is an inner sense of *vitality* (B.E.S. Vitality, 10a). Several *massages* of the arms and back help to *bring these areas to life* (10b), given that they had become withdrawn, closed, lifeless. *Intense movement* (10c), consisting in throwing the arms and legs outwards, carried to their extreme, and using an *open and decisive voice* (10d) allow her to feel her blood circulating more intensely, together with an energy that she feels needs to be let out and focussed on something real, and "even move mountains!". The therapist *emphasises* (10e) that these sensations are re-emerging.

In the meantime, Angela talks in therapy about *the sensations she experiences during the week* (changes, 11a). The therapist helps her to *understand their meaning* (11b) and to see how the course of therapy is progressing. Elements that represent evident changes in the direction of a new way of functioning are *emphasised* (11c) (sleeping better, changes in her menstrual cycle, her voice is becoming more open), and separated from elements where her old functioning is still manifest (tense jaw, tiredness when she's doing things, running away from people who are critical of her).

The therapist's *presence* (B.E.S. Containment, 12a), his *reassuring words* (12b), a *touch of the hand* (12c) on the arm or the back of her neck, provide a sense of containment and tranquillity which allow Angela to make progress in therapy.

At this point, we can start a process of authentic, genuine *reconstruction of the Basic Experience of the Self relating to Strength* (14), a fundamental Experience in child development.

It is necessary for us to repeat and rebuild the Basic Experience of Strength because it has been disturbed by other emotions in Angela that have blocked or altered it, as we have already seen. Only at this point in therapy are we able to do this, because the previous phases and techniques have prepared the ground. The patient's *Functions have been sufficiently mobilised* (13): breathing (13b), the autonomic nervous system (13c), muscle tone (13d), hormones (13e), inner sensations (13f) and the voice (13g); and then movements (13h) (although only a little), postures and body language (13i) with the help f the therapist, who adjusted Angela's position with his hands, getting her settled into a better position. The emotions have also loosened a fair amount (13j): both the negative and the positive ones. Her memories have been reopened quite a lot (13k); she has once again gained awareness of past events (13l). Angela's tender feelings towards the child she used to be have started to change the value that she attributes to herself (13m).

To reopen her Calm, direct Strength, we must start with its earliest roots, a more Archaic Strength, getting Angela to make very precise movements, such as *repeatedly pushing gently with her feet* (14a), *moving her legs* (14b), and *clearing a space around her more forcefully* (14c) by opening out her whole body after it has been closed in a foetal position.

These movements absolutely must, however, be *associated with other Functions* (integration, 15a): her voice, breathing and the emotional implications of the exercises must be in complete harmony with this Archaic, Gentle, not destructive Strength. This form of Strength is not "against" anything; rather it represents expansion and growth. The therapist *suggests what modifications are necessary* in the voice, or the movements (15b). He also *suggests the emotions* that correspond to Original Strength (15c), *describing the sense of this Basic Experience* (15d), just as a little girl would experience it if her growth and her relationship with her surroundings had been positive and full.

Angela finally starts to perceive *the first sensations* linked to Archaic Strength during therapy (effects, 16a): the pleasure of opening herself up and making way for herself without the paralysing presence of anger. The sensations are *consolidated by the therapist's explanatory phrases* (16b), which explain how they work at a physiological level. They are also reinforced by *breathing* (16c) and also by *massage* (16d) in the areas that are still struggling to recover the mobility of their muscle tone, or which have low thresholds of perception, restoring the vitality of the tissue.

Because this Basic Experience is rooted so early in child development, we can touch very deep vital functional processes (full recovery of the BES, 17a). We can go to an even deeper level, as well, if the *therapist creates a specific atmosphere using his voice and words* (17b). This is like telling a story to the little girl in Angela, a story about Archaic Strength, and the sensations that it brings about, and about what it is really like to be little and to be able to go through this experience in a positive way. The therapist talks to Angela whilst holding her in an intense, reassuring contact, just like when talking to a little child. The therapist *touches* her (17c), holding her shoulder, her hand, holding her head in his hands, *holding her in his arms* (17d), just as if she really were a little girl, to help her to recover that exact Experience, that goes back to such a remote moment in her development, and none other, in all its facets, characteristics and details.

Therefore, the patient goes through the Experience in a way that is completely different compared to the past – this time it is full and positive. The Experience can be further consolidated using a *guided visualisation sequence* (18a) that exactly reproduces situations of this type. The therapist's voice *guides the patient step by step* (18b) through the scene, which should be as exact as possible to help the patient to perceive Archaic Strength. For example, the patient is asked to imagine being curled up, wrapped in leaves. Inside the leaves, it is warm, welcoming, and she feels protected and calm. The colours are warm and there is a familiar smell. Then she must imagine the desire to open out, to start pushing with her arms, legs, and back. She feels how pleasant it is to open out her body, shift her wrappings, and come out into the open, the light, and the air. She pushes the wrappings open using Gentle Strength and opens the wrappings, opening out her body and her breathing.

The sky is blue and the sun is warm. She notices the colours, the smells, and the sounds. She opens up, expands, and spreads herself out.

Angela reports that over the last week she experienced the *return of an old symptom* (19a) from when she was 7 years old: she couldn't stop vomiting. The *therapist shows her* that therapy has managed to reach a very deep, very early functional process, at the root of the first set of symptoms tied to her horrible sensations of impotence and anger. The old symptom is a bit like being able to go back to the point just before her life took a wrong turn, before she took the road that lead to suffering and dysfunction.

We still need to *reopen old positive functional processes* (20a) using breathing, massage, and movements that help to recover direct, full Strength more and more. We proceed *one step at a time* (20b) with *increasingly intense movements* (20c), *integrated, as always, with the voice, breathing, emotions, and meaning* (20d). *The movements of Gentle Strength have been studied and honed* (20e) in such a way as to help the patient get as close as possible to the early Experiences that all children go through with regards to Gentle Strength. For this reason, the movements are simple and archaic, but at the same time extremely evocative.

We still have to *dissolve her old fears* (21a), *reassuring her using words* (21b), *eye contact* (21c), *tone of voice* (21d) and *touch* (21e).

Moreover, we must *further intensify her sensations* (22a) by opening up her *breathing* (22b), getting her to *listen to herself* (22c) and *describe all the sensations* (22d) that she feels in her body, no matter how small or how humble.

At this stage, the muscles that are still retaining old traces and old sensations are loosened with *deep massage* (23a).

As we can see, this complex, *integrated* procedure is much more far-reaching than autogenic training or techniques using suggestion, gestaltic therapy of the parts or symbolic elaboration.

Now we can *work directly on Angela's voice* (24a), helping her, during therapy, to produce an intense, open sound. *The therapist shows her how to do it* (24b), *telling her to open her mouth and throat wide* (24c), *he shows her what still is not working* (24d) and *suggests improvements* (24e). The voice is an important expression of Strength.

At the same time, we work on *Angela's throat with delicate massages* (25a) getting her to assume *postures where the neck is open* (25b).

Angela describes the feelings of Strength that she has recovered in therapy (26a), *as well as discussing her experiences of Strength in her life outside therapy* (26b), and she is able to *see clearly which elements are old and which are new* (26c) with the therapist's help, where necessary, who *explains even more clearly* (26d) what has changed in real terms and what elements are old traces.

Angela reports that she faced up to her boss at work for the first time without getting annoyed, without shaking; finally obtaining a transfer to a different office because her workload was unjustly and excessively heavy.

She also telephoned her brother and announced that she does not want things to continue the way they have been, she cannot stand it any more. However, they decide to talk about things calmly, face to face. When Sergio's aggression explodes yet again, she doesn't burst into tears as she used to.

She manages to *express Calm Strength in therapy* (27a). Calm Strength must be based on the *integration of all the Functions* (27b): an open, strong voice free from anger or fear, decisive movements, active (but not rigid) muscle tone, decisive facial expressions, an intense, strong-willed posture, breathing that is neither held nor breathless, pleasant sensations of Strength, images of Strength, memories of Strength.

If any of these Functions are not fully appropriate and congruent, *the therapist helped the patient to open those as well* (27c) by explaining which elements and how to improve them (27d), sometimes offering himself as an example.

Angela *reports a few more dreams about Calm Strength* (28a), but it is no longer necessary to highlight the connection between the elements of the dream to the Experience of Calm Strength, because the connection has become fully evident.

She reports episodes in her real life (29a) in which Calm Strength emerges more and more clearly. Every time that she manages this, she *receives praise* (reinforcement, 30a) and *encouragement from the therapist* (30b) just as she did when she managed to express Calm Strength in therapy (30c). The therapist's *face, voice, words, and touch* (30d) express his happiness to her (and all this is much more far-reaching than a behavioural reinforcement technique). In the end, *Calm, open Strength* will become an authentic *capacity* (31a) in Angela's life, which she will be able to turn to, without anger and without fear, whenever she wants.

The different techniques, objectives, and factors of change

As we have already mentioned in the introduction, the numbers in brackets stand for the various *factors of change* (or *modalities of therapy*, in other words) that have been used, moment by moment, in the phase of therapy described above. The letters, on the other hand, indicate the *techniques* relating to each factor of change. What we are talking about, in other words, are techniques and modalities of therapy that clearly belong to different theoretical models of psychotherapy which each touch on different levels of the Self.

What follows is a list summing up the different factors of change (otherwise known as modalities of therapy or partial objectives) and the techniques touched on during this phase in Angela's therapy.

1. *Gaining a full awareness* that she does not have full, open Strength, that she can use outwardly, and that her Strength is stifled by the anger that is mixed up with it. She fully realises, on an emotional level, how all this ties in with her past and her everyday life *(insight).*
2. *Elaborating and mentalising her behaviour* relating to the Strength in her life (especially in her relationship with her brother), realising that she makes cognitive generalisations and finding strategies to modify this.
3. *Reliving her old anger* during therapy, *connecting* it to events in her past, analysing *negative transference* and above all *eliminating it.*

4. *Letting out the anger* that is preventing her from using her Strength *(abreaction).*
5. *The therapist utilises countertransference, widened to all levels of the Self* (what he feels at an emotional level, what he feels on the physical plane and his memories, especially in relation to his own therapy).
6. *Deep contact between the therapist and the patient. Consolidating the real affective relationship* in a new adult-parent relationship, a "good" parent. The therapist must *avoid reacting automatically* to the patient, *perceiving what the patient is really like* below the surface.
7. *The patient reconstructs her past, working on old memories,* completing them with emotions and sensations. Sadness re-emerges for events that happened in the past, during her childhood or adolescence *(catharsis).*
8. *Analysis and interpretation of dreams,* highlighting progress made: what has already changed and what still remains of the old traces.
9. *Rediscovering the Basic Experience of deep-down well-being* as the real basis for Calm Strength, a strength that comes from deep down, instead of being produced by gritting the teeth and making a huge effort.
10. *Recovering the Basic Experience of Vitality.* Rediscovering energy, another fundamental elements of Strength, something that flows inside, moving the will to act decisively.
11. *Highlight changes* by examining the series of sensations that Angela experiences between sittings, in every day life. Look at the fact that the old elements are going away and the new elements are becoming established.
12. *Recovery of the Basic Experience of Being Contained.* The therapist acts as a container for the patient's fears and anxieties. The presence of the therapist calms her and allows her to get to the heart of the problem.
13. *Mobilising the Functions,* on all planes of the Self if possible; starting to give them a greater amplitude, and a more balanced presence within the Self as a whole, as well as the capacity to pass easily from one polarity to another (being tough ↔ being tender, sympathetic activation ↔ parasympathetic activation, soft muscle tone ↔ tense muscle tone, sadness ↔ happiness, painful memories ↔ pleasant memories).
14. *Recovery and Reconstruction of the Basic Experience of Original Strength and Gentle Strength.*
15. *Reintegrating the Functions, reconnecting* each Function to the others until we reconstitute the unitary nature of the Self and all the Functions start to contribute equally to the fullness of life's experiences again.

16. *Utilise the effects of work on Original Strength, consolidating the relative sensations,* underlining and intensifying the relative feelings.
17. *Full recovery of the Basic Experience, creating the right atmosphere,* paying attention to every detail to help the patient to reach exactly that Basic Experience and none other.
18. *Consolidate Original Strength through a guided visualisation sequence*, on various sensorial levels.
19. *Return of an "Old Symptom"*, the return to the way the organism functioned when it had just become altered, becoming pathological. The therapist receives confirmation that the therapy is proceeding in the right direction and he can use this to strengthen the patient's trust in the process.
20. *Recovery of the Basic Experience of Gentle Strength and Open Strength.* Opening old, positive functional processes still further.
21. *Further work on Being Held and Being Contained* and on dissolving old fears.
22. *Intensifying the Sensations. Basic Experience of the Sensations.*
23. *Loosening muscle tensions that are still preventing the full recovery of the capacities that have been stifled.* Dissolving the last old traces.
24. *Working on the voice as a further consolidation of Strength.*
25. *Opening the throat to open Angela's vocal expression in general.*
26. *Taking stock of Angela's recovered Strength.* Episodes of Strength in Angela's life.
27. *Recovery of the Experience of Calm Strength.*
28. *Dreams about Calm Strength (consolidation).*
29. *Episodes of Calm Strength in Angela's life.*
30. *Reinforcement, encouragement of Angela's Calm Strength.*
31. *Complete recovery of Calm Strength and Open Strength as real capacities*, modalities that have become an irreversible part of Angela's baggage.

Reconnecting, integrating, and transforming techniques

Angela's case history clearly shows us that the techniques used were not just techniques *placed* one after another – they were not merely *added together.* The techniques used have become part of an overall, *integrated* picture, in which each technique has been *strengthened* and *developed.*

Each and every technique contributes to what we consider to be *integrated objectives*: the overall factors of change upheld by an *integrated theory*, i.e. the rebalancing of the Self, the mobilisation of all the Functions on all levels and the recovery and reconstruction of the Basic Experiences.

What we have, therefore, is a *series* of factors of change and techniques that are interrelated. For this reason, each has been significantly strengthened, both because it has been freed of any elements that limited them, such as elements that were outdated, not having been upheld by advances in scientific knowledge, and also because it has been linked together within the context of a new, *integrated* theory.

To sum up, then, using techniques and factors of change in an *integrated* way means:

- that every technique or factor of change is linked to all the others, at all times;
- the techniques have all been modified so as to lead on naturally from one to another;
- each factor of change is profoundly linked to the overall factors of change of the theory as a whole, and each must contribute to that end.

The patient's awareness that she has not possessed Calm Strength since she was little, the analysis of her anger through transference, its subsequence release (abreaction), the catharsis of her old sadness and changing cognitive and behavioural strategies all pave way for the reconstruction of the Basic Experience of Calm Strength, and yet each one of these elements is a technique and an objective in its own right.

However, these techniques have taken on different meanings within the context of an *overall integrated theory*. We can therefore note that:

- insight in this case is not referred to anger in the sense of an innate destructive drive, but rather as a result of experiences in the subject's environment that have generated it and rendered it rigid;
- transference is not merely interpreted, but also dissolved by the therapist's real presence as a good parent, with a deep contact that is not just verbal;
- the release of anger is not considered to be an opportunity to "let out accumulated feeling" as if it were a tank being emptied, but rather an opportunity to perceive what's inside, compressed, so that the patient will be able to abandon it more easily;

- sadness and crying are not encouraged if they emerge with old, stereotyped modalities;
- the new strategies are not set off by purely cognitive action and then trusted to the willpower of the patient.

The techniques as a system of integrated elements

In effect, the techniques themselves assume a different guise, not just because they are always used in conjunction with one another, but also because they themselves take a different, wider, connotation, enlarged to various aspects of the Self. Each of them becomes *integrated*, in the sense that numerous Functions and functional processes are *integrated* within it.

Letters were added to the numbers in brackets in Angela's case history. These refer to the various elements, the various Functions, that each technique, when adapted to the overall theory, can integrate within it.

Let us look at how this happens in greater detail, using the same examples that were chosen in the previous section in reference to the different meanings assumed by the various techniques when they are used within the context of a greater, *integrated* theory.

- Awareness also arises from experiencing real movements of Strength during therapy, breathing and physical sensations;
- The negative transference resolves itself because the therapist is "close" to Angela, not just with his words, but also in the way he looks at her, the touch of his hand, his tone of voice and a body position consisting in leaning forward affectionately;
- The anger is expressed with the body as well as verbally, with direct movements as well as the imagination. Above all, it is resolved not because the therapist lays emphasis on "letting it all out", but because of the tenderness that Angela has recovered during therapy;
- Crying is not limited to tears, it is not tense and stifled, but comes from deep down, in a wave of sadness that is also sweet, at the same time. This sweetness is because the diaphragm is relaxed, the voice is no longer stifled, the eyes are mobilised. Furthermore, her crying is received by the therapist not just verbally but physically, holding her in his arms;
- The changes in the strategies for every day life are also the fruit of a capacity to start breathing in a different way when anxiety and immobil-

ity return in certain situations, from body movements experienced during therapy, plans shaped during guided visualisation sequences (devised with this specific aim in mind). The decision to face her brother is not an act that has merely been constructed artificially with her willpower. It is based on a deep wellbeing and a sense of vitality, prompting her to take action naturally;

– Above all, the full recovery of Strength is also founded in the specific objectives of the integrated theory, on the mobilisation of all the Functions, and on the complete reconstruction of a Basic Experience (not just on different techniques from various approaches); together with all the consequences that this implies – all the diffused, multiple, extremely intense effects that can arise from these Experiences and the integration of the Self.

Conclusion

For a course of therapy and a theoretical model to be truly *integrated*, they must be so on many levels, and they must be able to:

– unite the fields of investigation and clinical practise;
– construct an outline of individual functioning that is overall, global and multidimensional;
– formulate objectives, modalities of therapy, factors of change and techniques within the context of a more complex and complete vision, interconnected and integrated on multiple levels of functioning;
– integrate the positive contributions of the various clinical and scientific approaches in terms of techniques, objectives and factors of change;
– all the above must accompany a form of intervention that is complete and full, in order to make it more and more effective, profound and long-lasting, and as painless as possible;
– construct a genuine condition of wellbeing, in terms of both cure and intervention.

A protocol for assessment in Functional Psychotherapy

The assessment protocol for psychotherapy, developed by the author, is composed of 16 points representing the various Functional levels of the Self and of several important Basic Experiences. The different points are assessed on the basis of both the patient's answers to certain direct questions, and through observation made during the course of certain therapeutic techniques. For each one of the 16 points, there are 4 possible levels of functioning for the patient (which are described in detail, and are therefore standardised): from A, which represents the best, or most mobile level, down to D, which represents the worst, or most rigid, level.

In our research on the results obtained during therapy, we assigned a value of 4 to A, 3 points to B, 2 to C and 1 to D. This provides us with an overall score, from a minimum of 16 in the case of maximum intervention, to a maximum of 64 for a condition of full functioning.

1. ABANDONING ONESELF/LETTING GO ↔ CONTROL
Values range from a capacity to loosen control and abandon oneself (A) → to movements that are all controlled and forced (D).

2. PROJECTUAL IMAGINATION
Values range from a capacity to summon exact images at will, rich with details and sensations (A) → to poor or limited images, or images which are full of involuntary negative elements (D).

3. DREAMS
Values range from the ability to dream clear dreams that the patient himself is able to understand (A) → to the inability to remember dreams, or the presence of numerous, often frightening, dreams (D).

4. TENDER ↔ HARD/TOUGH VALUES
Values range from a good balance between hard/tough values and tender values (A) → to the distinct prevalence of hard values (D).

5. FEAR
Values range from a prevalent sensation of calm and pleasure, even if points of the body typically associated with old fears are stimulated (A) → to explosions of panic or anger associated with these selfsame points of the body (D).

6. ANGER
Values range from an open anger, expressed with directness, but without fury or rage (A) → to a compressed, rancorous anger (D).

7. SOFT, TENDER MOVEMENTS
Values range from a capacity to feel and express tenderness with tender movements (A) →

to difficulty in expressing or feeling tenderness due to an excess of hard/toughness and aggressiveness (D).

8. RELEASING BODYWEIGHT "DOWNWARDS"
Values range from the ability to throw the legs downwards with ease, completely loosening control over them immediately afterwards (A) → to the completely inability either to throw them down or to let go of them afterwards (D).

9. MOBILITY
Values range from an ability to break into a sudden leap or jump following a moment of calm (A) → to huge difficulty in coming out of the previous state of immobility (D).

10. CALM STRENGTH
Values range from strength expressed with calm movements, voice and breathing (A) → to a lack of strength, accompanied by agitated, angry movements and a weak voice (D).

11. HYPOTONIA ↔ HYPERTONIA
Values range from a relaxed muscle tone that allows the neck to follow the movements produced by the therapist as he moves the patient's head (A) → to rigid, controlled muscle tone that either prevents movement or anticipates it (D).

12. PAIN THRESHOLDS
Values range from a normal pain threshold, where the patient is able to feel pleasant sensations even when areas are pressed hard, but not violently (A) → to an alteration in the pain threshold, provoking high levels of pain or insensitivity to touch (D).

13. VOICE
Values range from a full voice, being open and sonorous (A) → to a closed, weak, strangled voice (D).

14. BREATHING
Values range from deep breathing from the diaphragm, with calm and wellbeing (A) → to shallow, thoracic breathing, closed and held (D).

15. YAWNS
Values range from a capacity to yawn, loosen tension, lessen hard, rigid control (A) → to few or no yawns, holding a forced, exaggerated vigilance (D).

16. DEEP DOWN WELLBEING
Values range from a capacity to relax at a deep level, being able to "just be", in a state of vagotonia after working with the therapist on diaphragmatic breathing (A) → to a state of vigilance with signs that the sympathetic nervous system is still in action even following work on deep breathing (D).

Polarity Diagrams

We can use the evaluations made using the assessment protocol to extrapolate a "polarity diagram". This is a 360° graphic representation of the state of the patient's functioning, where the axes of the 16 points of the protocol are placed like the spokes on a wheel and the 4 levels (from A to D) are placed in concentric circles across these "spokes"; D being the innermost circle, and A being the outermost ring.

Figures 9 and 10 show the case of a patient before and after therapy. This form of representation is evocative and immediate, because we go from a figure that looks collapsed in on itself (almost like the Self has folded in on itself), to one that is full and expanded.

Fig. 9. *Representation of the polarities before therapy*

Patient: Anna
Age: 38 years old

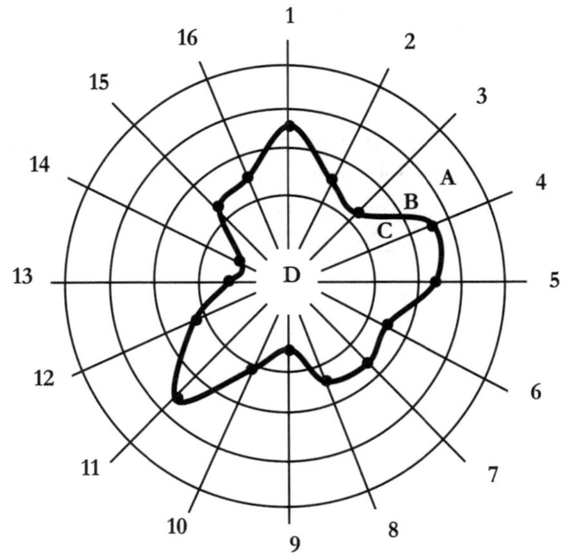

Fig. 10. *Representation of the polarities after therapy*

Patient: Anna
Age: 38 years of age

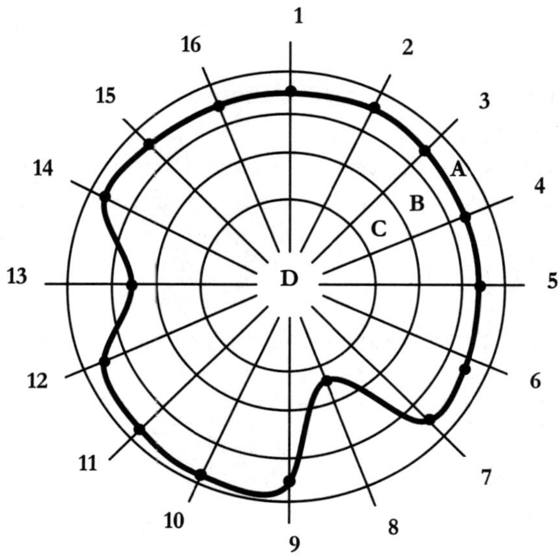

Furthermore, representing the polarities in this way allows us to take in, at a glance, which planes of the Self show greater alterations or contractions, given that, of the 16 points, 4 refer to the cognitive-symbolic plane, 4 refer to the emotional plane, 4 to the postural-motor plane and 4 to the physiological plane.

Chapter 8

Reconstructing the Basic Experiences in therapy

Reconstructing deep nuclei within the Self

The first thing that strikes us when we start talking about therapy is the question of *which part* of the patient's functioning we should be acting on. There are two basic ways of approaching therapeutic intervention.

There are forms of therapy that work separately on all the different events, behaviour patterns and situations in the patient's life as and when they occur. There are also, on the contrary, forms of therapy which focus on the functional processes which lie at the root of these things, instead of examining each particular situation in the patient's life in isolation. Using the Basic Experiences of the Self in therapy means bringing about real change in the individual's functional processes, which in turn lie at the root of all their behaviour in different situations, as shown in fig. 1.

Fig. 1. *The Basic Experiences of the Self in relation to specific situations*

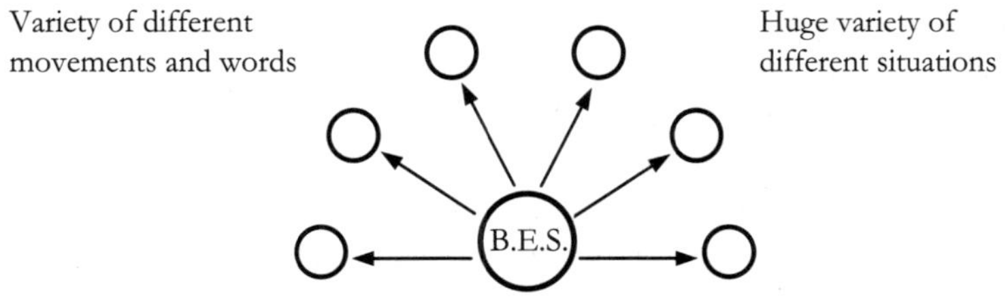

If we have to reconstruct the capacity for *Contact*, we won't go chasing after each and every situation in the patient's life that involves Contact, i.e. with their children, their partner, their friends, with their parents or even their colleagues at work. We won't need to trace back to each and every occasion in the patient's life where Contact has been good, or not good, or establish whether the patient experiences more complete contact with his friend than with his spouse, or in one particular set of circumstances more than in another. What we will do, rather, is work on the patient's *capacity* for Contact, pure and simple. This means working on *Contact for contact's sake*, the Contact with which the patient was familiar as a child, before any difficulties started. This is the Contact that every functioning living organism knows how to perceive and open. From then on, the individual will know how to utilise this underlying *capacity for Contact* in every situation (more or less fully depending on the level to which his surroundings facilitate or impede Contact). The patient will be able to establish Contact in love, in friendship, with family members, in his sex life, at work, etc.

Intervening right "at the root" of difficulties brings two significant advantages. By working with the Basic Experiences and intervening on the individual's profound nucleus, we are not obliged to track every event in the patient's life that involves that particular Basic Experience. If we recover the capacity to *Take*, the individual will be able to use this capacity whenever and howsoever he chooses. He can use it by asking clearly for a colleague's help, relighting a loved one's affection and sheltering in the warmth of this emotion, bringing others around to his point of view and winning them to his side, as allies, seducing that special person, successfully securing their love. All these cases imply the exact same basic capacity, that of *knowing how to Take.*

A second, equally important, advantage regards therapeutic techniques. By working on the Basic Experiences and on the individual's underlying functional processes, we can adopt clear, direct, linear techniques. These techniques, moreover, have the advantage of being as simple as the deep functional processes they deal with.

As we can deduce from fig. 1, the body movements, physiological activation, postures, ways of breathing and words that the patient is asked to use in therapy must not be those associated with specific, detailed situations or scenarios. This is not about reproducing the dialogue between the patient and their father in order to see what words come up, seeing what might be said in those circumstances. It is not about "acting out" a scene that brings back the past, such as a scene with the patient's mother or brother, to try to heal old wounds. It is not about finding particular cognitive strategies with colleagues at work, i.e. analysing what so-and-so said, what the patient replied, and what this might have meant and so on – or, at least, not in the deepest and most important phases of therapy. If anything, this can be done in one of the final phases[1].

During the delicate phases where change is most intense we will not modify the traces of the past through simulations or the imagination; no amount of "pretending" on the part of the therapist or the patient can really bring about changes; no acted-out scene or "as if" can be fully effective. What we really need to do, on the contrary, is really, genuinely modify the *traces* left by the events of the past. We must act on the individual's deepest, root functioning. This makes therapy far more effective, but it also means that techniques are clear and the processes within therapy are simplified (even though they are complex in terms of the overall picture).

To recover *Calm Strength*, the patient must find a way of breathing that allows him to feel completely and profoundly Calm while he accesses this Strength. He must find very simple movements that really express Strength externally (rather than acting out scenes with complicated or circumstance-specific gestures). The patient's muscles must be energetic and activated and his postures must express Strength. The voice must be strong, not strangled, nor feeble, nor angry. At the same time, the patient must be capable of using words that are concise, simple, and clear. The patient must have images and memories of Calm Strength. These elements are all equally important for us to be able to reconstruct a Basic Experience of the Self fully.

In this way, the techniques used to modify the underlying functional processes can be made to be extremely precise, and their effects can be very striking. The course of therapy is complex as a whole (because there are numerous Basic Experiences to reconstruct) but its logic and processes are simple and linear.

The configuration of the Functions within each Basic Experience

As we have seen, each Basic Experience is essentially made up of all of the different Functions of the Self – excluding none. For each Basic Experi-

1 See chapter 9: "The therapeutic process and its phases".

ence, the Functions concur with a different and specific configuration (see fig. 2).

Therefore, for us to reconstruct the Basic Experience fully, we must work as much as possible on all Functions, and not just on some of them. We have already said that a Function can have become altered in a sort of "short circuit", i.e. whilst it maintains a residual connection with the other Functions; it is no longer able to heal itself of any alterations if we do not work on it directly.

Fig. 2. *Functions and Basic Experiences of the Self*

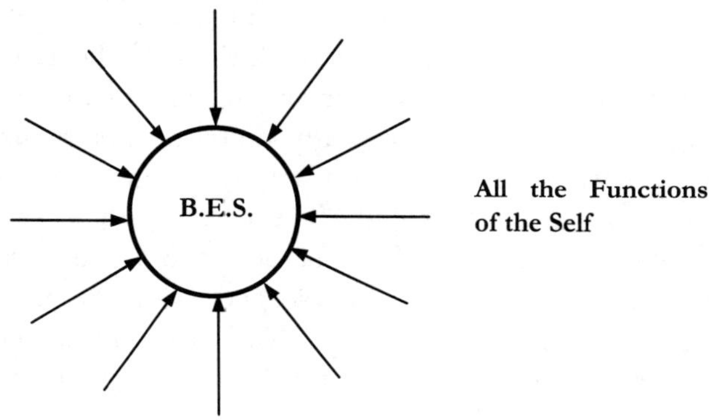

This is the reason why I have enhanced the techniques of Functional Psychotherapy with many details, so that they could succeed in touching on as many Functional levels of the Self as possibly at the same time.

One of the most important Basic Experiences to reconstruct in therapy is that of *Being Held, Being Contained*, which is often seriously insufficient. If we wish to involve more than one Functional level, we must not limit ourselves to recreating Containment using just words or eye contact. Rather, we will help this Basic Experience to be as complete as possible by actually touching the individual's body and taking it into our arms, just as if he were a little tiny child. We will talk to the patient with simple words, using the same tone of voice that we use with little children. We will help the patient to breathe serenely, just as a child does when it is being Held, we will give him the warmth of Being Held, the sensations of Being Held, and the images of Being Held.

This is what we mean when we use the term "integrated". We do not just work at a verbal, or cognitive, or a physical level, which would mean limiting ourselves to just a few Functional levels of the Self. An *integrated course of therapy* acts, as far as possible, *simultaneously* on all Functional levels: the emotions, postures, the symbolic plane, the imagination, movements, breathing, sensations, and so on. *Integrated therapy works at all these levels, not just to bring back their lost mobility, but also to bring back the integration that existed between them in the beginning, which is indispensable for a full and competent life.*

Work on the Functions is most meaningful when they all form part of one Basic Experience. Whilst it is without doubt very useful to work on the Functions purely to mobilise them (working on the voice, breathing, memories and movements), it is only helpful if the above is followed by the recovery of the Basic Experience they refer to and its respective capacities. Work on the Functions can be preparatory, and even pleasant, but at a certain point the preparatory work must lead to the concrete reopening and reconstruction of an archaic and deficient Basic Experience, getting back to the real meaning and reason for therapy.

The old traces

It is not always easy to open up a Basic Experience with all its original sensations. Throughout the various Functional levels that make up each Basic Experience, stable or chronic alterations will have built up over time: the traces of old negative episodes, and these are the very episodes that have caused this Basic Experience to become deficient or dysfunctional.

The old traces, as we can see in fig. 3, surround the original Basic Experience, making it hard to reach.

We could Hold a patient in our arms, with great tenderness and care, and he could still turn round and tell us that he had felt us to be cold and distant. What the patient is actually feeling are old sensations that have overwritten his real, present sensations.

Fig. 3. *Old traces*

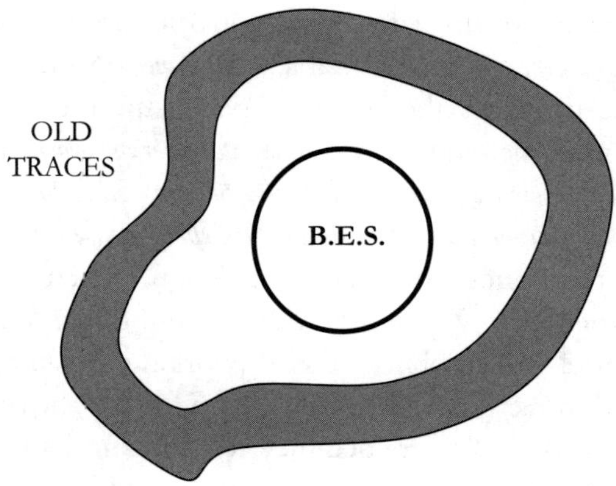

Figure 4 shows us how we can come up against old traces repeatedly in the attempt to enter into the heart of an old Experience, retrace its course and reconstruct its healthy functioning.

Fig. 4. *How to get down into the heart of a Basic Experience*

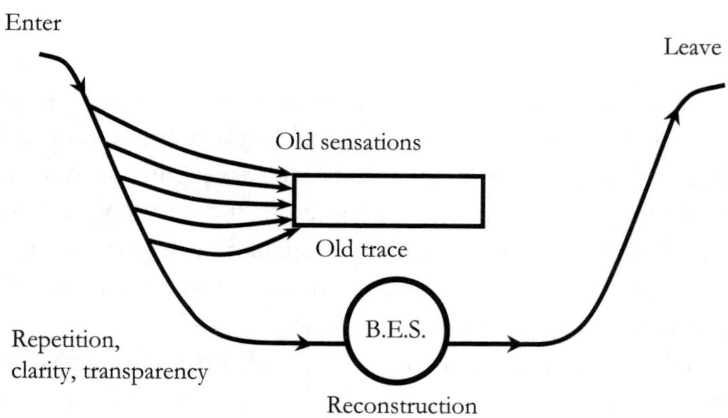

We must therefore try and try again, with patience and tranquillity, and each time we will get a little deeper down, getting closer and closer to our goal. *We must take the patient gently by the hand and lead them exactly where we want to go, i.e. the fullest expression of that archaic Basic Experience.*

Marco used to jump every time that anyone touched him. He hadn't the faintest idea of what "Being Held" might entail. His Basic Experience of Being Held had got mixed up with his old fears, his exasperated control, and a lack of calm sensations of Contact. Another obstacle was the negative fantasies that were automatically set off when anyone in the group came near him. When the group welcomed him into the centre of the circle he imagined he was being suffocated. Marco even found it hard being looked at by the others. Their gaze made him even more agitated instead of calming him down.

Marco's physical sensations were also few and far between, especially the pleasant ones. All this leads him to "tighten up", to shut himself off, and to have more and more difficulty in feeling the sweet and tender sensations of Contact that the group were offering him.

It was vital for Marco to interrupt this "short circuit", which was leading him further and further away from Contact. We needed to break down this incapacity to recover all the positive meaning, tenderness, and beauty of *Being Held.* The course of therapy needed to focus on eliminating the mechanisms that were blocking the old Basic Experience.

What we had to do, therefore, was to patiently, and precisely push away all the obstacles lying between Marco and the recovery of this Basic Experience. Calm Strength had to become disentangled from rage, distrust or fear; otherwise it would not be Calm Strength. Letting Go must no longer be mixed with alarm, excitement, or a lack of trust, and so on.

One step at a time

In figure 5, we can see how a course of therapy may proceed if it is taken *one step at a time.* We must proceed patiently, but at the same time, our course must be clear and decisive.

We enter more and more deeply into the Basic Experience in question, separating out the old traces and pushing them away, little by little. In this way, we can resolve problems and relive the Basic Experience in a positive way (which is very different to the way the Experience first unfolded in the patient's past), reopening it to its full capacity.

Fig. 5. *Proceeding one step at a time*

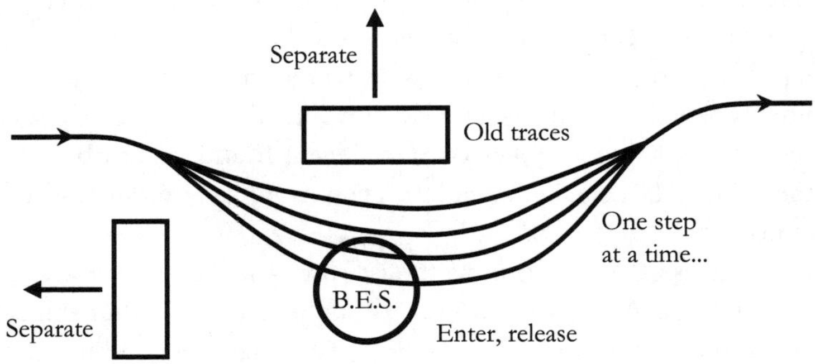

Figure 6 shows us a complete diagram, on several fronts, of the way in which a Basic Experience of the Self is reconstructed, i.e. preparatory work on various Functions, pushing away the old traces; and, lastly, the real, deep recovery of the Experience itself.

Fig. 6. *Proceeding on several fronts at the same time*

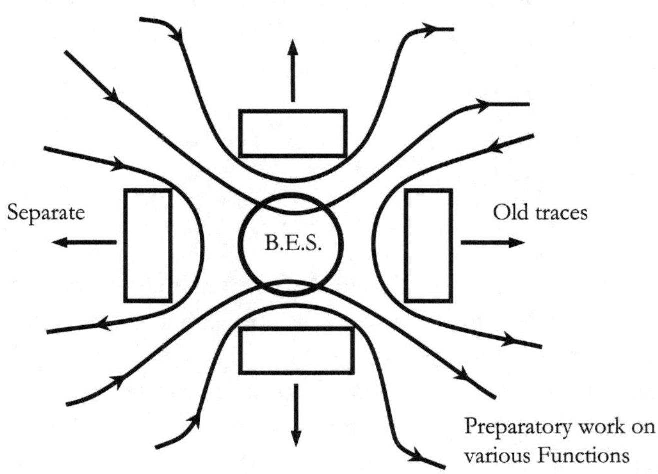

Repetition and transparency

When approaching a Basic Experience of the Self, and when actually entering into it, it is of vital importance that the patient is able to perceive as much as possible the positive sensations of the present (the same sensations that in fact characterise the original Basic Experience), going beyond the old sensations that are in the way. If we truly wish to overcome the old traces, therapy must necessarily include *repetition* and *transparency*. The positive signals that the "new parent" (either the therapist or the group) gives out must be reproduced over and over again, absolutely clearly and unequivocally, otherwise the patient will find it hard to perceive the signals in their real form, and they will always be distorted by old sensations. It is necessary that the current sensations become stronger than the old ones.

If we wish to make the patient feel understood, the message must be clearly defined and without ambiguity. It must be repeated many times, and it must be transmitted with words, eye contact, tone of voice and physical contact. Repetition does not just mean repeating the message many times. It also means that the message must be repeated *on all channels*: visual, audio, tactile, and proprioceptive.

If we are working on *Being Seen and Understood*, the patient must necessarily reach the real sensation of Being Seen, and the sensation of Being Seen must be positive, along with all the pleasure that this old Experience implies. The therapist cannot fake this: his interest must be genuine, and therefore *transparent*.

Precision and details

At this point, it is easier to see why we talk about *precision* in Functional therapy. Precision is indispensable if we wish to modify a functional process, and modify it in the quickest, most profound, and at the same time the gentlest way possible; and we need to use techniques that are able to do this. If the individual needs to recover his capacity for *Contact*, we must reach real Contact: we cannot pussyfoot around it forever. We can only reach it if the techniques at our disposal really do actually help us to reach real Contact, just Contact and nothing else. There must be no other elements mixed in with it, we must not create sources of confusion, we must not add additional elements that could lead in different directions, or which involve other Basic Experiences of the Self or other functional processes.

This is why our techniques are being honed to forms that are ever more precise and, at the same time, "uncontaminated": as finely tuned towards their objectives as we can make them.

We must also pay a lot of attention to the *details*: i.e. we must take care that the techniques really do modify the patient's Functions, that they succeed in intervening on the Functions on many levels, and, lastly, that they take in the exact direction of the Basic Experience in question.

When Marco was recovering his capacity for *Being Held*, he ended up feeling the group's touch as being that of just one big body that was holding him; he felt little, even in terms of his body weight, because he was lifted up by the group, just as if he were a child. His breathing was calm and deep, just like that of a person who feels calm and safe, his voice came out as a light sound of relief and relaxation. The words Marco heard were the sorts of words that we use when we talk to a baby lying in our arms, with the same tone of voice we use when talking to babies and the same inner sensations of calm and pleasure that are an intrinsic part of Being Held.

Naturally, the therapist's attention to detail must be neither obsessive nor coldly calculated. In reality, it is a way of feeling the patient "from within". The therapist must be able to realise when he has really entered into the Basic Experience itself, and he must be able to fine tune all the details that could help him to enter even further towards the very core of the Experience and fully utilise its beneficial effects.

It is also extremely important for us to pay attention to the way we speak, our facial expressions and the way we hold the patient (in addition to the content of the words we use and the detail which we have put into the organisation of therapy). This is an important element of the *Auxiliary Self*[2], a characteristic Function of integrated therapy. In his role as the auxiliary Self, the therapist complements the patient's modalities of expression where they are insufficient, being with him, sharing and confiding, as well as helping him to live this moment in all its fullness.

The ways in which the therapist expresses himself help to focus the therapeutic experience still more on the objective, making it even more

2 See also L. Rispoli (1993).

precise. Whilst working with Marco, we used a soft tone of voice, tender facial expressions and looks, the movement of rocking him in our arms and murmuring the right words. These are modalities that a "good" parent would employ, and they help to make the Experience of Being Held *cosier*, more *replete* and intense, richer with detail and more effective.

In group sequences, attention to detail takes the form of paying attention to all participants. The therapist intervenes to correct, to encourage, and to help the group overcome any further obstacles.

In the past, it was common to wait for change to occur on its own, but this often failed to come about, or it happened extremely slowly over the long term. At times this even lead to a worsening of the patient's condition. Today, on the contrary, we help all the members of the group to keep their breathing open so as not to cut off any sensations, we help them to make more suitable movements, we suggest sensations to them, we propose images that make the experience fuller, we encourage the expression of emotions that are appropriate to the situation[3].

The voice of the therapist, in its role as Auxiliary Self, perceives the deepest needs of the participants and accompanies them in the experience gently, step by step. This is not about "giving instructions". The therapist's voice simply gives vent to the group members' old, unsatisfied needs.

If the group is guided with great precision, it can in turn become one, big Auxiliary Self: with a hugely intense and dramatic evocative capacity.

Today, with attention to detail, with precise techniques and with gentle, flexible guidance, a group can reach levels of intensity and depth that were hitherto unimaginable over a short period.

Completeness

Continuing in my research on the relationship between technique and theory, I have paid more and more attention to the course of therapy as a

3 Research currently being carried out by our Institutes aims to identify how the way in which the therapist formulates his vocal message, the nuances in his voice and the linguistic characteristics of the message can help to make the techniques adopted more effective.

whole, in all its details, in order to make the experience as *complete* as possible.

Nowadays, it has become common practise to use lighting in the therapeutic setting, using softer lighting in moments of intimacy with ourselves or in moments that go far back in time. Similarly, the atmosphere is often completed by a suitable piece of music, which can echo the emotions of the present Experience. The therapist's voice takes on a soft tone in moments of tenderness and a more vigorous tone when the patient must experience Strength and energy. All these elements help to evoke the Basic Experience completely, intensifying it and intensifying its effects.

However, even when an individual or a group are already inside an early, deep Experience, we can pay attention to technique in order to make the Experience as complete as possible. The therapist accompanies the individuals with his voice, opening out and dilating the effects of the Experience itself. He can either do this directly, by underlining sensations and feelings in order to make the patients more aware of them, or he can indirectly suggest little adjustments in posture, movements, breathing and images that will help them to overcome chronically altered functional processes, ensuring in this way that the feelings linked to that Basic Experience of the Self are recovered and absorbed more completely and intensely.

There are methods that can be used to intensify the Experience and make it more exhaustive, exploring all its furthest limits, all its effects, all its consequences, before leaving it. Underlining the fact that there are only a few minutes left before we will be leaving the Basic Experience we are immersed in, for example, helps patients to absorb it with more desire and intensity.

Leaving an Experience is not painful if patients are able to preserve the feelings and sensations it gave them, to keep hold of them inside, so that they can take them up again when they need or wish to. The *positive continuity* of experiences makes them more complete, as well as more stable. Completeness ensures stability.

Sequentiality

Sequentiality regards the course of therapy as a whole, its progression by phases, and the fact that every intervention by the therapist must be introduced at the right moment and at the right phase[4]. A suppressed and explosive temper cannot be dealt with unless we have already gradually recovered Calm Strength. Rigid and stereotyped formality cannot be loosened without first having touched the patient's capacity for tenderness and, above all, trust.

We cannot however use general guidelines to outline the overall course of therapy. We must refer to each individual's personal history, the current organisation of their Functions, and the condition of their Basic Experiences. Only then can we produce fairly precise indications as to what must be dealt with first and what must be worked on subsequently.

To help us in this task, we have developed the *Functional Diagnostic Protocol*, an efficient tool that allows us to determine clearly and simply which Basic Experiences must be relived and reconstructed in therapy for each given patient.

Therapy is a process of evolution, which proceeds from a state of unease towards one of wellbeing. It moves from Functional alterations towards the overall rebalancing of the Self and from a condition determined by deficiencies towards the recovery of the Basic Experiences. Therapy is a process that moves in a very precise set of directions, and which is constantly modified as it goes along. Sequentiality means that the course of therapy proceeds along precise lines, rather than at random. This makes therapy shorter, more effective, and more satisfying.

However, each technique also has a sequentiality of its own. During so-called "group sequences", which are used to move an entire group towards a given Basic Experience, things are done in a specific order. Before we descend into the Basic Experience itself, we must perform a series of actions that are aimed at dissolving the barriers that prevent most of the group from accessing the Experience itself.

In group sessions, it is more likely that one patient or other might find himself unable to live the current experience to the full, compared to what he is able to do in individual therapy. He may find that the old traces which

4 See chapter 9: "The therapeutic process and its phases".

have not yet dissolved completely still form too strong a barrier. For this reason, the therapist must lead the group through different moments, one after another (hence the name "sequence"), which make it easier to enter into the deep Experience that we are trying to reach.

> The Leaning on Others sequence starts with the participants being asked to walk around the room more and more randomly, with no fixed goal or destination, loosening their control as much as possible.
>
> We then explore the feeling of not wanting Contact, wanting to be on our own, feeling irritated if anybody touches us, clearly expressing these feeling externally. We will even reach the point where we will positively avoid any contact with the others as we walk.
>
> In the third phase, the irritation is expressed even more evidently, even becoming open hostility. If one hand brushes another hand, it will push it away, we make way for ourselves among the others even if we have to resort to the occasional shove. We want to follow our own path without having to deviate because others are in the way. These shoves must only use a little Strength. They must not be collisions, rather continuous little thrusts that allow us to manifest our Strength a little without causing damage.
>
> Lastly, we start to feel tired. Our movements start to soften, and our breathing, too. The participants are brought to feel, ever more strongly, a desire to Lean on somebody. The therapist's voice says, "We want to Lean on somebody just a little, just enough to loosen the tension and the fatigue, so that we can leave this level of irritation and hostility. We already work too hard in our every day lives, we never allow ourselves to Lean on others. Now we want to Lean just a little of our burden on somebody else's shoulders, just a little. Yes! We have a right to! At least this once!"

It is only at this point that the real Basic Experience starts. The rest was preparation – overcoming and dissolving obstacles such as the fear of contact, bitterness, closure, overexcitement, and excessive self control. We can therefore say that the different phases that the group goes through within the same sequence have specific objectives and they must be performed in this precise order.

Lastly, there is an "intermediate" level of sequentiality that lies somewhere between that of the course of therapy as a whole and that of its single sequences. This is the sequentiality that allows each Basic Experience to be consolidated, by linking together individual sequences.

It is not always possible for us to touch all the Functions of the Self fully using just one technique or sequence. We can, therefore, place one technique after another, all aimed at the reconstruction of that same Basic

Experience, each however with different connotations for the Functions involved.

The Basic Experience of Tenderness can be reached, for example, through a group sequence exploring tender *movements*, where the members express tenderness above all to themselves. At the end of the sequence (which is carried out standing up, like many other sequences), the participants lie down, and they can go back, using their imaginations, to a moment of Tenderness in the past; to relive it in all its details and on all levels of sensation (colours, smells, sounds, facial expressions, movements). This second technique gives precedence to Functional levels such as the imagination, memories and reliving old sensations. A third experience might be that of massage in pairs: the person who is doing the massage should let himself be guided towards the parts of the other person that call for Tenderness, that need it, that suffer because they do not receive enough Tenderness. Thus, we can see that by linking together several individual sequences, in a series, we can consolidate the Basic Experience, by extending it to the largest number of Functions possible.

The sequentiality of Functional Psychotherapy has the same aim as all the other elements hitherto examined, in addition to the most recent research, i.e. *moving towards an ever greater understanding of the mechanisms underlying the process of therapy and the processes of change and care-giving – to manage them, first and foremost, and then to improve these processes more and more.*

Chapter 9

The therapeutic process and its phases

Subjectivity and objectivity

One of the principal problems at the centre of the debate as to whether psychotherapy can be considered "scientific" is that of assessment and evaluation.

Whilst the patient-therapist *relationship* is widely held to be the central element of clinical methodology, with the subjectivity that this entails, we cannot deny that there are elements that are objective both in the relationship itself and outside it. To deal with this problem with a sufficient level of complexity, we must allow for both the description of phenomena within therapy, and the analysis of the therapeutic relationship itself (from which these observations are derived). Similarly, we must consider both the participants' personal experience (unrepeatable and subjective) and the events that can be observed from outside the patient-therapist pair (objective). All of this makes it possible to study and evaluate the *therapeutic process* as it unfolds, by researching the extent to which observed phenomena can be *repeated* and *applied at a general level*, just like in any other branch of science.

Now, if we take more than one plane of functioning into consideration (as we do in integrated therapy), the principal difficulty lies not so much in the "mathematical" effort of identifying *all* the variables called into play in the therapeutic relationship, nor does it lie in an attempt to reduce the clinical method at all costs into strictly "quantitative" measures. The central difficulty lies rather in identifying elements that can be considered *repeatable* or *constantly present*, and therefore *scientifically communicable* within these essentially inter-subjective phenomena.

In every therapeutic process, there are a series of *interactions*, which can be *recorded* by the therapist and interpreted according to his theory or model of reference. Yet, psychotherapy, just like other scientific disciplines, may refer to both *single case histories* that change from situation to situation, as well as to a series of general laws. We could therefore state that although the particular fabric which makes up each single case of therapy is *unrepeatable*, there are certain elements that can be found in all courses of therapy – identical elements that appear every time that a course of therapy successfully reaches the goals that the therapist has set.

It therefore seems possible for us to identify *two different levels* in the therapeutic process. One level corresponds to that which is *unique* in every story, in every patient-therapist relationship (or group). This is the result of the specific nature of each participant's personal baggage of experience, knowledge, and formation. This can be referred to as *individual narration.* The other possible level is the one upon which we will base our assessment criteria – the level that refers to phenomena that are communicable and repeatable. We can call this *scientific narration.*

Undoubtedly, the passage from one level to another (they are profoundly interconnected, not separate) poses a series of delicate and difficult problems. Perhaps these problems are among the principal causes behind the awkward persistence of the dichotomy between the so-called human sciences and the so-called exact ones.

Fig. 1. *Individual narration and scientific narration*

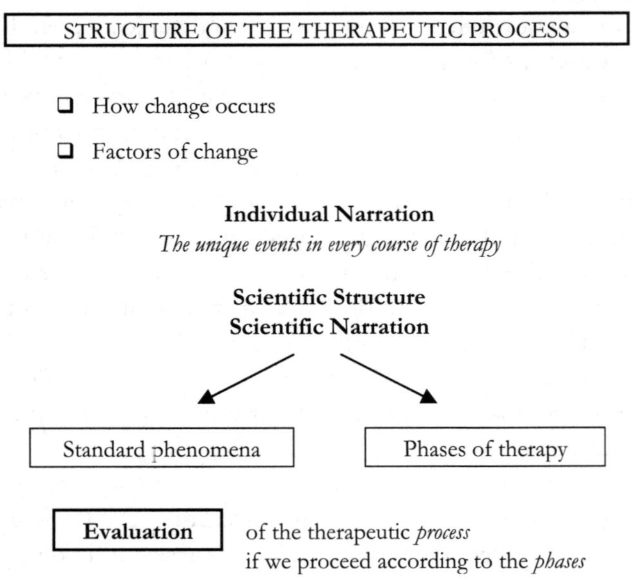

Phases during therapy

The scientific nature of psychotherapy should not merely be seen in terms of a cause and effect relationship linking the therapist and the patient's words and actions. There is no mathematical law that can provide *exact equations* for the infinite variations in the way in which the phases, sounds, and gestures occur. Rather, consistency can be found in the discovery that the therapeutic process is characterised by authentic phases that are identical in all forms of therapy (at the level of *scientific narration*).

We can clearly identify whole series of sessions where one particular modality of relation is predominant compared to the others, and we can find events that are common to all types of therapy.

Obviously, these phases do not have rigid or mathematically precise limits. They can be distinguished from one another, however, thanks to the different modalities adopted during each one, as the course of therapy progresses. These phases regulate, although not in a way that is strictly quantifiable, the way the course of therapy progresses from the initial state at the outset to a distinctly different conclusion.

During any course of therapy, there are moments when symptoms are initially greatly improved, there are characteristic relapses, phases where the patient negatively opposes the therapist, and phases characterised by a strong positive transference. There are moments in which the patient manages to trust the therapist, phases where there are deep regressions to very early experiences, periods full of new sensations, experiences of reciprocal understanding and closeness and moments where the patient discovers himself to be a fuller person than he had previously thought and he discovers that the therapist is a real person.

Starting from this basis, it has been possible to hypothesise a series of *observation criteria* aimed at identifying the various phases of the "psychotherapeutic process" in general, beyond single experiences or any particular clinical model.

Following this direction, we can hypothesise a possible form of evaluation for psychotherapy as being modular, i.e. a form of evaluation that follows the phases, tracing out the way the process unfolds by *modules*. Modular evaluation can be applied both to the criteria governing each specific, singular course of therapy from within; and it can also be used to analyse the patient-therapists' inter-subjective experience "from the outside", because these phases are present in any form of therapy, referring to standard phenomena that can be noted by any trained observer.

It is only by following the phases and the overall flow of therapy that we will be able to devise a method of evaluation capable of discerning between authentic psychotherapy and movements that are merely manipulation. Only in this way can we carry out a serious assessment of the results over the short and the long term.

Signs to look for in psychotherapy

Before we talk about the phases of therapy, we must address the problem of what to look for in the therapeutic process and which signs to observe, and this is even more necessary when it comes to an *integrated* course of therapy.

Given that *integrated* psychotherapy is characterised by a vision of the individual as a whole, a "bird's eye" view that overcomes the traditional distinctions between psyche and soma, verbal and non-verbal, emotive and cognitive, symbolic and motor (because it examines all of these aspects simultaneously), the traditional boundaries between the *visible* and the *invisible* also change significantly. What was formerly thought to be invisible can now be revealed by very evident signals on other planes of the Self (hidden anger can be read in an altered muscle tone, an apparently absent fear can be revealed by alterations in breathing and heart rate, and a completely subconscious weakness can be revealed by a lack of strong movements). The delicate relationship between concrete *signs* and what we *infer* about them can be completely revolutionised by an integrated approach, because this takes many more aspects into consideration than were formerly considered by the single therapeutic models. An expression or alteration that is *invisible* on one plane will nevertheless be *visible* on another.

However, before we can carry out this type of multidimensional analysis, we must make a leap forward at an epistemological level: we must look at the different *Functions*, not only because they are expressions of the *whole* individual (avoiding the risk of fragmentation), but also because they are the only way of avoiding being bogged down by the chaotic observation of thousands of signals: gestures, words, postures and movement. Taking the *movement* Function into consideration actually means observing any changes in the person's movement in general, and not in observing each one of the thousands of individual movements that the individual carries out. It means noting the *amplitude* of the various Functions by observing whether the range between the two polarities is full and ample or whether it is limited, whether the changes are predominantly fast or slow, whether movements are small and suppressed or ample too, and whether they are graceful or awkward.

We can talk in a more generalised way about *limitations* and *alterations* in the *mobility* of the subject's perceptive, motor, postural, cognitive, symbolic, emotive, and physiological Functions. A subject can present (in his relationships with others) the presence of certain physical, verbal, and emotive expressions and the lack of others, clearly demonstrating well-defined *limitations* and *alterations* in his mobility.

These limitations and alterations in *Functional mobility* tell us the patient's history (and the history of his relationships), but they also allow us to observe the flow of the course of therapy at a practical level, in its various phases.

The elements gathered during observation of an integrated course of therapy will therefore be relative to all the Functions of the Self (the extension of the range between polarities, the mobility of the Functions), but they will also refer to the presence or absence of all the capacities linked to the Basic Experiences of the Self.

The signs that the therapist must look for in his observation are as follows:

- What the patient knows and communicates verbally about his cognitive, emotional, imaginative, symbolic, motor, postural and physiological worlds, and about his capacities;
- The form his language takes (choice of words, sequences, tone...);
- The physical sensations that the patient is able to perceive;
- What the therapist is able to read in the patient's movements, postures and somatic structure, what he observes about the characteristics of the patient's physiological systems and apparatus (breathing, heartbeat, perspiration, skin temperature, muscle tone, musculature...), deficiencies observed in the Basic Experiences of the Self;
- The therapist's emotions, fantasies and thoughts;
- His kinaesthetic perceptions and physical sensations;

– The history of the patient's psychic and physical symptoms, their progression over time (especially with regards to old symptoms).

Observation criteria

The phases that punctuate the therapeutic process can be observed from several points of view. The criteria that we will examine represent different "lenses" through which we can observe the elements that make up therapy from the first session to the last.

We can distinguish two categories of criteria. The first can be considered as *diagnostic*, in the sense that they allow us to monitor the progress of the various phases and the therapy's gradual passage from one stage to the next.

On the other hand, we use what we define as *prescriptive (or therapeutic)* criteria to examine the various phases of therapy, assessing what changes must be made in the therapist's approach and methodology as therapy progresses, to bring the course of therapy ever closer to its objectives. First, we will examine the diagnostic criteria.

Diagnostic criteria

Criteria regarding transference and the therapeutic relationship

This criterion allows us to observe evolutions in the patient's experience of transference, and in his emotive expressions towards the therapist. The phases of therapy, according to this criterion, are as follows:

1) *Concentration of transferential experiences in the first sittings*
The individual seems to concentrate a whole series of memories, perceptions, experiences and emotions into his encounter with the therapist, which have been trying to find a way out for a long time, or which have

been welling up in a tumult since he first decided to start treatment or at least make an appointment.

2) *First phase of diffidence. Prevalence of the false Self*

Very early on, the patient falls into his old habits of closure and rigidity. His initial openness is smothered by the stereotypies of the false Self and by deficiencies in the interaction between the Functional planes. It is inevitable that distrust should return when the patient takes up the routine of his existence, following the exciting and unusual event of undertaking a new road towards overcoming his symptoms and problems.

3) *Reinforcement of the initial positive transference. First deep emotive contact*

This is the moment in which the patient starts to feel the first benefits of treatment. The patient is able to see that something good is happening at a practical level, and this can reinforce the positive sensations that had arisen in the first encounters. Dreams that we can define as "start of therapy" are a classic in this phase, and they show how the patient has only just started to feel that he is really "in therapy". He becomes fully aware that he is doing something important for himself.

Moreover, there is also a deep affective encounter with the therapist. Unlike the first emotive concentration, which was poured over the therapist almost as if it did not matter who he was, now the patient starts to feel helped reassuringly by that particular therapist, by that particular person.

4) *Second phase of negative transference (deep)*

This is a difficult, but important, phase. All the negativity that is buried deep down, and which was difficult to express because it was not tolerated by the patient's original family environment, can finally come out into the open. At first, this deep negative transference is not perceived or expressed directly. By degrees, this is perceived as a movement of opposition or negativity that the patient no longer has to repress because it can be expressed in a way that is not destructive.

It makes no sense to "interpret" the patient's negative behaviour as "resistance" to therapy, or as the manifestation of innate destructive impulses. The patient must simply continue to feel that he is not being judged, and that, on the contrary, his fragility and basic needs are fully accepted, because feelings of negativity are nothing more than a painful reaction to not having been sufficiently accepted and protected as a child, to not having gone through the Basic Experiences positively. It must however be made clear that these negative sentiments are never really aimed at the therapist. They are really aimed at the old parent-figures.

Today, whether it be because the tools of therapy have been honed, or because we now know much more about what really happens during therapy, and have consequently improved techniques, centring them still more on the objectives in hand, deep negative transference has diminished enormously, both in terms of duration and gravity, whereas the presence of positive transference has increased.

5) *Trusting, and the patient's capacity to abandon himself to others*

In this phase, the patient abandons himself completely to the therapist and their work together becomes very productive. After the second phase of negative transference has been overcome, it is much easier to get down to the earliest and most integrated functional processes, and the experience is more intense. There is now more material to work on, and it is more open, more accessible.

6) *Empathic movement. Profound Positive Transference*

Empathic contact and positive transference are already present but they become fuller in this phase. The individual can re-explore his movements of positive emotion without fear or anxiety. This phase deals with the reconstruction of the old Basic Experiences of the Self, very intense one-to-one work, and increasing the mobility of the various Functional planes. The patient feels that the therapist is "there for him", that he is protective, just like a new, good parent.

7) *Loosening the dependence*

This is the final destination of the therapeutic relationship. The relationship has become person-to-person, adult-to-adult. The patient is perfectly able to feel intense gratitude towards the therapist (for his help in the previous phases) but he also feels strong and independent. The patient will often remain to chat after the session has finished, to talk about plans, ideas, and everything that one would talk about with a friend.

Criteria regarding the therapeutic relationship

This criterion regards the phases governing the patient's relationship with the therapist, with particular reference to his subjective experience of the relationship.

1) *Relationship lived from the outside*

During this first (lengthy) phase, the patient does not deal directly with the questions relating to his feelings towards the therapist. At best, he touches on them indirectly, and refers mostly to events experienced outside therapy, in his daily existence. References towards what is happening in therapy are rare, and they are almost always of a cognitive nature: doubts or curiosity, what method is being used, the meaning of the first changes.

In the treatment of children, this phase is considerably shorter because they manifest an intense need for a direct relationship with the adult right from the beginning, given that the therapist represents a new affective figure to add to those that already exist. The child has a strong desire to know and understand to what extent the therapist really cares about him, if the therapist's interest and affection towards him are genuine.

The child shows a huge curiosity about anything the therapist does, not just in therapy with him, but also about any other little patients he might have, or what he does in his everyday life. The child becomes emotionally involved with everything that surrounds this new relationship and this new adult model.

2) *Centring on the relationship with the therapist*

This is a phase that the patient reaches gradually. There are numerous signs that prepare for it: the patient complains more and more about what we are doing or not doing in therapy; therapeutic "warnings" about possible negative reactions the patient might have; a deterioration in the patient's symptoms; significant relapses into old symptoms; dreams where the therapist is featured more overtly.

Everything is aimed at discovering what the therapist's real feelings are, what "makes him tick" and how important the patient really is to him.

The patient may refer to other therapists, or he may even talk about the therapist's "professionalism". The patient might close in on himself, sulk, avoid contact or feel uneasy, precisely when he most desires a more direct and affectionate relationship, thinking that the therapist is only interested in him because it is his job to be so.

In the Functional approach, given that we use all planes of the Self, the patient is able to put the relationship to the test right from the beginning, in a very direct manner. Physical contact, touch (reassuring and containing) and being taken up and held produce strong, unequivocal sensations. However, the disconnections between the various Functional levels are still too strong at this point to allow these sensations to create a stable sense of security. Moreover, the therapist's intervention still refers more to the patient's past than to the patient's relationship with the therapist himself.

Later, when this phase is at its full, the need to test the therapist's affections emerges on all levels of the Self and becomes explicit. It is of crucial importance at this point that the therapist has already elaborated and resolved the negativity produced by countertransference because it is impossible to pretend. His emotions, even the deepest ones, are directly absorbed by the patient, beyond any possible verbal dissimulation. Furthermore, only if there is a genuine capacity to love the patient can we actually hope to fully reconstruct the affective Experiences that were deficient during the patient's childhood and adolescence.

During the whole period that follows, the patient may present other crises of doubt, or other "peaks" of strong emotion. By then, however, it will have become possible to work on what the patient really feels during sessions, on his relationship with the *new parent*, the *good parent*, without confusing this with old traces and old sensations.

At this point, references to the patient's life outside therapy provide further confirmation of what is changing in within the therapeutic relationship itself.

3) *Patient's emotions shift to the world outside therapy*

Over the previous period, the patient's Functional organisation was examined and modified, starting from the therapeutic relationship itself. Now the patient's interest starts to shift towards his daily life again. He has rediscovered his lost mobility and capacities within therapy, and now he starts to test how far he can shift the boundaries of his old life, and to try out his new capacities in his relationships with others. This is the phase in which the patient applies what he has learnt in therapy to the outside world.

Even from this point of view, we witness the same "natural" attenuation in the patient's level of dependence and need, as mentioned above. Dependence and neediness should only be a temporary part of therapy, as they are the result of old, unsatisfied needs.

Perceptive criteria

It is easier to analyse the different stages of transference and affect if we also understand how the *asymmetry* of the relationship changes during the course of therapy, and how the patient's *perception* of the therapist changes over time.

1) *Perception of the therapist as a parent*

The patient's sensations throughout the whole initial phase resemble something that he has "already experienced". The fear and pain of revealing himself and repeating frustrating experiences yet again constitute the fundamental nucleus of all the patient's alterations and symptoms. The sentimental concentration of the first sessions, the negative transference and the old traces of early experiences on all the various Functional planes automatically reproduce these feelings.

The old traces and sensations continue to operate at a subconscious level, even though the patient may not believe this to be possible at a rational level, despite the fact that the present conditions are completely different from those of the past. The patient *reacts* to the therapist *almost automatically*, and he is stimulated to react exactly *as if the therapist really were* a figure from his childhood at perceptive, motor, and emotive levels.

In reality, however, the therapist is a completely different person compared to those old affective figures, and the more Functional levels we use in therapy the sooner the patient will come to perceive this. Some of these Functional levels (such as touch, eye contact, tone of voice and movements) transmit these new sensations very powerfully compared to the old ones. It is precisely this difference that allows the patient to immerse himself in his past with relative tranquillity. In this way, we can start to explore the patient's innermost feelings about his relationship with his parent figures (or with other figures of great importance to him): both the painful and the positive ones.

2) *The patient's perception of the therapist as a parent is modified*

Whilst the patient's *reactions* on several levels of the Self imitate early experiences in his "family" history, on other levels he is able to perceive that there are elements of the present reality that are very different from those of his past. Old fantasies are contradicted by the new sensations experienced in therapy. Automatic emotional reactions are mitigated by a reopening of the patient's perceptions, muscles and physiology; and the patient's emotionality is collocated once again in the present, in relation with what is going on around him, in the here and now.

We really can speak in terms of a genuine *corrective experience*, to use an old phrase coined by Alexander. In the present relationship with the "new parent", we can reconstruct the most important Basic Experiences and capacities. The "new parent" is very different, and he behaves in a completely different way, compared to the figures in the patient's emotional world as a child. The patient, however, does not just discover a form of behaviour that is the "opposite" of what he has previously experienced. What he really recovers are his own *positive* memories, perceptions and experiences, which had become trapped and crystallised within his organism, suffocated by alterations in his Functions and by the old traces which had continued to bring about the same effects, as if his situation were identical to that which he had suffered as a child.

Before therapy, the patient was unable to identify the altered and stereotyped signals that continued to be transmitted on one or more planes of the Self (in the form of traces deposited by old negative experiences).

Recovering the Basic Experiences that were deficient, renewing the mobility of the Functions and re-establishing contact with the correct signals, will allow the patient to get back into contact with his real surroundings, allowing him to work fully towards his own wellbeing and affirmation.

3) *Perception of the therapist as a "person"*

In the same way that a child mainly notices the aspects of his parents that are most useful to him, (because he is chiefly in contact with his own needs), the patient almost fails to notice changes and physical details in his therapist, and is unaware of any unusual behaviour, mood changes or moments of tiredness that the therapist might show during therapy.

After the descent into the deeper, earlier, and more integrated functional processes, there is a stage when the patient starts to feel his curiosity towards the therapist as a person grow inordinately. The patient might start to notice little details about the way he looks, the way he acts, or try to find out about aspects of his life. The way the patient greets the therapist and the way in which he takes his leave of the therapist before and after each session change, becoming friendlier, often becoming quite chatty and familiar.

His feelings towards the therapist also change, because he is no longer merely seeing him as a figure capable of absorbing his pain and fears, protecting him and magically setting off long buried echoes from the past, but as a real person, tenderly real, with his own suffering, his own little defects, manias, incongruences and difficulties.

4) *Collaboration*

This phase follows on closely from the last. The patient is capable of looking at things together with the therapist, together devising and examining how to proceed so as to obtain positive results. By now, the patient knows his own psychophysical processes, their old crystallisation, and their new mobility. He is aware of the downwards spirals and traps that he is prone to fall in, but he is also aware of the quickest way of overcoming little relapses or moments of rigidity. He is also now able to perceive which areas of the body need the most help.

Sometimes, the patient still pretends to be hanging on the therapist's every word, or he pretends to abandon himself completely to him in order to feel the comforting sensation of being looked after once again, but we must not let ourselves be deceived by this. It is only an affectionate habit. Some patients ask to go back into therapy, or they state wistfully that they wish therapy could carry on longer, but in reality, over the course of many years of practise, only a very few patients have returned to therapy, and if they did, it was for a very specific purpose.

Criteria regarding symptoms

One of the focal points of psychotherapeutic treatment has always been, besides resolving the patient's "problems", that of modifying and resolving his symptoms. Today, more than ever, people seek therapy because they want to be cured, to be able to feel good, to appreciate the joys of life, in as short a time as possible. It is obvious that healing the patient's symptoms also implies developing their potential. The two are interlinked and it does not make much sense to divide them. It is very rare, however, that someone seeks therapy just because they want to undertake an adventurous journey towards a better understanding of themselves.

Moreover, in Functional therapy we pay particular attention to the modification and remission of symptoms, not only because we act directly on the patient's psycho-physical conditions, but also because one of the characteristics of Functional therapy is to explore disorders and alterations in the patient's past, right back to his very first experiences.

1) *Anxiety about symptoms. Symptoms presented to the therapist*

Often, the decision to take a new direction in life, undertaking a new voyage to get to the heart of things and "resolve" them (rather than continue to patch them with useless palliatives) is due to the fact that the symptoms the patient suffers from have become intolerable. A symptom serves as an alarm bell, and when the patient first starts therapy, talking about his symptom in therapy serves precisely this purpose.

Functional alterations that do not produce symptoms are not perceived to be as strange and disturbing as the symptom itself. When the symptom fails to improve, it raises the patient's level of anxiety, upsetting the old equilibrium, and sparking off the desire to change.

During the first phases of treatment, the patient continues to focus most of his attention on his symptoms, considering them to be the only real way of approaching the therapist. He will relate his symptoms with unexpected meticulousness in his attempt to be understood and helped completely; especially with regards to his negative sensations, fear and anxiety, for which he is unlikely to find support elsewhere. The symptoms often intensify in a rash of explosions concentrated in the initial phases of therapy, corresponding to the initial phase of *concentration* of his feelings linked to transference.

Although the symptoms do not have a mechanistic correspondence with specific situations or periods during childhood, they nonetheless tell us how the equilibrium of the Self became altered during that period; what schisms, immobility, or stereotypies intervened. This does not mean that the symptoms are just a symbolic manifestation or a metaphor for "psychic conflicts". Functional alterations are present on all the planes of the Self, and the symptoms are a real, concrete effect of these dysfunctions.

The symptoms do however betray a breakdown in the old equilibrium: buried needs re-emerge, even though the form they take is virulent and unpleasant. A violent fever forces someone who never stops to take a break; dizzy spells loosen control in people who are always alert and tense. Symptoms are the body's way of trying to re-establish its lost mobility or to satisfy forgotten needs (recovering a part of its original integrity), but the attempt is too brusque, incomplete, and ultimately damaging.

2) *Initial improvement*

It is crucial that the patient receive unmistakable proof that the path he has taken, and the methods being used, are effective, and this can occur when there is an initial, significant decrease in the patient's symptoms. We are not talking about a "hysterical" improvement, nor are we talking about a "placebo" effect.

Functional psychotherapy's initial "first aid" treatments produce results that are clearly tangible. The symptoms that benefit from this kind of care in the short term are: headaches, tachycardia, anxiety and pains. They also produce evident beneficial effects with insomnia, dizzy spells and stomach and intestinal problems, although the effects take a little longer to appear in these cases. Some of these disorders can go into total remission and others show significant improvements. They also improve general mood, fears, brooding, and obsessive thought patterns.

By working on all the Functions of the Self, Functional psychotherapy unblocks the inextricable knot that of factors that go to make up the symptom, namely unexpressed emotions, immobile muscle tone (which "holds back" our capacity to communicate), altered breathing, suppressed body sensations and stereotyped images. Moreover, we unblock the zones of the body in which inadequate oxygenation, deficiencies in the flow of neurotransmitters, tissue vitality, cellular metabolism, alterations in posture, movements, and sensations have consolidated to form the basis for the symptom itself.

3) *Relapse*

Soon, however, the intensification of movement brought about by therapy, in both a physical and a psychic sense, causes the patient to deal with parts of himself of which he had not previously been aware, the innermost sources of his fear, the deepest and oldest roots of his symptoms. In the meantime, the course of therapy takes the patient deep down to where the Functional integrity of the patient is still present. On the one hand, then, the patient feels fear due to the surfacing of buried sensations, which he experiences, however, as if they were new, as if they came from outside himself. On the other hand, we also have positive emotions rising to the surface which are not accepted, and therefore cancelled out, bringing with them the sense of alarm with that they had been associated with during the patient's childhood. On yet another plane, the patient's urge to look for a way out increases, even though the organism is not yet able to keep up with demand. Moreover, the results obtained during therapy sessions seem to sink under the blows dealt by every day life, especially since the patient is more "sensitive" than before, and the patient often experiences this with fear and worry.

For these reasons, an intense relapse occurs. Symptoms worsen to the point of a genuine crisis, which the therapist must handle with great care and delicacy, and resolve with great patience.

4) *Symptoms arise during a sitting*

Not long afterwards, the moment arrives when the symptom occurs (in its most evident, acute form) in the therapist's presence, during a sitting. This is a fairly important turning point, and it determines a big step forward in the course of therapy (and in particular in the patient's level of trust and positive transference) given that the therapist can literally dissolve the symptom in that exact moment. When this occurs, therefore, it is indispensable that the therapist focuses all of his attention on the resolution of the symptom, trying to make the momentary crisis completely disappear.

The symptom's appearance during therapy is an important sign that progress has been made because we can now claim to have touched the patient's pain right at its source, the roots of his illness, the mechanisms underlying his symptoms.

5) *Sensations similar to the symptoms*

Another milestone during the course of therapy consists in the emergence (during a sitting) of sensations that are very similar to the symptoms reported by the patient. A dizzy spell, a "throbbing" in the abdomen, tiredness and numbness, a feeling of a sort of downwards flow, ringing in the ears and tingling in the hands are all effects and sensations that present themselves during therapy sessions when therapy is really working and we are successfully managing to mobilise and reopen blocked functional processes. The patient may find these sensations unexpected, or he might be surprised by them, but they are not as frightening or as unpleasant as the original symptoms, despite the fact that they move in the same direction. These new symptoms are similar to the original symptoms in that they are an attempt by the organism to resolve dysfunctions that have become intolerable.

The therapeutic process seems to be able to reach right back to the mechanism underlying the symptoms. The symptoms are the organism's attempt to react and finally re-establish a healthy equilibrium, but therapy succeeds where the symptoms on their own do not, because its action is effective and complete, instead of being explosive and damaging.

A dizzy spell is a way of relaxing control (and it is absolutely not unpleasant in the way that it was before therapy), numbness and torpor is a way of "letting go", deep down. The tingling is a result of the body's tissues regaining vitality; the sense of something flowing downwards is exactly what happens when the tensions in the upper part of our body dissolve (thoughts, worries, etc.). What the symptom only managed to achieve in an incomplete, brusque and damaging manner, therapy achieves completely by acting on the organism as a whole.

6) *Period of alternation between improvements and relapses*

As the number of reconnections between disconnected Functions increases, so the patient's imbalances diminish in intensity. In therapy, the patient often senses dysfunctions, which we are then able to loosen until they disappear. Alarm and anxieties diminish at the same rate. In this phase, the patient often alternates between periods where his symptoms improve and periods where they worsen, in rapid succession. These relapses are short-lived, however, and they are much less intense.

Towards the end of this phase, the alternations can be so rapid that they can even follow on from one another within the space of a day.

7) *Reappearance of symptoms from the past*

In connection with the phases 4 and 5, this phase highlights an equally important aspect of the descent into the patient's deepest and earliest Functions. The patient starts to suffer from symptoms that they had not experienced for years and years, since adolescence or childhood. The symptom is often of a "psychosomatic" nature, but we may also find sensations, fears, old fantasies, or old thought patterns.

Once again, the meaning of this lies in having touched the very root of the patient's unhappiness, as if we had managed to reach back to the first alterations, which were what led to the present symptoms themselves, as the problem worsened. All of this allows the organism to "return" to the "fork in the road" and take a new path, towards health and wellbeing. Once again, the patient is regaining the use of Functions that are very near to the deep, integrated and healthy nucleus of the Self.

8) *Original Functional symptoms*

In our voyage down to the deeps (because that is what therapy really is), we reach a point where we touch on very archaic dysfunctions, which cannot easily be described as symptoms, in the true sense of the word. They are the healthy and vital reactions of a little child when faced with unpleasant, frustrating, or stressful external situations. They are his way of feeling *not good* when his deepest needs are *not met*, and they are already a characteristic part of the individual. A newborn baby might vomit, he might alter his breathing, his muscles might contract, he might experience colics, etc., but these are all momentary manifestations linked to external causes.

These first alterations in the individual's Functional processes are evidently connected to negative experiences. For this reason, they do not seem as strange as later symptoms, nor are they expressed with the rigidity (or the characteristic traits, as we might call them) that they will acquire when they become subconscious. Our symptoms and our ways of expressing ourselves are, in a certain sense, "fused" together, and they represent an explicit, but also temporary, expression of the child's unease, just like the patient's unease during this phase of therapy.

9) *Symptoms soften and become mobile*

Even though the patient's symptoms and alterations have softened more and more, no patient can delude himself that he will never again experience moments of unease or unhappiness, especially if they are normal reactions to negative conditions in his surroundings or relationships. Moreover, they will always have "weak points", just like everyone; i.e. the propensity to fall back into old mechanisms. A downwards spiral can always reoccur. However, if the course of therapy has been conducted well, then it will also provide the patient with the tools necessary to prevent old mechanisms or spirals of unhappiness being set off.

The symptoms, which have *softened* at this point, can of course re-present themselves, but only in a non-virulent, flexible, and controlled form. The patient's reacquired Functional mobility allows him to focus on *real external conditions*, rather than old traces and old negative sensations, even though some events in his life may continue to provoke particularly intense resonances within him.

Renewing the integration and harmony of the Functions, together with the fullness and mobility of the reacquired Basic Experiences of the Self allow a continuous re-adjustment of the gap between the patient's childhood conditions and his present ones. The individual is now capable of choosing the nuances, emotive and expressive tones, and the types of interaction best suited to the circumstances in which he finds himself. Mobility gives the patient flexibility both in terms of adapting to the situation in hand and transforming the world around him, providing him with the consequent intense feelings of sharing emotions with others and success in his human interaction.

"Therapeutic" (or "prescriptive") assessment criteria

The distinction made here between diagnostic criteria and therapeutic criteria does not in any way mean that we should consider diagnosis and treatment as being two separate moments within therapy. Treatment is in fact based on a continuous evaluation of the signals produced between the patient and the therapist, placed in direct correlation with the diagnoses and observations that have accumulated over time.

Similarly, the following criteria generally deal more with how the therapist *can and must act* during the various phases of therapy, rather than dealing with the state of the patient or his perception of the relationship with the therapist. The aspects described in the last section, and their gradual evolution, give us clear indications as to how the course of therapy is proceeding, the transition from one phase to another, and so they are clearly of a diagnostic nature. Therapeutic criteria, on the other hand, tell us what the therapist must put into action at a practical level during the various phases of therapy, the different "modalities of therapy" to be adopted as therapy progresses if we wish to steer it towards a positive conclusion.

Criteria regarding Functional configuration

This criterion is based on a particular was of looking at the alterations that lead to psychophysical disorders. A patient's behaviour denotes a decreased mobility. His choices have been narrowed down thanks to negative experiences with their system-environment, and he presents automatic, coactive, and stereotyped responses, no longer suited to his real surroundings or situation. The patient's whole "Functional configuration" has become altered, assuming precise characteristics.

The part of this Functional configuration that is *most easily visible on the outside* is an authentic message that the individual transmits continuously to the world around him, with his whole being. This message is subconscious, however, and it is rigid and repetitive. We define this as the *Functional trait*, but it could also be identified as a "personality trait" or "character trait", as it was termed in Wilhelm Reich's first writings. The Functional trait nonetheless provides us with a first indication, although somewhat general, of the whole system of Functional processes of the Self.

1) *Receiving the trait*

Due to his Functional alteration, the patient finds it hard to perceive that he actually "exists", if not in the form of an inadequate, or unauthentic construction, unable to find appropriate ways of expressing itself. The sensation created by the sclerosis of the Functions (the False Self) is that of emptiness, a frightening nothingness, caused by the erosion of the central nucleus of the Self, which had originally been integral.

During the first phase, the therapist receives the "message" that the Functional trait has been sending out to the world incessantly. In this way, we communicate to the patient a sense of acceptance, a profound feeling of understanding about the fact that he feels ill, false, or not alive. Finally, for the first time in his life, the patient does not have to deny how he feels or force himself to demonstrate the opposite. The patient has already had too many experiences of not being understood or not being believed, because people almost always avoid entering into contact with suffering or the stereotypies caused by Functional traits, fleeing from these appeals, made so desperately and obsessively.

It is important, then, that therapy produce a new experience right from the beginning: that of being "seen" and "recognised" by the other person, really and truly, with all our stereotypies, anxieties, our sensation of inconsistency or unreality. It is as if the individual were finally being told, "I know you exist, I can see it, but I also know that you feel that you don't exist fully."

2) *Providing support for the motivations and profound needs underlying the trait*

When an individual feels that all his manifestations have been seen, even where he is least sincere, and he finally feels accepted and believed. He can start to relax and let his deepest nucleus emerge. This makes it much easier to reach the functional processes underlying his trait. The individual's intense need to be helped, the childlike tenderness, fears and fragility that the therapist has already felt, at the level of transference, during the first phase, can come to light and be received openly.

The Functional trait gives rise to a habitual, stereotyped and fixed body position; but it is the position that is the complete opposite from the patient's habitual one that is closer to the deeper emotions that have not been accepted in the patient's life. These emotions are hidden by the more visible habitual posture and therefore by the trait itself. In order to help the patient perceive these two conditions better, we must push these body positions "to the limit", until he goes beyond the point where his chronic, and therefore subconscious, postures become conscious and he is able to perceive them. Slowly, everything that had always been denied or hidden comes to light, and can be expressed and understood by the patient.

During this second phase, therefore, the therapist aims at putting the patient more in contact with his buried functional processes, through postures, emotive expression, and other related Functions. The therapist uses the "auxiliary Self" chiefly to praise and support parts of the patient that the patient does not yet know how to reveal and live freely.

3) *Therapeutic use of the Functional trait in the patient's relationships*

Whilst the previous phase was characterised by a decrease in how much the patient talks about the events of his every day life, in this phase he starts to do so again.

In the beginning, the patient tried to tell the therapist about every detail in his life, afraid that if he does not do this the therapist might not understand him, or that he could misunderstand something and make a mistake. His worry at that point is that if the diagnosis is not based on the exactness of every detail, then the cure might not be completely right. To use the correct term, he is afraid that he will not be Understood or Seen.

Now, however, by telling the therapist about his life outside therapy, the patient can assess what changes are occurring and how effective they are. Moreover, the patient also arrives at a better understanding of how his old Functional alterations, and particularly his trait, led him inevitably to a series of failures in his social and sentimental relationships. The traps that the patient always falls into are always strictly related to the Functional trait; and they always produce reactions in others that the patient finds incomprehensible, being responses to his own subconscious expressions or attitudes. This can become the object of very fertile and re-integrative exchange at this stage, where the patient cooperates actively with the therapist.

4) *Openly contrasting the Functional trait*

Here, the therapist is no longer an ally to the False Self, nor to the modalities or emotions that bring about the trait itself. At this stage, the therapist becomes an ally of the most integrated nuclei of the Self, which have been expanding during the course of therapy anyway, restoring consistency to the individual's original Functional configuration.

The reconnection and remobilisation of the Functional planes of the Self therefore allows us to consider the trait as a disorder that is just as external and damaging to the individual as the symptom was.

At this point, it becomes possible for the therapist to provide open opposition when the patient falls into the traps of his Functional trait.

The therapist can affectionately sweep away the residues of the Functional trait, or he can oppose them in no uncertain terms, with a serene but decisive movement. The patient can also see the old downwards spiral of his old Functional rigidity more objectively (when and how they are set off), thereby managing to modify them before he reaches the point of no return.

We are now at a point during therapy where we can joke about relapses, old conditions and what still needs to be modified. We can lighten the atmosphere a little, using irony, serene in the knowledge that we have already covered a lot of ground.

Regression and integration criteria

The most critical and central part of a course of psychotherapy, particularly Functional psychotherapy, is that of travelling to the deeps – a "regression". This does not mean returning to moments during the development of the individual when the child was not yet a complete or mature person. On the contrary, it means reaching back to when the individual's Functions were still integrated, as they certainly were at a given moment in his past. For us, regression is the guideline for a voyage towards areas deep down in the individual's personality, and the recovery of the Basic Experiences of the Self is the tool that we use to bring about stable change.

1) *Initial regression and the concentration of emotions in the first stage of transference*

During the first session (or during the first phases of the therapeutic relationship) we notice an unusual condition which brings to light what was gradually building up within the patient, breaking out into the decision to seek practical help and undertake psychotherapeutic treatment.

The Functional alterations and the Functional trait reveal the growing presence of emotions, memories and personal experience, culminating in the *concentration of emotions* in the *first stage of transference.* Regression is already underway when the patient comes to the first session, and the complex interaction between body memory and the patient's current emotional and relational feelings produce significant consequences, without the need for particular forcing or manoeuvring by the therapist.

2) *Deep regression*

Soon, however, it becomes necessary to proceed towards deeper areas of the Self. The most central aspect of treatment is to penetrate within these innermost functional processes, where they are still integrated. The methods of regression are the same ones that have already been indicated for the configuration of the Functions of the Self.

As therapy proceeds, a state of regression becomes ever easier and more accessible. Immersing ourselves over and over again in the integrated nucleus of the Self enables us to consolidate improvements that have already been made, such as the reconnecting different movements within the emotions, becoming aware of our sensations and a renewed integration between our expressions and our physiological activation. All of this takes us much further than the effects produced by sporadic or chance regressions outside therapy such as the intense emotions produced by a film, a reverie inspired by a novel we have just read, a moment of ecstatic contact with nature or a profound encounter with a work of art.

Profound changes can only occur thanks to a systematic programme of regression aimed at reconstructing deficient Basic Experiences, and it can only occur if the patient-therapist relationship is continuous. This is what distinguishes *psychotherapy* from the *therapeutic experiences* of which life is surprisingly full.

3) *Extending the integration*

The individual is led through a series of specific experiences of reconstruction and reintegration, patiently and continuously, mending the most damaging disconnections, rebalancing the altered Functions, and recovering the Basic Experiences of the Self. Our starting point and our strongest ally lies in the areas that are still intact within the original nucleus of the Self. We sweep outwards from these towards Functions that are more external and functional processes, reconstructing he foundations for sense, positivity, ability, and bio-psycho-social "movement".

The final part of therapy aims at assessing the level of mobility attained on all the polarities on all the perceptive, motor, postural, cognitive, emotive, and conceptual levels.

Criteria regarding the therapist's emotional response

The emotive resonances and processes of identification that the therapist is able to feel (amplified field of transference) allow him to recognise the patient through his own Self. He must be able to distinguish between his own feelings, experiences and sensations and those of his patient within his own sense of "com-passion" (feeling-with: feeling together with the other person).

This profound contact causes us to consider once more (although in the opposite sense) the problem of distance between the therapist and the patient. Should the therapist's emotional involvement be expressed or hidden? Should he show open emotivity or rather neutrality?

The hypothesis that we propose is yet again that of an *evolution* in the therapist's use of emotions. There are necessary differences in the way the therapist can present himself during the different phases of therapy. There are two opposing points of view (both of which are justified) regarding therapists' emotional involvement, one stating that therapists must establish an emotional bond with the patient, even at times intense, and the other stating that the therapist must maintain a distance between himself and the patient to avoid confusing or exaggerated emotional attachment. The concept of an "evolution" in the level of emotional involvement is the only way of reconciling these two positions, both of which are defensible. Both of these modalities are possible if we apply them at different times; taking into account what the patient is experiencing in the current phase of therapy, his current needs, and the objectives and goals of therapy at that given moment.

1) *The use of the emotions in countertransference*

During the first phase of therapy, the patient absolutely must not be made to bear the weight and the responsibility that he would feel were the therapist to render all his emotional reactions apparent. This doesn't mean that the therapist should be cold, sterile and unfeeling, but rather that he should mainly make use of his emotional reactions (on all levels, including physical sensations) to reach the other person in his state of need, below the level of his Functional stereotypies. The emotions become an extra sensory organ, the specific tool that helps the therapist to reach what the patient is going through.

Moreover, this is the only way of preparing ourselves to offer real "containment", to be a "new parent", and avoid being caught out by the patient's Functional trait. Avoiding reacting to the input coming from the patient cannot and must not be an "effort" based on a sense of duty or imposing our will over our feelings. As we have already seen, our interest and fondness for the patient cannot be anything other than genuine and profound. If this were not the case, then the course of psychotherapy (particularly a multidimensional type of psychotherapy such as this) would be destined to fail, because the therapist's real feelings and the falseness of this forced expression would get through one way or another. Our interest in the patient must not be false, and neither must it depend on the case in hand, circumstantially, such as a patient we particularly like, a pathology that we are particularly interested in, or Functional stereotypies that we find easier to deal with and accept.

Interest in the patient can only arise from a correct use of transference and countertransference (besides our experience of our own therapy and our type of professional training, naturally). Just like a mother (when there are no significant inner conflicts) whose love and interest for her offspring overcomes whatever opposition, negativity, tantrum or closure the child may present, the therapist shouldn't feel rejected by the patient's aggressive or negative actions, because he knows how to see beyond them. He is able to see the patient's fragility, his need for warmth and affection, his fears, his deep suffering, his angers, and his disappointments.

2) *Using emotions at a practical level*

The therapist does not have to control and contain his emotions throughout the whole relationship, because they are usually a very valuable tool in treatment.

In this phase, then, the therapist uses his emotions as an actual operative tool, by using various different "modalities of therapy":

- The therapist uses his emotions, bringing out the parts of himself that best correspond to parental or key figures in the patient's past. This is about stimulating responses that have gone into hibernation, or sensations that are subject to excessive control or which have been emptied by excessive explaining at a rational level. The patient's feelings are revitalised, and his mental and body memories put areas of his Self which had previously been inaccessible in motion;
- In other moments, however, it is necessary for the therapist to interpret his parental role in a way that is completely different from the figures in the patient's past. This is about providing *corrective emotional experiences*, managing to lay the correct amount of emphasis on the patient's present sensations, compared to those being radiated by the old traces, from deep down. Just like before, the therapist cannot "act" as if from a script, because his attitude is real, deriving from an understanding that goes beyond reactions, to touch the patient's innermost feelings;
- Lastly, the therapist's emotions can be used to give life and voice to the emotions that the patient himself suppresses, openly expressing what the patient is not yet able to render explicit. The patient's emotions are supported, and they start to take shape through the therapist's auxiliary Self, made up of his various expressive Functions, such as tone of voice, phrases, touch, and movements. The *auxiliary Self* breaks through the veil of emotional confusion, the patient's doubts about himself, his self-criticism and control, by providing the emotion that was trying to come out directly and strongly, where it had previously been trying to emerge with great difficulty and in an indirect way.

The use of feelings and emotions at an operative level requires a great many nuances and it is very complex, but the most important thing is not to lose the work done by the therapist on countertransference (amplified to all levels of the Self in the case of Functional therapy), which allows him to avoid contaminating therapy with feelings related to his own private life that have nothing to do with the current phase of therapy.

3) *Expressing emotions directly*

It is in the final phases of therapy that the relationship increasingly becomes that of an interaction between equals, one person to another. The therapist can show his own emotions straight away, calling them into play along with those of the patient. He can express displeasure, joy, fear; he can express his own fragility, get angry or cry, even, about something that is currently happening in the patient-therapist relationship. The therapist can make use of his own experience as well, to help the patient to feel similarities or that he is close to him, emotionally.

The difference between this and the relationship between friends lies in the fact that there has to be complete transparency so that everything is clearly understood by both parties, and also because the relationship must be used to give the patient still more balance and harmony of the Self. Friendship, on the other hand, may contain confusion or anxiety (also due to possible unresolved conflicts), and it does not have the aim of reconstructing health and well being.

Criteria for using the Self

To conclude this argument, we will analyse one last criterion which is already partly contained in the previous criteria, in some of its essential characteristics, but which nonetheless requires further specification.

1) *Acceptance of the patient's false Self*

This is present in the phase (which we have already mentioned) in which the patient feels that his inconsistencies and rigidity have been Seen, and he can therefore feel recognised and accepted even when it comes to his stereotypies or the fact that he doesn't feel he really "exists".

2) *The therapist uses the auxiliary Self*

In this function, the therapist must offer containment, as well as act on the patient's behalf, and he does this on various planes.

First of all, the therapist uses the auxiliary Self to assume the responsibility of recording everything that happens in therapy, "following the thread" so that, for once in his life, the patient does not have to worry about having to follow everything that happens or understand it all.

At other times, it becomes necessary to help the patient to reacquire specific body movements that he has lost, and at such times, the therapist can help the patient to move, almost as if he were a substitute for the patient's own muscles.

Another possibility is that the therapist can make important associations or connections himself, in the patient's stead, or he can make up for physiological dysfunctions by changing the patient's breathing, muscle tone, etc.

The person undergoing therapy feels that his atrophied Functions are being reanimated, and that these disconnections can be repaired, even though he is still in the hands of the therapist for now.

3) *Using the areas of the individual that are still integrated*

By descending to the deepest nuclei of the Self, we can make previously suppressed or inhibited Functions and capacities accessible again. The integrated areas of the patient must be developed and encouraged, not in the sense of an effort of will, or a duty, but rather as the result of a sort of synergetic flowing together of all the other planes as well as the cognitive plane. Part of the auxiliary Self provided by the therapist is gradually replaced more and more by the patient's expanding integrated Self.

4) *Mobilising and consolidating the Self, stability*

This phase is about not settling for the results (however significant) that are normally reached during the previous phases, but going the extra mile to obtain, with more little steps, modifications that are even more extensive and also more stable.

Here, treatment consists in widening the ranges of the Functional polarities (perceptive, motor, conceptual, emotional) still further, stopping to look at both the individual's central issues and the more peripheral ones.

In this phase, therefore, we turn once more to the Functions and the Basic Experiences of the Self that have not been sufficiently mobilised and recovered over the course of therapy and we try to increase the level of functioning, as well as the patient's awareness of them. Particular emphasis is placed on the capacity to carry on helping himself once therapy is over, experiencing ever wider nuances and tonalities on all planes.

On the other hand, the stability of the results is also ensured by the fact that adults have a very different capacity for survival than children do.

Adults do not have such an impelling and dramatic need for help, protection, and affection as children do, because they do not *die* if all this is missing (as can *literally* happen in the case of children). An adult can procure these things for himself later on, and he can find roads that will help him to reach the fulfilment of his needs sooner or later.

If new difficulties or frustrations arise after therapy is over, the patient can face them with a full, integrated Self at his disposal, without therefore having to find distorted ways of surviving or necessarily falling into Functional alterations.

Conclusions

None of the criteria that we have talked about must be taken in isolation. They must all be placed in relation to the others, interacting at all times, almost as if we were to lay several observation charts one on top of the other, each printed on transparent paper, to give us a depth of field which would, nonetheless, prove to be a long way away from the complexity of the real thing.

Furthermore, we must also stipulate that no phase can really be distinguished clearly from the others, because there are numerous shades of grey and returns from one to another. The therapeutic process is only linear when taken as a whole: if we go into detail, we can see that it is made up of zigzags and spirals.

The criteria taken into consideration must not be considered exhaustive by any means. The argument needs further development. However, the above criteria do provide a sufficiently wide and natural guideline for interpreting phenomena that are subject, by their very nature, to an enormous amount of variables.

Lastly, we can say that whilst on the one hand these criteria can be linked to one of the fundamental problems of clinical psychology, i.e. diagnosis, on the other hand they pave the way to a possible *analysis of the therapeutic process and its results*. They lead us towards the formulation of standardised elements, which determine the way the course of therapy progresses, dividing its course into a series of scientifically verifiable phases. We can in fact connect these phases to the *standard elements* observed in the last chapter, which render the subdivision of the therapeutic process more specific and concrete.

Studying the phases, together with the criteria aimed at identifying and interpreting them from a multidimensional perspective, is another step towards the construction of an *integrated theory* of psychotherapy, as well as human functioning and the phenomena related to care-giving in general.

Chapter 10

Manuela: a clinical case history

Diagnosis

Reasons for seeking therapy, as explained at our first encounter

Manuela is 31. She is pretty and well presented.

Five years ago, during a skiing holiday, she started to feel bad, feeling a lot of "irritability". At first, these bad spells came and went in cycles, roughly every four months, then they became more frequent, and for about a year and a half now they have been a constant presence.

During these bad spells, these crises, her thoughts lose touch with reality, causing her to doubt the people around her, even her friends and her boyfriend. Her negative thoughts reach the point where she feels threatened by everyone. In particular, she fears that her boyfriend is unfaithful and that all of his family are against her, and so she doesn't like going to see them.

She feels distrust towards everyone. In these moments, she feels that people are talking behind her back, they're against her, so Manuela draws in on herself, unable to talk to anyone, whoever they might be.

She has had a few appointments with doctors but she didn't feel safe with them. She wasn't sure they would abide by professional secrecy. She had been prescribed tranquillizers and antidepressants, but she lost faith in them after a while, and now she takes them in alternating phases. The drugs haven't had any noticeable effect anyway.

Besides these crises, Manuela actually has great difficulty establishing an independent life for herself, in which she is able to live the life of a self-sufficient adult, make friends, make plans for the future, or simply feel normal. She's never been able to do so, instead always living in the shadow of her family or her boyfriend, in a kind of non-life.

Present complaints

Manuela has a very high level of anxiety, with tightness in the thorax. She often suffers from tachycardia. Her feet and hands are cold, especially her feet.

Manuela's attention span has shortened and she keeps losing things. Her lack of attention sometimes takes her away from reality. She is often extremely indecisive.

She has relationship problems with her boyfriend, and she sometimes lets imaginary situations get hold of her. She thinks he is unfaithful, that he has other women; and she is unable to convince herself that it's only her imagination, even in spite of proof in some cases.

At times, she has problems with insomnia. A while ago, she suffered from a sensation of pins and needles in her hands.

Whilst on the one hand she has started to feel the desire to have a child even though she is not yet married, she's also worried that it would be a burden to her.

Early difficulties

She was often withdrawn as a child as well. She found it hard to express herself or socialise.

She was scared of ghosts and the dark. She was frightened when her parents' arguments went over the top – she suffered from a sense of impending tragedy.

Scary films left her with a high level of anxiety.

Family

Manuela's *father* was restless, irritable, and distant. He often created a disorientating sense of confusion because he had the habit of denying the existence of episodes that were true, he would suddenly change mood, or he wouldn't give clear explanations about what was happening to him.

Her *mother* was passive, and she was often sad and depressed.

Her parents ended up separating when she was 14.

She has a *sister*, four years older than her, who is more open and expansive, more sociable and more practical, and who was more able to communicate with their mother, to a certain extent.

The *atmosphere* at home was often one of agitation and chaos. Manuela never dared say anything for fear of upsetting what little equilibrium there was, and she continually suppressed her impulse to get involved. If she was unhappy or had a problem, she couldn't go to her father because he often shouted or made fun of her, and her mother wasn't the sort of person that one would seek comfort from.

She would have liked to receive support and guidance, especially from her father, but he was only capable of sporadic moments of closeness, without real affection.

Games

Manuela played a bit with her sister, but mostly she played with the other girls and boys in her apartment block. She played with dolls, hide-and-seek. She also liked unusual games where she used her imagination to frighten herself. For a while, she played boy's games, but she wasn't good at them and she often ended up losing.

What she was like when she was little

As a child, Manuela already felt a lot of sadness inside her. She was shy, a "good girl". She hardly spoke at all.

Anger

When Manuela was little she used to get angry but she used to keep it "inside": she suppressed her anger so as not to create further family upsets. The only person who she openly showed a little anger to was her sister, because she was jealous of the fact that she was able to get their mother to notice her. However, she only expressed this anger verbally, becoming agitated and shaking with tension.

Crying

She has cried on several occasions as an adult, but as a child she used to cry a lot, on her own, and she never told anybody.

School

She used to do her homework quickly, and then she would get to work modelling sculptures because she really enjoyed it. She also enjoyed embroidery. She often took up new activities, but she frequently left them half-finished.

Sport

She's only tried a few sports. Of the few she tried, she particularly enjoyed gymnastics.

A few chief points that are clear from Manuela's story

- She hasn't had the guidance she would have liked, and which would have done her a lot of good;
- Her sister established contact with their mother, preventing Manuela from doing so;
- She has had very negative fears and fantasies from a very early age;
- She doesn't easily become fond of people, ideas, or activities;
- She has had to exercise tight control in her life, but this has got blocked;
- She is indecisive, unassertive;
- She lacks real strength, outwardly directed and openly expressed;
- She is unable to loosen her tension and vigilance.

Functional diagram

Fig. 1. *Functional diagram of Manuela*

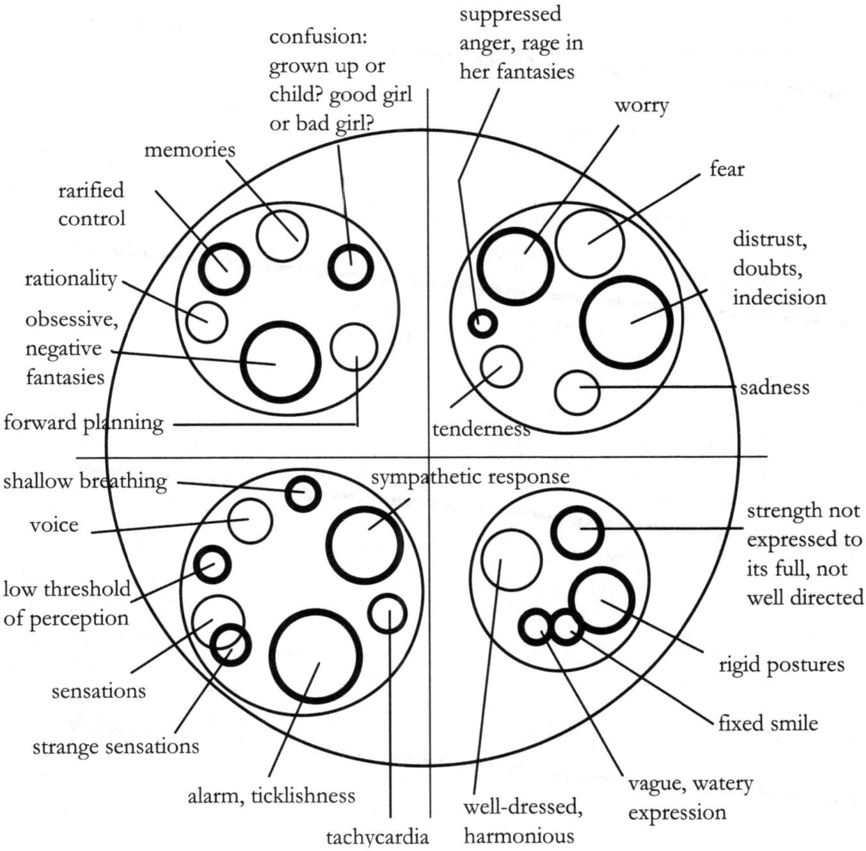

Figure 1 shows the configuration of Manuela's Functions when she first arrived in therapy. The alterations described in her diagnostic assessment are clearly represented.

Running themes in Manuela's life

Fig. 2. *Running themes in Manuela's life*

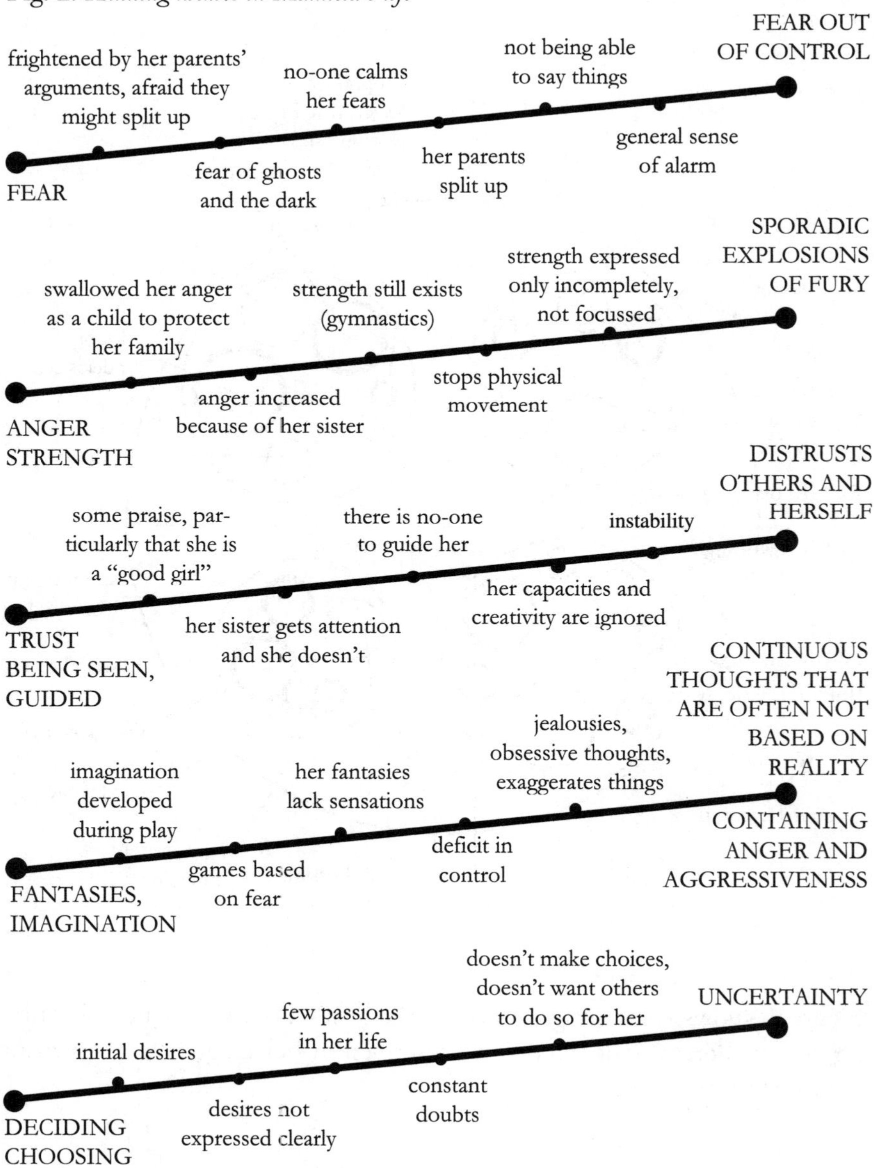

Program of therapy

1. Let go, Loosening Control
2. Being Understood, Clarity, Transparency
3. Little explosions
4. Contact
5. Clear, repeated explanations about what is happening and what will happen
6. Being able to tell things, Trust, Abandoning herself to
7. Being Held, Nourishment
8. Calm Strength
9. Being Guided
10. Caring for others. Maternity

The course of therapy

Manuela had already started a previous course of psychotherapy when she first came to me, but she was very confused about how it was going, because the sessions were very far apart and she didn't understand why. She therefore decided to suspend it so that she could try out a different path – this new type of therapy with a new therapist (2)[1]. However, despite having taken this decision, Manuela doesn't return to therapy for 23 days, and she only returns because her condition considerably worsens. She is still full of doubt, (in line with her overall distrust and confusion) but she promises herself that she will continue. She reports that she ended the other course of therapy for good when she had asked the therapist about the fact that their appointments were so far apart. Was it so that she would get used to difficult situations and rely more on herself? He replied, "If that is the way you feel about this, if that is what you think, then it's probably true. Good." This reply left Manuela speechless, as she was left yet again without guidance, clarity, or certainties.

1 The numbers in brackets indicate the number of sessions attended at that point in Manuela's therapy (the number 2 indicates the second appointment, and so on).

She starts a simultaneous course of pharmacological support, accompanied by a psychiatrist, who works in close collaboration with myself (4); but she is still a little worried about the effects that the drugs might have on her self-control, her eyesight (she's suffering from slight double vision), and her drowsiness.

She is already able to *let go* for the first time at her fifth appointment. She experiences fairly intense physical sensations but she still worries a lot. During the experience of "letting the arms and legs fall", she reveals an enormous level of *inhibition*, her huge difficulty in letting go. Nonetheless, she starts yawning, a clear sign that her tension is loosening, and she starts yawning a lot outside therapy, too (6).

In the 7th sitting, she reports one of those dreams that are typical of what we call "start of therapy": she dreams about the house she grew up in, her bed when she was a girl – and she really felt as if she were there, with the exact same sensations that she used to have.

Therapy is very focussed on letting go and on loosening control, through deep, long massages. The sensations quickly become more intense. There are clear improvements: she feels better, her obsessive thoughts are less frequent, she's more impulsive, and she feels alive. She feels so good that this almost "worries" her (8). We start to reduce the drugs.

Asides from the physical sensations, some indistinct emotions start to emerge during sessions, associated with an intense itching. The emphasis of therapy starts to shift towards an earlier functional process in her eyes and her mouth, but when she performs a motion based on "suckling" her mouth stays tight shut. Her way of relaxing or loosening control is still a kind of falling asleep, more than anything, a kind of drowsiness; as well as a way of not perceiving tiredness, pain, and cold.

Her symptoms start to worsen again for a time, in connection with a strange flu that lasts months. She dreams about her boyfriend cheating on her, but together with all of this, she also dreams about the house she grew up in, her childhood friend, her sister, and her mother. Her yawning has stopped a little, her feet are as cold as before, she has few sensations again and she suffers from intense pain in her ovaries – a pain which reminds her of a dramatic and dangerous inflammation that she once had, which had caused her enormous worry because it had not been diagnosed in time (11).

However, something is starting to change in her life, above all towards her sister who she seeks a different type of contact with, and with her mother because she starts to oppose her constant criticism. She no longer feels that they are united against her. Yet, she remembers when it really used to seem impossible for her to carry on living with her mother who was incapable of treating her with love and with her sister who stole her space, in alliance with their mother. When she was a teenager, she would have been happy to leave home, but she couldn't because she was sure that her mother "would die"; so she bore it all and kept her suffering hidden inside.

Manuela takes part in a therapy workshop where she relives her relationship difficulties very clearly, and straight afterwards her anxiety and old sensations increase: worrying about everything that is happening to her, moving in "slow motion" and suffering from tachycardia. She realises for the first time how unhappy her childhood was. In the end, she had had hardly any reassuring contact at all – neither from her mother not from her father who was too concerned with his own "absurdities".

The process of loosening tension continues, despite the re-emergence of painful memories. Her heart rate decreases from 84 to 74 after deep massage and the recovery of diaphragmatic breathing, even though she continues to talk every so often during treatment. She is only taking one medication at this time (13).

A cold that Manuela has been suffering from for a while seems s if it will never end (almost as if it were a continuous "outpouring" of something inside); and she continues to examine her own feelings about her mother and her sister during treatment. She dreams that the three of them to a hotel together: there are rooms booked for her mother and sister but not for her. They put her in a dingy room in the servants' quarters with no bathroom. Her sister says, "It's just right for you," and she manages to get angry and say, "Why don't you two go and stay in there?" (14).

She feels a stronger and stronger sense of "maternal" contact with the therapist. This helps her to regain her archaic desire to be at the centre of the family and the object of attention.

Around the 16th sitting, she gets a *cold sore* just like she used to when she was a child (classic return of an "old symptom"). There had been a period in her life when Manuela suffered from skin allergies, and she now suffers intense itching in several areas of her body during therapy: knees, diaphragm and forehead.

During a brief trip with her boyfriend and some friends, her anger and tension about her "illness" return because her boyfriend wants her to stop taking the medication and "make an effort" to get better. He wants them to get married and start trying for a baby. Manuela yet again feels that her fears and anxieties have not been understood.

Not long afterwards, however, she starts doing a creative job that she had often dreamed about: a real job making and decorating pottery. She feels good and she plucks up her courage and requests that we stop the drug therapy.

We start working on *Strength* in therapy, which isn't easy because Manuela's strength is not well focussed and it is suppressed. When she expresses her Strength, all her energy goes into the upper part of her body, so much so that her head actually starts spinning.

She soon worsens again (as is normal in therapy). She starts having negative thoughts, she is irritable and agitated, and she feels distrust not only towards her boyfriend but also towards the friend she had been thinking of starting up a pottery business with (21). The difference between this and the first relapse is that Manuela's negative "thoughts" are based, if we look closely, on negative events that are *real.*

Manuela's boyfriend has started insisting again, in an unpleasant and pressing manner, that she attend an English language course (which he already speaks well) even though he knows full well that she detests learning English. Her friend, on the other hand, already has a business making artistic objects. At a meeting with some potential buyers, who they wish to sell their ceramics to, her friend passes her off as an employee rather than as her partner in a new, separate business venture. As if that wasn't enough, Manuela's family start pressuring her to "get better" again, as if it depended on her own will. When Manuela calls her father to seek affectionate contact, he misses the point and asks her if she called because she needed something!

Manuela's thoughts and fantasies do gallop beyond reality, but not being understood, not being received, a lack of affectionate attention *really have happened* in the past, and it is these that *pave the way for, and set off her crises of withdrawal and negativity, even now.*

I speed up the process of therapy a little and I manage to *take her up* more fully, more than she had ever been before, as if she really was a little girl, and in so doing, we move into the important and delicate phase of recovering the most nourishing Basic Experiences (21). However, Manuela is not yet able to make positive use of this profound help, this archaic contact. Because of this, she starts worrying that she won't be able to cope without the help of medication and she calls the psychiatrist to request a prescription.

All the links in the chain of Manuela's innermost functional processes have now emerged and have become much clearer. She draws in on herself when she doesn't feel understood or received, or when she is afraid. She used to feel as if she were "sick", just as she does now. She used to have a recurring dream when she was ill as a child, and it was characterised by sensations of profound insecurity, horrible sensations, and it was permeated by a dull, uniform colour.

Yet, Manuela isn't really "sick"; she is only sunk into a more that comprehensible reaction made up of anger, sadness, and withdrawal. In this state, her thoughts become confused and unclear, which means that she is unable to express anything externally. We look at all of this calmly and at length, with tenderness, allowing her to see how painful it was for her at the time, the fact that all these factors are related to each other, the fact that she's not "mad" at all (22).

The cold sores continue to "explode" on her mouth, her chin, and she has itchy spots on her feet – further signs of small-scale explosions.

Now is the moment to help Manuela, using very precise modalities of intervention, to profoundly modify her breathing, keep her thorax low (whereas she tends to raise it continually, breathing upwards), to breathe with her diaphragm and her belly. Manuela starts to venture into a deep state of wellbeing, but she doesn't stay there long. She takes control again straight away, and her heartbeat increases until it reaches a state of tachycardia.

The dose of medication has been reduced again. Now she only takes one pill in the morning. Things are going better with her boyfriend's mother, her sister, and her boyfriend. Everything has become clearer.

Manuela starts talking more about these relationships in therapy, especially about her mother and her boyfriend's brother and the fact that they are oppressive and condescending.

I encourage her to express her thoughts and feelings a lot, and not just during therapy, and to find more space in her life where she can talk about her personal situations, and to give her opinion on the things that happen to herself and to others. I also encourage her to manage to change other people's opinions when they are wrong and change her own opinion when this is appropriate (24).

We work on calming the anxiety that Manuela often feels, but we also work a lot on her self-expression, using her face, her voice, and her movements. Her sensations during therapy become intense and full of life. Her physical pain during specific therapeutic "positions" also clearly emerges, but she does not express it outwardly – she keeps it shut up and hidden! When I talk to her now, I talk to her as if she were a "little girl", about how she draws in on herself, how she stays curled up in her "shell". I then talk for a long time about her sensations, tracing a clear picture of what little Manuela's life was like, sharing, in a moment of profound contact, her feelings and her fears. Who could Manuela talk to? Later, as an adult, who has she really been able to turn to? Who has she been able to open up to completely and be fully received? (26)

In July, Manuela and her boyfriend go on a 10 day trip with two other couples, and Manuela feels bad again: she falls back into her old withdrawal, in obsessive and negative thoughts, in her muteness and immobility. This time, however, she didn't feel agitated, nor did she suffer from tachycardia. Not just that, but her distrustful and hostile thoughts towards the others were a lot less violent.

Together, we again look at the fact that she has bottled up minor, *real* displeasures, frustrations, and delusions, sometimes without fully realising it. The fact that there is no one in her life that she can really confide in is also a great weight to her.

However, Manuela is scared, she thinks she'll never get through it, that she made a mistake decreasing her medication, even though the therapist reassures her a lot on this point. What she really desperately needs is *contact*: as a girl she had hardly ever been held in anybody's arms, and when she had been, it had never been just for the sake of reassuring contact, contact for contact's sake, with the sole purpose of providing affection and protection.

Once again, Manuela is unable to really feel taken up and held in therapy: she feels uncomfortable during contact, and she can't manage to feel small and protected in a pleasant and positive way – but she does manage to externalise this, confiding in the therapist! She talks about how contact has alarmed her at other times in her life. She has never had the courage to talk about it (27). She felt bad again all week, closed, shut off from everybody. She was unable to resist calling the psychiatrist to start taking the medication again. However, she is able to talk more calmly and serenely in therapy, and she even manages to smile! Even her closure, she notices, is different from before: less agitated, calmer (28).

We have got right down to Manuela's deepest nucleus, to the confusion between reality and imagination that she absorbed as a girl from her whole family situation, especially from her father: the way he denied real occurrences, and the closure that he transmitted to the whole family. We have got down to another part of the nucleus as well, to the fact that she never had a moment's support from her mother either: she was harsh and critical of her, and she was always against their father even when the girls were small. Manuela often feels like a child in the presence of a friend's "parent", as if her mother were a stranger who inspired fear and respect. Whenever she feels negativity, criticism, not being received, *non-joy*, she is unable to say anything.

The fact that Manuela attaches too much importance and pays too much attention to *words* is by no means a consequence: Manuela *had* to hold on to something when she was little, something that could remove her doubts; and so words took the place of other, more tangible, sensations that were more "physical", deeper. Today, as a result, Manuela is very sensitive when it comes to words – if they present even the slightest negative or ambiguous nuance her thoughts run away with her, reaching the blackest negativity.

During a session, Manuela manages to talk about all of this for a long time; and also about her boyfriend (without having to defend him, no matter what the cost, as she had done at the beginning with her mother and her sister), his inability to really understand her, help her, or receive her. Manuela, deep down, had always known what she really needed from a man: real, profound, calm Contact (28)!

All of this is what underlies Manuela's present difficulties, her obsessive, negative distrust, and her closure. The lines running from the past to her present pathology are very clear. Her present difficulties are not a discontinuous jump or a strange and incomprehensible event.

Manuela manages to overcome the crisis not so much because of the drugs, as the fact that the therapist has managed to get right down to her innermost needs, and the running threads that have led her from the past to today. The reconstruction of the Basic Experiences like Contact, Being Understood, Trusting, Being Guided, and being able to Express herself has had its effect. In this last crisis, something has already changed. The therapist does not remain neutral, external, impassable, but he moves in with huge warmth and deep emotional involvement in Manuela's fears, brushing away her last doubts, again revealing the connections between all the elements in her story, giving her trust and contact full of warmth, and receiving her as if she were a tiny, fragile child.

Manuela's disorder is no longer an obstacle to therapy. On the contrary, it is a tool for reaching back to her past and her innermost needs; her thoughts that everyone is against her have not prevailed over the new, positive sensations that she has received from the therapist.

Even a pathology like this, then, can be resolved by proceeding in the right direction, by recovering the most fitting Basic Experiences, taking up the patient's "path of development" from the point where it was threatened or altered.

Before leaving for her holidays, Manuela asks the therapist if he can talk to her boyfriend about her crises and closures, to give him a better understanding about what causes them, and to tell him to tolerate what happens rather than attack or blame her.

The summer goes well. Manuela sleeps a lot, she manages to be around the others without closing herself up too much, and her boyfriend manages to help her. When there is something that she really is not ok about, she manages to tell him openly. She was able to tell him openly when she was tired, when she did not feel too good, when something was upsetting her. She even managed to think of "exactly what she would have been thinking" (what fantasies would have been set off) if she had been in the same state, with the same difficulties, as she was before therapy (29).

Contact with me is now very good. Manuela smiles, she is happy to be held, she lets herself be hugged with serenity, and she feels understood and helped. Her relations with her mother and sister are also going a lot better. It's just her father. Manuela does not want to call him. She can't stand him. She can't stand the fact that he's as chaotic and confusing as ever. With her new ability to let herself go and talk, Manuela finally tells me at length about the fear that she had felt when her ovaries were inflamed that she would not be able to have children, her worries about getting married and having children, her possible future (30).

Now therapy is very productive. The program of therapy still calls for a period of nourishment, and the bolstering of early Basic Experiences relating to containment, before working on her Strength and her capacity for maternity. However, things are already well underway, even if she still doesn't quite think she can do without her medication; despite the fact that the dose has been reduced drastically to below the minimum quantity necessary to produce an effect. Many things have changed and many things are changing. Manuela says that she is now incapable of breathing without leaving her mouth *slightly open* – this is considerable progress seeing that she always used to keep her jaw tight shut (31).

Another period of ups and downs starts, and a little anxiety returns, which Manuela attributes to the fact that she has suspended the drug therapy. In reality, we are approaching an important turning point: establishing *Positive Continuity* through her relationship with the therapist. After intense work on breathing and Contact, Manuela is perplexed, she hardly speaks – she feels anxiety with me, because of the positive emotions that she feels towards me (35). I help her, and she rediscovers the pleasure of talking about her life: her games with her pillow before she fell asleep at night, her earliest sensations; and how she *never told anyone* about all of this, or about herself, not even her mother. In therapy, Manuela gradually rediscovers the capacity to *chat idly* about what happens to her during the week: lunch with friends, the boat trip, contact with her sister, and her conversations with her boyfriend.

We continue to lay emphasis on the Loss of Control and on her Sensations, which are still very anaesthetised, especially in her legs. In the meantime, Manuela is preparing her first exhibition in her new job making artistic ceramics. She is under pressure, the exhibition goes well, but afterwards new closures and negative thoughts are unleashed. This time, it is clear that all this is set off by lots of little negative incidents: people not giving her attention or even putting her down, people not placing their trust in her, people betraying her trust (just like when she was little), especially her business partner. Instead of expressing her anger towards the others openly and directly, she keeps swallowing it down, increasing her negative fantasies (she even reaches the point where she starts thinking that she will never manage to be what everyone else wants her to be) and she loses heart (44).

Nonetheless, there is a very clear distance between this and her previous crises. Manuela is able to talk to me about it all with great lucidity, and, more importantly, she remains in contact with me throughout. Her closure is only with the people that she has experienced unclear or uncomfortable situations with. This time, she feels absolutely no anxiety and her jealous thoughts are very limited, and only in relation to a real incident which really could have led her to think the worst. Manuela manages to talk at great length about how unhappy she was as a child, the sudden fears that used to seize her, and the confused and frightened fantasies about people who did not seem reliable. She talks about her difficulty in saying what she liked or did not like, even as an adult, the nervousness that her father made her feel with his agitation and his confusion, and how she had ended up feeling something similar with her boyfriend, too, when she was unable to express a preference.

We go through a phase when she feels better, and she manages to avoid taking the medicines, which she nonetheless wanted to take up again as soon as she started feeling bad again. She has not yet got through a central point in therapy, that of *full* Contact with the therapist, being able to completely Abandon herself, and the Continuity of the relationship above and beyond negative episodes, distances and thoughts. During the sitting, we yet again loosen her Control, and at the same time, she starts to absorb Protection and Contact, being Held and nursed, as she never had been as a child.

Manuela manages to get angry, openly, with her business partner, because she had tried to sell decorated ceramics on her own outside their business, and she breaks the partnership; but in the end, she breaks down again. She is in a bad way; she goes back to shutting herself off and not speaking to the others. She does not, however, close down her relationship with me, which is still very intense, which is very different from how it was in the initial stages of therapy. Yet, she feels discouraged. In reality, Manuela has already changed a lot, and even throughout this new, serious crisis, she stays in contact with reality, with her sensations, with her feelings and with me – she reports a dream about this that is very significant.

She sees a baby girl in a pram (her boyfriend's sister had had a baby girl a month ago and she hadn't seen her until a few days before). The baby girl is calm, serene, and very pretty. Manuela stands next to the pram and watches her. There is another person next to Manuela, a reassuring presence, but she cannot clearly see who it is.

The expectation of a beautiful and calm "new childhood" is clear, as is the identity of the figure who is present and helps all this to happen.

Yet again, Manuela goes back to taking the medication, because she is afraid she cannot get through this with just the help of therapy. In the meantime, she starts working on the confused and negative sensations from her past and on old thoughts, which she had never expressed, about her confusion with regards to ambiguous figures who used to visit their family, and about times when the atmosphere at home was not serene. Another dream undoubtedly reiterates the origins of her unease as a child, beyond any ambiguous fantasy: her feeling of being discarded.

In this dream, Manuela is in the old family house, in the kitchen. Her mother and sister are busy near the stove and she is on the floor, like a black, ugly mass letting out vulgar insults. A hand comes near her and she pushes it away.

Manuela's phase of anxiety and closure continues. Her boyfriend is tired of her unhappiness, saying, "There's no point carrying on being upset about her childhood. She should leave the past behind her. She should have got over it by now". He wants a girlfriend who is as active as he is. This time, however, Manuela does not take this criticism passively. She replies that at the beginning of their relationship she was the one who did a lot for him, who helped, reassured, and supported him! (53).

Manuela has alternating periods of improvement and deterioration. She starts to trust in her contact with me again but then when she is far away she loses it again. Now we work on both Loosening Control and on Strength. We are looking for a Strength that is Original and gentle, aimed at opening her up, making space for herself, regaining sensations of inner consistency and authority. Manuela goes back to feeling really good again (56). She can once more smell her own smell on her pillow in the morning, just like when she was little.

Manuela feels moved when she reads about one patient's relationship with his father in a book of mine. She feels less hardened towards her own father. She is more relaxed with her mother, too. She actually asked her to prepare a dish she fancied and asked her to make her a coffee, for the first time ever! Her boyfriend is changing too. He is a bit more attentive towards her. Before, he was either completely indifferent to what she did or he was always criticising her. Now Manuela does a few things on her own, autonomously, without asking him first whether it is the right thing to do. The work on Strength becomes more intense, sometimes explosive, trying to get her pleasantly out of control. Manuela feels really good, perhaps too good; and she is taking a tiny quantity of drops of her medicine, only in the evening, which she soon suspends again. She doesn't want to live according to too many rules, even in her eating habits. Most importantly, she does what she feels like doing (she bought a cuddly toy like a little girl), and she does it without worrying too much about it (61)!

A warning appears in a dream: she dreams about being ill again and having an argument with her mother and sister. She must be careful not to fall into situations where she loses contact, or in which she is left out by other people who make alliances amongst themselves: this is her weak point.

It finally becomes clear that when she was ill again it was basically because Manuela had ended up compartmentalising the whole course of therapy into narrow, limited categories, debasing this new, open contact with her therapist, blocking and suppressing her own fondness, just as she had done when she was little with her parents. In this way, she was devaluing what was really being opened up through this *new parent* figure. However, the Basic Experiences cannot be closed up again that easily once they are recovered, and the open flow with the new parent/therapist merely needs to find stability, with the full recovery of the Experience of Positive Continuity.

As confirmation of all this, Manuela realises that she even tends to shut herself off when an old, very "paternal" friend comes near and hugs her, as if even this lovely feeling that she has felt for a while could be misunderstood by others. This closure mostly starts off as a hidden and silent attitude of opposition, just as her bitter and rampant brooding is set off when she receives little attention, or she is treated with indifference or continuous, belittling criticism. When these things happen, it leads her to *shut off her emotions.*

Now, every so often, when Manuela is a little girl again, held in the arms of the therapist/new parent, she now no longer feels uncomfortable. She abandons herself and absorbs protection, warmth, tranquillity, and love. Her sensations are also more intense – relaxation, contact, a feeling of calm, pleasure and warmth which spread through her whole body, as well as a sense of expansion (68). When she was ill as a girl she used to feel the opposite of this: it was as if even her body was being *sucked* inwards.

A new relapse quickly passes without her having to go back to taking the medicine. Now all we have to do is finish working on her Strength and Authority, without losing touch with Contact and Wellbeing. We need to work on Contact more than any of the others, because Manuela has a tendency to lose it, going back to old thoughts and horrible sensations; neither of which are, however, as intense or as devastating as before. The changes that we have obtained allow her to open out and live a different life: fuller, more grown up, calmer, even though she still has difficulties. She can even start thinking now about the possibility of generating another life; about getting married and giving space to her own motherhood and a child of her own, a child to look after, *which is no longer herself.*

The road is clear now. It is not over yet but the way is straight and clear now. Despite further relapses, Manuela is set to completely reconstruct her life, grasping an Authority and an Autonomy that she had never possessed, patiently mending the fabric of all her relationships, meeting others like a normal person. She is looking back at her adult life and choices (or non-choices) with a critical eye in order to be able to reach the competency and fullness necessary to create a family, build up a career, weave together a social life and finally give life to another being. It all seems simple, but this finishing line seems like a dream to Manuela, which she would never have been able to imagine.

Chapter 11

Functional development in the prevention of childhood and teenage disorders

Childhood

As we have already seen repeatedly, there are many new discoveries about childhood, and about the functioning of very small babies, and all of them tell us that interaction with their surroundings and with adults is crucial for positive development. It has been proven that newborns have intense contact with their mothers, through eye contact, touch, and the voice. We know, in particular, that physical contact is hugely important for the newborn to continue to perceive the relationship with his surroundings in a positive way. We also know that children's healthy development is tied to the healthy development of all their Functions.

Figure 1 shows the Functional characteristics of a healthy and harmonious child, together with the most common risks that parents and childcare workers should take care to avoid.

In more general terms, we can say that certain primary Experiences are indispensable for the healthy[1] development of a child. These Experiences are at the root of life and are defined as the "Basic Experiences of the Self" by Functional Psychology

Nowadays, we know that all the basic needs during childhood (which are fulfilled in the Basic Experiences of the Self) absolutely must be met and satisfied in an uninterrupted "flow", which the child must not be concerned about, so as not to break the *continuity* of his existence, his innermost nucleus, too precociously.

1 By "healthy", we do not intend the absence of illnesses, but rather the individual's capacity to interact with their surroundings in a suitable way, enjoy their own life and conserve and develop wellbeing, positive sensations, harmony and joy.

Fig. 1. *Functional Diagram of the child and the risks of alteration*

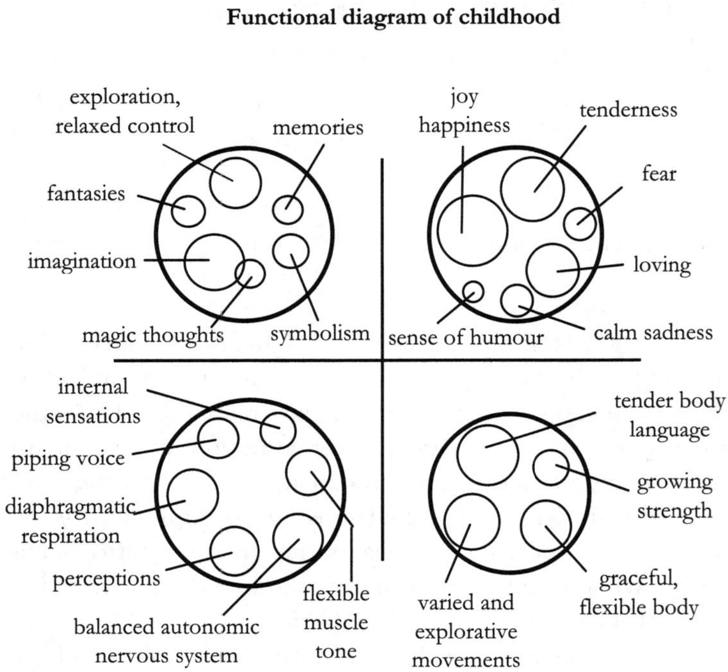

Risks of alteration

The child's movements have not been consolidated yet: we must not stop them
Do not let the child fool himself that he is stronger than the adult
Do not make wisecracks or plays on words when speaking to children
Do not suppress the child's imagination, do not stimulate it excessively
Leave the child his relaxed control
Let the child leap with joy
Allow him to regain his body's flexible and graceful appearance
Let him explore and study the world
Do not force him to beg for love
Allow his emotions to be mobile
Do not increase his fears
Don't let his tenderness dry up

The Basic Experiences of the Self must be undergone many times during childhood in a full, positive, and satisfying way. This is possible only if all the organism's psycho-physical (psychophysical) Functions concur in a unitary and integrated way, together with all the planes that make up the Self: from emotions to movements, from sensations to fantasies.

If these Experiences have a non-positive outcome, if they are not-full or there is a deficiency in the way in which they are experienced, they leave alterations on various planes of the Self, on the physical ones as well as on the psychological ones. Such alterations are signals that appear well before any disorder, symptom, or malaise, whether this is physical or psychic.

It is therefore important to "read" these signals, these traces left by the Basic Experiences that have not been experienced in a fully satisfying manner. These can be found both in the child's body and in his psychological processes; or they are to be found in all has *Psycho-physical Functions*, as the precocious warning signs of pathologies and problems. Outbursts of illness, behaviour problems, scholastic failures, linguistic disorders, the risk of drug addiction etc never appear without warning; rather they are the evolution of alterations which have already been underway for some time.

When we perform early, in-depth screening, we do not look for "symptoms" or *evident* pathological alterations, but rather a whole series of factors: elements that may be subtle, or deeply buried, which we are now able to reveal with sufficient precision. In this way, we can make fairly reliable predictions about the risk of future disorders, as well as formulate hypotheses about the type of disorders that could occur, and on what plane they might appear.

It is therefore possible to look at the child from different perspectives. We can examine the way he *moves*, for example (and not just to reveal whether he is a late developer compared to a normal child, or whether he has any physical handicaps). There are many signals that it is important to notice: whether the child has movements that are expansive or limited, whether movements are jerking or fluid, whether the child is able to let himself go or whether he is always "held back".

Another example can be that of the meaningful information provided by the child's internal physiological apparatus, e.g. basic muscle tone, deep and diaphragmatic as opposed to shallow and thoracic breathing or frequent sweating.

The congruence between the different planes of the Self is also important. When one Function does not move in the same direction as the others, it is disconnected, it goes into *short circuit* and reproduces an altered way of functioning that cannot return to normality unless we intervene directly on that specific Function.

Breathing can, for example, become chronically altered to become breathing that is subconsciously full of vigilance and fear. This characteristic remains even when the external causes for alarm have ceased. The individual does not even notice it, but in the long run, the altered Function will also have negative effects on the emotions, the fantasies, movements etc. – in short, on the whole Self, leading it towards more or less complex pathologies.

By observing the Functions, we can also observe the Basic Experiences of the Self. We can see whether the child is able to "Just Be", quietly and calmly, whether he is able to "Let Go", whether he experiences "Being Held" in a positive way, whether he feels "Curiosity", whether he "Abandons himself" readily to an adult's arms, whether he is able to use "Calm Strength". All this permits us to understand to what extent his "health-system", vital capacities, and joy of life are integrated or compromised.

There are numerous early signs that can reveal child's overall functioning. They are not always evident, and they are often very different from the ones that are traditionally taken into consideration (because they precede the actual disorder itself). Moreover, in order for us to be able to use these early signals to predict future disorders, they must necessarily observe all the organism's levels of functioning, all planes of the Self, a global and multidimensional vision.

Figure 2 shows a list of the *early signals* indicating alterations that can be taken into consideration in children.

Fig. 2. *Early signals indicating the presence of alterations of the Self*

ALTERATIONS OF THE SELF

EARLY SIGNS

Movements
Characteristic Uncontrolled

Way of moving
Slow Brusque Jerky Fast

Muscle tone
Hypotonic Hypertonic

Habitual postures
Shoulders Head Spine

Breathing
Thoracic Diaphragmatic

Autonomic Nervous System
Hands Hot Cold Sweaty

Loosening Control
Somersaults Leaps Sudden, happy movements

Just Being
Capacity to let go

Being Held
Being Taken Up Absorbing

Threshold of perception
Pain Insensibility

Voice
Open Closed Hoarse

Eye contact/Facial expression
Lively Unresponsive Eye-to-eye contact

Language
Vivacious Rich Poor Creative

Fantasies
Open Stereotyped

Games *Drawings* *Stories*

Using Functional theory, we have been able to develop, starting from these elements, real, genuine "assessment protocols" for childhood, a specific one for each different age group. By choosing the Functional levels that have proved to be the most important, these protocols provide us with a fairly reliable general outline of the children's capacity for health and well-being, and what their *real conditions* are, beyond their level of scholastic achievement, cultural habitat, social behaviour and conditioning, or their differing after-school activities.

Our children's real conditions are at the roots of pathologies, disorders and problems, but an absence of disorders and problems doesn't necessarily indicate that there aren't any *alterations* already underway. These alterations will produce problems and disorders later on whilst, on the contrary, children with deviant behaviour due to their social surroundings manage to make full use of the positive opportunities in their lives, reaching a state of balance and harmony later on.

Once this data relating to the child's real conditions has been obtained, we can plan to intervene with *early prevention* that is calibrated to the child's actual state, and therefore genuinely effective. The point of this intervention is not that of getting the children to perform activities (however interesting they might be), just for the sake of it. Prevention must consist in a *rebalancing* of the child's Functional configuration through the activities that are best *suited* to him, and most particularly through the *way* in which these activities are carried out. Swimming, dancing, pottery, music, photography and IT workshops and activities must be chosen based on the children's conditions, and they must be carried out placing emphasis on certain precise modalities of movement, posture, verbalisation, emotion and symbolisation that are deficient or which have been stifled in the children.

The act of prevention should usually, therefore, be present in all children's lives (and not just those considered to be "at risk"). It should become an integral part of the way society approaches child education.

To conclude, in order for prevention to be effective it must aim to:

1. Reconstruct the most deficient Basic Experiences of the Self, as well as any altered or disconnected Functions.
   The Functional vision allows us to identify where to intervene, and how, often working on Functions and planes that are far away from where the actual disorder has appeared.

2. Help parents, psychologists, childcare workers, and paediatricians to know how to spot the early signs of disorders, long before they explode into pathologies.
   A systematic use of "Functional Assessment Protocols" could significantly aid this important primary screening process.
3. Help parents to fully understand the importance of the Basic Experiences of the Self.
   A Project for Prevention should always, however, be of a scientific, focussed nature, as shown in fig. 3.

Fig. 3. *The characteristics of Prevention Projects*

INDISPENSABLE CHARACTERISTICS IN PREVENTION PROJECTS FOR CHILDREN

- *At the root of functional processes*
- *Precisely focussed intervention*
- *Multidimensional (all the various aspects of the individual, all the various Functions)*
- *Synergy (Parents, Teachers, Childcare workers, Children)*
- *Scientific (Overall theory, Evaluation of results)*

Adolescence

Premise

In the light of what we now know about the various phases in the life cycle, society has rightly placed adolescence at the centre of its attention. This is both because it happens over a *long period* of time (with preadolescence, adolescence and protracted adolescence, we are looking at a span of time that runs between 10 and 23 years of age), and because it is without doubt a delicate and important moment in the formation of the individual's personality (with well-documented risks of violence or social deviance).

Firstly, we must examine and underline several concepts which will provide us with an *overall outline of adolescence* and which will form a basis for any reasoning as to how to work with adolescents and their disorders.

1. There is an underlying *continuity* between the various phases in life; and therefore there is no break between childhood and adolescence, or between adolescence and adult life.
   We can no longer sustain (in the light of the knowledge we have acquired) that a child is merely something "waiting to become" a full human being, or a "non adult". This is also the case with adolescents. An adolescent is a *complete person* – an individual with his own particular characteristics. We cannot therefore say that the adolescent has a Self that is "immature", or that he must "reach maturity", even if several of his hormonal physiological Functions change significantly during this period. On the other hand, the process of maturation is in reality a process of expansion of the Self that never stops – lasting our whole lives.
2. We must not consider the condition of adolescence a pathology in itself. Unhappiness and malaise are not necessarily inevitable, neither is it true that a certain amount of "disorders" are an inherent part of that period.
   The truth is that this phase brings undeniable changes and transformations, which can be revealed at an objective level, but these must not be identified with, or translated as, pathologies. Rather, they are conditions that are typical at this time of life – typical shades of colour, specific modalities of perception, or the prevalence of specific nuances of emotion: in short, a specific, characteristic *configuration of the Self.*
3. These characteristic conditions of teenagers essentially need to be treated with understanding by the adults surrounding them. Adolescents need to feel that their needs and their specific way of being have been understood.
   It is therefore necessary that the transformations taking place be understood rather than ignored, "absorbed" gently rather than received as a trauma, respected and facilitated rather than hindered.
4. As a result, there must be another important form of *continuity*, and that is the smooth passage between curative intervention and preventative intervention, and between prevention and simply a culturally diffuse way of interacting with, and behaving towards, adolescents on the part of parents, educators, sports coaches, doctors, priests, and, in short, all those who come into contact with them.

5. The goal that we wish to set ourselves is one of *integration* as well as *continuity* – and integration between the adult figures that interact with adolescents, between the different professional figures that deal with them and between the many different scientific disciplines and theoretical approaches.

What we want to avoid is compartmentalisation, the idea that each person is "an expert" on a different aspect, each with his own, limited vision. Compartmentalisation means that we run the risk of neglecting important aspects in adolescents' lives, reducing everything to facts to be learnt or "educative" solutions, or slipping into the idea of adolescence as a pathology, or again aiming at dealing always and only with negative conditions.

Integration, in the first place, also means looking at the individual as a whole, the complexity of all his planes and psychophysical Functions, rather than as a vessel of emotions when it comes to his family relationships, as a body when it comes to sport, as the subject of fantasies in his visits to the psychologist, and so on.

Let us therefore try to examine the organisation of the Self during adolescence: what are the general characteristics, the changes that are underway, the relationships between the different Functions and levels.

Let us try, that is, to trace a general outline, to paint a picture of the whole, so that we can first *understand* what happens to an adolescent and to his relationship with the outside world. It is only in so doing that we will avoid the risk of separating our intervention at a material level from the reception of their basic needs, from their real necessities, or from the continuous and comprehensive attention that adults must pay towards adolescents, which ought to be affectionate, sincere and in-depth.

Functional Diagram of Adolescence

By following the indications of Functional psychology, we can trace as easy and immediately understandable diagram of the characteristic conditions of the organisation of the Self during adolescence.

The circles with the thicker borders represent Functions under rapid transformation, at risk of losing their healthy mobility.

Fig. 4. *Functional Diagram during adolescence*

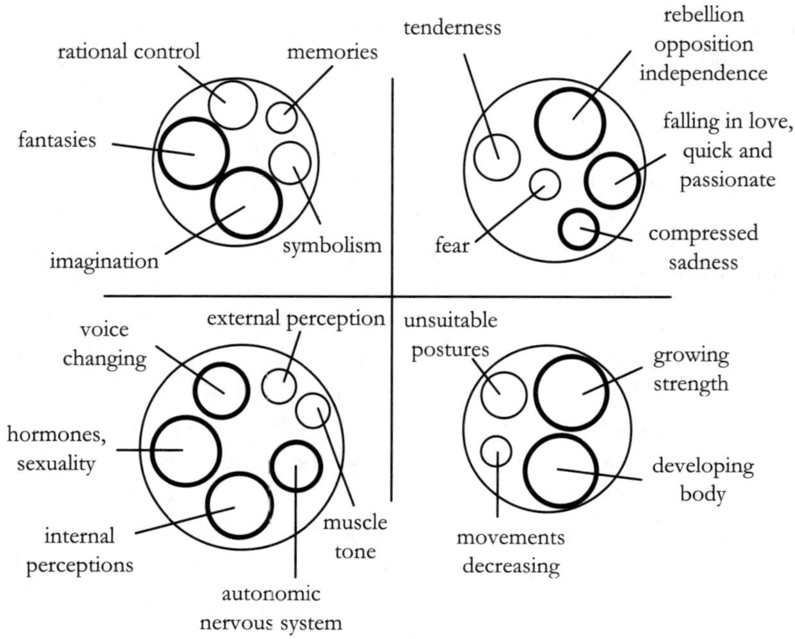

The postural plane

Starting in the section dealing with movements and posture, we note that the largest space is taken up by the rapidly developing body, which, together with the equally intense growth of physical strength, completely unbalances the way in which the adolescent had perceived himself in relation to adults, and to the way they in turn perceive him. Parents suddenly find themselves faced with a big body, which they find t hard to recognise as the "baby" they used to have. They are often scared by their grown offspring's size and strength or they are embarrassed by physical contact.

At the same time, body movements, especially the more expansive ones, (apart from sport and dancing) tend to diminish in the adolescent's life, especially in girls. They assume more composed, suppressed movements, movements that are much less chaotic or free, less "liberating".

Posture and body language also undergo alteration. They become less loose and casual in that they are neither sustained by the experience of an adult, nor are they yet a part of the adult world's codified behaviour.

The physiological plane

In the sector relating to the systems and the physiological apparatus of human functioning, we deduce that the voice is under significant transformation, together with the explosion of hormones and sexuality, naturally.

Adolescents feel a huge need to fully understand what is happening to them. This necessity takes the form of close attention to what is happening within their bodies and around them, to the detriment of their external perceptions. This produces that impression of inattentiveness and detachment from reality, although this is not really detachment at all.

The cognitive-symbolic plane

Huge attention is given to understanding the meaning of all the above changes: how to manage this new body, these overflowing desires and new sensations.

A lot of space is therefore given to thoughts relating to the body, and the fantasies and imaginings that accompany these processes are intense and vivid, such as the image of scenes that particularly struck the adolescent, which suddenly return, as well as the images of desired people or situations, and physical and tactile sensations.

It is not completely exact to assert that a sense of "forward planning" is absent in girls and boys of this age. This sense is turned rather towards the immediate future – managing to meet another person, the first conquests, getting accepted or being admired by their peers, finding the right clothes.

Memories of the past diminish significantly, leaving space principally for more recent memories which could help the adolescent get closer to what he currently desires, helping him to "improve his aim" in order to reach his goals and try out his new capacities.

Adolescents' value systems and their symbolic worlds find it hard to keep up with these changes and remain completely and consistently positive at the same time, especially when it comes to how they see themselves, their sexual role and their identity. Hence adolescents' terrible doubts about themselves and their own abilities.

It is inevitable that there is a huge desire to keep this whole series of changes under control. Since it is very difficult to manage this merely by using their *rationality*, adolescents find a shortcut (which is also present during childhood, however): that of *magic thoughts*. Emphasis is principally placed on strange coincidences, signs of destiny, and anything in the world around them that appears to refer to them, their life, and their thoughts.

The emotive plane

Within the field of the emotions, a considerable amount of space is taken up by rapid ad passionate crushes, which are needed to draw the adolescent's affectivity and sensuality beyond the confines of the family, to help him overcome years of having grown "used" to known sensations that have accompanied his life since birth: tone of voice, smells, tactile sensations and behaviour patterns which condition the child much more than is commonly thought.

The same amount of space is taken up by a strong feeling of independence, which often takes the form of opposition, regardless of circumstances. This rebelliousness is easily set off, and serves to redefine his territory and new achievements. He often falls back on rudeness, which is generally aimed at hiding the fact that the adolescent is still fragile and very much in need of help.

However, the fear of not being able to cope is hidden rather than being openly admitted. This is to avoid falling into a position of fragility that the adolescent no longer wants. This fear is also hidden because of pride, which pushes the adolescent to deal with the situation on his own.

In the end, this fear takes the distorted and much more serious form of a sense of inadequacy, a heightened sense of drama about anything that does not go well, and their own incapacity. This can reach the point where it manifests itself as extreme acts which are highly destructive for themselves and for others.

In reality, adolescents have a huge amount of tenderness inside them, and a huge need for tenderness from others. They also still need to feel strongly supported, and every so often, they need to feel "little" again, to lean on an adult, and feel sustained. Obviously, this must happen in a different way and with different timing from when he was a child, and above all, this support must be sought with greater discretion, because it must not be too evident, and no one must know about it.

Figure 5 shows the Directions in which the Self tends to expand during the life of an individual – in other words, the individual's basic needs. These are needs that we cannot live without if we are to maintain good health, positive potential, and "wellbeing" throughout our entire lives, and not just during childhood. We will always need contact, to be held and contained and to be "nourished", although obviously as an adult these needs are less urgent.

Fig. 5. *Basic Needs*

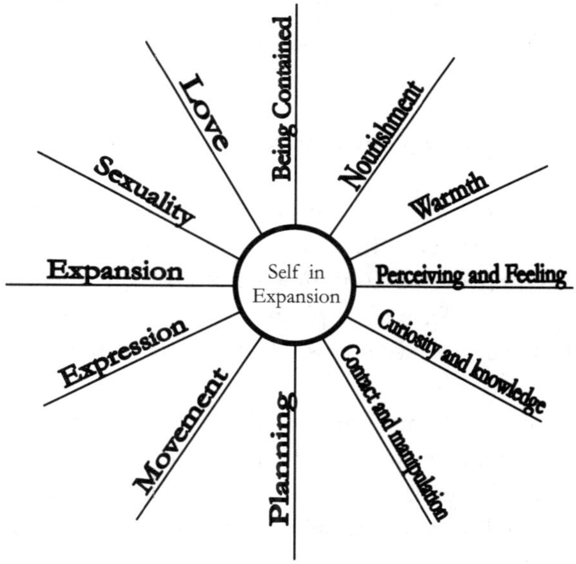

However, the more afraid teenagers are of giving in to these needs, the harder it is for adults (and especially parents) to overcome the distance that is created by their fear, embarrassment (especially towards offspring of the opposite sex). As a consequence, the child's sense of being misunderstood, his sense of tragedy and inadequacy, his hardening towards his parents grows, and he is unable to find the contact, the tenderness and the support necessary to avoid brusque interruptions in his existence, between the previous and current phases.

It is of no use that parents react in the opposite sense, denying the fact that the children have grown and insisting on treating them as if they were still a child, provoking inevitable reactions of intolerance and rejection.

Influence of the surrounding social conditions

Let us now try to trace the outlines of the various social scenarios in which our children are already growing. This means analysing the influence of the social, cultural and technological transformations of post-industrial society on the children and adolescents' ways of thinking, perceiving and being, in short on the whole organisation of the Self.

The growth of visual stimuli, video games, computers, and virtual reality

In figures 6 and 7, the effects of an ever more massive shift towards the culture of the visual image, often, moreover, limited to a restricted area such as the television or the computer screen, or the even tinier area of portable games consoles or mobile phones. These images can be created or distorted in whichever way we choose, further and further away from reality.

Without doubt, all of this amplifies the *imagination* and *creativity*, but it also creates a detachment from practicality, and an increased illusion of unlimited power, which ends up intensifying to become *magic thoughts*.

There is an overall increase in *speed*, to the detriment of *slowness*, the capacity to do things in their own time, and the ability to take long moments of contact with ourselves or for reflection. It is enough just to see how the action in films has speeded up, even when it comes to films aimed at children like cartoons.

Their attention has become more concentrated, more punctiform, they are more used to capturing single details rather than the overall picture, keeping up with the rapid and minuscule movements of computer games. The *movements* that are more commonly requested are also *small, rapid, and precise*, and children move the computer commands with incredible dexterity. *Expansive movements* end up decreasing, and these are the movements that we use to express our Strength to the full, or to expand, to occupy large spaces with our presence or use all our muscles and tire ourselves out to the point where we seek repose and abandon ourselves with huge pleasure.

Fig. 6. *Increase of visual images and computer games*

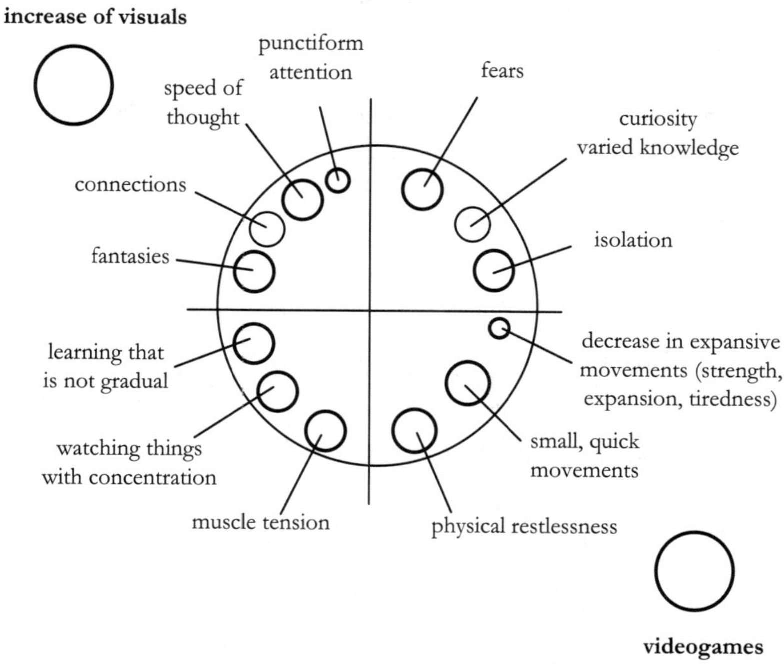

Fig. 7. *Computers and Virtual Reality*

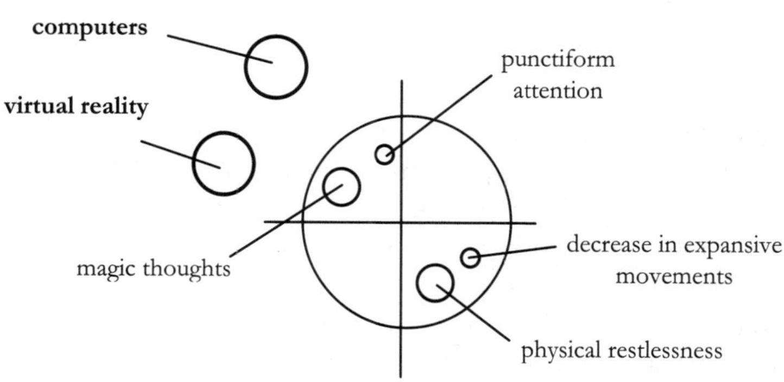

Often, one of the most visible consequences of these changes in children is the widespread phenomenon of restlessness on the motor plane, causing repeated, nervous movements that could almost be interpreted as tics.

The direct experience of the world is considerably lessened, together with their own way of moving within it. Assessment of their surroundings is trusted more and more to eyesight alone.

Exaggerated models of success, physical perfection, sexuality, and aggression

Fig. 8. *Models of success and physical perfection*

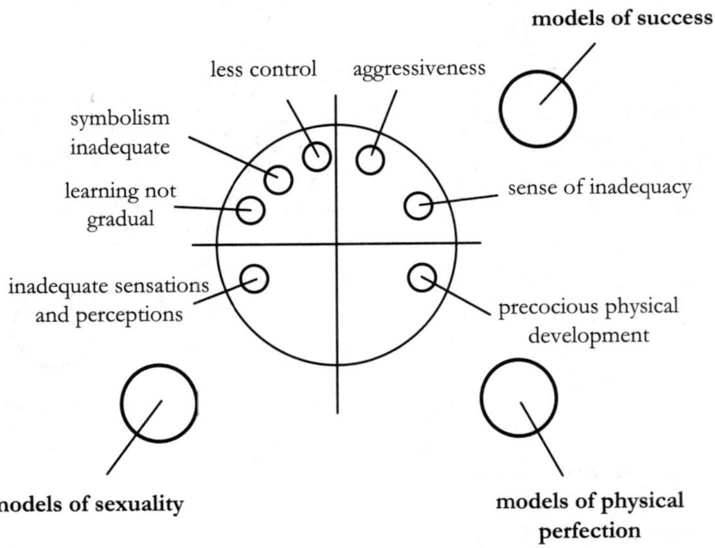

Growing children are endlessly bombarded with advertisements, films, soap operas and celebrity gossip, preventing them from satisfying the natural need to *learn gradually* about relations with the opposite sex, modify their self-image slowly, and arrive at a more accurate perception of their limits and potential in their own time.

The culture of the visual image implacably force-feeds us models of success, power, and false self-confidence. In films, we see young kids who are able to stop world wars and save the world from impending danger;

kids who are already experts in the art of loving, kids who are already on the road to success.

These models create a *sense of inadequacy*, a horrible sensation of being inferior in comparison, which insinuates itself dangerously into adolescents' psyches, together with the *illusion* that the world only works in a certain way – and this way is more and more detached from reality.

It is increasingly difficult, if not actually impossible, to *control* their existences enough to be able to emulate the models offered by the mass media, and adolescents' symbolic system is naturally unable to keep up with this climax of false and improbable values.

Fig. 9. *Models of aggressiveness*

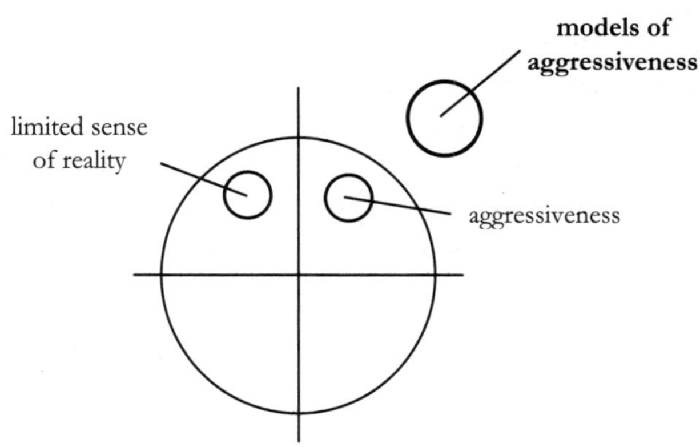

In addition, there is a strong desire to anticipate the natural stages of growth, precociously developing their bodies which do not actually have the corresponding ability as yet to *move*, *feel* and *perceive* as an adult does, because the adolescent has not yet accumulated enough experience to have a real mastery of his relations with others. There is enormous pressure to do what they have seen performed in films, and to be good at it straight away.

On the other hand, all of this also prompts adolescents to procure as many *status symbols* as they can, as soon as possible (otherwise they're nobody). It forces them to "grasp" for as much as they can get, and pushes them towards widespread aggressiveness and violence, which they learn directly from the mass-media, becoming an example to be followed, completely immersed in unreality, completely separated from any pain and suffering it might cause.

This is why we read about things like young kids "playing" by throwing stones at passing cars from the bridges over the motorway with reckless superficiality. Death is only an image on a screen, with no smell, no taste, divorced from the acute pain that accompanies it. One could even say that death is no longer something which is experienced as a part of our every day normality, given that it is shut up in hospitals and retirement homes.

Small, single-parent families

The number of adult figures the child can turn to is drastically reduced with the small family units in today's society. Often there are just two parents, or just one, rather than a network of extended family to turn to, such as grandparents, aunts, and uncles.

Smaller family units are inevitably characterised by having less support and deficiencies in the protection and care of children, which ends up eroding the child's positive nuclei and Self-confidence.

Fig. 10. *Small, single parent families*

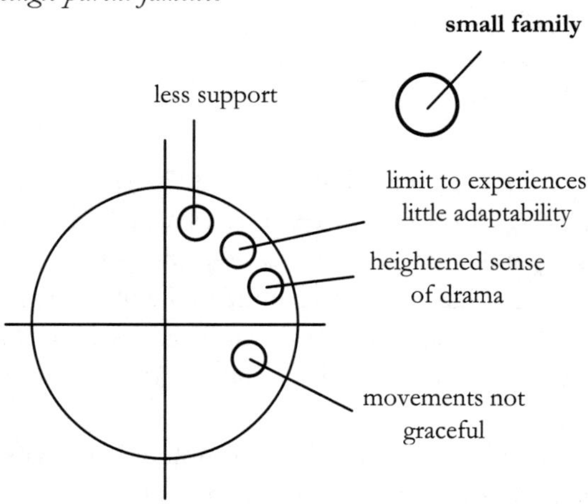

Secondly, the limited nature of the possible experiences that the child can have, in the fact that there are fewer adults present, prevents the child (unlike in the extended families of the past) from being able to juggle easily between adults, moving from one to another as the need arises; being able to seek consolation from a grandfather, a sister or an aunt if someone else in the family has been distracted, rigid, unjust or excessively severe with him.

The lack of diversity in family relationships leads to an increased difficulty in *adapting to each other's ways*, a certain rigidity in roles and movements, a certain difficulty in knowing how to deal with things *fluidly*, as well as a strong and overpowering sense of drama. The relationship between the child and the parent is no longer mediated by any other figure: either it goes really well or it becomes difficult and painful.

The precariousness of the planet

For the first time, a whole generation has grown up immersed in the sensation that the survival of life on this planet could be uncertain, with a sense of impending disaster, of a planet that is polluted and ill, with the possibility of nuclear destruction. We are not yet fully able to evaluate the consequences of these altered conditions on the personality of the new generations.

Fig. 11. *The Precarious future of the Planet*

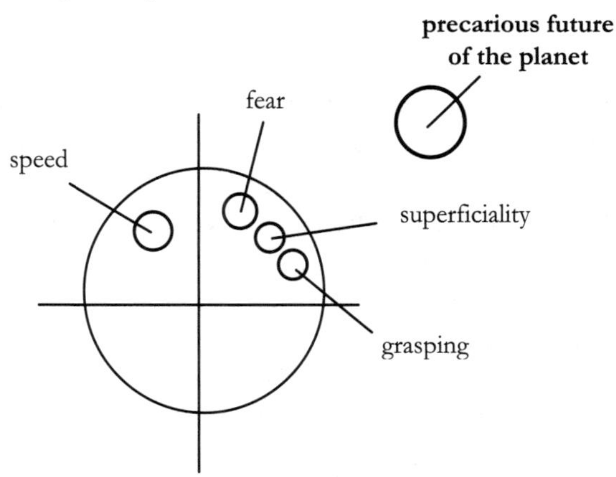

However, we can hypothesise that there is a constant background fear that had previously been absent. In these conditions, it is unlikely that young people will be moved by great ideals or utopias like those (for better or for worse) of their predecessors.

The risk is that tendencies towards self-centredness, superficiality in dealing with existence, attitudes aimed at taking as much as possible and grasping what they can, when they can, without worrying about others, will take the upper hand. It is also possible that this widespread sensation of precariousness will provide a further reason to increase the *speed* of life, achieve everything quickly, and obtain as much as possible as early as possible, accelerating even further the already frenetic pace of life; as it used to be in wartime when people did not know whether they would be alive the next day.

Understanding prevention and cure

Given that adolescence creates disharmonies that cause a few difficulties (although they are not pathological); we should move in such a way that the social context doesn't make these momentary imbalances more acute, leading them from conditions that are simply "physiological" to pathologies or disorders.

The social context surrounding adolescents should be capable of thoroughly understanding the changes they are going through. This should be true of all the contexts they live in (from family to school to free time); and, moreover, these changes should be absorbed by the surroundings very softly, counterbalancing and softening momentary imbalances, favouring the reintegration of the Self as quickly and as serenely as possible.

Even though changes in technology are leading teenagers towards further possible imbalances, we should not *demonise* new technology. Instead, we should try to *counterbalance* the effects of these changes effectively and intensely by sustaining those Functions and Basic Experiences which tend to diminish dangerously, such as expansive movements, looking at the bigger picture, slowing down, serenity, deep emotions and sensations, practical and varied planning, deep support, tenderness and contact.

The Basic Experiences must be "positive" not just during childhood but also during adolescence. These Experiences include being able to be contained and protected, letting themselves go, being loved, being seen, contact, movement, curiosity and knowledge and they must be given a lot of attention by the adult world.

If these Experiences were already deficient when the adolescent was a child, then they have left negative traces. The adolescent's imbalances accumulate in these points, creating profound alterations, disorders, and authentic pathologies. However, although we are talking about cure, we must not neglect prevention. Every cure should be a direct continuation of prevention activity, and it should be part of a more general outlook in the way we deal with adolescence.

To do this, it is crucial that we have a clear and detailed outline. We must have a global, multidimensional vision of human functioning in general, and more specifically of the way adolescents function, to which we can refer, without neglecting any of the aspects underlying life, or leaving out any of the planes or psychophysical Functions upon which the organisation of the Self is based.

Only by utilising all planes can we *make predictions* with a high level of accuracy, enabling us to intervene at an early stage, well before the appearance of disorders or symptoms, suffering or social deviance.

An overall vision will also allow us to look at adolescents' "healthy" needs with greater precision, together with the way they evolve thanks to social and technological changes. We will establish the best way to behave with them, understand them, talk and with them, as well as how to deal with situations undergoing constant change, which are perfectly normal in the end, but which require attention, rebalancing and love while they are underway.

Perhaps in this way we will finally be able to discover that behind their search for their own identity, adolescents can hide huge *lovability* (as opposed to suffering and drama). We can discover that separation from their parents can include huge *tenderness*, rather than a need to replace their parents or "kill" them in order to grow. We might discover that kids can grow up *alongside* adults rather than against them, that they can receive good things from the adults around them and make them a part of themselves, perhaps even trying to go beyond the example they have been given. Kids can learn that the world is a big place, and they can find new people to support them, but they can also use old support figures, if and when they choose to do so. They could learn that Strength is never *against* anyone, and it never will be, if it is used in conjunction with tenderness and gentleness. They could learn that joy and play don't necessarily have to leave our lives when we grow up, and that independence doesn't mean self-centredness: on the contrary; human beings naturally live within certain biological and psychological limits, in which solidarity represents a vital and hugely important element.

Violence, abuse and male and female stereotypes

Violence and abuse in the family environment

According to both past research and current research[2], we are discovering a fact that we have already known for some time, but which has unfortunately been reconfirmed, i.e. that most cases of violence and abuse against women take place *within the family environment.*

There is a significant difference between occasional rape (set off in isolated episodes, on the street) and the subtle and continuous kind perpetrated within the family environment. Whilst occasional rape is deplorable (not just because of the act itself, but also because of a context of further aggression in the way society deals with rape victims), it is easier to deal with than abuse within the family, because the rapist is a stranger, and the event is a one-off. It causes damage, but never as much as that caused by abuse in the home, which becomes a place of aggression when it should be a safe haven.

What are most damaged are the principles right at the root of the family bond: "the possibility of being protected", "being able to trust", and the "possibility of being looked after". All this is even more devastating when it is done to little girls (the majority of cases), and when carried out by close family members (father, brothers, or sometimes a grandfather or an uncle).

How can a little girl who has suffered abuse in the family environment confide in anyone? Whom could she confide in?

2 For example, see research projects carried out by the *"Onda Rosa"* Association in Naples, and the *"Progetto Urban"* of 2001.

The growth of violence

What is certain is that there is a significant rise in incidences of rape, and it has been proven that violence towards women is set off by a more generalised climate if widespread violence, linked to various factors.

First of all, there are more and more restricted families, with little extended family, who are less able to provide children with support, less able to be protective and to "envelop" the child.

Furthermore, the family is much less able to act as a filter when it comes to negative messages arriving from the outside world. Children and adolescents, exposed to the dominant culture's mass media, construct altered desires and behaviour patterns, like the desire to have everything straight away. The ideals of power, success, and beauty that are constantly offered to children and young people give them the sensation that they are not good enough. These ideals make young people feel frustrated, and they accumulate a sense of underlying rage, which can easily transform itself into a tendency to stop at nothing to achieve these models, or at least something that resembles them.

The pressure exerted by the world of the visual image produces yet another negative consequence, however, i.e. a dangerous confusion between reality and virtual reality, the latter being characterised by continuous violence. All computer games are steeped in violence, incredible violence. The main characters kill each other, weapons make them literally explode, and everyone dies all the time, repetitively. We no longer know what violence against living beings really means because violence has become an obsessive virtual image. Violence has also increased on the television and in films. Its overpowering, constant presence is presented as "normality".

To all of this, we must also add that a sense of justice has been gradually declining, just as great ideals or the concept of a moral and ethical code of conduct. The only possible consequence of this is a decline in our respect for others, nature, and life, together with the increase in outbursts, aggression and violence.

Lastly, a further element of deterioration is a decreased capacity to receive children's basic needs or aid the Basic Experiences of human life such as *unhurriedness*, *serenity and tranquillity*, *the ability to relax*, *profound contact*, *the ability to trust* and *being held*. All of this is diminishing more and more within the family, not just because of the frantic pace of modern life, but also because we have forgotten how important these Basic Experiences are to our children's development.

The profound division between male and female traits and their subsequent sclerosis

Aggressiveness develops differently in men and women because of the division that society continuously operates between male and female characteristics.

Gender identity is not just the result of a biological component. It is also the result of messages, guidelines and rules of daily behaviour that are gradually absorbed by little boys and little girls; often transmitted unawares. Public opinion has not yet been made sufficiently aware of the extent of the impact that these messages have on gender differentiation within the structure of the personality, and the effects that these messages have on children at a profound level.

To understand this phenomenon better, we must look at what happens, for example, in the mechanisms at the root of *aggressiveness*, and how these are structured in both sexes.

In girls, the most common experience during childhood and adolescence is a whole series of educative rules, which have the effect of *removing* the capacity to feel and express their *Strength* fully. It follows that their capacity to "assert themselves" or "throw themselves into" important or ambitious enterprises or projects is also diminished. This has a negative effect on self-esteem, the ability to deal successfully with difficulties and a positive self-image.

How does society remove these elements? It does so through the continuous messages that are given to little girls to restrain their *movement*, not to test their *Strength*, to be *composed and calm*, to keep to their *place*. Girls *must* be delicate, more restrained, and more composed. Even when this behaviour is not explicitly requested, it is silently approved of as being the most "suitable" for girls.

On the other hand, in boys, a completely different attitude reigns. "Masculine" games are encouraged, and toys based on warfare. We are tolerant towards (if not actually pleased by) strong, brusque manners, barefaced aggressiveness, riotous movements, and exaggeratedly raised voices. Boys are granted more liberties and given much wider freedom.

As we can easily understand, a characteristic of fragility and passivity is gradually "produced" in women, on different planes of the Self, especially on those relating to movement, posture and body language and Strength. This characteristic takes on the guise of a genuine role, which is attributed to women as if it were the result of "nature".

On the contrary, the aspects of aggression, strength, and domination are seen as positive values in males. Praise is given to intense movement, the externalisation of aggression, kicking, fighting and violent games. Often, families really boast about boys that are aggressive and they clearly encourage these aspects.

At the same time, from a certain age upwards, experiences of tenderness and fragility, as well as the possibility of feeling small or the need to be looked after are actively discouraged in boys. However, *when Strength is deprived of its tenderness, it becomes violence or domination.*

There is, then, a forced differentiation between men and women, a precocious distinction between the characteristics that both sexes are expected to have with regards to Strength, aggressiveness and tenderness.

The following two figures show the results of research into childhood that has been underway for a few years. The data was obtained using *multidimensional assessment protocols*, specifically calibrated for childhood, for primary school children, as developed by Functional Psychology. The circles represent the different Functions of the Self in varying states, the extent to which they are expanded or atrophied (see the diameter of the circles), to what extent there is sclerosis or stereotypy (see the thickness of the outline).

The diagrams in figures 12 and 13 clearly demonstrate the fact that there are already alterations and imbalances underway at this age in both males and females.

According to these results, girls are much more controlled, but they also have a greater capacity for sensation and perception. We note that their body language and posture is more controlled and restrained, whilst their Strength is not expressed. Girls' games therefore tend to be more static, more repetitive and at times obsessive.

Fig. 12. *Diagram of the stereotypies present in boys*

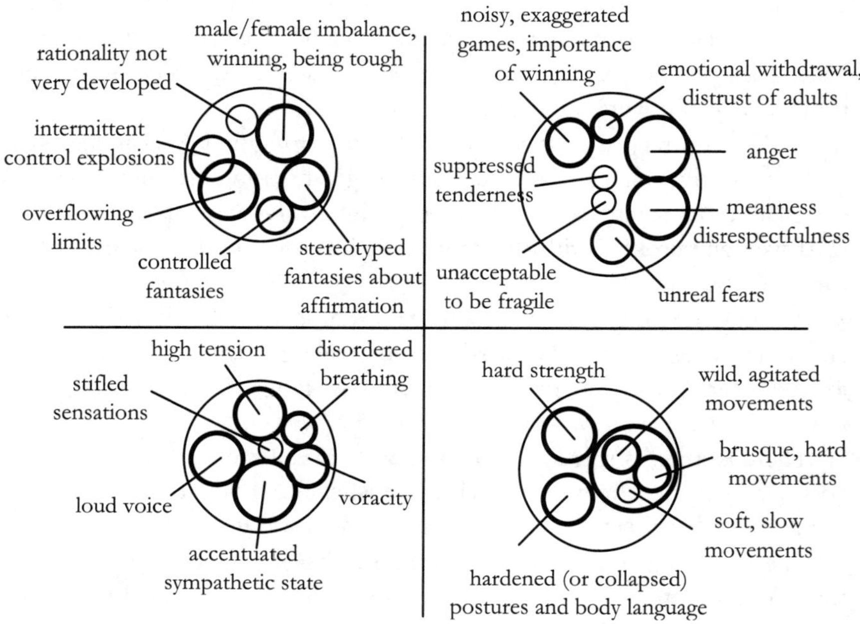

Fig. 13. *Diagram of the stereotypies present in girls*

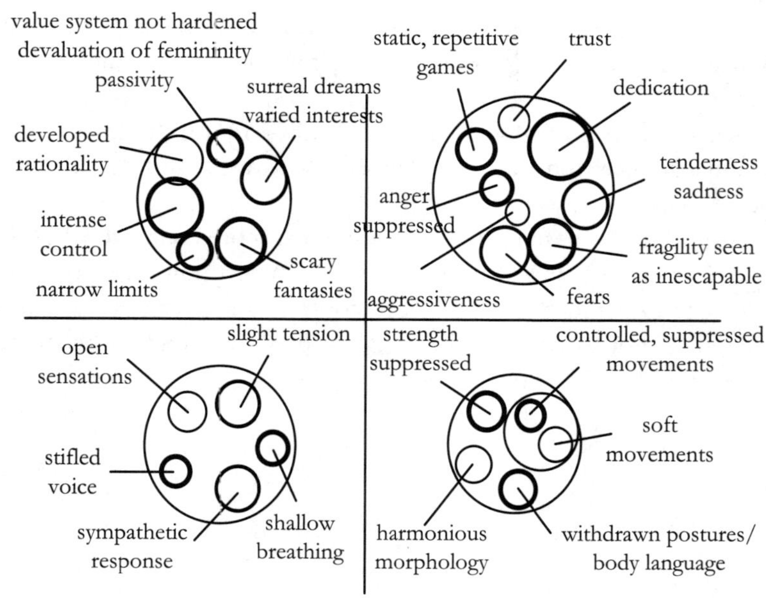

On the emotive plane, anger is limited and compressed, whereas the girls' fears are much less controlled and stifled than in boys, and they are expressed more openly. Girls preserve their trust in adults fairly well. However, girls' aggressiveness progressively diminishes, becoming internal, transforming itself into a tendency to devote themselves to others, which is, however, another way of creating a space for themselves. Doing things for other people represents a residual opportunity of playing an important role and gaining a position of (relative) strength.

If we compare this with the characteristics of boys of the same age, we find that the latter have less ability to reflect on things. Their self-control is less rigid and more intermittent, allowing sudden explosions.

On the other hand, boys' fantasies are less dramatic and carry out fewer flights of fancy: the imagination does not feed concrete or varied projects. Boys' interests are more limited, and they are fairly stereotyped: almost all boys love football or want to become pop stars.

This can be clearly seen in the results obtained from the application of the "assessment protocol" to a class of primary school children (see figure 14).

Fig. 14. *Results of the observation protocol applied to a class of primary school children*

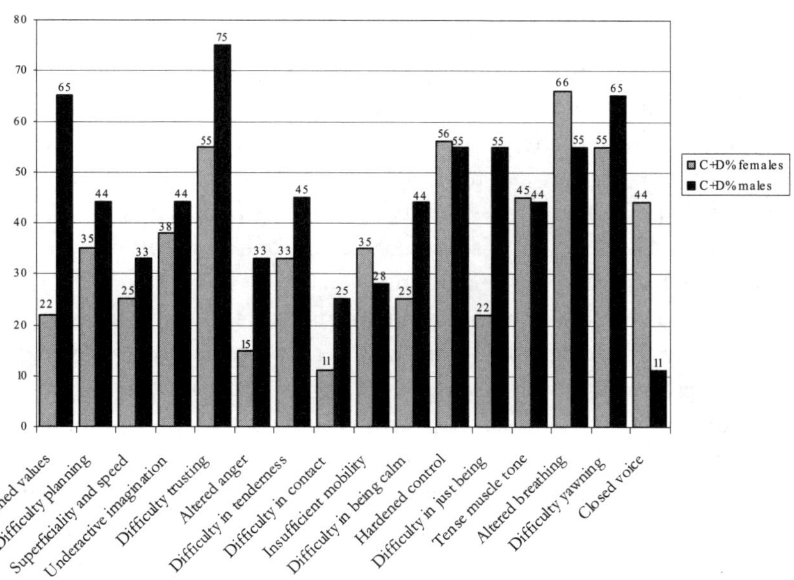

We note that there is a significant imbalance between boys and girls. Alteration is already very clear when it comes to the results for tenderness and the level of flexibility-rigidity. In males, the values and the Functions for tenderness and fragility are considered unacceptable. They are limited and held inside. The boys' inner sensations are also stifled, together with external perceptions. Boys tend more towards greater levels of tension with intense breathing, a loud voice, accentuated activation of the sympathetic nervous system. Their strength is hardened, their movements are generally agitated and their postures less relaxed. All this suffocates and crushes their sensations and the ability to perceive others with subtlety.

Furthermore, boys already show distrust towards adults at this age, which is absent in girls, together with a strong dose of anger and disrespect.

The consequences of Functional alterations in males and females

The consequences of these precocious alterations, these male-female stereotypies, lead to the situations that we have already mentioned, first in children, and then later in adults. We end up with women who have great difficulty expressing strength and aggressiveness and who are forced to live in a situation of chronic submissiveness, incapable of defending themselves or reacting and therefore forced to suffer everything passively.

All women's groups dealing with domestic violence and abuse know that there is a *core problem* that they always meet. Even women who manage to come as far as their help centres and talk about their problems, even those who manage to ask for help, are often unable to stand up to their oppressors or muster their strength. They are often unable to do anything to change their situation at a practical level, such as report the abuse to the police, react, or ask for a separation.

What we are dealing with is women's inability to use *positive aggressiveness.* They are unable to use this because it is reduced, shrunken. Their positive aggressiveness has become suppressed anger. There is little movement, and they are unable to use what little there is, and so it becomes submissiveness, weakness. They suffer passively, not knowing how to defend themselves.

Even dedication towards others can take on the quality of submissiveness. It reveals a basic incapacity to act positively for themselves, the tendency to be passive. There are women who are ill treated first by their fathers, then by their husbands, for their whole lives, completely unable to escape from this mechanism.

These women could get out if only they could just explore new modalities of movement and expression, rediscover their strength, which can be both calm and at times playful, which is effective without falling into destructiveness, ill will or hardening. Women have huge strength, but they use it to cope with their daily tasks, such as looking after their children, the household, and their job. They do not use it (at least, not as much as they could) to defend themselves, to relate positively with the outside world, to assert themselves or create high profile, active positions for themselves in society.

Conversely, the opposite occurs in males. Their strength becomes hardened and tough, losing its component of tenderness and sensitivity, its calm and its playfulness. It is transformed into an exasperated search for power, and overpowering others. This is why it is always the men who assert themselves in powerful circles, whatever the position in hand.

How we can intervene

Again, our proposal for a possible form of intervention is something that really does get down to the roots of the phenomena of violence, well below the surface behaviour patterns of the individuals in hand.

Today, we are able to spot *early* signs of the disorder that is taking root. We can already see what is going wrong in children and adolescents. We can see what is happening at a deeper level on many different Functional levels of the Self, because all the signs and alterations that we have mentioned can be observed, concretely, on each Functional plane, right from the moment when they first develop.

The reconstruction of the Basic Experiences of the Self constitutes a course of profound intervention that is truly preventative. The Basic Experiences of the Self are being revealed increasingly deficient in recent generations, but they are indispensable if they are to conserve their full vitality, to develop a serene and rounded personality, without dangerous distortions. Children must have the capacity to *Just Be*, to *Relax*, to perceive their innermost *Sensations*, to be *Held*, to be *Listened to*, to recover full *Contact* and to keep their *Tenderness* open.

Conclusions

It is very important for us to understand how violence is created and structured within the family nucleus. If we do so, there is a real possibility of avoiding this division, given that aggressiveness is the same in all human beings and it is essentially a positive characteristic; at times playful, often calm and serene, often aimed at reaching concrete goals and results, but never destructive.

Yet aggressiveness gets channelled differently in men and women, losing its positive connotation, becoming either violence or passivity, precisely because of the alterations that are produced in the Functions of the Self, in the movements, in games, in body language, voice and the emotions by continuous subconscious messages and behaviour.

Often, children (especially girls) suffer continuous aggression and violence within the family, without even realising it; through indifference, being put down, being forced to do things, anxiety and agitation, and also at times through irony, which little children are never able to understand and which they anxiously interpret to the letter.

However, adults do not often realise this, and this is why parents must be helped to avoid damaging behaviour. We must set up a widespread support system for parents with two principal aims: to help parents to understand these dynamics serenely and completely and to rediscover the Basic Experiences of the Self and their profound significance as an aspect of life and development that we simply cannot risk losing.

The dynamics of learning and the pedagogical relationship

The complexity of the learning process

Babies experiment with their environment right from birth. To them, their surroundings are never neutral or grey. On the contrary: every object has strong affective connotations and the entire world is coloured by their emotions. The child discovers the world gradually, with wonder, joy, and close attention.

When we say that babies "experiment", we do not just mean that newborns evaluate what they observe, rather that they *move around* in the world, with their whole Self. This movement leads babies to gradually identify what are known as "invariants", i.e. a *series of stable experiences* that constitute a form of learning. These stable experiences are made up of various elements that are profoundly interconnected. The simultaneous presence of these elements creates knowledge.

A child learns to perceive all the characteristics that distinguish an event that is repeated in his life. Let us use the evening bath as an example. The child notices a change in his mother's tone of voice and the way she moves, in addition to the specific movements that she uses to prepare the bath. He notices that night is falling, he hears the water running, and he can smell soap and perfumes.

Moreover, the child also notices his own physical sensations that announce that it is bathtime: a whole day's tiredness, his skin feels the need to feel refreshed, the wetness from his nappies that has not completely dried. He feels the need for water, the weightlessness, the warmth, the wellbeing, the caresses, the cream, and the talcum powder.

The memory of other bathtimes animates him, and together with that memory, he feels a pleasant sense of expectation for the moment to come. A slight excitement comes over the whole organism, from breathing to heart rate, a reddening of the skin.

Lastly, there is the emotion: a joyous and happy mood as the moment of pleasure, games and the exchange of affection with his mother gets nearer. The face expresses these moods; the movements of the arms and legs become excited and every so often they become faster – just like newborns do to express joy.

All of this is a learning process, i.e. an *integrated* experience that the child participates in intensely with his whole self and his whole organism. This takes place at a cognitive level, certainly, but also, and above all, with his emotions, body movements, body language and posture, with internal and external perceptions, with his memory and his imagination; as well as internal physiological systems and apparatus, from breathing to the autonomic nervous system, from muscle tone to the neuro-endocrine circuit.

Now, every time that we put the learning process into action, we will necessarily touch all these functional processes, i.e. attention, understanding, but also showing ourselves, interest, curiosity, making others happy, the need for gratification, the desire to be seen and receive just recognition and so on.

Every time we put the learning process into action, it is grafted onto the experience of much older learning, on top of the mechanisms that we have described for a little baby. The process follows *traces* of these experiences, running along the grooves made by the *outcomes* of these initial learning relationships, which always implies the relationship with adults. These traces are reactivated, relit, and they obviously exert a strong influence over the individual's current learning processes.

Communication from the Functional perspective

Even the most specific processes of teaching and learning are based on numerous *levels of communication* between two people. Messages run along these different channels constantly, from the Transmitter to the Receiver and vice versa.

Fig. 15. *How communication works*

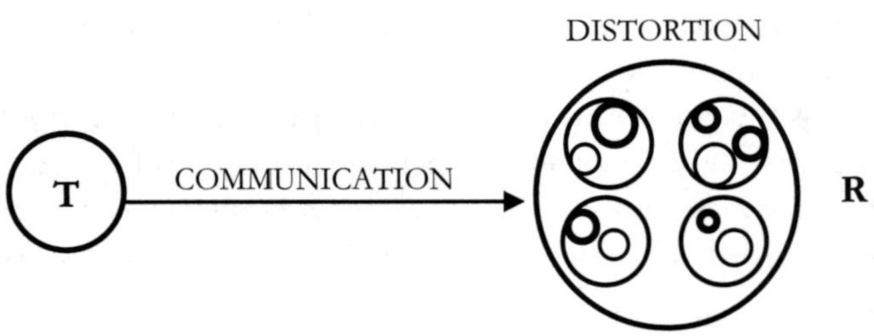

Communication can therefore be seen as a bundle of interconnected pathways uniting the person who is communicating with the person who is receiving, i.e. between the person who is teaching and the person who is learning. If we look at one of the two subjects, we know that below the surface there is a complex and extremely well-articulated world, made up of Functional processes that are not always visible, i.e. what we defined as the *Functional organisation of the Self*; sometimes made even more complex by the presence of alterations, hypotrophisms or sclerosations. In order, then, to understand others fully, we must look beyond appearances, beyond the more superficial part of communication, and try to perceive what is being communicated deep down, on all levels of the Self. This means looking not just at words and their meanings but also tone of voice, facial expressions, movements, postures and body language right down to the signals arriving from the physiological levels such as blushing, muscle tension, shiny skin and so on. Only in this way, can we really "understand" others, and arrive at a perception of which processes may be dysfunctional and which, therefore, prevent open, direct, clear communication. The Functions of the Self, as a whole, whether altered or not, constitute the "receiving system", and we must look at the Functions, keeping any alterations in mind, if we really wish to enter into contact with the other person and aid him in the learning process.

Fig. 16. *The Organisation of the Functions in Leonardo*

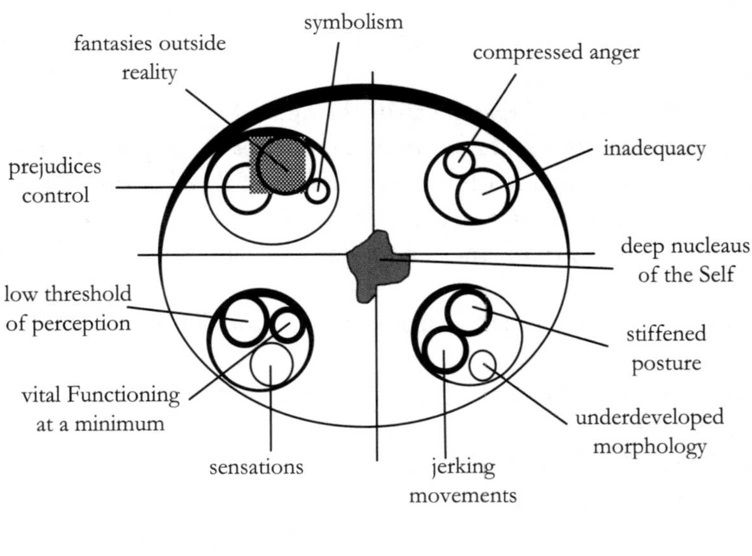

Fig. 16 is a practical case of one of the "receiving systems" represented in fig. 15. To enter into profound communication with Leonardo, we must try to understand what the real *functional processes* are on the different levels of the Self (see diagram), beyond the way he relates at more superficial levels. Only this profound communication will help Leonard profit from a valid and positive learning process.

Leonardo has serious problems at school. Alterations of the Self always lead to learning difficulties. There is no longer the mobility on all the Functional planes that you would find in a small baby or in an individual who has conserved health and wellbeing. The emotive plane, without which learning of any kind is impossible, is full of rigidity and sclerosations. In addition, there are also alterations in his attention, his memory, the ability to listen on the one hand, and his curiosity, interest and desire on the other.

Furthermore, the situation is worsened by the sensation of not being understood, which diminishes his gratification, and with it, the desire to change, to do well at school, to study and to show off what he has learnt and display his knowledge.

The Basic Experiences of the Self

As we have said, all learning during the years of schooling is grafted onto the old Experiences of the Self, and if these have not been positive then learning is necessarily affected.

Many of these Basic Experiences of the Self are, moreover, an integral part of the learning process. It is enough to think of the importance of *being see*, or *being listened to*, or the central role played by *assertiveness* in scholastic success, or yet again, the *pleasure of showing oneself*, the need to *be liked by others*, or to give pleasure to others as a central motivation on the child's relationship with his teacher.

However, there are other Experiences, less obviously related to the scholastic process, that play a hugely important role, such as the ability to *just be*, i.e. allowing ourselves brief pauses in our activation so as not to let the level of interest fall, or even *abandoning ourselves*, which forms the foundations of the child's trust in his teacher.

If these Experiences have not been sufficiently positive during childhood, (i.e. lived fully, without impediments, in an environment which favoured their positive outcome by giving them the exact meaning they were supposed to have and no other), then the teaching-learning process is considerably hindered.

The experience of "trusting" must not be contaminated by other situations that have nothing to do with trust, such as having to follow or obey, being controlled by an adult or being forced to do things. It is unlikely that a child will be able to "just be" if he has always been encouraged to be active or do something to make his parents happy, or because breaks and idleness are seen as useless or to be discouraged. If a child has not been "looked at" with affection, or if he has been looked at without actually being *seen*, then he will find it hard to believe that the teacher will notice him. If this is the case, he may misbehave to get himself noticed, or he will behave badly in the certainty that he will not be noticed, or he will feel that the teacher's observations about him are unjust. This is because he is sure (even if he is mistaken) that the teacher has not seen him properly or has got it wrong – "it's not true that I was talking", "she mistook me for someone else".

If, on the other hand, a child has lived through the Basic Experiences in a generally full and positive way, they constitute a significant store for his future behaviour, a wealth that he can access whenever he needs to, that will allow him to concentrate and be attentive whenever he wants to. They will allow him to feel seen, to make himself heard and understood, and manage to change the teacher's opinion about him when his or her judgment doesn't satisfy him or he doesn't feel that it corresponds to his actual behaviour, he will be able to show himself with pleasure, when necessary.

Children that show themselves off constantly have just as many problems as the ones who never show themselves at all. Children who are always attentive should make us stop to think as much as those who can only concentrate for a few brief moments.

Reading the various planes of the Self

Let us go back to figure 15. It is clear that alterations of the Self create *distortions* in communication.

The first necessity for T (the teacher who is Transmitting) is therefore to perceive R (the pupil, who is Receiving) as correctly as possible, reaching his complex configuration at a profound level. This implies that the teacher has been trained to capture the various Functional levels, the various planes of communication, which most teachers are not trained to read.

However, even in R → T communication, the teacher must obviously try to receive everything that the pupil is sending to them. Once again we must not limit ourselves to the content of the words used but we must look at the emotive planes, movement, postures and body language, as well as the reddening of the skin, sweaty palms, breathing and tone of voice, which are just as important if we are to understand what is really happening within the pupil's Self.

It is equally important that the teacher learn how to read himself, too, on the various Functional levels. He or she must have a certain awareness of the various planes of his own Self. When he is functioning as a "receiver", in fact, he may find that the pupil's personal condition may "resonate" excessively with certain of his own emotions, given movements or a particular tone of voice. On the contrary, he might develop a certain difficulty in "feeling" those aspects that correspond to characteristics that he is not fond of in himself. This can lead to a sort of opacity and insensitivity.

When transmitting, the "contents" of the teacher's words and discourse might express given concepts, but at the same time, he could be transmitting contradictory messages with the "modalities" of his expression (tone of voice, facial expression, eye contact, body movements, body language and postures and breathing) without realising it.

How often does it happen that whilst talking to a class or a group of people, we tend just to look at the listeners who are showing the most interest and attention or who show that they agree with us, transmitting negative sensations to the others, who feel neglected? Non-verbal communication has the strongest impact on the listener, in that it does not work at a conscious level (or at least only marginally) and is therefore very difficult to control (as has been demonstrated in experiments on subliminal messages).

Redundancy

The figure below shows a preliminary didactic and pedagogical indication, as can be deduced from the outline we have drawn.

To try to overcome the pupil's difficulty receiving and diminish the risk of distortion as much as possible, the only thing to do is to introduce a lot of *redundancy* to what we are saying. We cannot say that we are happy with a pupil's results if we then add that these results can improve if he takes more care over presentation. If the child has intense emotive alterations and low self-esteem and trust, then he will inevitably end up thinking that the teacher looks down on his work and the effort he has made. He could even end up coming to the conclusion that there is no point continuing to make the effort.

For a child with problems, it is not enough for a teacher just to express a positive judgment, to be able to perceive positivity. The message must be extremely redundant for it to break through the child's stereotypies, both in terms of quantity (repeated many times), but above all, it must be redundant in the sense that the message is repeated on many levels of the Self.

Fig. 17. *Redundancy in Communication*

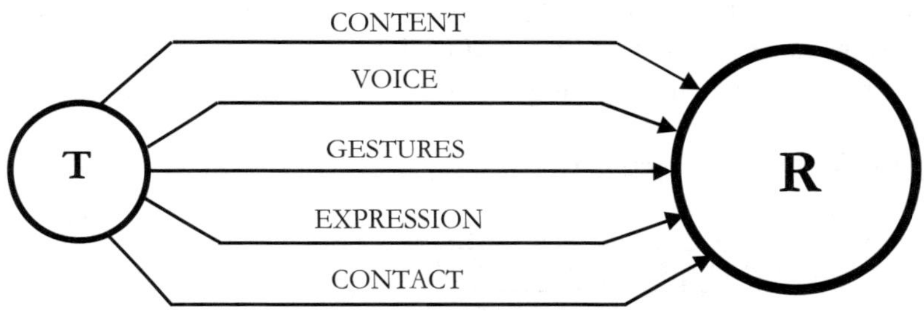

The message must arrive not only through the contents of the teacher's words, but also with his tone of voice, looks, gestures, facial expressions, his whole body, and even with physical contact. Leaning a hand on a student's shoulder with deep and sincere emotional contact can say a lot more than a cold, sterile word.

Only redundancy can offer us the hope pf penetrating beyond the hardest and most defensive parts of the Self.

Mobilising the polarities and the Basic Experiences

Another indication aimed at improving the teaching-learning process is that of the *polarities*, i.e. the polarities of the various Functional planes and Basic Experiences of the Self. This is the most recent discovery in applied research, and it has perhaps the widest range of possible methodological implications.

If we take the polarity *exploring on our own ↔ being guided we* soon realise that a good method of teaching should allow the pupil to range between one pole and another. If children are merely guided, they might feel guidance to be as a form of intrusion, regulation, or oppression; however, having to discover everything on our own is extremely painful and discouraging. However, staying exactly half way between the two positions is completely useless.

Real *mobility* is when a child can pass calmly from the moments in which he seeks guidance to the ones in which he tries out his capacities on his own, returning to seek guidance only when necessary or when he really needs it. Life's flow is a process of constant modulation between two poles: a sine wave, which passes by first one pole and then the other.

We can cite numerous examples like the one above, because there are numerous ranges and polarities involved in teaching-learning. Figure 18 shows the ones that are most important for the didactic process.

Fig. 18. *Polarities in teaching-learning*

POLARITIES. FALSE OPPOSITES

Relaxation	⟷	Concentration
Attention for ourselves	⟷	Attention towards others
Weakness	⟷	Strength
Tenderness	⟷	Rigidity
Exploring on our own	⟷	Receiving Guidance
Being Assessed	⟷	Assessing Others
Logical Thought	⟷	Creative Thought
Unconditional praise	⟷	Criticism
Empathy	⟷	Differentiation
Teacher's Decision	⟷	Class Decision
Small Movements	⟷	Expansive Movements
Attention to detail	⟷	Attention to the big picture
Influencing flow	⟷	Influencing Process

As we can see, the polarities touch on numerous crucial points in teaching. These points have often been at the centre of clashes between scholars in pedagogy and those who work in the field as teachers. As we have said, truth and virtue do not lie in a "happy medium" between the two poles, because the more able a child is to go towards one of the polarities, the easier he will find it to have full access to the other.

Fig. 19. *Teaching tools linked to the polarities*

OPERATIVE TOOLS

- 1. Welcome, praise, containment. Empathy. Affection for the "little one"
- 2. Moments of Relaxation

3. Psycho-physiological questionnaires
4. Creation of questionnaires
5. Evaluation of the various Functional levels →
   - *Movement*
   - *Tone of voice*
   - *Posture*
   - *Skin*
   - *Autonomic Nervous System*

6. Expansive movements
7. Seeing the overall picture
8. Complete project

9. Finding different strategies when faced with difficulties in learning
10. Moments of creativity
11. Realistic, gratifying steps

12. Letting pupils make decisions
13. Letting pupils make assessments

- 14. Modularity →
  - *Letting them decide for themselves ↔ guiding*
  - *Praise ↔ criticism*
  - *Tenderness ↔ toughness*
  - *Affection ↔ tasks*
- 15. Bringing out details about their personal lives

The more children are able to experience pleasant and effective moments of relaxation, the more they are able to concentrate when the need arises. If they are always concentrated, their concentration reveals itself false and ineffectual. If they are always relaxed, in reality they are not calmly relaxed but rather immobile and impotent. The poles are, in other words, "false opposites".

We can carry out a similar reasoning for all the polarities represented in the diagram.

Some dimensions refer solely to students, others solely to the teacher, and others to both of them.

Now, if we set ourselves the task of *opening up the polarities* and helping students to regain complete use of the whole range of each of them, it is easy to find just as many fertile techniques which could be applied at a scholastic level. There is just a short step between this and the development of real teaching tools to be used at an operative level. In figure 19, we briefly list a series of suggested techniques for the teaching-learning process.

Conclusions

School is an important "second chance" in young people's lives to heal the wounds and lacerations of childhood.

On the other hand, if we look at the general outline of all the levels that make up the Self, we fully realise that the "cognitive" part is only really a *small part* of our complex personality. School must not, therefore, work only at this one Functional level. The cognitive level, no matter how much society and traditional scholastic methods place emphasis on it, cannot reach the deep nuclei of the individual on its own and create real knowledge.

It is therefore of fundamental importance for us to take up the entire scope of the Basic Experiences of the Self in our battle against scholastic failure, marginalization and truancy. It is something else as well, i.e. the positive and concrete prospect of a project for the prevention of disorders and difficulty in children and adolescents in general. This means that we really can offer a new chance to children and adolescents who have lived the oldest experiences of the learning relationship in a problematic way, and who therefore carry traces of this difficulty within them, with the risk that this could lead to further difficulties.

Opening up the school environment to these prospects also represents a good opportunity for us to redirect learning and studies back to their natural course, i.e. to the level of playful attention (none the less serious for that) that the child puts into action when he studies the world around him.

We must fully recover what is profound and natural in all of us: the need for knowledge, the pleasure of learning, the taste of curiosity towards new things, and the desire for new intellectual horizons.

Prevention scheme: The Child and Adolescent Wellbeing Project[3]

The Child and Adolescent Wellbeing Project started in 1998-99 financed using funds provided by Naples council bylaw 285/97 for child welfare, and it is still underway. Over the years, the project has expanded to include several schools and year groups, and even now, it involves a huge number of teachers, parents, and children. The quantity of data that has been accumulated is now both impressive and of great value, since it regards the real conditions of children in various neighbourhoods and differing social conditions in Naples. It also examines the efficacy of the prevention work being carried out. The project is still the most significant attempt that has been carried out successfully, aimed at the real prevention of disorders and problems in our children.

Figure 20 illustrates the essential characteristics of the project.

Fig. 20. *The Child and Adolescent Wellbeing Project*

CHILD AND ADOLESCENT PREVENTION-WELLBEING Project within a wider network

SURVEY Observation of the children. Surveying the children's real conditions on all the levels of the Self. Specific, standardised, 16 point assessment protocols. Revealing deficient modalities and capacities, but also strong points to be encouraged.

3 Originally called the Progetto Benessere Infanzia e Adolescenza.

WORKING WITH ADULTS
Working with parents in a seminar-experiential type workshop (based on understanding, but also on feeling and living), centred around the Basic Experiences, those necessary to live life fully.

The same type of workshops with teachers; enriched with training and refresher courses aimed at acquiring and exploring the multidimensional methods necessary for assessment and rebalancing.

Workshops with figures involved in extra-curricular activities.

REBALANCING ACTIVITIES AND WORKSHOPS
Planning of teaching units and workshop activities aimed with precision at the recovery and rebalancing of the children's Self. Pedagogical tools which take us in the direction of development of a full and complete personality.

The importance of child development

We now know which are the difficulties that impede child and adolescent development and the construction of the identity with certainty.

It has been scientifically proven that children must find protection, warmth, serenity and, above all, the satisfaction of their basic needs for them to be able to conserve vitality and wellbeing as adults, otherwise dangerous alterations are formed in the deep nucleus of the Self, such as the loss of contact with vital capacities in life, disorders or unhappiness.

If the nucleus of the Self is made fragile and insecure, it grasps on to external images of strength and security, and tries to compensate its profound deficiencies by chasing after false certainties, i.e. power over other people, domination over others, easy success, violence, money at any cost. The other alternative is to give in to anxiety and fear and end up feeling weak, overcome, crushed; therefore allowing himself to be so.

The necessity of intervening

It is absolutely crucial that we find innovative and wide-reaching answers to the difficult conditions that new generations are facing. The episodes reported in the media every day (rape, suicides, child killers, drugs) are just the visible part of a widespread condition on unease and unhappiness.

We must intervene right from the age at which this unhappiness takes root and at which people's personalities lose their initial positive characteristics, losing track of the meaning of their existence, solidarity, and respect for others, for nature and for themselves.

Figure 21 shows the fundamental points that underline the indispensable nature of prevention projects.

Fig. 21. *The necessity of Prevention Projects*

THE NECESSITY OF PREVENTION PROJECTS

- *Truancy and school leaving*
- *Increasing violence* — *Bullying*
- *Victims of violence* — *Paedophilia*
- *Educational failure and difficulties in life*
- *Diminution in certain Basic Capacities, in certain Polarities*

PREVENTION

Takes on the multidimensional and complete nature of

WELL-BEING

What follows is the proposal for the prevention project, as it was presented to and approved by the Naples Town Council.

The Change in Social Conditions

Constructing an identity is undeniably difficult in today's society. We are "losing" some of the aspects of human functioning that are indispensable for a correct equilibrium (i.e. serenity, unhurriedness, relaxation, listening to our inner sensations, knowing how to just be, and contact).

Emotional support for children is becoming increasingly deficient due to the reduced size of the family unit (sometimes just one parent and one child) and their increasing isolation from the social context, which is seen as dangerous. What is missing is a support network comprising a variety of adult figures (which children used to be surrounded by when families were larger).

However, other aspects of society are also significantly changing.

More and more space in our lives is taken up with videogames, the television, computers, virtual reality, high speed, competitiveness, and technology. These are not always negative elements in themselves, but they do undoubtedly cause imbalances in the structure of the Self in children, causing an increase in punctiform attention, tiny movements, high speed, the amount of fantasies, attention to detail, the level of excitement and frantic activity.

Moreover, children are bombarded with improbable and unobtainable "models" by the mass-media, and models of easy success, all of which make young people feel increasingly inadequate. They are no longer allowed to grow up gradually, calmly building on their own experiences, creating their own space and their own identity over time.

The continuous exposure to scenes of violence, put across as if they were something habitual (or even as if they were positive) does not help children to create a healthy idea of reality. On the contrary: this phenomenon, together with a general absence of ideals, contributes to the closure of children's personalities, shutting out tenderness, calm, the importance of being able to show fragility and the ability to listen to their real physical sensations.

Recovering mobility between male and female roles

We must also take action to preserve the positive characteristics of masculinity and femininity before they are lost due to the increased rigidity and stereotypes linked to their respective roles. In other words, we must prevent aggressiveness, competitiveness, toughness, and domination from taking on essentially negative connotations within the male role stereotype, without the opposite characteristics of tenderness and softness to counteract them. At the same time, in women, tenderness, sensitivity, and fragility tend to lose their positive qualities when deprived of expansive strength. They instead tend to be transformed into an incapacity to assert themselves, an increased dependence, shutting themselves up in private life and what they are familiar with, resignation.

A project within a wider social network

This project must be widened at much as possible to other areas of society. It must involve the scientific community, government, the institutions, civil society, and public opinion.

An integrated project

This project must be *integrated*, in that it must examine human beings in all their complexity, all their Functions (such as the emotive, cognitive, imaginative, postural, motor and physiological Functions), the equilibrium among all these aspects, their harmonious development, a vision of all the planes that make up not just individuals but also groups and societies.

Assessing children's real conditions: observation

Our observation methods make it possible, for the first time, to decipher the *real conditions* of children and adolescents in today's society. We can see the trends and changes that are currently underway and predict the possible future profiles of up-and-coming generations.

The *mobility* of the various Functional planes of the Self is taken into consideration. We use innovative, multidimensional *functional assessment protocols* to see whether the individual is lacking any of the functional processes or aspects of the personality, which are necessary for health and wellbeing, and also to see which of them are present and active.

Our observation provides us with a *primary evaluation* of the children and adolescents' conditions, as well as a *secondary evaluation* after we have worked with the children and adults (both teachers and parents), in order to determine the effectiveness of the prevention work carried out.

Re-establishing equilibrium as a form of prevention

Using the results of our observation of children and adolescents' real conditions, we can plan teaching units, finely-honed activities and specific workshops that work towards rebalancing the altered conditions of the Self and recovering the Basic Experiences that our assessment has revealed to be lacking or deficient. In this way, we can stop the unscientific and damaging practise of proposing activities for children and adolescents without knowing what effect they may have on them, instead of honing our action towards their real wellbeing.

Working with adults

The first stage of prevention is that of working with the adults who play a part in the children and adolescents' development, i.e. parents and all those who work with children. Our intervention must take the form of an actual sequence that these individuals must experience (rather than just furnishing them with cognitive concepts), aimed at the basic problems in child and adolescent development.

Working with teachers

We try to work as far as possible with teachers who teach children of the same age groups as the children and adolescents in our sample group, if not with the actual teachers of the group in question.

Our intervention takes the form of weekly group sessions conducted by a psychotherapist who is an expert in these themes and who has been trained specifically for this role. The workshop includes both practical experiences and theory.

The *points dealt with* will be the ones that have emerged from our observation, with particular reference to:

- children and adolescents' basic needs;
- the Basic Experiences of the Self as the basis for a healthy and harmonious development;
- any anomalous increases in violence, aggressiveness, negative fantasies, high speed, intolerance and distrust in the younger generations;

- any anomalous decrease in tender emotions, contact, positive relationships with their own bodies, calm and serenity, ideals and goals;
- the stereotyping of male and female gender roles.

Support for parents

Our parental support is characterised by group workshops that are based on both theory as well as practical experiences. Each session is comprised of two parts, a seminar and a workshop, with similar characteristics to those used with the teachers, but specifically aimed at the particular nature of the parent-child relationship, whereas the teachers' sessions are aimed at the specific nuances of their professional role and the learning-teaching process.

Paedophilia

Some of the themes relating to the basic needs and the Basic Experience of *deep contact* will be used as the real basis for an effective prevention of child abuse and paedophilia.

Overcoming male/female stereotypes, boosting women's role in society and equal opportunities

A specific aim of the project, which runs through all the points described above, is to carry out work on the female world. We aim to work on their symbolic worlds, their specific values, freeing up the body, and reopening movement in girls. We also aim to aid the re-evaluation of the history of our society, examining the important contribution that women have always made to it, and examining and promoting positive female role models, both contemporary and historical.

Rebalancing workshops

Particular attention is paid to the possibility of carrying out workshop activities with the pupils themselves. However, they must not merely be activities for the sake of it. These activities must possess a real *capacity to rebalance* any conditions of harmonious overall development that have been less than satisfactory, and the *capacity to recover* the processes that are crucial to success in life.

The most important thing when planning workshop activities or teaching units is not so much planning what type of activity to offer, but rather the *way* in which the activities are carried out, and the *direction* that they move in, i.e. what areas of the overall functioning of the Self and which polarities we need to recover.

The final evaluation

The final evaluation is carried out according to the following criteria:
- the interaction between the participants;
- the results obtained using the assessment protocols;
- how specific and how practical were the workshops and teaching units to the indications given following the primary assessment?
- interviews and conversations with the teachers;
- a specifically prepared assessment protocol.

The Functional Profiles of several children, together with the rebalancing workshops carried out in each case

A girl in her 4th year of primary school[4]

Emotive Plane

A very early, very strong fear has been buried and held at bay over the years. Even today, she still seeks reassurance although she tries to let it

4 Translator's note: Primary education in Italy starts at the age of six, not five, as it does in England and America.

show as little as possible. She has never fully experienced the feeling of *being held and calmed.*

Despite everything she has been through, her tenderness is still open and her softer feelings are still open.

She really wants to be with the others but at times she is clumsy and childish. This is in part due to her underlying insecurity. She has a reasonable capacity for experiencing contact.

Cognitive Plane

She has managed to make use of her intelligence and her capacity for understanding to pluck up courage, although she is still missing a little speed and concentration. She studies quite well, she is curious about new things and she even looks at books to find things out on her own. Her imagination and creativity are fairly well developed, but they are not concrete enough.

Motor-postural Plane

She is a little clumsy when it comes to making small movements, and she is still slightly uncoordinated when it comes to filling up the space around her. Her physical appearance denotes a lack of harmony and the lack of calm, deep strength. She finds it quite difficult to let herself go, let herself be led, or to accept help.

Physiological Plane

She has a considerable level of anxiety but this has not yet led to somatisations. Her breathing is not open or calm. The emotions that are not very open (especially her fear and pain) could lead to future alterations in the physiological systems that regulate the organism.

Capacities to be encouraged (Strong Points)

Tenderness, soft feelings, the desire to be with others and help them.

Capacities that require further development

She wants to let herself be led, but she is not completely able to do so.

Capacities that need to be recovered

Contact with her emotions, especially pain and fear. She must be completely reassured, as well as held and completely calmed and soothed in order for her to be able to reach real calm.

She must recover her strength and her flexible movements. This will also enable her to recover her coordination.

Strategies and workshops

Trust her with the leadership of a little work group so that she can assert her will over the others and help them. Encourage and amplify her tenderness and gentleness with a research project on the importance of being tender instead of being tough (violence among kids in the rougher areas of Naples, etc.).

Keep her very close to the teacher, as if she were a part of her, for a while, making her feel that the teacher is keeping her close not to keep an eye on her, but because she is fond of her, regardless of how well she does scholastically.

- Workshop on letting go and being held. Workshop on gentle movements.
- Workshop where she has to tell the group about one sad thing, and one fear.

A boy in the 2nd year of primary school

Emotive Plane

The only way this boy has been able to counteract the terrible, difficult conditions of his life has been to construct an underlying toughness. His insecurity is badly hidden behind an attitude of provocation. Despite his efforts to be tough, his face and body betray a profound unhappiness.

Cognitive Plane

His capacity to understand things suffers because of his emotive world and his extreme state of agitation. He studies badly, without a method. He remembers things by set phrases and words. His ideas have no originality or creativity. He is unable to ask or plan. He doesn't read. However, he still manages to socialise fairly well, but when he tries to communicate he is confused and distracted. His conversation is unfocussed and is disconnected from his body language. He has had to become tough and acquire strength, but he still managed nonetheless to conserve a few elements of tenderness.

Motor-Postural Plane

He is agitated, with jerking movements and restless eyes, with no capacity for deep contact. His bowed head and hunched shoulders betray his sadness, his sense of defeat and dejection.

Physiological Plane

His strangled and exaggerated voice and his permanently shallow breathing show that he is trying to show strength, but that this is not really real, it doesn't come from deep down. The tension in his muscles is evident from his stiff movements. He's anxious, nervous. He is unable to relax and 'stop' himself. He avoids direct eye contact. His emotive and physiological conditions have led him to somatise quite a lot.

Capacities to be encouraged (strong points)

His ability to resist hardship and keep going in spite of everything. His ability to look for friends.

Capacities in need of further development

His social life must be developed, but this must be based on clear, shared rules. We must take up his remaining tenderness and re-open it fully before it is too late.

Capacities that need recovering

We must recover his calm, the ability to let go and completely relax. We must reconstruct the capacity to establish intense, as opposed to fleeting, contact with people. We must reconstruct his capacity to concentrate calmly over long periods of time, and develop his visual memory. He must recover happiness and joyousness. He must recover soft, gentle movements.

Strategies and workshops

We must maximise his capacity to be with others, putting him in charge of planning and running collective games. He must be the referee, the one who makes sure that the rules are followed.

Group work. Everyone stands in a circle, and each person is asked to talk about him or herself, and the things that have hurt them.

- A workshop where each child reads aloud a story that he has written;
- Workshop on letting themselves go, and Just Being;
- Workshop on Tenderness (the cat game, etc.) and on gentle movements;
- Workshop on joyful movements and playing;
- Plan a board game in a group, step by step;
- Plan and carry out a drawing in a group. Playing at drawing.

A girl from the 2nd year of primary school

Emotive Plane

The emotions are very positive: happiness, strength, and trust are present, although there is a slight overtone of anger. A good balance between tenderness and strength.

Cognitive Plane

She has a quick, sparkling intelligence and an organised and systematic method of study. Her memory is above all visual. She is coordinated, she is able to plan and she is adequately practical. She gets enthusiastic and interested about new things. She reads enough.

Motor-Postural Plane

Her body expresses positive emotions: happiness and curiosity, open postures, tenderness and gentleness in her movements. A slight closed-in sadness has started to appear which must be released as soon as possible. She also has a good ability to socialise.

Physiological Plane

She has a good capacity to relax. She is capable of Just Being. She has a slight hyper-emotivity in her blushing. She has good contact with others and her calm facial expression and eye contact confirm this. Her voice is open and it gives a sense of authority. There are no negative situations stratified which could lead to somatisations.

Capacities to be encouraged (strong points)

Intelligence, equilibrium, confidence, contact, happiness.

Capacities in need of further development

A greater capacity to be in situations involving confrontation. Tranquillity about negative emotions and other people's judgement. Capacity to let go even more.

Capacities to be recovered

Capacity to overcome sadness without forcing herself too much. Less need to show off all her abilities.

Strategies and workshops

Give her the opportunity to evaluate her teachers to help her lose her worries about being judged.

Get her to compare projects prepared by her schoolmates on a teaching unit to be invented.

- Workshop on losing control very much, on losing concentration and intelligence at times.
- Drama project on emotions that are not totally positive.
- Strength that is even more calm.

A child from the 5th year of primary school

Umberto's teachers describe him as not serene. They report that his movements are agitated, especially his head and eyes. His declarations are repetitive; he shows uncertainty, distrust and fears. He often places himself near the teacher's desk. He is characterised by a certain victim complex and has darting, restless eyes. He has a shrill voice.

The teachers' observations have been integrated with an *assessment protocol of the Self*, compiled by the teachers and verified on site in afternoon encounters with the project's operators. Following the evaluation, a *Dynamic Profile* of the student was laid out.

- The prevalent emotions are sadness, insecurity, fear, which upholds the victim complex identified by the teachers;
- His movements are accelerated. He is restless both verbally and in terms of movements. He is unable to "let go";
- He presents few somatisations;
- He shows very inconsistent capacity for contact. Yet when he does manage to enter into contact he remains "very contained" and he manages to "keep still", unlike the accelerated movements described above;
- The capacity to socialise, in the sense of a capacity for openness and communication, is almost nil;
- Reading: he reads little, mostly comics;
- Comprehension is severely impeded by his habits of talking mindlessly and beating about the bush that take the listener away from the focus of his discourse;
- His study method is disordered, basically dictated by a "personal inner categorization";
- His memory would need to be developed and yet observers were struck by his surprising mnemonic capacity during a play organised by the school;
- His fantasies are very repetitive and stereotyped;
- Values: he tends to attribute the most value to strength and toughness, but this is counterbalanced to a certain extent by his tenderness.

Capacities to be developed

The capacity for Contact that the pupil managed to express, even though it was in an alternating fashion, must, without doubt, be encouraged and developed, by getting him to experience a profound sense of Containment. The experience must allow him to recover relaxed, non invasive contact, without generating fear ("immobilism") and/or fleeing ("restless" movement, incapacity to "let go"), instead allowing him to act in a way that is more confident and creative, and at the same time less repetitive and stereotyped.

Strong Points

In order to develop Umberto's strong points, we must emphasise the "surprising" mnemonic capacities during experiences, which he has found particularly interesting and involving. We must also emphasise his desire for tenderness and his relative capacity for Contact with adults and with his peers. It has been suggested that drama activities should also induce him to follow movements and speeds that are different from the stereotyped ones he puts into action automatically.

Capacities that need to be recovered

In order to recover mobility and modularity with respect to movements and contact, as well as to develop the pupil's strong points, we have also suggested workshops for the children on "movement" and "contact", which we conducted together with the teachers.

A description of several rebalancing workshops

Below, we will report a few suggestions for workshops to carry out with the children, some with a full description of the whole sequence.

Workshops on:

- Intense, expansive movements-Letting Go;
- Relaxation-Concentration;
- Being Guided-Exploring on their Own;
- Facing each other, Open Strength;
- Affectionate, playful Strength;
- Tenderness;
- Automatic movements, movements that are not controlled;

- Voice;
- Breathing.

A few techniques

The Blind Man

In pairs. One person is the blind man and the other person has to guide him. The blind man explores his guide to get to know him better, to hone his tactile sensations and to be better aware of the other person. Then the guide takes the blind man to explore the space around him. He is the blind man's eyes; he takes him to explore the most important things in the room and the objects that are different to the touch. The guide introduces the blind man to a whole series of sensations that he had never felt before. He also helps him to discover contact with other people and to perceive them through touch. Then the guide makes the blind man go a bit faster, walking, turning, losing his sense of direction, so that the blind man has to trust his guide completely. The pair step in time with each other and they walk in the same way. The walking gets faster, at times the pair even run. For a while, the pair has to escape, run fast, move away from where they are, seek shelter, a refuge where they can finally stay, protected, and rest after their run. The blind man is held tightly by the guide, who protects him, hugs him and reassures him. Slowly their fear ebbs away and the tension leaves them. After a while, they can face the world again, and go to take a walk again together. They start walking again. They start exploring again. They meet other people, other blind men. They enter into contact with them, tenderly and sweetly. Now the guide can allow the blind man more freedom of movement, and the blind man knows that his guide is always there. The blind people can even start playing among themselves, trying out more open movements, moving further, even without being in contact with their guides, who follow them without touching them. The blind man can start moving freely because as long as their movements are gentle they cannot hurt themselves or crash into each other violently. Feel the joy of being free, with movements, turning, jumping, sometimes spurting forwards, with no more fear. When the blind men are tired, they can return to close contact with their guides and enjoy the affection and closeness once again.

Open voice

Bring the voice all the way up from the diaphragm; first softly, then increasingly strongly, without strangling it or tightening the throat, even when it is very loud. The breathing must also come from the diaphragm.

Head voice, throat voice

Become aware of the differences between the diaphragmatic voice, the throat voice and the head voice in order to better open up the diaphragmatic one. This can be done better by asking the participants to imagine that they are moaning gorillas (a low voice and suitable movements); cheeky baboons (throat voice and faster movements); and lastly that they are budgerigars (high, head voice, lightness). Then we return to a soft voice from the diaphragm.

Baby animals

Everyone is lying face down. They are asked to get up again slowly onto their knees and hands, without raising their level of vigilance, without losing the relaxed sensations from the previous activity. The head still hangs low. "Imagine that you're baby animals: puppies, kittens or fauns. Imagine that you are discovering the world around you with joy and pleasure. You can meet other baby animals and start getting to know them. You can start to play together. Test your strength a little bit, with some play fighting. Then you stop for a minute to rest. And you take a walk around. After all this moving around, the baby animals are really hungry! They go and look for food (some object that represents this, a bean bag, a cushion, etc.). But some people are taking other people's food as well as their own. You have to fight to take the food from them, and defend what's yours. You have to threaten them and sum up your determination. The baby animals have to eat at all costs. They compete for it. In the end, everyone takes their food to a corner to eat it in peace, at last! Night is coming. You take a last little walk. You stop somewhere to sleep. But the night is dark, it's scary. You can hear wolves howling and the cries of strange animals. The baby animals are small and defenceless. They are alone; there are no other baby animals in sight. Go and look for shelter, where there are other baby animals. The howling of the wolves and the cries of the other ferocious animals are getting louder and nearer. It's dangerous out there. You have to run to where the other baby animals are, everybody under shelter, everybody squeezed together. We can feel how safe it is here. We can feel how calm the group is. We curl ourselves up, within the group among the others. We can finally sleep calmly. The night is over, the light returns, a new day has dawned. The baby animals start to wake up, stretch, move around and then venture out again. It's a new day. The baby animals feel safe, full of energy and wanting to get on with things. They make happy, lively movements, they have a little run, they speed up and slow down suddenly. And finally they start playing together again.

Assessment protocols for children and adolescents

The child and adolescent assessment protocol that I have developed is made up of 16 points, each of which represent the various levels of the Self and several important Basic Experiences. The score in these points are give on the basis of both the replies given by the children and adolescents to a series of questions, and of direct observation trained staff, who guide the children and adolescents through a series of activities which are presented as a sort of game. For each of the 16 points there are 4 possible Functional levels (which are standardised, because they are described in great detail), from A, the highest level with the most mobility, down to D which is the worst level, with the most rigidity.

The protocols have been adapted to suit different age groups: 4–7 years, 7–11, 11–14 and 14–18.

1. VALUES
From a good balance between "tender" and "rigid" values (A) → to a prevalence of "rigid" values (D).
2. PLANS
From a capacity to imagine and plan in detail, at a practical level (A) → to a, incapacity to plan, with vague, stereotyped projects (D).
3. SPEED, SUPERFICIALITY
From an interest in a variety of television programs with diversified characteristics (A) → to superficiality, stereotypies, shows that are violent, fast and frenetic (D).
4. IMAGINATION
From a good imagination, able to follow suggestions and reproduce appropriate details (A) → to difficulty in reproducing the images requested, stereotypies, and/or fears (D).
5. TRUST
From the capacity to turn to adults, trust (A) → to closure and distrust (D).
6. ANGER
From an open anger, expressed directly, without, however, the presence of fury (A) → to a suffocated, rancorous anger (D).
7. TENDERNESS
From the capacity to feel and express tenderness with tender movements (A) → to a difficulty in expressing tenderness, with toughness, aggressiveness (D).
8. CONTACT
From an ability to be "in Contact" with others, with adults (A) → to avoiding contact, uneasiness or restlessness when with other people (D).
9. GENTLENESS
From the capacity for gentle, slow movements (A) → to jerking, rigid movements (D).
10. CALMNESS
The ability to do things calmly and unhurriedly, applying oneself with serenity (A) → to agitation, confusion, restlessness or isolation (D).
11. CONTROL
From an ability to loosen control, let go, lose coordination (A) → to rigid, forced, exaggerated control (D).
12. JUST BEING

The capacity to stop, just be still, abandon himself, tired and tranquil (A) → to the inability to take a break, relax or abandon himself (D).
13. MUSCLE TONE
From an inability to loosen the muscles, allow himself to be moved by the other person, relaxed/flexible muscle tone (A) → to an inability to abandon himself, tense muscle tone (D).
14. BREATHING
From diaphragmatic breathing, from the belly, characteristic of calm and wellbeing (A) → to shallow, thoracic, closed and suppressed breathing (D).
15. YAWNS
From the ability to yawn, release tension, let go of rigid control (A) → to few or no yawns, keeping control forcedly, exaggerated alertness (D).
16. VOICE
From a full, sonorous open voice (A) → to a closed, weak, strangled voice (D).

Analysis of the overall results obtained from the Evaluation questionnaires on the Functions of the Self

Introduction

In graphs 1–6, we have summarized data obtained over 3 years of practise in the Child and Adolescent Wellbeing Project. However, we have only included the data relative to primary school children, because the results obtained were more numerous and complete.

Graph 1 shows the total number of *alterations, as a percentage* (the total percentage of C and D values) as revealed by the protocols *on entry into the scheme* (i.e. before the start of the activities proposed by the Project) subdivided into *males* and *females*. Graph no. 2 gives us the total percentage of alterations following the project's activities (*exit* protocols), again divided according to *gender*. The subsequent graphs show the same results subdivided by age group.

Graphs

Graph 1. *Total results obtained using the Assessment Protocol before project*

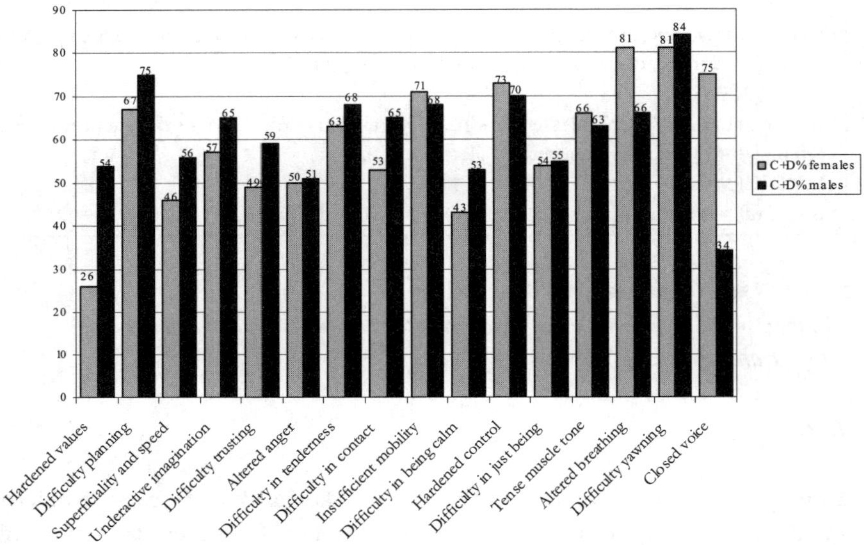

Graph 2. *Total results at end of project*

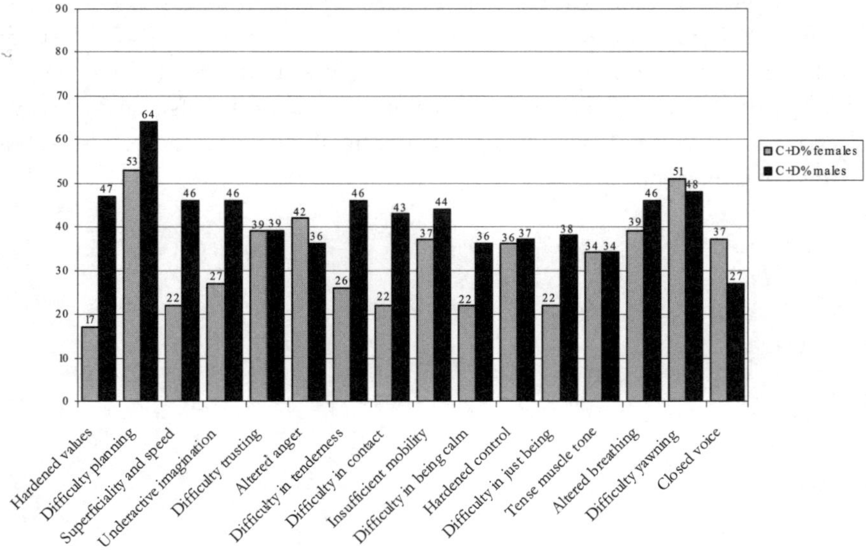

Graph 3. *Total results at beginning of project, age 5–8 years*

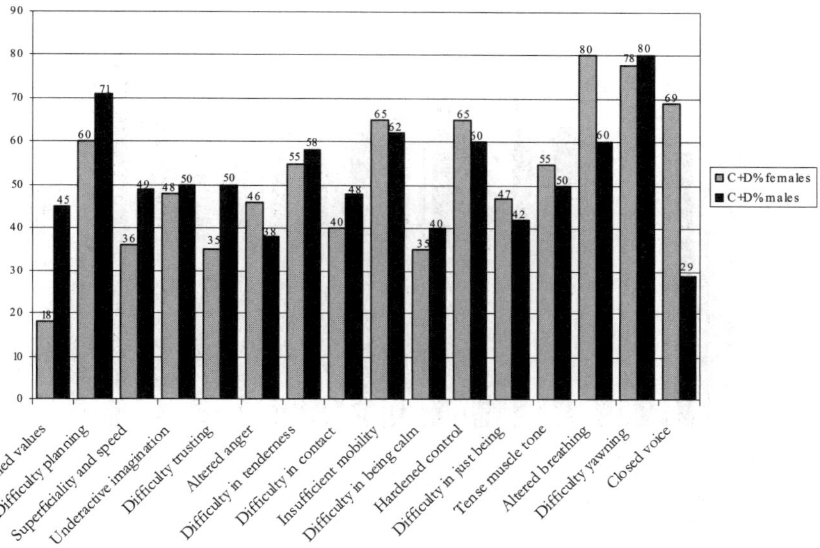

Graph 4. *Total results at end of project, age 5–8 years*

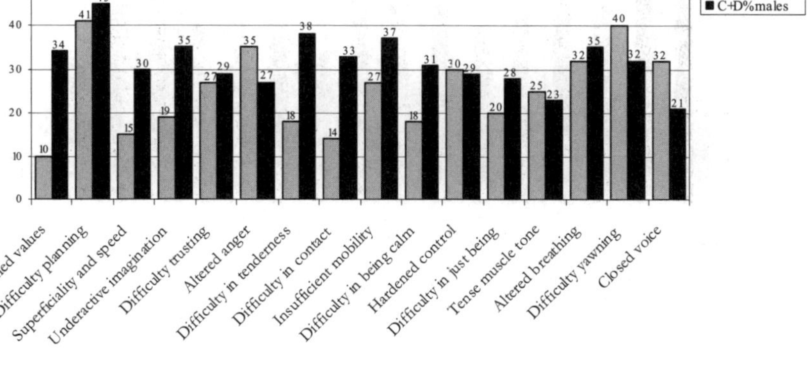

Graph 5. *Total results obtained using Assessment Protocol before project, age 9–11 years*

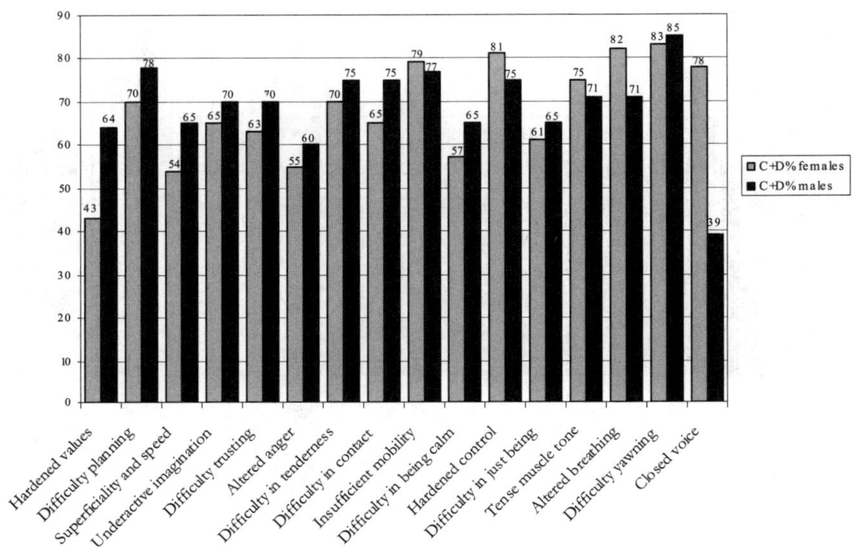

Graph 6. *Total results at end of project, age 9–11 years*

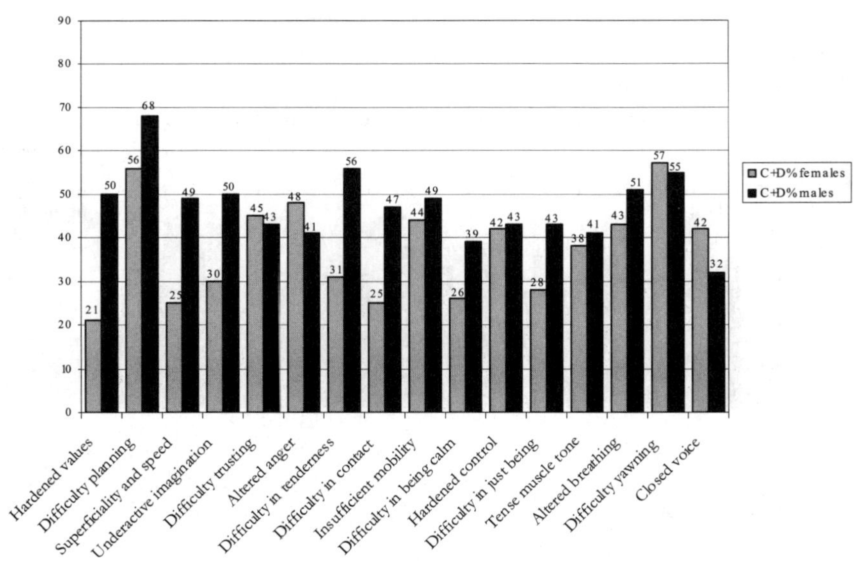

Conclusions

- There is a clear worsening in all the variables as we pass from the younger to the older age groups;
- We note that there is already an early hardening of the *values* that the children consider to be the most important. Few children gave a positive value to crying, and there was a lot of uncertainty with respect to values such as culture and knowledge. In any case, *hardened* values are more present in boys than in girls;
- The ability to *make plans* at a practical level (especially when detail is required) in order to proceed step by step to the desired goal is considerably compromised, especially in boys. The desires they expressed were almost always stereotyped, dulled down to values of easy success from the television. The girls were more able to make plans, but at times they got lost in desires that are too dreamy and vague;
- The *guided visualisation sequence* captured the interest of almost all of the children. Apart from the huge difficulty they experienced at first in "just being", and lying calmly on the mats with their eyes closed, the images that were created were rich and vivid when the sequences were well guided. However, the ability to imagine was more limited in the boys;
- There was a strong difference between boys and girls when it came to what *television programmes* they were interested in: apart from stereotypes like football matches and soap operas, the girls tended towards programmes with deeper values, and were interested in a greater variety of elements. In any case, smaller children still had more varied and multiform interests, because they had not yet been caught up by high speed, superficiality and violence;
- The *trust* element was very worrying, and it showed a clear division between girls and boys. In boys, distrust was already spreading, whereas girls still showed a certain ability to trust adults. The ability to ask for help seems however to exist when it comes to parents, but it becomes hidden from other adults, especially if they are family;
- *Anger* is fairly open in the smaller children. It is not even limited or suppressed in the girls. Later, it becomes more restrained and bitter, exploding in emotive outbursts. In girls, the *voice* denotes a further difficulty in openly expressing *Strength*, becoming closed and suffocated very early on, whilst it is still open and sonorous in boys of the same age;

- It was a pleasant surprise to discover that there is still a fair capacity for *tenderness* in both boys and girls, beyond what we might have expected. In terms of *softness*, the boys have greater difficulty than the girls from much earlier on. They are "hardened" and much more "awkward". Later, though, it seems to become much more difficult to express tenderness outwardly, especially for the boys: there were a lot of jokes and gags to get over the embarrassment, often accompanied by aggressive, harsh or jerking movements. The greatest difficulty is with *contact* in general, which provokes a high level of agitation, often masked by aggressive behaviour such as challenging others or fighting;
- The capacity for *calm* and *quietening down* are still fairly present (more so in the girls). The difference between girls and boys lay more in the high level of *agitation* and *anxiety* that prevented nearly all the boys from calmly making suggestions or contributing to a group task, even though they attempted to give their opinion many times. On the other hand, the girls who did not manage to get their suggestions heard gave up trying;
- The level of *control* is growing. The children's biggest difficulty is with *uncontrolled* movements. They find it hard to completely let themselves go, both when it comes to making uncontrolled movements and when it comes to lying still for a few minutes;
- On the physiological plane, a certain muscular hyper-tonicity is starting to present itself, especially regarding the chest, shoulders and neck;
- *Anxiety* is already present in smaller children, reaching high levels. This is shown by fairly compromised *breathing* (shallow, thoracic) and huge difficulty relaxing (few yawns).

Scholastic Observation Protocols

These protocols are a very useful tool for teachers and childcare professionals when more standardised, "technical" tests, such as the Assessment Protocol of the Self, are difficult to apply. Furthermore, these protocols also provide us with information on the pupils' study methods and other, more specifically scholastic, activities.

After completing the observation using the 12 point questionnaire below, we can draw up a Dynamic Scholastic Profile for each pupil, based on the relative protocol.

SCHOLASTIC OBSERVATION PROTOCOLS

1. *Emotions* Open or Hidden
2. *Movement* Which movements are prevalent?
   Mobility:
   Writing:
3. *Postures and body language*
   Prevalent facial expression, habitual postures, eye contact
4. *Physiology*
   Tone of Voice, Breathing, Muscle Tone, Blushing/reddening
5. *Symbolism*
   What the child considers to be very important, or not very important.
6. *Use of the imagination in making plans*
   Imagine that one of your plans or wishes could come true next year. What would you like to happen? Describe in detail the steps you would take to make it come true.
7. *Communicative capacity*
   Communication in pairs, with a third person watching.
8. *Study Method*
9. *Type of memory*
10. *Comprehension of a television message*
    Advertisement or Talk show about young people (5 minutes recorded)
    Three pupils: each takes turn to explain, decode the message.
11. *Comprehension of a written text*
    Reading a page (3 pupils) until they understand it (the rest of the class also does the exercise, for comparison). Explaining the content.
12. *Using a computer*
    Procedures, written texts, ways of correcting mistakes.

DYNAMIC SCHOLASTIC PROFILE

1. *Emotions*
   (Verbal, face, postures/body language, physiology)
2. *Calm ↔ Agitation, Anxiety*
   (Movements, way of talking, physiology, mobility)
3. *Somatisation*
4. *Capacity for Contact*
   (Eye contact, understanding, listening to others, stopping to enter into Contact)
5. *Socialisation*
   (Talking to others, open body language/postures, frank voice, communication)
6. *Reading*
7. *Comprehension*
   (Decoding, focussing on the problem, asking why, understanding texts)
8. *Study Method, Level of Organization*
9. *Memory*
10. *Imagination, Creativity*
    (The ability to get enthusiatic about new things and to plan. Curiosity. Themes. Computer.)
11. *Value System*
12. *Capacities, Strong Points*
    Capacities and strong points to be encouraged.
    Capacities that are in need of further development or reconstruction.

Chapter 12

Psychotherapy with children and adolescents

Introduction

So far, we have traced the basic outlines that characterise a typical, integrated course of psychotherapy, and these general outlines are valid whatever the situation or single case. We can say that the way the therapeutic process unfolds is essentially identical each time when it comes to the underlying functional processes that are brought into play.

However, there are situations in which we can also outline very *specific* details about the way the therapeutic relationship unfolds, one of which is psychotherapy with children and adolescents. This is because therapy comes about in a different way, because the person who decided to seek help is not the person undergoing therapy, rather a parent or guardian.

A further point of interest in these particular situations lies (aside from the fact that treatment is carried out very early, and so it is more effective and much more akin to prevention than it is to cure) in the fact that the development of the Self is still underway in these subjects. The therapeutic treatment of children and adolescents naturally reunites, in one area, the two dominant themes of this book: *development* and *therapy*.

Child therapy

General methodology according to age

When we welcome a child into therapy, it is important to understand that the parents play a crucial role in the therapeutic process.

Fig. 1 (first part) shows general strategies for intervention with parents and children, according to age.

With small children, it is crucial that intervention be carried out essentially through the parents themselves. Undeniably, their relationship with the child is central to the successful outcome of therapy, given that children are deeply immersed in the family atmosphere at that age, and they absorb most of the *functional processes* they will need in the future from it. The parents must, in this case, be closely followed by the psychotherapist, and must be given very precise and detailed indications and advice, because they themselves are the therapist's *hands and eyes*. The parents meet regularly with the therapist, but they do not undergo a full course of therapy themselves (either as individuals or as a couple) unless they themselves feel the necessity.

In tandem with parental intervention, we can also work directly with the child using group *workshops* (this has proved to be very useful). These workshops must move in a precise direction, in that they must contribute to the recovery of the Basic Experiences that have already started to become altered or deficient. As we have seen in chapter 11, workshops must be enjoyable and fun, and so they can include activities involving movement, the use of theatre, stories, painting, clay modelling, and games. However, the aim of these workshops is not that of teaching the children the techniques themselves. The workshops employ these techniques, but each time they use them in a specific way, in order to help the child move towards Calm Strength, Just Being, Playfulness or Being Held, Being Taken Up or Being Led.

From age six onwards, the necessity emerges for us to undertake a course of individual psychotherapy with the child. The characteristics that distinguish this from psychotherapy with adults will be discussed fully in the next section. However, the parents still play an important role. For this reason, the therapy will be accompanied by regular meetings with the parents, who will reinforce the work carried out in therapy at home, in harmony with, rather than working against, the progress made in therapy.

From 12–13 years onwards (preadolescence), therapy has the same modalities and characteristics as with adolescents.

The characteristics of individual therapy

The second part of fig. 1 shows a summary of the main points that characterise individual psychotherapy for children compared to adult psychotherapy.

The child is still developing, exploring his capacities, and going through the various Basic Experiences in different contexts and situations. His relationship with his parents is ongoing rather than being an event from the past. As a result, rather than *relive* past events in the patient's relationships with adults and create a different outcome, we *live* present events. The therapist is an authentic *third parent*: another emotionally important adult figure in addition to the ones that are already present in the child's life. For this reason, the therapist must not be in disagreement or conflict with the other two figures.

Fig. 1. *Psychotherapy with children*

THE MODALITIES OF CHILD PSYCHOTHERAPY

WHO WE WORK WITH

Small children below 6 years of age → Work through parents, giving precise indications, workshops.

Children between 6–12 years → Working directly with the child + Intervention with the parents.

From 13 onwards → As with adolescents: a complete alliance

CHARACTERISTICS

Therapist → T is a third parent – the children are still developing.

Relationship → The child is very interested in the therapist as a person – there is curiosity; he puts him to the test.

Memories → Not a "recovery" of the past – we change things straight away, taking a new path: "that's the way it was, now things have to be different."

Therapy →	A lot of fun – no responsibility in therapy – no directives – no duties – pleasure and wonder – no symbolic interpretation.
Games →	A number of very varied games and toys – on all polarities. They should not be "symbolic".
Techniques →	A lot of playing (although always in connection with the B.E.S.'s). Games are modified for the purposes of therapy.
Diagnosis →	Diagnosis through the parents (what they report), direct observation of the child, rather than "tests" – diagnosis is verified as therapy progresses through the things the child says.
Program of therapy →	Less "sequential" than adult therapy. We can work on several Basic Experiences at the same time.
Regressive B.E.S.'s →	Use stratagems to reach them (tiredness, guided visualisation, specially devised games).

Only as a third parent can he reinforce certain Basic Experiences that risk being lost or becoming altered, or recover fundamental emotive experiences that have not been sufficiently opened in the child's life.

The child sees the therapist as another sentimental figure that has entered his life and is interested in him. In therapy, therefore, the child will be curious and want to understand what the therapist is like, what games they will play together and how he will respond to his displays of affection, right from the beginning.

In child therapy, we do not have to worry so much about recovering the past. What the child has to feel is that things are changing right now, that they can go well in his life in the present. At most, he might feel that "things in the past used to turn out differently from the way they are turning out now, but who cares – it is now that is important

Play is the central activity in child development (on all Planes of the Self). Therapy must therefore be one big game, it must not be seen as "treatment". Therapy is experienced as a natural part of the child's every day life, just as the therapist is seen as just another important adult figure, who he bonded with immediately and who offers him interesting and fun activities (as adults often do). The child cannot and must not feel responsible for the outcome of therapy or the way it proceeds, otherwise the experiences would no longer have the desired effect, provoking in the child a sense of having to procure them for himself. For the same reason, he must not be given *directives* (as his parents do) rather he must simply be offered moments to be experienced, and he often experiences these with a great sense of wonder and novelty if the situations lead to a different outcome from the ones the child normally experiences. Change is not brought about by the symbolic interpretation of the games or the way he plays them, but rather the fact that, during play, he can once again Abandon himself completely to the adult, Be Taken Up, Be Seen, use Gentle Strength and Calm Strength and his whole Self.

Because the Basic Experiences and the Functions that need to be brought into play are extremely varied, it is a good idea to use many different toys, and a wide variety of games, in order to involve the child's whole being, fully, and not just his cognitive and symbolic plane.

With children, we can still think in terms of Diagnosis, a Program of therapy, and proceeding by Phases; but there are differences compared to therapy for adults.

First, the Diagnosis is gathered from the parents' stories when they come and report the problem (without the child being present). The child is not able to remember and talk about his whole life. There are very early events that he is unable to report, or he may have dysfunctions of which he is unaware, which only his parents can relate. However, the parents' story must always be associated with direct observation of the child by the therapist, carried out when the two are together during play-therapy, without putting the child through particular tests. The stories that the child tells over the course of therapy about what happens at home and in his life are equally important. This serves as a way of verifying the real state of things (in addition to the parents' reports), and of continually monitoring the changes in the parent-child relationship, and the little patient's everyday life.

The Program of therapy derived from Diagnosis is nonetheless made up of phases, each of which is linked to a different Basic Experience, but this is less "sequential" than the Plan drawn up for adults. A child is intent on exploring all the different contexts in which he can experiences the *positivity* of Being Held, Calm Strength, Loosening Control and Loving, over and over again. Each time, he consolidates his ability to do so successfully, with the approval and help of the adults around him. With children, therefore, we can work on more than one Basic Experience at the same time, during the same Phase in therapy. The sequentiality here lies in the fact that as therapy progresses we must consolidate these Experiences more and more, making them fuller and more stable.

Some Basic Experiences can be introduced directly into therapy, in the form of a game. With other, more *archaic,* or *passive,* Experiences, the therapist may have to fall back on some preliminary expedients to help the child to reach them. For example, with children who have trouble in Just Being, we need to arrive at the opposite polarity of movement and completely tire the child out before he can start to feel the *pleasure of stopping.* Ironically, restless and *hyper-kinetic* children must be helped to go right to the other extreme of movement and be encouraged to make movements that are no longer stopped half-way or repressed, truncated or controlled. On the contrary, they must be encouraged to make wide, expansive, intense movements, carried right to the extreme. At times, the movements are even chaotic and uncoordinated.

Often, *visualisations* can help a child to enter into a Basic Experience that is difficult for him. Pretending to be a mummy bear and a baby bear that are going into hibernation can help the child to curl up right inside the therapist and explore the Experience of Being Held and Contained with greater ease. Telling stories based on a given Basic Experience allows the therapist to enter more easily into the Experience of Giving Love, or Drawing Others to you, in the guise of one of the characters in the story: a duckling, a kitten, or a little bird.

Pre-existing or invented games can often act very well as preparation for entering into a specific Basic Experience. A game about *fear* can help the child to run to the therapist's arms to seek Protection and Abandon himself to him. Playing with *cuddly toys* or *puppets* can provide inspiration for moving in such a way as to Lose Control.

Therapy with Adolescents

Figure 2 shows a summary of the main points characterising therapy with adolescents.

When an adult decides to seek therapy, he has already been worried about the state of his health for a while, so when he starts the process he is particularly careful to describe all his difficulties to the therapist, and give him the fullest possible understanding of the situation, providing detailed information about his life.

The first thing that an adolescent wants to do, by contrast, is understand who the person standing in front of him really is, what the therapist's ideas, judgements and opinions are, especially with regards to the adolescent world to which he belongs. This is also because adolescents almost never arrive in therapy of their own accord. Adolescents are usually brought to therapy by their parents when they notice something alarming in their child's behaviour. We must not forget, however, that parents are often alarmed by forms of behaviour that differ from their ideas and the norms conditioning their family. For this reason, it is very important for the adolescent to feel he can trust the therapist, and that he understands him, for the therapeutic process to be effective. The adolescent must be sure that the therapist is completely on his side, that he is not conditioned by his parents' expectations and that he is not going to be used as a tool in their plans.

The therapist must maintain the fragile equilibrium between expressing his position as clearly as possible to the adolescent (which must result as completely independent from the requests that the adolescent's family make of him) and the fact that he has to answer to the family in some way about what is happening, because they are the real "customers", they are the ones who pay, and so they often feel that they have a right to be informed about what is happening or to interfere directly in the progress of therapy.

Furthermore, we must not forget that, just as with children, adolescents are also still developing, that the relationships that are crucial to their formation are still underway instead of being memories of the past, and we must therefore remember that the therapist represents, just as with children, an additional adult figure to refer to. Unlike with children, however, this new adult figure must be able to be more of a *role model*, someone who can show the adolescent how to live, guide him and provide him with an example to follow, because this is what the adolescent really needs.

Fig. 2. *Psychotherapy with adolescents*

MODALITIES OF PSYCHOTHERAPY WITH ADOLESCENTS

Interested straightaway in what we will be doing during therapy – Interest in the therapist (his opinions, ideas, judgments), even if not outwardly expressed.

Need to TRUST the other person – Confidence that the therapist is on his side – Transparency about the therapist's position in relation to the family.

Subject is still developing – Therapist is seen as a "different" kind of adult figure – Need to follow this figure as an example.

Detailed reports on the experiences of his present life – Trying to understand, find strategies. Little interest for his childhood.

Danger of contact being distorted by sensations → understand them, live them, don't suppress them.

Anger needs to be treated with great respect, as well as the adolescent's individuality.

The adolescent is brought by his parents and cannot decide autonomously whether or not to continue therapy.

The adolescent also however has problems with Strength.

Once the adolescent has learnt to trust the therapist, he will tend to provide him with a richly detailed account of all the events in his everyday life, particularly concerning budding relationships or relationships with his peers. Adolescents are not very interested in their childhood, being more projected towards their future as adults. The detailed accounts of everything a patient said when he met a girl (in the case of a boy), and what she replied, and what this or that friend told him, help the adolescent to try to understand how peer relationships work, find strategies to make his first conquests, and to understand how to be accepted by his friends.

The huge number of psychological changes that adolescents go through create the risk of a distorted form of contact with their internal physical sensations. This is also because there are no opportunities for correct and reassuring information in today's society: on the contrary, there is an ever greater tendency to encourage kids to concentrate on what is external to them, rather than to stop and listen to their sensations. Therapists must therefore concentrate on helping the adolescent to return to himself, to understand his own sensations, to listen to them rather than stifling them.

Another desperate need specific to adolescents is the need for others to recognise their motivations and frequent anger, because the latter is almost always justified, often arising from incomprehension from the adults around them or wrongs suffered. This anger must not therefore be undervalued (as parents often do), considering it merely to be a characteristic phase of growing up, something irritating and unreasonable. A psychotherapist who works with adolescents has to *feel* all of this and treat the adolescent's anger, or the deep hurt he carries inside, with great respect.

However, every time that there are problems with anger, what the therapist really needs to do is to focus on Strength. Working on Strength takes a central role in therapy with adolescents. Only by recovering their full Strength, in all its forms, can adolescents recover the confidence and tranquillity that will allow them to feel that they can go out into the world and get what they expect from life, without feeling crushed or set aside.

Conclusion

Functional thought

Functional thought in its present form could be a significant contribution towards the formation of an epistemological approach more in line with modern scientific advances. It offers us a new phase of thought, which overcomes previous theories, uniting and integrating them; a way of seeing things based on the notion of *complexity*.

Our attention is drawn to the concepts of the *Functions* and the *Underlying Functional Processes* (the *Basic Capacities* and *Experiences*) because of their extreme versatility and their huge operational and descriptive effectiveness. The Functions and the Functional Processes are not structures, per se, but rather a way of describing how the system is organised and how it continues to organise itself.

On the other hand, a Function is not a part of the system, but rather an operation of the *system as a whole*. Morin's theories move in the same direction when he states that each part possesses, in addition to its own identity, a common identity, or common characteristic of the whole system. However – Morin states – a system is made up of a series of actions carried out between one complex unit and another, each of which is itself made up of *interactions*. "The organism is not made up of cells, but rather the interactions between cells. The sum of such interactions constitutes the system's organisation... The concept of the system, without the concept of organisation, is as mutilated as the concept of organisation without the concept of systems" (Morin, 1982).

The Functional vision allows us to approach the system from a new angle, not just considering it as a whole, but also examining the complex relationship between the whole and its parts. More than parts, however, it considers the system in terms of its *organisation*, and the interactions that comprise it.

However, as we have already underlined, this organisation must not be seen in terms of a "structure" or entity. "Organisation is not an institution, rather it consists in the permanent activity of regeneration and generation on all levels" (Morin, 1982).

The Functions and the Functional Processes allow us to examine the organism in question in detail, right down to the smallest particulars, without losing sight of its essential unity, This is precisely because they are not pieces of a complex whole, rather the complex whole itself, operating through each and every Function or Functional Process in its entirety.

Rather than just considering the organism in its own right, what the Functional model allows us to do is consider the organism's *Functional organisation* in relation to both internal and external conditions, both stimuli and responses, and in relation to the degree of organisation that the organism itself currently possesses.

We are not moved by *drives* that prompt us to satisfy them when their energy has accumulated beyond a certain point. What we are moved by, on the contrary, are a series of constant *directions* that the Self develops along; a series of Basic Needs that accompany us our whole lives, This is a "qualitative" vision of human impulses and drives that avoids both pure determinism on the one hand and also the concept of an indefinable chaos on the other.

Children are not subject to magma-like forces that they are unable to control and are therefore forced to suppress. Nor are they a blank page where new experiences etch rules that are pre-constituted deterministically. A child is not a genetically predestined being, but nor is he a totally random presence in nature. He is not a system that is closed in on itself with all information already contained in his DNA, nor is he the exclusive product of his environment.

Functional psychology as a model is centred on the way in which the system's elements of organisation gradually modify themselves over time and over the course of the subject's life. This is not a simple feedback model with "linear flow charts" and simple return actions that act on a single part of the diagram. It is a complex feedback model, which we can think of as a "circular" diagram in which the returns (created by the Functions and the Functional processes and therefore the individual's own personal history) have an effect on the whole circle, the whole organisation, the whole person. If we were to draw a diagram of the human-system, therefore, we would have to substitute each line or flow chart with a circular one, or better still a spherical one, each one completely and continuously interacting with each and every one of the others, in a way that is both specific and complex.

The Functional approach allows us to look at the whole, as well as at how each single Function has evolved over the history of the entire system. We can "photograph" the system in a given moment, showing how every Function presents itself, its history clearly evident in its present configuration. However, we can also follow the way each Function and Functional process progresses over time, as it continues to evolve, with precision. Prigogine states that a complex system cannot be understood without taking its history and course into consideration.

We have discovered that life is not always *homeostatic*. The organism does not seek to return to fixed values every time a change occurs; rather it modifies itself, with a *wavelike* motion over time. Life is like the Mayan *snake-god*, *Quetzalcoatl*: continuous ups and downs between one pole and another of the various ranges that make up the Functions and the Functional processes. Life is a continual movement between tenderness and toughness, between pleasure and pain, strength and fragility, between holding and letting go, fast and slow movements, alarm and tranquillity, the sympathetic and the parasympathetic state and so on and so forth. Life does not lie in a "happy medium" between these polarities. On the contrary, it lies in the possibility of flowing fully and freely from one extreme to another.

A Functional approach must not create rigid models that are limited to certain variables or just a few aspects of the system, despite the fact that current knowledge is not yet ample enough to allow us to range freely in all directions. It is not necessary to have a "complete" knowledge of human functioning right away. The Functional model is essentially an *open* model. Other Functional levels can be added as they are discovered and other processes can be added as they emerge or take on greater significance, thanks to the fact that this is not a model based on parts or categories. The model is comprehensive because the whole is already present, given that the whole is interwoven into each and every Function and Functional process. The discovery of new Functions or Functional processes would not cancel out any previous knowledge about the system. It would merely enrich it. You cannot add complexity to something that is already complex, but you can add additional facets to something that is already essentially multifaceted.

Functional thought could prove to be useful in taking scientific thought a step further on the road to complexity. Perhaps it would just be a small step, but it would be one of the many steps that humanity is currently taking, with greater and lesser degrees of difficulty, in his comprehension of the way Man works, in close relation both to both external and internal conditions.

In our search for understanding, we must increasingly seek to avoid pigeonholing knowledge into rigid, absolutist structures. Similarly, we must avoid the danger of separating knowledge into stagnant compartments, losing sight of the whole. "The problem is not that of constructing a general theory to comprehensively explain every atom, every molecule, every star, every cell, every organism, every artefact or every society. The problem consists in taking into consideration every atom, star, cell, artefact, or society... (and basically every reality, including, above all, the realities of human existence) in a richer way, in the light of systemic/organisational [*we would say Functional*, author's note] complexity" (Morin, 1982)

A scientific discipline must no longer therefore remain closed in its own separate box and be blind to the collateral effects that it has on the disciplines surrounding it. Similarly, we can no longer afford to uphold hypotheses as being "true" which may have huge effects, for a given period, on conceptions about the health of the environment or the individual, only to realise too late that the theory in question was mistaken and dangerous. Similarly, a scientific discipline cannot consider its ideas and contents as being absolute without taking the point of view of other disciplines into consideration, to avoid risking limiting itself to a flat, mono-dimensional vision, without complex and multidimensional points of view.

The conditions for life on this planet, at both a general and a specific level, have are being put more and more at risk. There is an increasing necessity, then, for us to unite scientific disciplines into a unified, multidimensional whole. Man's actions are no longer a drop in the ocean whose impact is easily absorbed and counterbalanced by nature if damage or mistakes occur. Today, man's actions have a massive impact on a planetary scale, and the effects are often irreversible.

Today, Science has a new duty: that of repairing the profound, dangerous alterations that it has itself generated within biological, human, social and ecological systems, and of seeking to prevent further errors in the future. By now, indeed, it has been widely accepted that life can survive (in the highest and most noble sense of the word) only in a very restricted set of conditions, and these conditions are not merely chemical or physical, they also apply to our emotions, our perceptions, the senses and our affections.

Bibliography

Alexander F. (1956), *Psychoanalysis and Psychotherapy*, Norton, New York.

Alexander G. (1985), *Eutony: the holistic discovery of the total person*, Felix Morrow, New York.

Alexander F. M. (1932), *The use of the self*, Methuen & Co., London.

– (1969), *The resurrection of the body*, Dell Publishing Co., New York.

Ambrosi J., Beaudoux M. C. (1976), *La thérapie de la respiration*, Editions du C.R.E.B., Paris.

– (1980), *L'energia dell'umano*, Feltrinelli, Milano.

Andolfi M. (1977), *La terapia con la famiglia*, Astrolabio, Roma. [*Family therapy: an interactional approach*, translated from the Italian by Helene Raff Cassin, Plenum Press, New York, London, 1979]

Angell J. R. (1907), "The province of functional psychology", *Psychological Review*, 14: 61–91.

Attili G., Ricci Bitti P. (1983), *I gesti e i segni*, Bulzoni, Roma.

Baldaro Verde J. (1987), *Donna, Maschere, Ombre*, Cortina, Milano.

Baldaro Verde J., Pallanca G. F. (1984), *Illusioni d'amore*, Cortina, Milano.

Balint M. (1965), *Primary Love and Psycho-Analytic Technique* (New and enlarged edition), Tavistock Publications, London.

Basch M. F. (1988), *Understanding psychotherapy: the science behind the art*, Basic Books, New York.

Bateson G. (1972), *Steps to an ecology of the mind: collected essays in anthropology, psychiatry, evolution and epistemology*, Paladin, St. Albans.

Beck A. (1976), *Cognitive therapy and the emotional disorders*, International Universities Press, New York.

Berne E. (1964), *Games people play: the psychology of human relationships*, Penguin, Harmondsworth.

Bertalanffy L. von (1968), *General System Theory*, Braziller, New York.

Bertherat T., Bernstein C. (1977), *The body has its reasons: anti-exercises and self-awareness*, Collins, London.

Bibring G. L. (1959), "Some considerations of the psychological processes in pregnancy", *Psychoanalytic Study of the Child*, 14: 113–121.

Blurton-Jones N. B. (1972), *Ethological Studies of child behaviour*, Cambridge University Press, Cambridge.

Boadella D. (1985), *Wilhelm Reich: The Evolution of His Work*, Routledge & Kegan, London.

– (1987), *Lifestreams: an introduction to biosynthesis*, Routledge & Kegan, London.

Bovo P., Duguid A. (1992), *Il modello Funzionale nella prevenzione perinatale*, Riza Scienze, 62.

Bower T. G. R. (1972), "Object Perception in Infants", *Perception*, 1: 15–30.

– (1977), *A Primer of Infant Development*, Freeman, San Francisco.

Bowlby J. (1969), *Attachment and Loss, Volume I: Attachment*, Hogarth Press, London.

– (1973), *Attachment and Loss, Volume II: Separation, Anxiety and Anger*, Basic Books, Inc., New York.

– (1980), *Attachment and Loss, Volume III: Loss, Sadness and Depression*, Basic Books, Inc., New York.

– (1988), *A Secure Base: Parent-Child Attachment and Healthy Human Development*, Basic Books, Inc., New York.

Boyesen G. (1985), *Entre psyché et soma, introduction à la psychologie biodynamique*, Payot, Paris.

Bruner J. S. (1977), "Early social interaction and language acquisition", in H. R. Schaffer (Ed), *Studies in mother-infant interaction*, London Academic Press, London.

Carr H. (1925), *Psychology: A Study of mental Activity*, Longmans, Green, New York.

Cremerius J. (1991), *Limiti e possibilità della tecnica psicoanalitica*, Bollati Boringhieri, Torino. [*Limits and possibilities of psychoanalytic technique*].

Dewey J. (1896), "The Reflex Arc Concept in Psychology", *Psychological Review*, 3: 357–370.

– (1917), *Democracy and Education: An Introduction to the Philosophy of Education*, Macmillan, New York.

Downing G. (1994), *The Body and the Word*, Routledge, New York.

Eagle M. N. (1991), "Cambiamenti clinici e teorici in psicoanalisi: dai conflitti ai deficit e dai desideri ai bisogni", *Psicoterapia e Scienze Umane*, XXV, 1.

Ekman P., Levenson R. W., Friesen W. V. (1983), "Evidence for Autonomic Reactions in Specific Emotions", *Science*.

Emde R., Sameroff A. (1989), *Relationship disturbances in early childhood: a developmental approach*, Basic Books, New York.

Erickson M. H. (1982), *My Voice Will Go With You: The Teaching Tales of Milton H. Erickson*, Norton, New York.

Erikson E. H. (1982), *The Life Cycle Completed: A Review*, Norton, New York.

Feldenkrais M. (1972), *Awareness through movement: health exercises for personal growth*, Harper and Row, New York.

Ferenczi S. (1926), "Contraindications to the 'active' psycho-analytical technique", *Further Contributions to the Theory and Technique of Psycho-Analysis*, Hogarth, London.

– (1930), "The principle of relaxation and neocatharsis", *International Journal of Psycho-Analysis*, 11: 428–443.

Fornari F. (1963), *La vita affettiva originaria del bambino*, Feltrinelli, Milan.

Fromm E. (1976), *To have or to be?*, Harper and Row, New York.

Gadamer H. G. (1960), *Truth and Method*, Crossroads, New York.

Galli P. (1982), *La prospettiva olistica in psicologia*, Unicopli, Milan.

Galimberti U. (1983), *Il corpo. Antropologia, psicoanalisi, fenomenologia*, Feltrinelli, Milan.

Gill M. M. (1984), "Psychoanalysis and psychotherapy: A revision", *The International Review of Psychoanalysis*, 11: 161–179.

Greenberg J. R., Mitchell S. A. (1983), *Object Relations in Psychoanalytic Theory*, Harvard University Press, Cambridge, MA.

Grünbaum A. (1984), *The foundations of psychoanalysis: A philosophical critique*, University of California Press, Berkeley, CA.

Guidano V. F. (1991), *The Self in process: Toward a post-rationalist cognitive therapy*, Guildford Press, New York.

Hall E. T. (1966), *The Hidden Dimension*, Doubleday, New York.

Hinde R. A (Ed.) (1972), *Non-Verbal Communication*, Cambridge University Press, Cambridge.

– (1974), *Biological bases of human social behavior*, McGraw-Hill, New York.

– (1977), *La comunicazione non verbale nell'uomo*, Laterza, Bari.

– (1979), *Towards understanding relationships*, Academic Press, London.

Jacobson E. (1964), *The Self And The Object World*, International Universities Press, New York.

Jacoby R. (1983), *The Repression of Psychoanalysis: Otto Fenichel and the political Freudians*, Basic Books, New York.

James W. (1890), *The principles of psychology* (2 vols), Holt, New York.

– (1892), *The stream of consciousness*, Psychology (chapter XI), World, Cleveland & New York.

Jung C. G. (1961), *Memories, dreams, reflections*, Ed. A Jaffe,Vintage Books, New York.

Keleman S. (1987), *Embodying experience*, Center Press, Berkeley.

Kernberg O. F. (1976), *Object relations theory and clinical psychoanalysis*, J. Aronson, New York.

Khan M. M. R. (1983), *Hidden Selves: Between Theory and Practice in Psychoanalysis*, Hogarth Press, London.

Kohut H. (1984), *How Does Analysis Cure?*, Ed. A. Goldberg & P. Stepansky, University of Chicago Press, Chicago.

Kreisler L., Fain M., Soulé M. (1974), *L'enfant et son corps*, P.U.F. édit., Paris.

Kuhn T. S. (1970), *The structure of scientific revolutions*, University of Chicago Press, Chicago.

Kurtz R. (1990), *Body-Centred Psychotherapy*, LifeRythm, Mendocino, CA.

Laborit H. (1979), *L'inhibition de l'action*, Masson, Paris.

Le Boulch J. (1971), *Vers une science du mouvement humain: introduction à la psychocinétique*, ESF, Paris.

Leboyer F. (1975), *Birth Without Violence*, Wildwood House, London.

Lowen A. (1994), "Respiration, mouvement, sensation, sentiment", *Les lieux du corps* n. 1, Morisset, Paris.

Luborsky L., Crits-Christoph P. (1990), *Understanding Transference: The CCRT Method*, Basic Books, New York.

Mahler M. S., Pine F., Bergman A. (1975), *The Psychological Birth of the Human Infant*, Basic Books, New York.

Maslow A. H. (1962), *Towards a Psychology of Being*, Van Nostrand, Princeton, N. J.

Meltzer D. (1975), "Adhesive identification", *Contemporary Psychoanalysis*, 11: 289–310.

Meltzoff A. N., Borton W. (1979), "Intermodal matching by human neonates", *Nature*, 282.

Miller A. (1983), *For Your Own Good: The Roots of Violence in Child-Rearing*, Virago, London.

– (1986), *Thou Shalt Not Be Aware: Society's Betrayal of the Child*, Meridian Books, New York.

Miller G. A., Galanter E., Pribram K. H. (1960), *Plans and the structure of behavior*, Holt, Rinehart & Winston, New York.

Mitchell S. A. (1988), *Relational concepts in psychoanalysis: an integration*, Harvard University Press, Cambridge, MA & London.

– (1991), "Contemporary perspectives on Self: Towards an integration", *Psychoanalytic Dialogues*, 1, www.pep-web.org.

Montagner H. (1978), *L'enfant et la communication*, Stock, Paris.

– (1983), *Les rythmes de l'enfant et de l'adolescent*, Stock, Paris.

Moreno J. L. (1934), *Who shall survive?: a new approach to the problem of human interrelations*, Nervous and Mental Disease Publishing Co., Washington D. C.

Morin E. (1982), *Science avec conscience*, Fayard, Paris.

– (1986), *La méthode. III. La Connaissance de la Connaissance*, Editions du Seuil, Paris.
– (1990), *Introduction à la pensée complexe* [Introduction to Complex Thought], ESF éditeur, Paris.
Morris D. (1971), *Intimate Behaviour*, Random House, New York.
– (1977), *Manwatching: A field guide to human behavior*, H. N. Abrams, New York.
Odent M. (1984), *Birth reborn*, Souvenir Press, London.
Onnis L. (1988) (a cura di), *Famiglia e malattia psicosomatica*, La Nuova Italia Scientifica, Roma.
Painter J. W. (1986), *Deep Bodywork and Personal Development*, Bodymind Books, Mill Valley, CA.
Peresson L. (1991) (a cura di), *Il corpo in psicoterapia*, CISSPAT, Padova.
Perls F., Hefferline R., Goodman P. (1951), *Gestalt Therapy: Excitement and Growth in the Human Personality*, Julian Press, New York.
Pesso A. (1969), *Movement in Psychotherapy*, University of London Press, London.
Petzold H. G. (1977), *Die neuen Körpertherapien*, Junfermann, Paderborn.
– (1993), *Integrative Therapie. Modelle, Theorien und Methoden für eine schulenübergreifende Psychotherapie*, Junfermann, Paderborn.
Piaget J. (1966), *The birth of intelligence in the child*, (M. Cook, Trans.), International Universities Press, New York.
– (1968), *Structuralism* (C. Maschler, Trans.) Basic Books, New York, 1970.
– (1978), *The Development of Thought: Equilibration of Cognitive Structures*, Blackwell, Oxford.
Pine F. (1990), *Drive, Ego, Object and Self*, Basic Books, New York.
Polster E., Polster M. (1973), *Gestalt therapy integrated: contours of theory and practice*, Bruner/Mazel, New York.
Popper K. R. (1963), *Conjectures and Refutations: The Growth of Scientific Knowledge*, Routledge & Kegan, London.
– (1972), *Objective Knowledge: An Evolutionary Approach*, Clarendon Press, Oxford.
Popper K. R., Eccles J. C. (1977), *The Self and Its Brain: An Argument for Interactionism*, Springer International, Berlin.
Radnitzky G. (1986), *L'epistemologia di Popper e la ricerca scientifica*, Borla, Roma.
Raknes O. (1970), *Wilhelm Reich and orgonomy*, Universitetsforlaget, Oslo.
Redl F., Wineman D. (1951), *Children who Hate: The Disorganization and Breakdown of Behavior Controls*, Free Press, Glencoe, IL.
– (1952), *Controls from within, Techniques for the Treatment of the Aggressive Child*, Free Press, Glencoe, IL.
Reich E. (1977), "Emotional First Aid", *Energy and Character*, vol. 8, n. 3.
Reich W. (1942), *The Function of the Orgasm*, Panther Books, London, 1968.
– (1948), *The Cancer Biopathy*, The Orgone Institute Press, New York.
– (1949), *Character Analysis*, The Orgone Institute Press, New York.
Ricci Bitti P. E., Cortesi S. (1977), *Comportamento non verbale e comunicazione*, Il Mulino, Bologna.
Rispoli L. (1985) (Ed.), *Il corpo e le psicoterapie*, Idelson, Napoli.
– (1993), *Psicologia Funzionale del Sé*, Astrolabio, Roma.
– (1996), "Le esperienze fondamentali del Sé come nucleo centrale della psicoterapia", in Piccini F., Bavestrello D. (Ed.), *Insuccessi in psicoterapia*, Franco Angeli, Milano.

– (1998), "La psicoterapia corporea e il suo sviluppo Funzionale", in Cionini L. (Ed.), *Le psicoterapie. Modelli a confronto*, Carocci, Roma.
– (1998), "La psicoterapia Funzionale: verso un modello complesso e multidimensionale", in Lo Verso G., Ceruti M. (Ed.), *Epistemologia e psicoterapia*, Cortina, Milano.
– (1998), "La valutazione degli effetti e del processo in psicoterapia Funzionale Corporea", in Di Nuovo S., Lo Verso G., Di Blasi M., Giannone F. (Ed.), *Valutare le psicoterapie*, Franco Angeli, Milano.
– (1999), "La capacità immaginativa: un ulteriore elemento di integrazione nella psicologia Funzionale", in Di Nuovo S. (Ed.), *Mente e immaginazione*, Franco Angeli, Milano.
– (2000), "La valutazione integrata dello stress", in Cuffaro M., Garofano P. (Ed.), *Nuove frontiere della psicodiagnosi*, Franco Angeli, Milano.
– (2001), "Functional Psychology and the Basic Experience of the Self", in Heller M. (Ed.), *The Flesh of the Soul: The Body we Work with*, Peter Lang, Bern.
– (2003), *Il sorriso del corpo e i segreti dell'anima*, Liguori, Napoli.

Rispoli L., Andriello B. (1988), *Psicoterapia corporea e analisi del carattere*, Bollati Boringhieri, Torino.

Rispoli L., Belloni Sonzogni A., Fumagalli A., Nava P. (2002), "Paziente Alzheimer e teoria Funzionale del Sé", *Ciclo Evolutivo e Disabilità* [*Life Span and Disability*], Vol 5, n. 1, 9–28.

Rispoli L., Di Nuovo S., Genta E. (2000), *Misurare lo stress*, Franco Angeli/Linea Test, Milano.

Rispoli L, Saviane Kaneklin L., Festini Cucco W., Fischetti R., Malagoli Togliatti M. (1991), *Psicologia clinica: psicoterapia e formazione*, SIPs, S. Marino.

Rogers C. (1951), *Client-Centred Therapy: Its Current Practise, Implications, and Theory*, http://elearn.pri.univie.ac.at/pca.

Ruggieri V. (1987), *Semeiotica dei processi psicofisiologici e psicosomatici*, Il Pensiero Scientifico, Roma.
– (1988), *Mente, corpo, malattia*, Il Pensiero Scientifico, Roma.

Sandler J. (1987) (Ed.), *Projection, identification, projective identification*, International Universities Press, New York.

Schaffer H. R. (1977) (Ed.), *Studies in mother-infant interaction*, Academic Press, New York.

Sapir M., Reverchon F. et coll. (1975), *La relaxation: son approche psychanalytique*, Dunod, Paris.

Schachter S., Singer J. (1962), "Cognitive, Social and Physiological Determinants of Emotional State", *Psychological. Review*, 69, 379–399.

Schultz J. H., Luthe W. (1959), *Autogenic training: A psychophysiologic approach in psychotherapy*, Grune and Stratton, New York.

Schwartz-Salant N., Stein M. (1986) (Ed.), *The Body in Analysis*, Chiron Publications, Wilmette, IL.

Selye H. (1974), *Stress Without Distress*, New American Library, New York.
– (1976), *The stress of life*, McGraw-Hill, New York.

Skinner B. F. (1959), *Cumulative Record*, Appleton-Century-Crofts, New York.

Siani R. (1992), *Psicologia del sé. Da Kohut alle nuove applicazioni cliniche*, Bollati Boringhieri, Torino.

Siegel D. J. (1999), *The developing mind: toward a neurobiology of interpersonal experience*, Guilford Press, New York.

Stern D. N. (1977), *The first relationship: infant and mother*, Fontana/Open Books, London.

– (1985), *The interpersonal world of the infant*, Basic Books, New York.
Venturini R. (1979), *Sistema neurovegetativo e personalità*, Bulzoni, Roma.
Vygotskij L. S. (1973), *Lo sviluppo psichico del bambino*, Editori Riuniti, Roma.
Watson J. B. (1924), *Behaviorism* , Norton & Co., New York.
Watson O. M. (1970), *Proxemic behavior: A Cross-Cultural Study*, Mouton, The Hague.
Watzlawick P., Beavin J. H., Jackson D. D. (1967), *Pragmatics of human Communication: A study of interational patterns, pathologies and paradoxes*, W. W. Norton, New York.
Weiss J. (1990), "Unconscious mental functioning", *Scientific American*, 262 [trad. it.: "I processi mentali dell'inconscio", *Le Scienze*, 261].
– (1993), *How Psychotherapy Works: Process and Technique*, Guilford Press, New York.
Woodworth R. S. (1918), *Dynamic Psychology*, Columbia University Press, New York.